D0554242

ROTTING FACE
Smallpox and the American Indian

ROTTING FACE
Smallpox and the American Indian

R. G. Robertson

CAXTON PRESS
Caldwell, Idaho
2001

Library of Congress Cataloging-in-Publication Data

Robertson, Roland.
  Rotting face : smallpox and the American Indian / R.G. Robertson.
    p. cm.
  Includes bibliographical references and index.
  ISBN 0-87004-419-2 (alk. paper)
    1. Smallpox--United States--History. 2. Indians of North America--Diseases--History. 3. Indians of North America--Missouri River Valley--History--19th century. 4. Fur trade--Missouri River Valley--History--19th century.   I. Title.
  RC183.49 .R63 2001
  616.9'12'008997073--dc21

                                                        2001032376

Lithographed and bound in the United States of America
CAXTON PRESS
Caldwell, Idaho
166979

ACKNOWLEDGEMENTS

I am particularly grateful to my wife, Karen Robertson, first for persuading me to write about the smallpox epidemic of 1837-38, and then for photographing the historical sites where much of the tragedy took place.

For answers to my questions, I thank Mike Casler, National Park Service librarian at the Fort Union National Historic Site; Dorothy Cook, interpretive specialist at the Knife River Indian Villages National Historic Site; Randy Kane, National Park Service ranger and historian at the Fort Union National Historic Site; Dennis Northcott of the Missouri Historical Society Archives; Jannett Wesley of the Technical Information Center of the NPS Denver Service Center; and the staff at the Ketchum, Idaho, Community Library, who processed my numerous requests for inter-library loans.

I also thank my agent, Cherry Weiner, who brought Caxton Press and me together.

Finally, I thank all the people at Caxton Press and especially my editor, Wayne Cornell, who saw in *Rotting Face* a story that had to be told.

TABLE OF CONTENTS

ILLUSTRATIONS

Introduction

It is doubtful the Europeans could have so easily defeated the native people of North and South America without the help of Old World diseases.

When the Spanish conquered the Caribbean and Latin America, and during the initial French, English, and Dutch inroads along the eastern seaboard, European military technology was about equal to that of the Native Americans. Compared with the host of warriors the Indians could field, the Europeans were hopelessly outnumbered. The shock of hearing the discharge of a musket wore off quickly when the Indians realized a soldier had only one shot. Until he reloaded, his weapon was merely an unwieldy club. A trained gunner needed sixty seconds to load and fire a smoothbore flintlock. Older weapons such as the harquebus and wheel-lock musket took longer. While his European adversary fiddled with his powderhorn and ramrod, an Indian could let fly up to twenty well-aimed arrows.

Rough terrain gave the Indians another advantage, particularly in the dense eastern woodlands where European troops readily bogged down. When a skirmish between Indians and whites occurred, it more often resembled a melee instead of a large, set-piece battle, such as Blenheim.

The white invaders never would have conquered the Americas so readily had they not had a far more lethal weapon than their primitive guns and Old World tactics. European disease vanquished the New World's natives, not powder and ball. Of all the contagions the Europeans introduced, the most efficient killer by far was *Variola major*—more commonly known as smallpox.

In North America, trade—especially the fur trade—was the primary means by which smallpox reached the Indians of the interior. Moving inland from the Atlantic coast and northward up the Mississippi and Missouri rivers, smallpox diffused along tribal trading networks, far in advance of the first white traders. In its wake, the disease left countless dead. Yet beyond the toll in lives, smallpox also destroyed an elaborate Indian trading system that had prospered long before Columbus set sail from Spain. Around the St. Lawrence River and Great Lakes, and along the Mississippi and upper Missouri, smallpox wiped out the native middlemen who provided the underpinning to this far-flung trading scheme. As the tribal trading structure fell apart, French, Dutch, and English traders stepped into the void, increasing Indian dependence on European-manufactured goods.

Smallpox and the fur trade combined in one of history's most tragic pairings. The fur trade spread smallpox, and smallpox eliminated Indian competition, allowing the fur trade to spread.

While the European traders were supplanting native traders, a partnership existed between them. In the early days of the fur trade, Indians held the upper hand, but as smallpox whittled away the tribal middlemen, white traders gained the advantage. Although smallpox eventually allowed the Europeans to monopolize the fur trade, an individual white trader gained nothing if his Indian customers perished. The incongruity between the negative short-term effect that small-pox had on a single French, Dutch, or English trader and the positive long-term effect the disease had on the overall expansion of the European fur trade is an irony of economics. An outbreak of smallpox that killed most of an Indian band at the beginning of a trading season left its white trader with no furs and an unsold inventory of merchandise. Such a trader faced financial ruin. But if the smallpox also snuffed out a large number of Indian middlemen, it opened an avenue for other Europeans to enlarge their share of the overall trade. The marriage of smallpox and the fur trade won the Europeans an empire, but in doing so, it nearly annihilated the Native American people.

* * * * * * *

I have divided the story of smallpox and the fur trade into two parts, interweaving them in alternating chapters. Odd-numbered chapters chronicle the devastating smallpox epidemic of 1837 and 1838. As the culminating union between small-pox and the fur trade, this epidemic changed the tribal power structure of the Great Plains and ended any hope that the Native Americans had in retaining their freedom.

Even-numbered chapters relate the early history of smallpox and the fur trade in the western hemisphere. Because the modern world is—thankfully—unacquainted with smallpox, I start with its description. I feel readers must understand the terrible nature of the disease before they can empathize with the Indians who endured its horror.

Subsequent even-numbered chapters trace the introduction of smallpox to the New World, initially by Spanish conquistadors and then by early fur traders on the Atlantic coast. I also recount the spread of horses and metal products along the Native Americans' vast trading network, telling how smallpox diffused through this aboriginal distribution system, far ahead of the European traders. Since so much of the book details the destruction of the Mandans, Hidatsas, and Arikaras, I have included background about their villages and how they lived. Finally, I describe the great smallpox epidemics of 1780 through 1781 and 1801 through 1802, explaining how they crippled the Indian nations and altered tribal hegemony across the upper Missouri.

The dates given for the various Indian tribes acquiring horses are an approximation. Nomadic tribes, such as those of the Blackfoot Confederation, were made up of many bands. Often, several years passed between when horses first reached an outlying portion of a tribe and when they were acquired by all its members. Anthropological estimates of the date a particular tribe adopted horses may vary by over one hundred years. Readers wanting details about these estimates are encouraged to consult Frank Gilbert Roe, *The Indian and the Horse* (Norman: University of Oklahoma Press, 1955).

Throughout the book, I employ the term "buffalo" instead of the scientifically correct *Bison americanus.* My decision to do so is arbitrary; I think buffalo reads better. When referring to aboriginal North and South Americans, I use "Indian" and "Native American" as I think it fits the text. I do not consider the word Indian derogatory, especially since most of North America's native people use it to describe themselves. I avoid the hyphen-ated-American names that are so popular in the age of political correctness. I find that terms such as Euro-American make tedious reading and prefer to use "white" or "black" when refer-ring to Europeans or Afro-Americans.

My primary source for the smallpox epidemic of 1837 and 1838 is the journal kept by Francis Chardon, the trading post commander at Fort Clark. The copy I consulted is F. A. Chardon, *Chardon's Journal at Fort Clark, 1834-1839,* ed. Annie Heloise Abel (Pierre: Lawrence K. Fox, Superintendent, Department of History, State of South Dakota, 1932; Lincoln: University of Nebraska Press, Bison Book Edition, 1997). In order to keep my endnotes to a reasonable number, I have not provided endnote references for events that can easily be found in *Chardon's Journal.* All other attributions are duly noted.

Because smallpox progresses through its stages at a pre-dictable rate, it is possible to describe a victim's probable condi-tion at any point during his illness, including when the histori-cal record is silent about the details. I use this timeline—which is outlined in chapter two—when recounting the story of specif-ic people who endured the epidemic of 1837 and 1838. Where I think my dates are open to a different interpretation, I discuss it in an endnote.

References to the right or left side of a river assume the read-er is facing downstream. When writing about business partner-ships, such as Pratte, Chouteau & Company, I occasionally use Pratte & Chouteau. Whenever two or more formal names are separated by "&," the text refers to a business partnership. When the names are connected by "and," as in Pratte and Chouteau, it means the individuals, in this example, Bernard Pratte Sr. and Pierre Chouteau Jr.

Finally, while researching this book, I found that I had stepped into a heated debate concerning how many Indians were living in the western hemisphere when Columbus first vis-ited the Americas. Depending on which source I checked, the numbers ranged from eight million to over 120 million people.[1] Proponents of the lower numbers argue that many of the "High Counters"—a term coined by historians who disagree with large Indian population estimates—have a hidden agenda. Namely, they seek to paint the European invasion of the New World with the brush-stroke of ethnic genocide. By inflating the pre-contact Indian population estimates, the High Counters attempt to make the subsequent deaths—from disease, war, and slavery— more terrible than they were.

This book does not resolve the High and Low Counters' debate, nor do I intend that it should. I do not know if the High Counters are right, or if the Low Counters are; perhaps the correct number lies halfway between their extremes. Where I give population estimates, I usually offer a range and provide my sources in an endnote. Readers are cautioned to view all population figures and death rates with skepticism. Numbers that appear absolute—in this book and elsewhere—could be off the mark by twenty percent or more. The point is, no one can say for sure how many Assiniboines were on the upper Missouri in 1779, how many Hurons were in Canada in 1620, or how many Aztecs were living in Mexico when Cortéz invaded. The farther back in time historians go, the more their population estimates become out-and-out guesses.

Although such estimates add a dynamic to the story of small-pox and the fur trade, I am less concerned with actual numbers—which cannot be known with certainty—than I am with the role the fur trade had in spreading disease. Whether the total Indian population of the western hemisphere declined by 100 million in the centuries following 1492 or by only seven million, the result is no less tragic.

Introduction notes

[1.] David Henige, *Numbers from Nowhere: The American Indian Contact Population Debate* (Norman: University of Oklahoma Press, 1998), 23.

"My Friends one and all, Listen to what I have to say—Ever since I can remember, I have loved the Whites, I have lived With them ever since I was a Boy, and to the best of my Knowledge, I have never wronged a White Man, on the Contrary, I have always Protected them from the insults of Others, Which they cannot deny. The 4 Bears never saw a White Man hungry, but what he gave him to eat, Drink, and a Buffaloe skin to sleep on, in time of Need. I was always ready to die for them, Which they cannot deny. I have done every thing that a red Skin could do for them, and how have they repaid it! With ingratitude! I have Never Called a White Man a Dog, but to day, I do Pronounce them to be a set of Black harted Dogs, they have deceived Me, them that I always considered as Brothers, has turned Out to be My Worst enemies. I have been in Many Battles, and often Wounded, but the Wounds of My enemies I exhalt in, but to day I am Wounded, and by Whom, by those same White Dogs that I have always Considered, and treated as Brothers. I do not fear Death my friends. You Know it, but to die with my face rotten, that even the Wolves will shrink with horror at seeing Me, and say to themselves, that is the 4 Bears the Friend of the Whites—

"Listen well what I have to say, as it will be the last time you will hear Me. think of your Wives, Children, Brothers, Sisters, Friends, and in fact all that you hold dear, are all Dead, or Dying, with their faces all rotten, caused by those dogs the whites, think of all that My friends, and rise all together and Not leave one of them alive. The 4 Bears will act his part—"

Purported speech of Mah-to-toh-pa (Four Bears),
Mandan War Chief, July 30, 1837,
the day he died of smallpox.

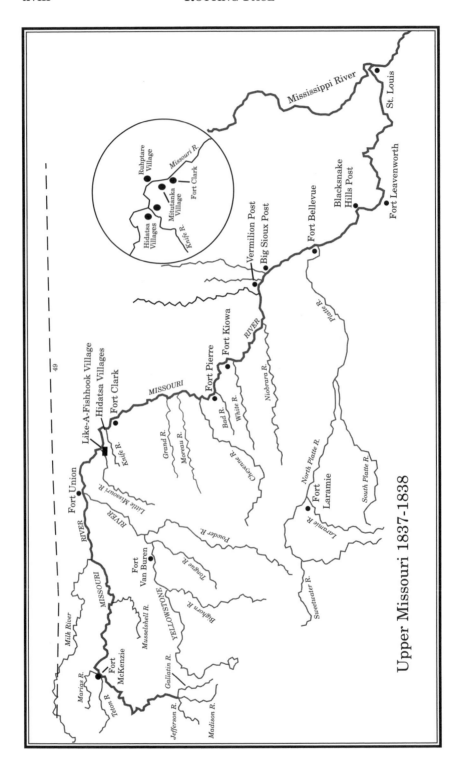

Upper Missouri 1837-1838

Chapter One

Early Spring 1837

On Wednesday, April 12, Francis Chardon could say that spring had finally come to the upper Missouri. An hour past noon, the Missouri River's frozen surface fractured in a thousand places. The air crackled with the sound of splintering ice as the river awakened from its winter slumber.

At Fort Clark, where Chardon served as the trading post commander—or *bourgeois* as he was more commonly called—and at the nearby Mandan village of Mitutanka, people paused as the sound caught their ears. Then, as if drawn by a giant lodestone, Mandans and whites, singly and in twos and threes, walked toward the river, their pace quickening as they descended the fifty-foot embankment that leveed the floodplain.

While the crowd gathered along the shore, the Missouri's frozen center buckled as if blown apart by gunpowder. No longer held in check, the water heaved, slamming its muddy torrents against the ice and pitching up pieces the size of dance floors. God help the man or buffalo that happened to be crossing when the Missouri cut loose, for they had no other hope.

This year winter had gripped the upper Missouri with a tight fist, and until today had shown no sign of letting go. By mid March, most of the snow had melted on the prairie, but that meant little to Francis Chardon and the men he supervised at

Fort Clark. Melting snow did not spell the start of spring; that was reserved for the day the Missouri River began shucking its frozen mantle. Each year the personnel at Fort Clark placed bets on the date the ice would break. When it did, they greeted the occasion with fanfare, for the Missouri always put on a show.

Mandans from Mitutanka Village lined the Missouri's right bank, watching the spectacle alongside Chardon and the other men from the fort. Like the whites, the Mandans were happy that spring was at hand, but for them, the ice breakup offered more than the promise of fair weather. It meant they could see an end to their hunger.

Each autumn during the first freeze, buffalo broke through the thin ice while attempting to ford the Missouri. Those too weak to reach shore drowned and were frozen in place until spring. At the end of winter, more buffalo were caught as they tried to cross the thawing river. Occasionally, a panicked animal or two would ride an ice floe for over a mile before being pitched into the water.

Every year thousands of animals died, unable to swim out of the roiling current. When dead buffalo floated past Mitutanka Village, young Mandan men carrying braided-leather ropes dived into the Missouri, lassoed the carrion, and dragged them to shore. Their tribesmen then cut open the animals' bloated skin and ate their raw innards. To say the meat was high is a gross understatement. The Mandans and their neighbor and ally, the Hidatsas, relished dining on buffalo that had been dead for months.

Over the past three years, since becoming the *bourgeois* of Fort Clark, Chardon had watched Indians eat meat that was so rotten it could be scooped with a spoon. The stench from these banquets was enough to turn the stomach of the most hard-bitten mountain man. Chardon had lived among Indians since 1815, when he began trading with the Osages in western Missouri, but he had never acquired a taste for rancid meat. It was probably something a person had to be born to. Certainly, his sisters and mother in Philadelphia would have recoiled from such a meal.[1]

For three hours the Missouri ran two feet above normal as it carried the ice downstream. Despite Chardon and the Indians wishing that winter would go, it seemed determined to draw out its parting. As the afternoon wore on, the northwesterly wind that had been buffeting the prairie throughout the day grew colder. The Mandans snugged their blankets and buffalo robes around their shoulders, and the whites flipped up the hoods on their wool capotes and tightened their belt sashes. A few of those looking on reckoned that winter still had some teeth in its bite. Spring had arrived, but winter refused to surrender without a struggle.

At 4 p.m. the water level fell, and the ice stopped moving. The crowd lining the shore was visibly disappointed, since everyone had anticipated that the river would flush the ice away. The Mandans filed up the bank toward their village, knowing they would again go to bed on empty stomachs. Their young men had failed to recover a single drowned buffalo.

Set 300 yards upstream from Fort Clark, Mitutanka—the Mandans' main village—shared an expanse of land with the trading post, terrain that bordered the Missouri's right flank. About a mile and a half south, stretching to three miles away in the west, a low band of hills girded the site but did nothing to mute the wind that continually swept down from the prairie.

Fort Clark and Mitutanka Village occupied the northeast corner of the broad terrace, a position that kept them safe from the periodic floods that inundated the bottomland. The location was eight miles below the mouth of the Knife River, which was home to the Hidatsas. Ruhptare, Mitutanka's smaller sister village, sat on a level bench on the left side of the Missouri, two miles upstream from Fort Clark. With upwards of eighty lodges, Ruhptare was less than half the size of Mitutanka.

That night the Missouri rose four feet. At sunrise the Mandans and men at Fort Clark were heartened to see the ice flowing. It gave them hope that by dusk it would be gone. Later in the day, while Francis Chardon kept an eye turned toward the river, two Arikaras reined in their horses at the fort and announced that their band was camped about forty miles away. If their story was accurate, the tribe could soon visit the post and barter its winter harvest of buffalo robes. The Arikara robes would go a long way toward helping Chardon meet his trading quota, especially since the Mandans were too frightened to hunt. But rumors about the Arikaras coming to trade had been floating on the Indian telegraph for seven months. Although the warriors could be telling the truth, the *bourgeois* was skeptical.

Overnight the river again froze, but at daylight, the Missouri reasserted its vigor and once more pushed the ice downstream. As they had done for the past two days, Mandans lined the bank, searching for drowned buffalo. They saw none. It was as if the herds had deserted the upper Missouri, perhaps heading for pastures where winter was not holding spring at bay.

The following day—Saturday—Fort Clark and Mitutanka Village awakened to a fresh blanket of snow. It had snowed several times in recent weeks and would probably snow off and on well into May, but at least the ice was still moving. For that, everyone was thankful. Around midmorning, a Mandan scout spotted a small herd of buffalo grazing on the prairie a short distance from the trading post. Putting aside their fears, Mandan hunters mounted their ponies and galloped onto the plain, their stomachs rumbling with the prospect of food. That afternoon the hunters returned to Mitutanka with meat from four bulls. Although the bounty was too small to feed the entire village, those Indians who received a share thanked the Manitou spirit for his kindness.

Despite the failure of Fort Clark's hunters to kill any buffalo during the chase, Chardon found the day full of promise. A few more Arikaras rode past the trading post as they headed for the Mandan village, offering evidence that the main body of Arikaras was indeed somewhere in the vicinity. Perhaps the trading season could be salvaged after all.

By Sunday, April 16, the Missouri had cleared enough ice so an *engagé* (a manual laborer working for wages) could make a canoe trip downstream to Fort Pierre, the largest trading post on the river. Chardon felt there was little danger the Missouri would refreeze. The *bourgeois* of Fort Pierre had sent word that he was running short of nails and had asked Chardon to forward some when the ice broke.

Forts Clark and Pierre belonged to the Upper Missouri Outfit of Pratte, Chouteau & Company, the dominant fur trading partnership in St. Louis. Rumor had it that the firm's managing partner, Pierre Chouteau Jr., intended transferring the operational headquarters of the Upper Missouri Outfit from Fort Union to Fort Pierre now that the Outfit's longtime manager, Kenneth McKenzie, had retired. Fort Union sat on the Missouri's left bank, about five miles above the mouth of the Yellowstone River (100 yards east of the Montana-North Dakota border), whereas Fort Pierre was located on the Missouri's right side, three miles above the mouth of

Courtesy University of Nebraska Press,
The American Fur Trade of the Far West, Vol. 2
Pierre Chouteau Jr.

the Bad River (across from present-day Pierre, South Dakota). Fort Clark occupied the middle ground between its larger cousins (about four miles southeast of Stanton, North Dakota), though it was closer to Fort Union than to Fort Pierre.

Fort Clark was almost two years younger than Fort Union. The acclaimed fort builder and trader, James Kipp, had established Fort Clark for the Mandan and Hidatsa trade in 1831. Named for William Clark of Lewis and Clark fame and now the Superintendent of Indian Affairs in St. Louis, the cottonwood trading post measured 120 by 160 feet, making it a good deal smaller than either Fort Union or Fort Pierre. Yet despite its size, Fort Clark was an important part of the Upper Missouri Outfit.

When the post had first opened, the Upper Missouri Outfit was a major piece of John Jacob Astor's powerful American Fur Company. The UMO, as the division was called in company documents, had been formed in 1827 when Astor absorbed Kenneth McKenzie's competing Columbia Fur Company. After the merger, McKenzie had taken charge of all trade above the Missouri-Big Sioux River confluence (near Sioux City, Iowa). Tradition called the country northwest of the Big Sioux the upper Missouri,[2] and McKenzie's command was named the Upper Missouri Outfit.

Although semi-autonomous, the UMO was part of the American Fur Company's Western Department, which had its headquarters in St. Louis. The two branches divided responsibility for the Missouri fur trade at the Big Sioux confluence, with the Western Department managing everything downstream, and the UMO handling everything above. At the time, Bernard Pratte & Company supervised the Western Department as Astor's agent, but for all practical purposes, the Pratte partnership was merely another American Fur Company division, a division headed by Pierre Chouteau Jr.

John Jacob Astor sold his fur interests in June 1834, the same month Francis Chardon became *bourgeois* of Fort Clark. Pierre Chouteau Jr. and his partner, Bernard Pratte Sr., bought the Western Department and Upper Missouri Outfit. They also reorganized their partnership, changing its name from Bernard Pratte & Company to Pratte, Chouteau & Company—or Pratte & Chouteau, for short.

On April 1, 1836, Bernard Pratte Sr. died, and his interest in Pratte & Chouteau went to his son, Bernard Jr., who worked for the firm as a riverboat captain. During the nearly three years that had passed since Bernard Pratte Sr. and Pierre Chouteau Jr. made their acquisition, Francis Chardon had seen no difference in how he conducted his trade. Chouteau still expected his *bourgeois* to turn a profit. Any who failed were quickly demoted to clerk—or worse.

On Monday, April 17, Chardon wrote in his journal that at sunrise a drowned buffalo had floated past Fort Clark. Wryly, and perhaps with a smile, the *bourgeois* noted that the Mandans at Mitutanka Village had slept late and "missed their breakfast." He often added tidbits such as this to his chronicle of daily life on the upper Missouri. He had begun the log on June 18, 1834, the day he first arrived at the trading post, and he had kept at it ever since. His entry about the drowned buffalo was certainly no less newsworthy than his monthly tally of the rats he had killed. Through March of this year, he had dispatched 1,510, which averaged out to more than forty dead rats per month.

No doubt the Mandans would sorely miss this morning's breakfast of drowned buffalo, especially since they were starving. The four tough bulls they had butchered the previous Saturday had been hard chewing and were now only a memory—and memories made thin gruel. Normally, village hunters would be scouring the prairie for buffalo, but not this spring. These days the Mandans sat inside their lodges, paralyzed with fear. In Chardon's opinion, it served them right to go hungry. After all, they were the ones who had tricked a group of Yankton Lakotas into coming to Mitutanka Village last winter for a peace parley. On January 18, a combined Mandan and Hidatsa war party had ambushed the Yankton ambassadors within the shadow of Fort Clark. In addition to killing the five male members of the delegation, the Mandans and Hidatsas had also taken the group's lone female captive. Ever since, the Mandans had been wary of leaving their village to hunt, for fear the Yanktons could be waiting to extract their revenge. Although Chardon did not do so, he may have been tempted to write in his journal that if the Mandans were famished, they could always eat rats. He had eaten one for supper two years earlier and had suffered no ill effects.[3] It certainly beat starving.

Adding a final entry to his journal for April 17, Chardon noted that his *engagés* had put up ten packs of buffalo robes that day. With ten robes per pack, each of the bundles weighed about ninety pounds. As they did with beaver, fox, wolf, and other skins, the workmen used a fur press to squeeze the robes into tight, uniform bales, which were easy to transport. That afternoon the *bourgeois* had ordered several other *engagés* to sharpen their axes. The next morning he intended sending them for firewood, since the fort was about out. The heat of summer was still weeks away, and despite the breakup of the river ice, the weather had continued unseasonably cold. This year, winter was taking its own sweet time in leaving.

Soon the traders would arrive at Fort Clark from the outlying Indian camps, bringing in the buffalo robes and furs they

had bartered for throughout the winter. As with the breakup of
the Missouri's ice pack, the appearance of the traders also
marked the beginning of spring. Everyone at the fort from the
bourgeois through the clerks, blacksmith, cooper, cooks, and on
down to the lowest ranking *engagé* always looked forward to
their return, for it meant that Pratte & Chouteau's annual
steamboat would begin its voyage to the upper Missouri.

On April 17 in St. Louis,[4] Captain Bernard Pratte Jr. watched a
line of workmen struggle across the narrow, plank gangway
that led to the main deck of the steamboat *St. Peter's* (occasionally spelled *St. Peters*). The gangway extended over a sharply-raked
bow, making the steamer resemble a beached narwhal whale.
Because spring floods and upcountry thunderstorms continually
altered the water level of the Mississippi and its tributaries—often
by forty feet or more—river towns found it impractical to build
wharves.

Bent beneath the heavy parcels that they balanced on their
backs with tumplines, the laborers inched their way onto the
steamer. They looked less like men than two-legged beasts of
burden. A couple of them rolled large wooden barrels up the
gangway, then muscled them into position for the voyage. No
matter how many days ahead the loading began, the clerks of
Pratte & Chouteau were always adding last-minute supplies.
The firm sent only one steamboat a year to the upper Missouri,
so everything from blue glass beads to casks of gunpowder was
top priority.

The *St. Peter's* unenclosed cargo hold was bursting with
freight, and every spare inch of deck space was crammed with
boxes and hogsheads, each packed with either blankets, bolts of
muslin and calico, metal knives, copper and iron pots, axes, bar
lead and shot, muskets, fire steels, scissors, brass wire, tobacco,
or a host of other truck. Some of the goods were intended for
Pratte, Chouteau & Company's trading posts, whereas the rest
were Indian annuities, the annual fee the United States government rendered to the Omahas, Lakotas, Poncas, and other
tribes who lived along the Missouri River. The fur company
earned a substantial profit from transporting the annuities,

George Catlin painting, Smithsonian American Art Museum.
St. Louis, as it looked about 1832, was the jump-off point for the frontier.

and it fell to Captain Pratte to ensure they reached their destinations.

The St. Louis waterfront was jammed with white-painted steamboats, their tall, black smokestacks standing like denuded trees after a forest fire. The 119-ton *St. Peter's* was a side-wheeler—as were most steamboats on western rivers—propelled by twin, high-pressure engines that operated two large paddle wheels, which were located amidships. It had been constructed in Pittsburgh, Pennsylvania, the year before.[5] Compared with the smaller stern-wheelers, side-wheelers had greater maneuverability. By running one paddle wheel forward while its opposite ran backwards, a side-wheeler could turn on a dime. The dexterity was invaluable on meandering rivers such as the Missouri, although it came at a cost.

Side-wheelers sacrificed space to their engines and boilers, leaving less room for cargo and passengers. In addition, the double paddle wheels made side-wheelers wider than stern-wheelers, which restricted the tandem-wheel boats in narrow channels. All steamers had broad beams and flat bottoms without keels. Boatbuilders did everything possible to reduce a vessel's weight, thereby increasing its carrying capacity. The newest steamers hauled nearly a ton and a half of lading for every measured-ton of boat weight and still drew only thirty inches of water.[6] The low-displacement allowed steamboats to negotiate shallow rivers where the beds were littered with shifting sandbars. If a boat with a rounded hull grounded on one, it would heel over. In contrast, a flat-bottomed side-wheeler could reverse its engines and back off.

Squeezed in around the *St. Peter's* and the other steamers were keelboats, pirogues, and mackinaws—the backbone fleet of America's western waterways—all scrunched as tight as sardines in a can. Although they were slowly being replaced by steam, these smaller craft had opened the Missouri to commerce, and they were still an important cog in riverine transportation. Most of the steamboats tied up beside the *St. Peter's* plied the Mississippi, shipping freight and passengers north from New Orleans and Natchez or south from Fort Snelling and Prairie du Chien. A number of the steamers had come down the Ohio, bringing furniture, tableware, grain alcohol, and a myriad of other items from cities as distant as Louisville and Cincinnati. The Mississippi River was the commercial bloodstream of western America, and St. Louis was its heart.

As Captain Pratte watched the workmen carry their loads across the *St. Peter's* gangplank, he probably glanced at the boisterous throng of men milling about on The Levee, awaiting the signal to board. Officially known as Front Street, The Levee separated the riverbank from the town. Most of the men standing on The Levee looked like castoffs from Falstaff's Legion. A number of them were drunk, though it was Monday. They gave no thought to abstaining on the Sabbath, so it was not surprising that they continued their binges into the workweek. No doubt they had started drinking soon after signing on for the voyage. St. Louis was a fine town for a spree, and men such as these saw no reason to stay sober.

If Captain Pratte looked closely at the milling throng, he may have picked out the smattering of men who were free trappers. Known as *hivernans,* they had earned the descriptive French title by wintering beyond the settlements. Doing so gave a man swagger and set him apart from the greenhorns who had never been above the mouth of the Platte. The *hivernans* had a term for such men: *mangeurs de lard,* eaters of pork, neophytes who subsisted on hog instead of living high on buffalo hump ribs and elk.

Perhaps one or two free trappers among those waiting to board had the wherewithal to buy their berths, but most intended working their way upriver by chopping wood for the *St. Peter's* fireboxes and unloading cargo at the Indian agencies and trading posts. It was backbreaking toil, but it beat squandering money on passage that was better spent on traps, gunpowder, and a drunken frolic.

By far the largest portion of the crowd were employees of Pratte & Chouteau. Most were *engagés,* hired hands who would spend the next year or two tending camp for one of the firm's trapping brigades or performing menial chores at a trading fort. The work was hard, dull, and occasionally dangerous, but it offered uneducated frontiersmen the opportunity to earn a decent wage. If a man were frugal and did not waste his $150 to $200 annual income on watered-down whiskey or gewgaws at the company store, he could save enough to buy a small farm. Although such a wish kept a steady line of men knocking at the fur company's door, experience told Captain Pratte that few *engagés* possessed that much willpower. Most would return to the settlements as broke as the day they left.

Among the other men standing on The Levee were skilled craftsmen—carpenters, blacksmiths, coopers, and cooks. Pratte & Chouteau paid them $300 to $400 per year to build warehouses and cut shingles, repair traps and hammer out metal hinges, piece together wooden pails and barrels, and bake hardtack and roast geese. They were a step above the *engagés,* to be sure, but their labor was no less demanding.

Every year Pratte, Chouteau & Company sent an army of recruits up the Missouri. Attrition in the ranks of its trapping brigades and among the men who staffed its trading posts produced a continual need for fresh bodies. The firm required not only trappers, *engagés,* and skilled artisans, but also traders, interpreters, hunters, clerks, *partisans* (trapping brigade leaders), and *bourgeois.* Perhaps the crowd waiting to board the *St. Peter's* contained men for every one of these billets. At some time or other, individuals filling all these positions had journeyed up the Missouri, many of them traveling on steam-boats such as the *St. Peter's.*

The clerks and *bourgeois*—if any were standing there that April morning—would have been easy for Captain Pratte to pick out. They dressed to their station. Despite the warm spring weather, they favored white shirts with high collars that were tied with either white or black cravats. Over their shirts they wore square-cut waistcoats, topped by knee-length, skirted frock coats. And they covered their heads with hats, made from the felted underhair of beaver. Compared with the thrown-together wardrobes of the trappers, *engagés,* and other mem-bers of the firm's lower rungs, the attire of the clerks and *bour-geois* spelled authority. They were the junior officers of Pratte & Chouteau. To these mid-level managers fell the duty of culti-vating order and profit in a land that was as untamed as the buffalo and its native inhabitants.

Most of the assembly was well armed, something Captain Pratte undoubtedly appreciated. Indian tribes along the Missouri River usually posed no danger to steamboats, but it was wise to be prepared. In contrast with the clerks and *bour-geois,* who usually carried pistols beneath their coats, nearly everyone else had either a flint- or caplock rifle, a skinning knife, and a hand ax, which was worn in the small of the back and held in place by a belt or colorful sash. Trappers and *engagés* who could afford it also sported big bore pistols, forty-four caliber at least. The upper Missouri was no place to go lightly armed.

French Canadians dominated the rank and file of those who were awaiting passage, although there were also men from Kentucky, Illinois, Virginia, and a host of other states. Two or three free blacks may too have been in the group, as well as men of mixed parentage. Most of these "half-breeds," as they were disparagingly called, were the human by-product of the fur trade. Fathered by the white employees of the fur companies, the mixed-blooded men had been born of mothers who were Crees, Ojibwas, Mandans, Omahas, or some other tribe. These men who were both Indian and white shared a common goal with the free blacks. They all hoped to make their mark beyond the prejudice of the settlements. On the upper Missouri it was

Sidewheeler steamboats were preferred in winding, shallow western rivers because they were more maneuverable than sternwheeled craft.

the man who counted, not the pigment of his skin.

Inland from The Levee and its armada of boats, St. Louis bustled with commerce. The business part of town occupied a gravel bench that nature had wedged between the Mississippi River and a limestone bluff. Pratte & Chouteau had its warehouse and offices "under the hill," as this oldest part of the city was called. Here too were the taverns and grog shops frequented not only by *hivernans* just back from the Rocky Mountains but also by Mississippi rivermen, Army dragoons, lead millwrights from Herculaneum, and Missouri farmers. The roots of old St. Louis were French and Spanish, but the town's expansion since the Louisiana Purchase was an amalgamation of nationalities that was pure American.

New arrivals to St. Louis increasingly built their homes atop the limestone bluff that overlooked the river. Much of the city's gentry lived up here in great houses that enjoyed commanding views of the Mississippi. A broad plateau stretched away from the bluff, giving the town elbowroom for growth. Above the "hill," the pace slowed from the frenetic clamor of The Levee and narrow roadways of lower St. Louis.

"Under the hill," St. Louis pulsated with energy. Where the streets were not cobbled, horses, mules, oxen, and wagon wheels churned the dung and dirt byways into choking dust during the dry season and a sticky gumbo when it rained. No matter the condition of the streets, the town's citizenry was usually too busy to notice.

St. Louis thrived on trade, and the most important trade was fur. Between the city's founding in 1764 and 1832, beaver pelts had ruled the fur trade like a king. Hatters in New York, Boston, London, Amsterdam, and Paris pressed the underhair of North America's largest rodent into felt for making men's hats.[7] Then in the early 1830s when an army of trapping brigades was in danger of hunting the beaver to extinction, hatters started switching to cheaper nutria fur from South America. About the same time, fashion-conscious gentlemen in Europe and the eastern United States embraced a new style of top hat that was made from silk. The market price of beaver began a slow but steady slide. Trappers continued flocking to the mountains, vainly hoping that demand would recover, but beaver's downward spiral merely accelerated. Fortunately for Pratte & Chouteau, as hatters turned to nutria and silk, eastern consumers discovered that Indian-dressed buffalo robes made ideal lap covers and coats. Each year since its 1834 reorganization, the company had shipped more robes than it had the year before.

As soon as the loading crew finished stowing away the final boxes and casks, Captain Pratte signaled the men on The Levee that they could board. Eager to be under way, they noisily clambered across the gangplank and crammed into the few remaining bits of open deck space, all the time shouting and waving to those on the riverbank who had come to see them off.

The departure of Pratte & Chouteau's annual steamboat always generated excitement. Undoubtedly a number of clerks and laborers from the home office were on hand to bid Captain Pratte and the *St. Peter's* good-bye. A company partner or two could have dropped by The Levee, as well, including the senior partner, Pierre Chouteau Jr. Wives, sweethearts, friends, the curious, and hangers-on also made up the gathering that waved and gawked from shore. Reporters from the *Daily Missouri Republican* or one of St. Louis's other newspapers may have been in attendance, too. They often visited departing steamboats in order to see what famous personages were on board.

Since the *St. Peter's* was transporting government rations for the Missouri Indian tribes, it would have been natural for someone from William Clark's jurisdiction to stop by. As superintendent of Indian Affairs, Clark may have been tempted to come in person, especially since his agents, Joshua Pilcher and William Fulkerson, were accompanying the annuities. Pilcher managed the newly expanded Lakota-Cheyenne-Ponca Agency at Fort Kiowa, while Fulkerson had charge of the Mandan subagency at Fort Clark.

The Lakota-Cheyenne-Ponca and Mandan agencies were part of the Upper Missouri District, which was administered by Clark. All Indian agencies and Superintendents of Indian Affairs answered to the War Department. Pilcher and Fulkerson reported to senior agent, John Dougherty, who ran the Upper Missouri District from its headquarters at Council Bluffs (near present-day Omaha, Nebraska). In years past, Dougherty had located his office at the Army's Fort Leavenworth (in eastern Kansas), but pressure from Clark had forced him to move upriver to be closer to the tribes under his supervision. It was no secret that Joshua Pilcher coveted Dougherty's job and had whispered in Clark's ear, inducing the former general to push Dougherty into relocating.[8]

The forty-seven-year-old Pilcher had as much experience with Indians as any agent on Clark's staff, and more than most. He had begun working in the fur trade soon after moving to St. Louis in 1814. Within five years of his arrival, he became a partner in the Missouri Fur Company, at the time, the dominant American fur trading partnership west of the Mississippi. In 1820, following the death of the company's senior partner, Manuel Lisa, Pilcher took command of the firm's field operations, locating his headquarters at Fort Lisa near Council Bluffs (about nine miles north of Omaha, Nebraska). Over the next five years, Pilcher struggled to keep the Missouri Fur Company out of receivership as Arikara and Blackfoot war parties attacked its traders and trapping brigades, and competitors such as William Ashley, the Columbia Fur Company, Bernard Pratte & Company, and the American Fur Company chipped away at its markets.

In 1825, the Missouri Fur Company's partners reorganized as Pilcher & Company, but their fortunes failed to improve. Following an unprofitable foray to the western beaver grounds in 1827, the partners dissolved their association. In the early 1830s, Joshua Pilcher joined the American Fur Company and took charge of its affairs around Council Bluffs. Then in March 1835, Pilcher secured a government appointment as subagent to the Lakotas. His office was located on the Missouri River at Pratte & Chouteau's Fort Kiowa (about ten miles northwest of Chamberlain, South Dakota). Estimated to be 14,000 members strong, the Lakota subagency stretched from the Missouri to the Black Hills, and from the Moreau River south to the mouth of the Niobrara, and west to the North Fork of the Platte.[9]

Pilcher had left Fort Kiowa in the autumn of 1836, traveling downriver to St. Louis. As Christmas approached, he became so ill that he was confined to bed for the winter. Early the following year, President Martin Van Buren recommended to the Senate that the Lakota subagency be abolished and its duties merged into a larger, full agency that would include not only the Lakotas but also the Cheyennes and Poncas. As agent, the president proposed Joshua Pilcher. By the time Pilcher learned the Senate had approved his appointment, his health had recovered. With Pratte, Chouteau & Company's steamboat, *St. Peter's,* set to begin its voyage up the Missouri in mid April, Pilcher booked passage to Fort Kiowa and his new position, no doubt drawing strength from his recent promotion and expanded responsibilities.

Located upriver from Pilcher's sector, the Mandan subagency of William Fulkerson was the most remote of any Indian agency on the upper Missouri. Although his headquarters was located among the Mandans at Fort Clark, Fulkerson was also responsible for the Hidatsas, Arikaras, Crows, Assiniboines, Crees, Ojibwas, and a few bands of Yanktonai Lakotas.[10] Fulkerson had replaced John F. A. Sanford as subagent in early 1835. In his last few years with the subagency, Sanford had married the daughter of Pierre Chouteau Jr. and, as a result, been accused of being more interested in furthering the interests of his father-in-law than those of his Indian charges.

After taking control of the subagency, Fulkerson annoyed the partners of Pratte & Chouteau by eliminating Sanford's guise that government annuities were presents from the Upper Missouri Outfit. Being part owner of Pratte & Chouteau, Captain Bernard Pratte Jr. no doubt resented Fulkerson as much as did everyone else in the firm. But Pratte and his fellow partners valued their trading license and the money they made delivering Indian annuities. Fulkerson was a thorn in the company's side, but he was a government thorn, and government thorns needed to be handled with kid gloves.

When the last passengers had boarded, Captain Pratte ordered his crewmen to pull in the gangway and cast off the *St. Peter's* lines. Pilcher, Fulkerson, and others of their station waved from the rails of the hurricane deck, while the trappers, *engagés,* and rest of the steerage passengers crowded onto the guards (lateral appendages of the main deck that extended it beyond the hull) and fired repeated rifle salvos to celebrate their departure. On Captain Pratte's command, the pilot eased the steamboat away from the bank and turned its bow into the Mississippi's current.

Above St. Louis, the Mississippi flowed as if it were two rivers. About eighteen miles north of the city, the Missouri River shouldered into the Mississippi with the rawboned exuberance of a teenage boy barging into a church social. Below the confluence, the western, Missouri side of the combined rivers ran muddy brown, reminding some of creamed coffee. Toward the Illinois shore, the water glistened with the jaded green of a lazy summer day. At the center of the channel, the chocolate waters from the Missouri gradually surrendered to the Mississippi's greater volume, but the Mississippi needed many miles to erase the last vestige of its largest tributary.

When the *St. Peter's* neared the Missouri's mouth, Captain Pratte no doubt cautioned his pilot to keep a sharp lookout for sawyers and other debris. Along its length, the Missouri's current whipped back and forth across its channel, forming eddies

and undercutting banks. Where the river passed through
stands of cottonwoods, cedars, and the like, it often eroded the
soil holding them in place. Sawyers were trees that had fallen
in the water and were anchored to the muddy riverbed by their
roots. Those with their tops exposed were called planters. In
deep water, the hydraulic sometimes drove the limbs beneath
the surface, causing them to bob up when the flow suddenly
slackened. Because sawyers could appear in an instant, they
were particularly hazardous to steamboats. Thunderstorms and
the surging snowmelt often tore them loose, allowing the
Missouri to hurl them like battering rams. Many an unsuspecting boat had sunk after being skewered. Some sawyers had once
grown along the shores of the distant Musselshell or Marias
rivers, and a few had come to maturity in the shadow of the
Rocky Mountains.

In addition to trees, the Missouri's upcountry tributaries
occasionally ripped away chunks of riverbank and whisked
them downstream as miniature floating islands. Steamboats
such as the *St. Peter's* were especially vulnerable to having
their side-mounted paddle wheels shattered by this water-
borne refuse. Sawyers and driftwood that collected in confused
jumbles against the upriver edges of sandbars and islands were
called *embarras,* a name given them by French-Canadian
voyageurs. If the *embarras* grew large enough, they could con-
strict the channel, making it impossible for boats to pass.

As the *St. Peter's* swung into the Missouri's five-mile-per-
hour current, Captain Pratte knew the river could throw up
many obstacles that could spell disaster. It would take a steady
head as well as a keen eye to ensure the voyage was a success.
More than lives were at stake if the steamer sank or were
wrecked and failed to complete its mission. The future of Pratte
& Chouteau could also be in jeopardy. Although the company
controlled the lion's share of the upper Missouri fur trade, its
hold was as tenuous as gossamer. Competitors on both sides of
the forty-ninth parallel would love the firm to stumble so they
could grab its business. Bernard Pratte Jr. clearly understood
that the fate of the partnership rested in his hands.

About fifteen miles above the Missouri's mouth, the *St.
Peter's* churned past Portage des Sioux, a narrow strip of land

that separated the Missouri from the Mississippi. Except at their confluence, this was the closest the two rivers came to touching. Fifteen miles farther upstream, the steamer reached St. Charles, which sat at the base of some small hills.[11] While the *St. Peter's* maneuvered to the left bank, the trappers and *engagés* fired rifle salvos, saluting the onlookers who welcomed the boat from shore. It was a performance the rowdy passengers would give at every hamlet and trading post from here to Fort Union.

The *St. Peter's* probably stayed at the river town just long enough to take aboard more passengers. Men with families in the vicinity typically joined the voyage in St. Charles instead of St. Louis. When the steamer pulled away from the landing, the air again erupted with the discharge of rifles and pistols, while on shore, wives and sweethearts dabbed their eyes as townsmen and boys shouted "Godspeed."

From St. Charles to Jefferson City, the Missouri was placid, allowing the *St. Peter's* to travel during the nights the moon reflected off the water. Without moonlight, the lookouts and pilot were unable to see the sawyers, *embarras,* and other hazards that could send the steamer to the bottom. When the boat had to stop for the night, the pilot usually moored on the west or southwest shore. Given the prevailing westerly wind, there was less danger on that side from storm-whipped waves.[12]

Beyond the river and its accompanying swale, the rolling countryside was green with fresh-leafed trees and a carpet of spring grass. Paralleling the Missouri, the flat bottomland meandered with the river, narrowing where limestone cliffs pinched it thin, then spreading to a mile or more when the crags receded. A discerning eye could see the traces of old channels. They crisscrossed the floodplain, a testament to where the current had once flowed. Every year, snowmelt and thunderstorms pushed the Missouri beyond its banks, submerging the bottomland beneath acres of mud-charged water. When the flooding abated, the river often carved a new channel, at times abandoning whole stretches of shoreline. Sun and time would then dry the deserted riverbed, allowing it to be claimed by the willows and grass.

Aboard the *St. Peter's,* important passengers, such as Joshua

Pilcher and William Fulkerson, occupied the gentlemen's cabin, which was located on the boiler deck, sandwiched between the main and hurricane decks. Their quarters consisted of a rectangular-shaped saloon, where they and the other first-class passengers ate their meals, played cards, and tried to relax. Vibration and noise from the engines were as constant as tobacco smoke and the sour smell of sweat and whiskey-breath.

At night the cabin passengers slept in cramped, double-tier berths that lined the long sides of the saloon. Curtains shielded the sleeping compartments from view. The beds were barely thirty-two inches wide, and the pillows were stuffed with corn shucks.[13] The steamer's cabin boys and waiters slept on the saloon's carpeted floor. Most of the trappers, *engagés,* and other less privileged passengers—together with members of the deck crew—slept amid the freight on the main deck or in the open-air cargo hold. Rain often made their nights miserable. When it was not raining and the boat slowed or stopped, swarms of mosquitoes descended, seeking exposed skin. Smudge pots were lit in defense, though the choking lungs and watering eyes produced by their acrid smoke were almost as irritating as the mosquitoes.

Life on the 139-foot riverboat was a crush of bodies, the word crowded in no way adequately describing the lack of privacy.[14] If the first-class saloon and sleeping quarters did not leak when it rained, their bulkheads and ceilings sweated with condensation, caused by the breath of so many men. Passengers feeling the need to bathe used a small washroom just off the saloon. The tiny compartment contained a wooden bench and a couple of tin washbasins that were filled with water dipped from the muddy Missouri. The men scrubbed their faces and hands with a communal bar of soap and dried themselves on a single towel that was looped around a wooden roller. White when the *St. Peter's* departed St. Louis, the towel soon became as brown as the river. After a few days into the voyage, it was impossible to tell if the towel had been woven from cotton, flax, or hemp. The washroom may also have been furnished with a hairbrush and comb, and possibly a shared toothbrush. The privy—which resembled a typical rural outhouse—was located over the stern and emptied directly into the Missouri.

Pilcher and Fulkerson had little to do while the boat was under way besides play euchre or some other card game and look forward to the next meal. Breakfast was served at six-thirty in the morning, dinner at half past noon, and supper around seven p.m. The cabin passengers ate at a long table in the center of the saloon. Although the food was plentiful, most of the dishes consisted of meat and ran the gamut from fried pork and chicken; to baked duck, turkey, and ham; roasted venison; and boiled buffalo tongue. The meals also included rice, potatoes, bread, and cheese, and were topped off with pastries and pies.

Although sounding delicious when described on the bill of fare, the food was seldom hot when the passengers sat down to eat. Cooks were hired for their ability to turn out a vast quantity of dishes instead of their culinary skills, so most of the cuisine floated in a reservoir of grease. It did not matter, since the passengers devoured their meals as though they were starving. Conversation was forgotten as the diners sought to get their money's worth by shoving the food into their mouths as fast as they could work their knives and forks. Many began their meals with what was closest at hand, even if it happened to be dessert.[15]

In contrast with the accommodations for the first-class passengers, those for the steerage passengers and deck crew gave new meaning to the word spartan. Because only one steamboat journeyed to the upper Missouri each year, freight took precedence over the comfort of those traveling second-class. Not only was the cargo room filled to the brim with boxes and casks but so too was the main deck, where the lower ranking passengers were left to shift for themselves. Privacy and sanitation were nonexistent. Men slept atop crates of trade goods and Indian annuities, amidst the boat's fuel supply of cordwood, or while reclining against hogsheads filled with flour or 200-proof alcohol.

Open as it was to the elements, the main deck offered no protection from the hot sun or pelting rain. Steerage passengers furnished their own food, cooking it on a small iron stove that provided their only heat when the weather turned raw. Most of the men subsisted on bacon, sausages, cheese, dried fish, and pilot bread (hardtack), which they washed down with their own store of whiskey. In contrast, the steamboat provided meals—usually leftovers from the first-class passengers' table—for the deck crewmen, which they ate wherever they could find a place to sit.[16]

Second-class passengers were expected to work their way upriver, cutting the endless cords of wood needed to fire the *St. Peter's* boilers. Under a full head of steam, the boat consumed one and a quarter cords per hour. When possible the *charrettes,* as the wood cutters were called, harvested fence rails from abandoned homesteads. But most of the time, they chopped the trees that choked the bottomland. Although dry mulberry produced the hottest fires and was the preferred choice, much of it had already been cleared from the lower Missouri to power other steamers, leaving the men from the *St. Peter's* to make do with what was left. Once the boat moved farther upcountry, the *charrettes* would occasionally salvage logs from deserted trading posts. Where there were no trees, old fences, or vacant forts, the work crews collected driftwood. It was usually damp and would burn only if treated with a healthy coat of resin.

Above Jefferson City, the Missouri's current strengthened. At times it worked in harmony with the wind, holding the *St. Peter's* stationary or pushing it downstream while the pilot screamed for the engineer to give him more steam. When the boat could not make headway, Captain Pratte put in to shore and waited—often for hours—until conditions improved and the steamer could proceed. On a good day, it made fifty miles, but when the wind and river refused to cooperate, the miles could be as few as a dozen.

About 200 miles above the mouth of the Missouri, the *St. Peter's* passed Boonville, a hamlet that had been founded about eight miles from a salt lick thought to have been discovered by Daniel Boone. Hugging the bluff on the river's right side, Boonville was a bustling steamboat port. The farms bordering the settlement were purported to be on some of the richest soil on the lower Missouri. Across from Boonville was the site of Old Franklin, a fledgling village that had seemed destined to eclipse Boonville until the Missouri washed it away in the late 1820s.[17] About thirty miles above Boonville, the *St. Peter's* passed the settlement of Glasgow, and then that of Brunswick near the

Library of Congress
Fort Clark on the Missouri. Painted by Karl Bodmer.

mouth of the Grand River.

When the *St. Peter's* stopped to take on firewood, passengers wishing to stretch their legs went ashore, their ears always listening for the steamer's bell. A crewman rang it when Captain Pratte was ready to leave. Anyone not heeding the signal had to race across the next bend in the river, praying the overland shortcut would put him ahead of the boat. To miss it meant being left behind. On the lower Missouri such a happenstance could cost a man some lost time, but at least he could return to St. Louis by flagging down one of the many pirogues, keelboats, mackinaws, or packet steamers that plied this section of the river.[18] These boats were the workhorses of the lower Missouri, continually ferrying cargoes as varied as wild honey, salted buffalo tongues, rendered bear oil, and swan feathers. In contrast, missing the steamboat in Lakota country, farther upstream, could cost a man more than inconvenience. If a Yankton or Santee war party found him, he could lose his scalp.

While the *St. Peter's* churned up the Missouri, life at Fort Clark continued in the dull, humdrum manner it did at all trading posts this time of year. A work detail chopped and hauled firewood, while another pressed buffalo robes into ninety-pound packs. Francis Chardon bartered for a couple of beaver pelts, the first of the season. They were worth a lot less than in years past, but Pratte & Chouteau continued buying them in case their price ever recovered.

The two Arikaras who had arrived at the fort on April 13, announcing that their band was camped forty miles away, left Mitutanka Village, heading back to their people. Chardon hoped they had been telling the truth and that the main Arikara tribe would soon be in to trade. Meantime, the Mandans found renewed courage and were again launching raids against the Lakotas. A canoe had arrived from Fort Union, its crew bringing no news of import. To everyone's delight, the boatmen had brought hams from six pronghorns they had killed along the way. The meat was welcome, since buffalo continued to be scarce.

Within the *bourgeois's* house, Chardon's Lakota wife, Tchon-su-mons-ka, lay sick in bed, her condition worsening by the day. No matter what nostrums Chardon gave her, she showed no sign of recovery. Tchon-su-mons-ka had been a good wife, bearing her husband two sons, Francis Bolivar and Andrew Jackson. The years had faded her beauty, but that was common on the upper Missouri.

Back in 1832, when the visiting artist George Catlin had painted her portrait, Tchon-su-mons-ka was a striking young woman. When she undid her braids, her long black hair cascaded over her shoulders like waves of glossy silk. She delighted adorning herself with rings, bracelets, and necklaces—*foofuraw* that Chardon had provided.[19] Indian husbands could rarely afford to give their wives such finery, but white traders could. Tchon-su-mons-ka was especially proud of a deerskin dress that she had decorated with dozens of brass buttons. She had worn it for Catlin, who took pains to paint the buttons into her picture.

As with many marriages, that of Tchon-su-mons-ka and Chardon had not been all bliss. In mid July 1835, Chardon had tarried too long at Mitutanka Village one evening, watching the Mandans perform their Medicine Dance. His wife greeted his return to Fort Clark by pummeling him. Whether she used her fists or a switch, Chardon did not say when he recorded the episode in his journal. A year later, Chardon's behavior again displeased Tchon-su-mons-ka, who once more chastised him with a whipping.[20] He accepted his punishments without complaint, indicating that he probably thought they were deserved. Still, arguments such as these were rare. For the most part, theirs was a loving marriage. Chardon would miss her when she died, an event he had thought would not come for many years. Now deathly sick, she failed to respond to his remedies, forcing him to admit that her end was near.

On April 20, the fourth day of the *St. Peter's* voyage up the Missouri, Chardon rode to the Knife River to check on the trade among the Hidatsas. At the tribe's main village, he noted a pile of buffalo robes that his traders at the Hidatsas' winter camps had sent downstream the evening before. Although the stock of robes was less than he had expected, it was a start. Perhaps if the Arikaras brought their robes to Fort Clark, he would yet meet his trading quota. He hated to think what Pierre Chouteau Jr. would say if he came up short.

The next dawn, Tchon-su-mons-ka was no better. Resigning himself to her death, Chardon rode across the prairie, searching for buffalo. He enjoyed hunting and did so at every opportunity. A good chase always lifted his spirit and made the tedium of post life easier to endure. No doubt, he figured a day in the saddle would make him forget his wife's illness. All morning he topped rise after rise, each time expecting to spot a grazing herd. But the buffalo were nowhere to be found. Seeing no game except a few pronghorns, he shot two and tied their carcasses on his packhorse.

A bit after noon, he ended his hunt and turned his horses toward Fort Clark. In the distance where the two Arikaras had said their band was camping, smoke from a large grassfire billowed over the plain. Indians often torched the prairie, both to drive the buffalo and to burn off the previous year's dead grass. Doing so gave the spring growth a head start and produced richer pastures for the Indians' horses. The fire was the most reliable indication yet that the Arikaras were close. Most of the Hidatsas were upriver in their winter camps, and Mandan hunters were still too wary of the Lakotas to venture more than a couple of miles from their homes. Because a Lakota war party would not be foolish enough to announce its presence by burning the grass, the fire must have been started by the Arikaras.

Two days later, four Hidatsa warriors stopped by Fort Clark, announcing that the Arikaras would come to the trading post within the week. The Hidatsas were members of a raiding party that had gone to the Heart River to steal horses from the Lakotas. On their return, the Hidatsas had visited the Arikara camp.

Five years earlier, the Arikaras had lived in two villages just above the mouth of the Grand River (near present-day Mobridge, South Dakota). In autumn 1832, the tribe at last grew weary of fending off the encroaching Lakotas and abandoned their homes. The Arikaras headed southwest, joining their Skidi Pawnee relatives on the Loup River (a bit west of Columbus, Nebraska). For three years, the Arikaras dwelled among the Skidis, harassing the Arapahos and Northern Cheyennes and lifting the hair of any trapper foolhardy enough to come within range of their muskets and bows.

In the summer of 1835, the Arikaras said good-bye to their Skidi Pawnee cousins and migrated north to the Black Hills (in northeastern Wyoming and western South Dakota). Twenty-four members of the tribe then separated from the main body and joined the Mandans at Mitutanka Village. Some months later, about five dozen more Arikaras moved to the town.[21]

Through the years, the Arikaras had maintained a shaky truce with the Mandans and Hidatsas. Although the tribes often stole one another's horses and occasionally fought, they readily put aside their differences in order to repel the Lakotas—their common foe. Lakota threats made the addition of an ally, including a fickle one such as the Arikaras, welcome.

At eleven o'clock Monday morning, April 24, Chardon's wife passed away. That afternoon the *bourgeois* asked two *engagés* to take her body downriver to Fort Pierre so Tchon-su-mons-ka could be buried in the land of her Lakota people. Two-year-old Andrew Jackson, Chardon's younger son, accompanied his mother and the *engagés* in a canoe. The boy's older brother, Francis Bolivar, would miss the funeral, since he was living

with his paternal grand-
mother and two aunts in
Philadelphia, where the
women were supervising
his education.[22]

That evening when
Francis Chardon entered
the day's events in his journal, he kept his grief hidden. He noted that his men
had pressed fifteen packs
of buffalo robes. He reported that a Mandan hunting
party had returned to
Mitutanka Village with a
large store of meat, and he
lamented that the season's
fur trade had started so
slowly. But other than
writing that Tchon-su-mons-ka had died and that he had sent
her body to Fort Pierre, he made no mention of how he felt
about his wife's death.

George Catlin painting from Smithsonian Art Museum, gift of Mrs. Joseph Harrison, Jr.
Tchon-su-mons-ka, Lakota wife of Fort Clark *bourgeois*, Francis A. Chardon.

The next day, the Arikaras arrived at the Hidatsas' main village on the Knife River. The Arikaras gave the Hidatsas tobacco and shared their hosts' food. Meanwhile, the Hidatsas
showed their friendship by performing the Dance of the
Calumet.

A bit after noon, April 28, the main band of Arikaras—250
families—rode down from the prairie to the broad bench that
was shared by Mitutanka Village and Fort Clark. As the tribe
neared the trading post, Chardon ordered the Stars and Stripes
hoisted atop the flagpole. At the same time, he signaled a gun
crew to salute the Indians with the fort's cannon. To the delight
of the Arikaras, the gunners fired ten rounds from a four-
pounder. Chardon could not have been happier. The trading
season and his reputation within Pratte & Chouteau were
saved. The Arikara chiefs let it be known that their tribe had
brought 3,000 buffalo robes and ninety pounds of beaver. The
Arikaras were eager to trade.

Riding past Fort Clark, the Arikaras continued toward Mitutanka Village. Although a dozen or so Mandan young men had galloped to the prairie to provide the Arikaras an escort, the main Mandan welcoming party waited just outside the town's palisaded walls.

Among the Mandan greeters was undoubtedly Mah-to-toh-pa, the Four Bears. This most famous of Mandan chiefs had been given his name by his Assiniboine enemies, who said he fought them with the fury of four bears.[23] Fierce in battle, Four Bears had time and again proved his bravery. Lakota, Cheyenne, and Arikara warriors had tried to kill him in hand-to-hand combat, but he sent them all to the spirit world. In total, fourteen foes had died by Four Bears's hand.

The Mandan chief had been shot countless times—by musketballs as well as arrows. He had captured prisoners and stolen horses, but by far his most daring feat was slaying the famed Arikara warrior, Won-ga-tap, who had killed Four Bears's brother. After vainly waiting several years for a chance to meet the Arikara on open ground, Four Bears had stolen into his village under the cover of night. Moving as though he were a shadow, Four Bears slipped into Won-ga-tap's earthen lodge. Finding the Arikara asleep in his bed, Four Bears impaled him with the same spear Won-ga-tap had used to kill Four Bears's brother. It was a great coup, one still celebrated around Mandan council fires.

Revered by his tribe for his selfless leadership and generosity, Four Bears struck fear into the hearts of his enemies, but he had never harmed a white man. Francis Chardon and the other men at Fort Clark were his friends, and Four Bears would risk his own life in order to keep them safe. He could imagine nothing that would turn him against his white brothers.

As Four Bears bid his Arikara visitors welcome, he may have worn a buffalo robe with paintings of his many coups. Five years earlier, he had given such a robe to the artist George Catlin, and it is likely Four Bears would have painted another. No taller than most other Mandan men, Four Bears stood out from those around him because of his noble bearing. Alerted that the Arikaras were coming, he would have donned his finest war shirt, a tunic made from two mountain sheep, its seams and borders trimmed with porcupine quills, ermine pelts, and locks of hair taken from the scalps of his victims. His legs were encased in deerskin leggings that reached from the waist cord holding his breechclout down to his quill-patterned moccasins. Around his neck hung a string of fifty grizzly bear claws, which further attested to his prowess. Only the most audacious hunters dared challenging a grizzly.

When the Arikaras approached Four Bears, their eyes would have been drawn to his eagle feather headdress, which cascaded down his back until touching his heels. Attached to its top and crowning his head was a cap of curly white fur and a pair of buffalo horns. Polished black and tasseled with hair, the horns jutted from his head as though he were an incarnation of the Minotaur. The buffalo-horn headdress proclaimed his status as a war chief. Among the Mandans, its use was restricted to the bravest of the brave. And among the Mandans, the only warrior deemed worthy to wear it was Mah-to-toh-pa, the Four Bears.

After their initial greetings, the Mandans invited the Arikaras into Mitutanka Village. The few dozen Arikaras who had begun living among the Mandans in 1835 and 1836 were reunited with their relatives. All afternoon and into the evening, the Mandans feasted their visitors with corn and the last of the meat that the Mandan hunting party had procured the previous Monday. Old quarrels were hidden away as the two tribes displayed their best behavior.

The same day the Mandans welcomed the Arikaras to Mitutanka Village, aboard the *St. Peter's,* a black deckhand lay wrapped in a woolen blanket, his lower back a spasm of pain and his body burning with fever. The remainder of the crew and the trappers, *engagés,* and other second-class passengers paid him little mind. The unsanitary condition of riverboat travel, particularly in steerage, taxed the strongest constitutions. It was not unusual for several people to become sick during a trip up the Missouri. Most of the illnesses lasted only a few days.

On April 29, the steamer came in sight of Fort Leavenworth. Manned by the Third U.S. Infantry, the post sat on the west side of the Missouri, approximately 600 miles above the river's mouth and twenty-three miles upstream from the Missouri's confluence with the Kansas River. The fort had been established in 1827, and took its name from its founder, Colonel Henry Leavenworth. Charged with safeguarding the Santa Fe Trail, the garrison was also responsible for ending the trade in contraband liquor. Federal law prohibited the fur companies from giving or selling alcohol to the Indians. To enforce the statute, the War Department required all boats to stop at the fort for inspection. The Army was ordered to confiscate any stores that exceeded the allowance permitted the firms' white employees.

Chicanery and a lenient definition of what could legally be carried doomed the law to failure. It was the unimaginative riverboat captain who lost his 200-proof cargo to government sleuths. If falsely identifying spirits on a boat's manifest and mislabeling barrels of liquor failed to prevent their discovery, a bribe usually persuaded an inspector to look the other way. In order to save space, trade whiskey was shipped as pure grain alcohol. At the trading posts, *engagés* diluted it with water, then laced it with cloves or other spices. Indians who developed a taste for the white man's "firewater" cared more for potency than flavor. Despite the searches, Pratte & Chouteau's boats regularly shipped enough liquor to intoxicate any Indian who wished to tip a cup.[24]

When the *St. Peter's* eased up to the bank at Fort Leavenworth and the deckhands ran out its landing plank, the ill black crewman's temperature hovered around 106 degrees. Compounding his backache and overall malaise, his head pounded with the tempo of an Indian war drum, and the sunlight hurt his eyes. If someone had informed Captain Pratte about the man's condition, he was not worried. The symptoms were those of any number of maladies. If Pratte had to wager on a diagnosis, he would put his money on ague. On nearly every voyage up the Missouri, someone developed the river fever. In Pratte's experience, the disorder usually subsided by the time the boat reached the Grand Detour.

Soon after the *St. Peter's* made land, government agents came aboard and began checking its manifest and cargo.

Captain Pratte probably joked with them and perhaps offered them food from the boat's galley and brandy from his legal supply. Any contraband liquor he had on board was no doubt labeled flour or gunpowder. The inspectors were free to poke around, but Pratte knew it would take a miracle for them to find where it was hidden. If they did stumble across a barrel or two, the steamer's strongbox carried bribe money for unforeseen emergencies.

While the *St. Peter's* underwent inspection and the passengers stepped ashore to exercise their legs, upriver at Fort Clark the newly arrived Arikaras invited Francis Chardon to a feast. Before leaving for Mitutanka Village, the *bourgeois* directed his cooks to heat ten kettles of corn. After the Arikaras fed him, protocol dictated that he reciprocate.

The Arikaras honored Chardon by serving him boiled dog. Following the canine banquet, the *bourgeois* and a number of Arikara chiefs smoked the calumet and made speeches proclaiming friendship. Afterward, the Arikaras accompanied Chardon to Fort Clark and ate corn mush that the cooks may have sweetened with molasses.

The following morning, April 30—while the *St. Peter's* with its feverish deckhand steamed away from Fort Leavenworth— the Arikaras came to Fort Clark to trade. For much of the day, Indians filed into the trade room, their arms loaded with buffalo robes and the occasional beaver pelt. The Arikara men and women bartered slowly, savoring the process. A few warriors squandered the labor of their wives on liquor, but most of them bargained hard, striking fair deals for the muskets, lead, buttons, blankets, kettles, muslin, and other manufactured wonders that would ease their lives. By day's end, the fort's traders had procured 350 buffalo robes and a few other assorted furs. If business continued at this pace, Chardon would have no trouble meeting his quota.

That afternoon when the trade was finished, the Arikara women celebrated their newly acquired mirrors, ribbons, and beads by performing a spirited dance. Chardon and the other men at the fort watched the women prance and sway to the cadence of the accompanying drums. Most of the whites enjoyed these cavorting entertainments, which customarily earned the dancers a gift from their audience. Chardon probably rewarded the women with food or a few trinkets, especially since their tribe still possessed over 2,600 buffalo robes, which he hoped to acquire.

Before going to bed, the *bourgeois* recorded the day's events in his journal, noting as he always did on the last of the month the number of rats he had killed. This April, he had dispatched sixty-eight, bring his total since he had taken command of Fort Clark to 1,578.

As May began aboard the *St. Peter's,* the black deckhand felt better than he had in days. Although he still ran a fever and his muscles continued to ache, his temperature had dropped a few degrees and his head no longer throbbed. If he could improve some more over the next day or so, he would probably return to his duties. As the rhythm of the *St. Peter's* engines lulled him to sleep, on the undersides of his forearms and on his cheeks, a faint rash slowly darkened his brown skin. Unknowingly, he began to scratch.

Later that day while the steamboat pushed toward the Blacksnake Hills Trading Post of the Robidoux clan, Indian agent William Fulkerson visited the sick deckhand, asking him how he felt. Despite the crewman saying he was better, Fulkerson could not shed a suspicion that had been gnawing at him since first hearing about the man's condition. Leaving his side, Fulkerson searched out Captain Pratte, determined to tell him what he feared.[25] Although the early symptoms were similar for chickenpox, scarlet fever, and measles, the agent was certain the deckhand had smallpox.

Chapter one notes

1. Readers who question the Mandans' fondness for rotten meat are encouraged to read Edwin Thompson Denig, *Five Indian Tribes of the Upper Missouri: Sioux, Arikaras, Assiniboines, Crees, Crows,* ed. John C. Ewers (Norman: University of Oklahoma Press, 1961), 48-9; and Charles Edmund DeLand, abst., "Fort Tecumseh and Fort Pierre Journal and Letter Books," ed. Doane Robinson, in *South Dakota Historical Collections* (Pierre: South Dakota State Department of History, 1918), 9:105-06.

2. Modern historians and archaeologists are split about the dividing line for the middle and upper Missouri. Some look at a map and logically refer to the North and South Dakota portion of the Missouri River as the middle Missouri, whereas others defer to tradition and label it the upper Missouri. This book follows the traditional practice.

3. May 4, 1835.

4. It could also have been April 18.

5. Michael M. Casler, *Steamboats of the Fort Union Fur Trade: An Illustrated Listing of Steamboats on the Upper Missouri River, 1831-1867* (Williston, North Dakota: Fort Union Association, 1999), 35.

6. Louis C. Hunter, *Steamboats on the Western Rivers: An Economic and Technological History* (New York: Dover Publications, 1949), 82, 170, 652, table 9. During the 1830s, nearly all steamboats on western rivers were side-wheelers. Until the Civil War, stern-wheelers were typically used on smaller streams and in periods of low water.

7. Beaver have two layers of hair. The outer guard hair, which is up to two inches long, protects a thick layer of fine underhair. Each underhair filament contains microscopic barbs that bind with the barbs of other filaments when they are compressed during the felting process. Hatters then mold the resulting felt into a hat.

8. John E. Sunder, *Joshua Pilcher: Fur Trader and Indian Agent* (Norman: University of Oklahoma Press, 1968), 97. At the time the *St. Peter's* was preparing to head up the Missouri River, the War Department administered all Indian affairs, as it had done since George Washington was president. In 1849, Indian matters were reassigned to the newly-created Department of the Interior.

9. Ibid., 110-11, 113.

10. LeRoy R. Hafen, ed., *Fur Traders, Trappers, and Mountain Men of the Upper Missouri,* compiled from *Mountain Men and the Fur Trade of the Far West,* ed. LeRoy R. Hafen, 10 vols. (Glendale, California: Arthur H. Clark, 1965-72; Lincoln: University of Nebraska Press, Bison Book Edition, 1995), 52-3.

11. John Bradbury, *Travels in the Interior of America in the Years 1809, 1810, and 1811* (London, 1819; vol. 5 of *Early Western Travels, 1748-1846,* ed. Reuben Gold Thwaites; Cleveland: Arthur H. Clark, 1904; Lincoln: University of Nebraska Press, Bison Book Edition, 1986), 39 n. 9 puts St. Charles twenty-one miles above the Missouri's mouth. Although the channel has no doubt changed over the years, this is probably a straight-line measurement. By my calculation, the distance is closer to thirty river-miles.

12. Hiram Martin Chittenden, *History of Early Steamboat Navigation on the Missouri River: Life and Adventures of Joseph La Barge,* 2 vols. (New York: Francis Harper, 1903), 1:85.

13. John James Audubon, *Audubon and His Journals,* ed. Maria R. Audubon, with

notes by Elliott Coues, 2 vols. (Charles Scribner's Sons, 1897; New York: Dover Publications, 1960), 1:451.

14. Casler, *Steamboats*, 35.

15. Hunter, *Steamboats*, 400-03.

16. Ibid., 422-6, 451-2.

17. Dale L. Morgan, *Jedediah Smith and the Opening of the West* (Indianapolis: Bobbs-Merrill, 1953; Lincoln: University of Nebraska Press, Bison Book Edition, 1964), 32, 322.

18. Robert L. Dyer, "A Brief History of Steamboating on the Missouri River with an Emphasis on the Boonslick Region," *Boone's Lick Heritage* 5, no. 2 (June 1997); published on line: http://members.tripod.com; and William E. Lass, *A History of Steamboating on the Upper Missouri River* (Lincoln: University of Nebraska Press, 1962), 7-8 report that in 1836, between fifteen and twenty packet steamers cruised the lower Missouri, transporting goods and passengers from St. Louis to Boonville and Glasgow, with a few boats going as far as Fort Leavenworth. By 1838, the number of steamboats on the lower Missouri had swollen to twenty-two.

19. George Catlin, *Letters and Notes on the Manners, Customs, and Conditions of the North American Indians: Written during Eight Years' Travel (1832-1839) amongst the Wildest Tribes of Indians in North America*, 2 vols. (Philadelphia: published as Field Notes, 1841; London: 1841, 1844; New York: Dover Publications, 1973), 1:224. Catlin's portrait of Tchon-su-mons-ka (spelled Ychon-su-mons-ka by Catlin) appears in the volume as plate 95.

20. On August 30, 1836 (Chardon, *Journal*, 78), Chardon wrote that his wife's anger stemmed from him having "Committed fortification." Since his spelling often missed the mark, perhaps he meant fornication, an act Tchon-su-mons-ka may have felt warranted a whipping.

21. Roy W. Meyer, *The Village Indians of the Upper Missouri: The Mandans, Hidatsas, and Arikaras* (Lincoln: University of Nebraska Press, 1977), 89-90. Denig, *Indian Tribes*, 59 n. 27 says that the Arikaras sent a delegation to the Mandans in the fall of 1836.

22. Catlin, *Letters*, 1:225 n. (n.n.). Although Chardon did not mention in his journal that Andrew Jackson journeyed to Fort Pierre with Tchon-su-mons-ka's body, there is no other reason for the lad to have gone, a conclusion reached by the editor Annie Abel in Chardon, *Journal*, 315-16 n. 478.

23. Catlin, *Letters*, 1:154 attributes the naming of Four Bears to the Assiniboines, whereas Chardon, *Journal*, 296 n. 348 cites Helen Clarke—the daughter of trader Malcolm Clarke (usually spelled Clark) and a Blackfoot woman—who wrote that the Blackfeet called Four Bears Ne-so-ke-i-o because he had killed four bears in a single day.

24. R. G. Robertson, *Competitive Struggle: America's Western Fur Trading Posts, 1764-1865* (Boise: Tamarack Books, 1999), 26-8.

25. Joshua Pilcher to William Clark, February 5, 1838, reprinted in "An Ethnohistorical Interpretation of the Spread of Smallpox in the Northern Plains Utilizing Concepts of Disease Ecology," by Michael K. Trimble, *Reprints In Anthropology* 33 (Lincoln: J & L Reprint, 1986): 68-71, states that "a gentlem[a]n of the Indian department suggested to the Capt[ain] of the boat, that it would be well to put the man ashore." Most historians conclude the gentleman was probably William Fulkerson. I assume that in order to make the recommendation to put the black deckhand off the *St. Peter's*, Fulkerson would have had to examine him.

Karen A. Robertson

The Mandans, Hidatsas, and Arikaras built their lodge entrances large enough for a warrior to take his favorite horse inside.

Karen A. Robertson

Lodge interior, showing the fire pit used for cooking. Smoke escaped through a hole in the ceiling above the fire pit.

Karen A. Robertson

Lodge interior, showing a buffalo robe-covered bed, a warrior's bow and shield overhanging the bed and a painted parfleche storage case. Beds were shielded with animal hide curtains to provide some privacy.

Karen A. Robertson

Mandan, Hidatsa, and Arikara bull boats were typically made from the skin of one buffalo and could carry two or three adults.

Chapter Two

Variola Major

From its genesis 3,500 years ago until its eradication during the latter half of the twentieth century, smallpox reigned as one of mankind's most lethal killers. Caused by the virus *Variola major* (*Variola* comes from the Latin word *varius,* meaning spotted), the disease mutated into three distinct strains. Unfortunately for the human race, its mildest form, *Varioloid*—or as it is also called, *Variola minor*—evolved late in the virus's life, after medical science had learned how to tame it. For most of its history, smallpox existed only as the deadly *Variola vera* and *Variola hemorrhagica* viruses.[1]

Immunologists define a virus as a simple submicroscopic infectious agent—a bit RNA (ribonucleic acid) or DNA (deoxyribonucleic acid) encased in protein—that can reproduce only in the living cells of plants, animals, or bacteria. Most other living things contain both RNA and DNA, but a virus has either one or the other. The polio virus is made up of RNA, whereas *Variola major* and the other pox viruses are composed of DNA. RNA and DNA viruses replicate by invading an organism—man, for example—and finding an appropriate host cell. The smallpox virus initially goes after cells in the mucous membrane of the human lung, then spreads to cells in the body's other organs. After locating a suitable cell, the virus pierces the cell membrane and injects its own genetic code. The cell then ceases its normal work and begins to manufacture viruses—depending on the strain, upwards of 100,000 of them. Cells infected by viruses other than *Variola* usually die after a short time. *Variola* viruses, on the other hand, keep their host cells alive far longer than do other viruses, maintaining them as virus "factories." Replicated viruses leave their factory cells to search out healthy cells and begin the process anew.

When enough cells are affected by the spreading viruses, the organism becomes ill, often fatally. Vaccines, such as polio vaccine and the modern world's annual flu shot, allow cells to create antibodies that protect them from infection, but the antibodies cannot cure cells after a virus has successfully invaded them. Once a virus has taken over a cell, it can be destroyed only by killing the cell, which leads to risky side effects. Scientists continue to debate whether viruses are extremely elementary microorganisms (less complex than bacteria) or intricate molecules. They may be among the earth's oldest types of life.

It is theorized that one or more ancient pox viruses evolved in a single species of wild animals over millions of years, then mutated and infected domestic animals soon after they began living with humans, a few thousand years ago. Some of the viruses mutated again within the domestic animals and jumped to man, where they evolved into smallpox, chickenpox, and the other modern pox viruses.[2]

Occasionally called "true" or "ordinary" smallpox, *Variola vera* is the most common type of the disease. Highly communicable, it is one of the most infectious pestilences known to man. Although its virulence can range from mild to severe, a benign attack will devastate its victim. *Variola vera* and the other two strains of smallpox typically enter the body through the respiratory tract, usually when a non-immune person inhales the infected breath from someone who is contagious. This also occurs when an infected person sprays the air with a cough or sneeze.

In a dry state, the virus can maintain its potency outside the human body for as long as two years. Corpses of those who have died from smallpox are still infectious. Cremation destroys the virus, and interment in a deep grave isolates it until it is no longer lethal. But burial is only a safeguard if no one unearths the cadaver. A susceptible individual can inhale the virus and catch the disease after handling the pus- or scab-contaminated clothing or bedding of smallpox sufferers. It is also possible to contract the virus from the dead bodies of smallpox victims or from their winding-sheets. Although dry smallpox pus and scabs can remain potent for many months—especially in cool, arid climates—the *Variola* virus can propagate only within man. Non-human animals are not carriers.

The incubation period from the time a person becomes infected until the first symptoms appear varies from eight to fourteen days, with twelve being the most common. Once the virus completes its incubation, the onset of the disease is sudden, and its effects are cataclysmic. After the virus attains a critical mass within a new carrier, the patient experiences extreme fatigue and a temperature that often skyrockets to 106 degrees. A debilitating backache, pounding headache, chills, nausea, and convulsions compound the misery. Many victims are delirious, and a few become comatose.

On the fourth day of illness, the fever normally subsides, and the victim feels as if the worst has passed. This short-lived respite is merely the eye of a hurricane. Foreshadowing worse suffering to come, flat, red blotches—called macules—now creep across the patient's cheeks and forearms. Spreading slowly, as though they are a scarlet dye diffusing through a pristine pond, the macules eventually discolor the face and arms, then inch their way over the victim's abdomen, chest, back, and legs. Unconsciously, the patient will scratch the blotchy rash, vainly attempting to relieve its annoying itch.

Now infectious (a smallpox carrier is infectious from immediately before the appearance of his rash until he sheds his scabs), the victim unwittingly discharges the virus with every breath, poisoning the air for many feet around. Soon the fever returns, and the backache—both with vengeance. Moaning in agony as his head pounds with the tempo of his pulse, the patient thrashes amid his bedclothes as his mind slips in and out of delirium. Every heartbeat begets an explosion of pain.

After a few days, the flat red lesions elevate, then ripen into clear blisters that slowly fill with pus. The face swells into a hideous mass of pimply flesh, barely recognizable as human. For many victims, the pustules become so thick they appear to run together like a giant, oozing sore, a condition that is termed confluent smallpox.

In some patients, the disease attacks the mouth, throat, and windpipe, forming pus-brimming ulcers in the mucous membrane. For these sufferers, eating and drinking are nearly impossible, since ingesting a bite of food or sip of water feels like swallowing a hot coal. Coughs can cause such patients' tracheas to hemorrhage, thereby drowning them in their own gore. If the victims live, a week or so after their skin pustules mature, they split open and dry into scabs. Within a month, the scabs fall off, leaving deep-pitted scars that are patterned in a centrifugal distribution, as if they have been etched into a spinning dinner plate.

Death can occur at any time after the incubation, often from secondary infections such as pneumonia, encephalitis (an inflammation of the brain), myocarditis (an inflammation of the muscular layer of the heart), and viral osteomyelitis (an inflammation of the bones and the destruction of the surrounding tissue). The disease can also ravage the lungs, liver, and intestines.

As their bodies are eaten away by the canker, smallpox victims exude the sickening odor of rotting flesh. Following the smallpox death of King Louis XV of France, his body stank so much, one of his pallbearers died from convulsive vomiting.[3] About one percent of *Variola* victims lose the sight in one or both of their eyes as the virus ulcerates their corneas. During the sixteenth through eighteenth centuries, smallpox was a major cause of blindness in Europe, Africa, and Asia.[4] As a final agony, many surviving male victims are rendered sterile. Individuals who live through the disease face a long convalescence, during which they remain susceptible to secondary infections.

The most malignant type of smallpox is *Variola hemorrhagica,* also called the black smallpox. After the incubation period, persons suffering from this strain experience the customary high fever and severe head and backaches. Within two or three days, such victims will start to bleed from their gums and internal organs; women sometimes bleed from their vaginas. In some hemorrhagic patients, the virus forms the itchy rash and pustules that characterize *Variola vera,* while in others it causes their capillaries to burst, swelling and darkening their skin with clotting blood. Virtually all victims of black smallpox die between the fifth and seventh day after incubation, often before any pustules have a chance to form. Rarely does anyone with hemorrhagic smallpox live longer than a week.

Like other pathogens, *Variola major* preys heaviest on the weakest members of a population, reserving its most severe attacks for the very young and very old, the malnourished, and the feeble. For those who contract the disease, there is no cure. If their bodies' immune systems cannot defeat the onslaught, they die. And throughout history, countless millions have.

The one blessing that survivors enjoy is lifetime immunity. Once a person has had any kind of smallpox, including the mild *Varioloid,* he can never again catch any type of it, nor can a former patient ever transmit the disease to another person. Yet such a benefit carries a steep price. Many a comely damsel has weathered the disease only to forsake the company of men, ashamed of her disfigured beauty, her once-lovely face forever scarred by an ugly brand. Too often these pockmarked maidens have chosen to live out their remaining days behind dark veils or within the cloistered walls of a monastic order.

Variola major is thought to have evolved around 1500 B.C. when the population of certain locales reached sufficient numbers for the virus to survive. In other words, smallpox is a crowd disease. Some epidemiologists think it originated in India, perhaps in the Indus River Valley, before spreading along the coastal trade routes to Egypt. Ramses V may have been the most famous early victim of the pestilence, since his mummy shows evidence of pustules, though modern scientists and Egyptologists are far from certain about what caused his death.[5]

By 1000 B.C., smallpox was endemic in India and Egypt, sustained by the large population densities that it needed to keep from dying out.[6] Endemic means that a parasitic microorganism dwells within a population. The population must be big enough to continually produce new, susceptible hosts so the chain of infection can be perpetuated. Repeated outbreaks of the microorganism-caused disease hold the population's overall immunity in balance. Despite these outbreaks, the population as a whole has no risk of becoming extinct. Epidemics occur when the microorganism mutates, or when it invades a virgin population. In these instances, the disease races through the populace, consuming victims as fast as they are exposed.[7]

From Egypt, traders—especially seafaring traders—eventually carried the virus to the villages and city-states bordering the eastern Mediterranean Sea. In time, overland trading caravans introduced it to Asia Minor. During the Peloponnesian Wars in ancient Greece (431-404 B.C.), a disease that was possibly smallpox so weakened the Athenian army that Sparta managed to emerge victorious.[8] One hundred years later, another epidemic that may have been smallpox struck Alexander the Great's army during its invasion of India.[9]

An epidemic generally thought to be smallpox was introduced to the Roman Empire A.D. 165 by its legions that had been warring in Mesopotamia. The Greek physician Galen lived through the scourge and wrote about its symptoms, which included fever and pustules. For fifteen years, the Plague of Antonius—as the epidemic is called—swept Rome's vast domain, eventually killing between three and one-half million and seven million people. Most famous of the dead was the Roman emperor and philosopher Marcus Aurelius.[10]

Another multi-year epidemic struck the Roman Empire A.D. 251, creating manpower shortages and opening the Roman frontier to increased raids by the Franks and Goths. At its height, this epidemic killed an estimated 5,000 people a day within Rome itself.[11] As with the Plague of Antonius, many historians think this later epidemic may also have been caused by smallpox.

By the time the Visigoths' King Alaric sacked Rome A.D. 410, smallpox was endemic across most of southern Europe and Asia Minor. Isolated outbreaks continued to occur, particularly among outlying bands of people who were being infected for the first time, but there were no more pandemics (epidemics that affect a large proportion of the population within a wide geographic area), such as the Plague of Antonius.

Foreign armies that invaded Europe and Asia Minor from regions where smallpox was not endemic were at great risk from the contagion. Sixty thousand Ethiopian soldiers perished from a poxlike sickness while laying siege to Mecca during the Elephant War A.D. 569 or 570. Many historians think the disease was smallpox.[12]

Variola major probably reached China sometime between A.D. 37 and 653, with 317 being the most likely year. One tradition says the disease infected Chinese soldiers who had been fighting barbarian invaders in the northwest.[13] From China, the virus migrated to Korea. It is thought that Buddhist monks from Korea first carried smallpox to Japan A.D. 552.[14] During the decades that followed, repeated epidemics swept the Japanese islands until *Variola major* became endemic.

In Africa, smallpox spread south from Egypt along the western Red Sea coast until it infected the sub-Sahara. By the ninth century, it had crossed to the Atlantic Ocean, reaching the natives of central west Africa.[15] In fourteenth-century Europe, bubonic plague—the black death—ravaged the continent, eclipsing smallpox's morbidity, and eventually killing twenty-five million people, about one-third of the population. But *Variola major* did not die out. By the fifteenth century, it had diffused to all but the farthest corners of the Euro-Asian and African landmasses.

In regions where it was chronic, smallpox became a childhood disease. The transition of *Variola major* from an indiscriminate killer among all age groups to a malady of the young followed the same evolutionary sequence in Europe, Asia, and Africa. The only difference was in what year the disease reached a particular locale.

After the fall of Rome, smallpox visited the villages of medieval Europe every five or ten years, exacting its toll from those who had been born since the last outbreak. Most adults of childbearing age had survived the virus and gained lifelong immunity from future attacks. In a process that evolved over many generations, immune parents passed to their offspring an increased resistance—but not immunity—to the illness.

A lot of children who caught *Variola major* died, but far fewer than had they been members of a virgin population. Parents took it for granted that a number of their sons and daughters would perish before puberty—from smallpox or other causes. High infant and adolescent mortality encouraged parents to have large families, ensuring that some of their progeny reached maturity. As smallpox came to kill primarily the young, its impact on European, African, and Asian society subsided. Though the deaths of children were certainly tragic for their mothers and fathers, a community could absorb their loss easier than had smallpox claimed a great part of its older, producing members.

Around A.D. 1000, towns began to gain importance across Christendom, especially those that grew into coastal and inland trading hubs. Children living in larger towns and cities were far more likely to catch smallpox and other childhood diseases— such as measles and whooping cough—than were their country cousins. Cities were so unhealthy, they needed a continual stream of rural emigrants in order to grow.[16] Provincial villages occasionally went ten or twenty years between *Variola* outbreaks. As a result, scattered reservoirs of vulnerable young adults dotted the landscape, waiting for the disease to strike. When pressed into military service, strapping farm boys who had never had smallpox often took sick and fared worse than their undernourished—but immune—kin from the city.

In contrast with Europe, Asia, and Africa, the western hemisphere—isolated by the Atlantic and Pacific oceans—had no knowledge of smallpox. Having crossed the Bering Strait land bridge thousands of years before the *Variola* virus first established itself on the Asian subcontinent, the native people of North and South America had had no time to build their resistance to the disease.[17] Their bodies were ripe for the killer virus. For them smallpox meant almost certain death.

The science of genetics reports another reason for the extreme susceptibility of Native Americans to smallpox. Unlike whites, blacks, and Asians, New World Indians are genetically uniform. Recent empirical research on measles shows that when an individual catches the disease from a member of his own family, the attack is normally stronger than if he had been infected by someone who was unrelated. Being similar to the measles virus, *Variola major* is programmed to search out hosts who are genetically akin to the one in which it was incubated. Finding such victims, the smallpox virus gains strength. Therefore, in addition to being a virgin population for the *Variola* virus, the natives of North and South America were all the more vulnerable because of the similarity of their genetic codes.[18]

U ntil the early sixteenth century, Europeans called smallpox simply pox or by its Latin-derived name—*Variola*. But around that time, an epidemic of syphilis swept Europe and became known as the great pox. Before long, people began calling *Variola* smallpox to differentiate it from its sexually-transmitted relative, which produced much larger pustules than those caused by smallpox.[19]

During the sixteenth and seventeenth centuries, London, Paris, Vienna, and other large European cities suffered through major smallpox epidemics every few years. Young children were the principal victims, since most adults had survived the disease in their youth and were immune. But smallpox did not confine itself to the young nor to the poor. Anyone who had not had it as a child was vulnerable.

Variola major ravaged twenty-nine-year-old Queen Elizabeth I in 1562, although she survived. Succeeding English royalty were not always so lucky. On December 28, 1694, thirty-two-year-old Queen Mary II died of the most lethal brand of smallpox, *Variola hemorrhagica*. Some years before, her husband, William, Prince of Orange, had lost his mother and father to the disease. In May 1774, confluent smallpox claimed France's Louis XV when he was in his mid sixties. By the time he died, his body was so rotten and smelled so bad, his physician declined to embalm it—as was required by law—and instead doused the deceased king with alcohol and quicklime as his corpse lay in a lead-lined casket.[20]

Americans—both Indians and those of European stock— were particularly vulnerable when they visited the Old World. The famed Pocahontas, who had saved the Jamestown settlement from annihilation by the Powhatan Confederation and later married planter John Rolfe, went with her husband to England, where she charmed the court of King James I. She never again saw her native land. Some historians claim she died of smallpox at the approximate age of twenty-two. Others blame her death on pneumonia (a possible complication of smallpox) or tuberculosis. In any case, the young Pocahontas coughed away her life in 1617 at Gravesend, having boarded a ship that was to carry her back to North America.[21]

Americans of European ancestry who had not had smallpox were also at increased risk of catching the virus when traveling abroad. Because the disease was less pervasive in the American colonies—despite periodic epidemics—than it was in Europe, many colonists avoided smallpox altogether. As a result, colonial fathers and mothers were reluctant to send their clear-skinned sons and daughters to the Old World where they could die from the disease. The impetus to build Harvard, Yale, and William and Mary colleges came, in part, from a desire by the colonists to protect their sons from the health danger of being educated at Oxford, Cambridge, or some other European university.[22]

The fear of smallpox was so great, it handicapped the Church of England from expanding its North American congregations. Young colonial men wanting to enter the Anglican ministry had to be ordained by a church bishop, all of whom resided on the east side of the Atlantic Ocean. Making a voyage to the British Isles required not only money but also an exceptional faith, especially for those who had so far escaped smallpox. Because few men had such a strong spiritual calling, the Church of England lost out to denominations and sects that commissioned their clergy in North America.[23]

Although there was no cure for those who caught smallpox, a mitigating treatment—acquired immunity—had been used in India for over 1,000 years and in China since the Sung Dynasty (A.D. 960-1279). Recognizing that those who had survived smallpox, including its weaker strains, were immune from ever catching it again, Indian and Chinese healers inoculated non-immune individuals by blowing the dust of ground-up smallpox scabs up their noses. The procedure worked best if the scabs were taken from a person with a light case. Another method of inoculation required rubbing the pus from a mildly sick patient into a scratch made in a healthy person's skin. The inoculee caught the disease, but it was normally a less severe case than the person would have acquired had it been contracted naturally. As an added benefit, scarring was usually less pronounced, as well.

Compared with this scientific approach for dealing with smallpox, the standard treatment in Europe was bizarre. Although European doctors recognized the necessity of quarantining smallpox victims in order to protect the general populace from becoming infected, they sought to cure the sick by bleeding them and making them drink concoctions that used sheep or horse dung as their central ingredient.[24] Such remedies merely added to the patients' suffering.

Fortunately for the Europeans, in 1700 an East India Company trader named Joseph Lister described Chinese inoculation to some English physicians. A short time later, the Greek doctor Giacomo Pylarini of Smyrna inoculated a non-immune volunteer by placing *Variola* pus in a scratch he had made in the individual's skin. The volunteer developed a mild case of smallpox, but lived, forever after immune. Although Pylarini's procedure appeared in the *Philosophical Transactions* of the Royal Society of England in 1714, it took another seven years for the British medical community to embrace it. Even then, its adoption required the efforts of a most unlikely participant, the wife of the English ambassador to Turkey, Mary Wortley Montagu.

Smallpox had blighted Lady Montagu's beauty when she was a young woman and had killed one of her brothers. Knowing personally the emotional scars that remained long after the disease had shed its last scab, she sought to spare her five-year-old son from a similar experience. In 1718, while living in Constantinople at her husband's posting, Lady Montagu enlisted a local female practitioner to inoculate her boy. The embassy physician, Dr. Charles Maitland, witnessed the procedure, which was a complete success.

On returning to England in 1721, Lady Montagu asked Dr. Maitland to inoculate her daughter to protect the child from a smallpox epidemic that was raging through London. Dr.

Maitland performed the inoculation before several court physicians, including Sir Hans Sloane, president of the Royal Society and doctor to the king. Following the girl's recovery, reports of the treatment reached the newspapers and came to the notice of Princess Caroline, wife of the Prince of Wales and future King George II. After witnessing the favorable inoculation of seven convict volunteers at Newgate Prison and eleven orphans at the St. James Parish, the princess permitted her two children to be inoculated.

Word of the princess's bold experiment gained acceptance of the practice among much of the English aristocracy. Egged on by the clergy, the merchant and lower classes were less willing to embrace such a newfangled idea. British ministers, such as the Reverend Edmund Massey, railed against inoculation, arguing that it was sinful for man to work against the will of God. Smallpox was a test, the Reverend Massey preached, and man was meant to bear it just as Job had endured God's challenges of him during Biblical times.

Faced with such superstition and benighted logic, Lady Montagu became an eighteenth-century publicist for inoculation, directly soliciting physicians to perform the procedure and writing newspapers, praising its benefits. Her tireless efforts gradually broke down the opposition and brought inoculation into the British medical mainstream.[25]

Across the English Channel, the French did not endorse the practice until the 1760s. In 1768, inoculation came to Russia when Catherine the Great hired an English physician to inoculate her and the Crown Prince, but the czarina did nothing to encourage the remedy among the general populace. In contrast, during the 1770s, Frederick II ordered Prussian doctors to learn the procedure so they could shield his armies from the dreaded disease. In this way, smallpox protection finally reached the peasant classes.[26]

European inoculators found far more business in rural communities than they did in cities. In the large population centers, smallpox had evolved into a childhood disease. By contrast, small country villages could go several years without being infected. When *Variola major* finally appeared in them, it often struck as a mini-epidemic, assailing young adults who had hitherto eluded its scourge.

Unlike the urban masses, provincial European men and women—especially those in England—often sought out inoculators and "bought the smallpox" rather than chance catching it naturally. Across the Atlantic, North American colonists also embraced inoculation more readily than did the residents of Amsterdam, Liverpool, and Paris. Unlike cities in Europe where children were routinely exposed to smallpox at a young age, many American communities—such as some rural European towns—escaped the disease for years before being ravaged by an epidemic that claimed infants and non-immune adults alike. Far more fully grown Europeans were at risk of *Variola major* in the New World than in the Old. As a result, colonists in Boston, New York, and other American coastal cities came to see inoculation as a reasonable means of protection.

Although inoculators took great pains to use the pus or scabs from a person with a mild case, the procedure involved considerable risk. Because inoculees actually caught smallpox, they needed to be quarantined lest they pass the disease to others. Adding to the danger, two or three percent of all inoculees died, a sobering statistic that prompted anyone who was considering the practice to think long and hard before submitting to the physician's lancet.

Prior to administering the treatment, inoculators prepared their patients. The good practitioners ensured their charges had plenty to eat and were in good health. Such planning was important if the inoculees were to survive the disease's fever and secondary infections.

Unfortunately, many inoculators looked to the medicine of the day when readying their subjects. In 1757, an eight-year-old English lad named Edward Jenner, who would later become a famous physician, underwent inoculation in his home county of Gloucestershire. The local apothecary, a Mr. Holbrow, who was to perform the operation, readied Jenner by repeatedly bleeding him over a period of six weeks. In addition, Holbrow gave Jenner purges that produced violent vomiting, in order to cleanse his body of harmful "humors." The apothecary also forced the boy to fast, prescribing sweet herb tea instead of food. By the time Jenner was ready to be inoculated, he was so weak, he could hardly stand.[27] It is a wonder he survived.

The complete inoculation process required between one and two months to complete. Inoculees spent the first half of the time resting and improving their diet if they had a competent inoculator, or bleeding, vomiting, and starving if they did not. During the second half of the procedure, the inoculees were bedridden with smallpox. Fresh, nutritious food and inoculators cost money, quite a lot of money. Further, it was the rare tradesman or common laborer who could afford to forgo a month or more of income, provided his employer would allow him a non-paid leave of absence.

In the large cities of Europe, inoculators rarely found work among the poor. Wealthy urban parents could pay to have their children protected from smallpox, but the penniless could ill afford the luxury. Most impoverished families had an excess of hungry mouths, so the death of one or two infants among a dozen or more sons and daughters was accepted as God's will. As a result, inoculation was generally restricted to the rich. Among the underclass, smallpox continued to rage.

From 1660 to 1800, smallpox ravaged Europe with more intensity than it had shown for centuries. In its peak years, *Variola major* caused over seventeen percent of London's fatalities,[28] and between 1731 and 1765, the city's Bills of Mortality blamed the disease for nine out of every 100 deaths.[29] During the last twenty years of the eighteenth century, smallpox accounted for one out of every ten Londoners who died. In Glasgow, Scotland, the ratio reached one out of five. As has been pointed out, children made up most of the dead, since the majority of European adults had survived the disease during childhood and were immune to further attacks. As the century approached its close, smallpox was killing one out of ten French and Swedish babies, and in Russia, one out of seven.[30]

On the Great Plains of North America, many Indian tribes believed that internal illnesses could be traced to the supernatural. They were a punishment levied by the spirits for disobeying tribal rituals. Indians could not fathom a sickness being passed from one person to another any more than they could imagine a warrior with an arrow in his leg transferring the wound to another. Native shamans treated broken bones, sprains, snake bites, and puncture wounds in a logical manner, similar in many ways to the procedures used by European doctors of the day. But smallpox was beyond Indian understanding. (To be fair, Europeans had little understanding of the disease either.) Accordingly, Indian medicine men often sought to treat smallpox victims with prayers and magical incantations.

When the disease first showed itself within a tribe and few were sick, a patient's family usually summoned a shaman, hoping he could divine a cure. As the family members looked on, the shaman would dance beside the feverish victim while tapping a small, hand-held drum. As the medicine man bowed and cavorted in rhythm with his beat, he would sing to the tribal spirits, asking them to grant him the power to heal. During the dance he would raise and lower his voice, matching the cadence of the drum. Every few minutes he would cease dancing and blow a reed whistle while shaking a dewclaw rattle over the patient. Believing that illnesses were caused by a malevolent spirit, he would pray for the strength to cast the evil from the victim's body. At this point in the ceremony, the shaman often brought out a couple of eagle feathers, which he had anointed with mystical rites, passing them four times—a magic number to most Plains tribes—over the length of the patient.

With the ritual now approaching its climax, the shaman would pull a hollow bone—perhaps made from an eagle's wing—from his medicine bag and hold it aloft for the family to see. Making a fist, he would tap his hand against his lips, secretly placing a pebble or some other object in his mouth. Proclaiming his triumphs as a healer, he would ratchet up his voice until the litany reached an ear-splitting crescendo. Suddenly falling mute, the shaman would let the lodge fill with silence. Bending down, he would place the hollow bone in the patient's mouth and suck, as if to draw out the evil pathogen. A few moments later, he would spit the concealed pebble into his hand and hold it forth for everyone to see, announcing that the patient was cured.[31] But there was no cure for smallpox. By repeatedly performing such rituals, Indian medicine men unwittingly spread the virus.

Another common Indian treatment for smallpox that added

to the death toll was induced sweating. Indians with high fevers were often placed in hot sweat lodges. A typical sweat lodge was made from a domed lattice of willows or saplings that was overlaid with hides, forming a dark, airtight enclosure. An outside helper heated rocks in a fire, then passed them to Indians inside the lodge, who sprinkled them with water. Shaved willow bark—a source of salicin, which is a component of aspirin—or other herbs were sometimes added to the water.[32] The resulting steam turned the lodge interior into a sweltering sauna. Participants thought that heavy perspiration purified body and soul. Vision seekers typically cleansed themselves in sweat lodges before going on their quests, as did warriors before setting off to raid their enemies. Because Indians sweated to rid their bodies of corrupting influences, most viewed the practice as a logical way to cure smallpox. After feverish smallpox victims had spent some time in a sweat lodge, their friends or relatives would usually carry them to a stream and submerge them in the icy water. If the shock did not kill the patients outright, it certainly increased their misery.[33]

If the Indians had understood the concepts of germ theory—something Europeans of the time did not comprehend either—the idea of quarantining the sick was foreign to everything they believed. Indian culture was clannish. Families crowded together in wooden or earthen lodges or in buffalo-hide tipis, where everyone breathed the same air. No better crucible for smallpox contagion could have been devised. As a general rule, nomadic tribes fared better than their village neighbors. But despite the migratory life of the nomads screening some bands from *Variola major,* infected hunting and war parties ensured that the virus was spread far and wide.[34]

Anglo-society in North America began protecting itself from smallpox in July 1721, when Dr. Zabdiel Boylston performed the colonies' first inoculations by rubbing scabs from a smallpox patient into scratches made in the skin of his six-year-old son and two black slaves. Dr. Boylston had learned about the procedure from his friend, Cotton Mather. Fourteen years earlier, the famed clergyman had purchased a slave named Onesimus, who was newly arrived from Africa. Before his capture, Onesimus had been inoculated by his tribe. When asked by Mather if he had ever had smallpox, Onesimus told him about his inoculation and showed him the scar it had left on his arm.[35]

Cotton Mather and Dr. Boylston, who had both contracted the disease as young men, knew the treatment was risky, but they hoped widespread inoculation would stem a smallpox outbreak that raged that year in Boston. The virus had arrived in April 1721 aboard the English sailing ship, *Seahorse.*[36]

After inoculating three members of his household, Dr. Boylston—with Cotton Mather's support—published the event, intending to spur public acceptance and quell the mounting epidemic. The response was not what they had envisioned. Many of the city's citizens railed against the practice, claiming it was unchristian. The clamor grew louder after Mather permitted Dr. Boylston to inoculate his grown son, Samuel Mather. The muckrakers believed it was God's prerogative to make people sick—which inoculation did—not that of man. One protester became so incensed that Boston's leading clergyman had slipped into blasphemy and heathenism, he pitched a bomb through Mather's window, attempting to blow him to kingdom come. Luckily for Mather, the perpetrator's bomb-making skills were as flawed as his theology.[37] Mather survived. Despite such protests, 247 Bostonians underwent inoculation before the epidemic ended in the spring of 1722. Among that group, only six died—a fatality ratio of 2.4 percent. In contrast, of the town's 5,980 citizens who caught smallpox naturally, 844 died—a death rate of fourteen percent.[38]

Because inoculated patients actually caught smallpox—albeit a mild case if the procedure worked as planned—they needed to be quarantined while contagious, lest they infect others. In addition, inoculees were in danger of having their controlled bouts explode into full-blown attacks, which carried the risk of death. Out of nearly 400 Bostonians who were inoculated during a smallpox epidemic in the early 1730s, twelve died. During an outbreak in Charleston in 1738, sixteen out of 441 inoculees passed away.[39] Although these death rates were under four percent—as compared with twelve to fifteen percent for whites who caught the disease naturally—inoculation remained controversial. As was the case in Europe, in North America it was most often used on the wealthier members of society, blue bloods such as Martha Washington and Abigail Adams, both of whom were successfully inoculated.

Inoculees were bedridden during the worst phases of the disease, which made the practice time-consuming as well as expensive. If not too indisposed, they occasionally visited with friends, either at home or in public. The lack of a proper quarantine often made inoculation more of a danger to an inoculee's healthy—but not immune—acquaintances than to the patient. A colonial inoculator named John Smith unleashed a mini-epidemic in the late 1760s, when his lax quarantine allowed his charges to infect the Virginia countryside. Several people died before the disease was contained. Although Charleston, New York, and several other cities enacted ordinances prohibiting inoculation, most communities sought to regulate the practitioners rather than forbid the procedure. Town councils usually suspended any laws banning inoculation if smallpox broke out naturally. Boston's selectmen did so during epidemics in 1776, 1778, and 1792.[40]

In contrast with their affluent brethren, the lower classes in America—like their impoverished relations in Europe—rarely had the wherewithal to "buy the disease." If the poor could scrape together the three-pound fee practitioners such as those in Philadelphia charged,[41] the month or more required for them to be away from their work was an impossibility. Most penniless whites, black slaves, and Indians had no more chance of being inoculated than they did of going to the moon. Consequently, *Variola major* had an unending reservoir of people to infect.

During the Revolutionary War, colonial recruits feared smallpox more than they did the fire of British muskets. The disease raked George Washington's troops in New York and New Jersey, as it did the Continental soldiers under generals Benedict Arnold and Richard Montgomery during their siege of Quebec City. After Montgomery was killed, the Americans retreated from Canada in June 1776, their ranks reduced by half from the 10,000 men who had boldly marched north earlier that year. Because of wounds, smallpox, and other illnesses, the brigade's effective strength was far less than the 5,000 soldiers that Arnold led back to Crown Point, near Fort Ticonderoga. That December, troops at Fort Mount Independence on Lake Champlain (in New York State) also suffered from smallpox. One soldier lying alone in his tent, his body racked with *Variola* fever, drowned when rainwater puddled beneath his pallet.[42]

By 1777, Army recruiters found it nearly impossible to fill their enlistment quotas, so frightened was the citizenry of catching smallpox. Faced with a shortage of troops, General George Washington pressured the Continental Congress to pay for inoculating the Colonial Army. Yet despite Washington's good intentions, a shortage of resources kept many soldiers from ever receiving treatment. Washington had no worry of contracting the virus himself because he had had it years earlier while in Barbados. In 1781, fourteen-year-old future president Andrew Jackson came down with smallpox, as did his brother, Robert. They were British prisoners of war in Camden, New Jersey. Unlike Robert, Andrew survived the disease, as well as his war wounds.[43]

Around the time of the American Revolution, a few Englishmen recognized that milkmaids who had contracted cowpox were immune from smallpox. Cowpox caused a mild rash in humans and was non-fatal. Its virus entered the body through cuts and scratches, usually on the hands of those who milked cows that had cowpox pustules on their udders. Since nearly every European adult bore a face pockmarked by smallpox, attractive women—those with few or no scars—were described as being "pretty as a milkmaid."[44]

In 1774 in Dorset, England, an individual deliberately contracted cowpox in order to protect himself from smallpox.[45] The experiment proved successful, although no one knew why. During the next two decades, the relationship between cowpox and smallpox remained a puzzle, ignored by all but a handful of scientist-physicians. Then in the 1790s, English country doctor Edward Jenner—the same Edward Jenner who had been bled, purged, and inoculated as an eight-year-old boy—began his own investigation of the cowpox virus. After performing several successful tests in which he vaccinated healthy children with cowpox, then exposed them to smallpox, Jenner wrote a pamphlet in 1798, titled *An Inquiry into the Causes and Effects of Variolae Vaccinae, a Disease, Discovered in some of the Western Counties of England, particularly Gloucestershire, and known by the Name of Cow Pox.* The publication received wide notice in England and the United States. Jenner called his procedure vaccination in order to differentiate it from inoculation (inoculation was also called variolation; the word vaccination comes from *vacca,* the Latin word for cow).

Though providing a safeguard from smallpox, vaccination is not foolproof. It does not grant lifelong immunity. Unless the treatment is periodically renewed, its protection fades. If exposed to *Variola major,* adults who were vaccinated in their youth can catch the disease, albeit in a milder form than had they never been immunized. Such patients normally recover, but while sick, they can pass on a full-strength case of smallpox to unvaccinated people with whom they come in contact.[46] Even so, Jenner's remedy was superior to inoculation.

Although Jenner had proved cowpox vaccination to be safer and much less costly than inoculation, inoculators fought the new procedure in word and print. (Cowpox can be passed from one person to another only by taking the pus from an infected individual's blister and rubbing it in a scratch on someone who is well. Unlike smallpox, which man can catch by inhaling *Variola*-infected air, a person cannot catch cowpox from the breath of someone who has the disease.) Inoculators correctly saw that vaccinations would ring the death knell for their lucrative profession.

Among educated—hence wealthy—Europeans, vaccination gained rapid acceptance though the doctors and scientists of the day had no understanding of why it worked. Many physicians held that epidemics were caused by miasmic vapors that affected people with weak constitutions. Although Girolamo Fracastoro (or Fracastorius) had written about contagion in 1546, his work remained controversial, and the germ theory of contagious diseases awaited proof.

Louis Pasteur, whose study of microbiology in the 1870s and 1880s would eventually give rise to the science of immunology, had not been born. Quarantining had been used to control the spread of disease for some time, but physicians could not agree on why it contained smallpox but not malaria. Therefore, when Jenner demonstrated that cowpox vaccination prevented small-pox, late eighteenth-century Europeans embraced it, despite the medical profession's inability to explain the science behind its success. In increasing numbers each year, the European pop-ulace—particularly the English—submitted to Jenner's treat-ment. By 1801, nearly 100,000 English men, women, and chil-dren had received cowpox vaccine.[47] But no one rushed to send the miracle drug to those who needed it most—the Indians of North and South America.

Chapter two notes

[1.] These definitions come from Wagner E. Stearn and Allen E. Stearn, *The Effect of Smallpox on the Destiny of the Amerindian* (Boston: Bruce Humphries, 1945), 15 n. (n.n.). Other writers call these smallpox strains by different names. For simplicity sake, this text usually does not differentiate between *Variola vera* and *Variola hemorrhagica,* and instead refers to them both as *Variola major.* During the past two centuries, a fourth smallpox-related virus has evolved, called *Vaccinia.* Scientists suspect it mutated from cowpox vaccine sometime after physicians began using it to immunize people from smallpox. Not found in nature, *Vaccinia* exists only in the laboratory and is the agent used for modern smallpox vaccinations; for more, see Joel N. Shurkin, *The Invisible Fire: The Story of Mankind's Victory Over the Ancient Scourge of Smallpox* (New York: G. Putnam's Sons, 1979), 32.

[2.] Aidan Cockburn, M.D., *The Evolution and Eradication of Infectious Diseases* (Baltimore: Johns Hopkins Press, 1963), 58, 96-9, 197.

[3.] Donald R. Hopkins, *Princes and Peasants: Smallpox in History* (Chicago: University of Chicago Press, 1983), 72.

[4.] Shurkin, *Invisible Fire,* 26.

[5.] James Cross Giblin, *When Plague Strikes: The Black Death, Smallpox, Aids* (New York: HarperCollins, 1995), 57.

[6.] Hopkins, *Princes and Peasants,* 14, 16, 20.

[7.] Ann F. Ramenofsky, *Vectors of Death: The Archaeology of European Contact* (Albuquerque: University of New Mexico Press, 1987), 139.

[8.] Hopkins, *Princes and Peasants,* 19. Henige, *Numbers from Nowhere,* 261-2 are critical of Hopkins, arguing that he attributes a number of ancient epidemics to smallpox—including the Plague of Athens (430-429 B.C.)—without corroborating evidence. William H. McNeill, *Plagues and Peoples* (New York: Doubleday division of Bantam Doubleday Dell, 1976; New York: History Book Club, Monticello Editions, 1993), 100 points out that the known writings of the Greek physician Hippocrates (*ca* 460-*ca* 377 B.C.) make no mention of smallpox, leading McNeill to think that smallpox did not invade Greece and her immediate Mediterranean neighbors during Hippocrates's lifetime. On page 105, McNeill recounts the Plague of Athens without determining its cause; also see page 318 n. 34. Part of the problem historians have identifying ancient diseases is because medical observers of the day often could not tell them apart. Abu-Bakr Muhammed ibn-Zakariya´ al-Razi (Rhazes), a Baghdad physician (A.D. 864-930), was the first person to differentiate smallpox from measles.

[9.] Cockburn, *Infectious Diseases,* 86.

[10.] Hopkins, *Princes and Peasants,* 22-3; and McNeill, *Plagues and Peoples,* 116-17. Hopkins is more certain than McNeill that the Plague of Antonius was smallpox. While inconclusive, Galen's written description of the disease lends some support to a diagnosis of either smallpox or measles. According to McNeill, *Plagues and Peoples,* 117, European physicians were unable to tell them apart before the sixteenth century, despite Abu-Bakr Muhammed ibn-Zakariya´ al-Razi (Rhazes) having learned to do so 600 years earlier.

In contrast with Hopkins, McNeill (page 118) discounts the view that smallpox had spread to the northern Mediterranean countryside before the Plague of Antonius. McNeill argues that the disease—he thinks it could have been either smallpox or measles—killed so many people because it was attacking a virgin population. As was discussed in the introduction to this book, readers ought to be skeptical about accepting numbers such as those given for the total of smallpox dead. Although history tells us that a large number of people died during the Plague of Antonius, it is impossible to know if the count should be one million or ten million.

11. McNeill, *Plagues and Peoples*, 116.

12. Cockburn, *Infectious Diseases*, 86 dates the epidemic A.D. 569; Hopkins, *Princes and Peasants*, 165 uses A.D. 570; and Shurkin, *Invisible Fire*, 49-50 cite A.D. 568.

13. McNeill, *Plagues and Peoples*, 133-5, 323 n. 80 hold out the possibility that the epidemic of A.D. 317 was measles. Hopkins, *Princes and Peasants*, 18 disputes McNeill, arguing that smallpox arrived in China with the invading Huns around 250 B.C. This seems far too early, since the *Variola* virus did not reach Korea before the sixth century of the common era.

14. McNeill, *Plagues and Peoples*, 140.

15. Hopkins, *Princes and Peasants*, 171-2.

16. McNeill, *Plagues and Peoples*, 275 states that it was 1900 before major cities could increase their populations without a steady influx of emigrants from the countryside.

17. Archaeologists differ on when the first Paleo-Siberians entered North America via the Bering Strait land bridge, also called Beringia. Originally thought to have occurred about 10,000 B.C., it is now considered to have happened around 50,000 B.C. or earlier; see Carl Waldman, *Atlas of the North American Indian* (New York: Facts On File, 1985), 1-2. At the end of the last ice age about 10,000 B.C., the oceans rose, submerging Beringia and isolating the western hemisphere and the Paleo-Siberian invaders. McNeill, *Plagues and Peoples*, 27 reports that by 8000 B.C., these ancient people had extended their domain to Tierra del Fuego at the tip of South America.

18. Robert McCaa, "Spanish and Nahuatl Views on Smallpox and Demographic Catastrophe in the Conquest of Mexico," *Journal of Interdisciplinary History* 25, no. 3 (winter 1995): 397-431; published on line: http://www.hist.umn.edu/~rmccaa/vircatas/, 12.

19. Giblin, *When Plague Strikes*, 59 states that the strain of syphilis that first invaded Europe in the mid 1490s was much stronger than modern strains.

20. Shurkin, *Invisible Fire*, 83-91, 96, 100.

21. Alvin M. Josephy, Jr., *The Indian Heritage of America* (Boston: Houghton Mifflin, 1968; revised, 1991), 301 attributes Pocahontas's death to smallpox. John F. Ross, "Picturing Pocahontas," *Smithsonian* 29, no. 10 (January 1999): 34-6 says she died from pneumonia or tuberculosis.

22. John Duffy, *Epidemics in Colonial America* (Baton Rouge: Louisiana State University Press, 1953), 109; and Shurkin, *Invisible Fire*, 179.

23. Alfred W. Crosby, *Ecological Imperialism: The Biological Expansion of Europe, 900-1900* (Cambridge, Great Britain: Cambridge University Press, 1986), 284-5.

24. Hopkins, *Princes and Peasants*, 32. Several centuries earlier, the noted Baghdad physician Abu-Bakr Muhammed ibn-Zakariya´ al-Razi (Rhazes) had prescribed treating a smallpox patient's eyes with mouse, starling, and sparrow feces. In addition, he advocated bleeding to reduce fever; see Giblin, *When Plague Strikes*, 63; and Shurkin, *Invisible Fire*, 55.

25. Frederick F. Cartwright, in collaboration with Michael D. Biddiss, *Disease and History* (New York: Thomas Y. Crowell, 1972), 123; Duffy, *Epidemics in Colonial America*, 25; Giblin, *When Plague Strikes*, 79-83; Hopkins, *Princes and Peasants*, 12, 46, 49, 51; and McNeill, *Plagues and Peoples*, 252-4. Shurkin, *Invisible Fire*, 122-7 also recount these events, but list the age of Lady Montagu's son as six, not

five, and the number of inoculated prisoners as six, not seven.

26. McNeill, *Plagues and Peoples*, 252.

27. Shurkin, *Invisible Fire*, 120.

28. Hopkins, *Princes and Peasants*, 59.

29. John Duffy, "Smallpox and the Indians in the American Colonies," *Bulletin of the History of Medicine* 25 (1951): 327. Bills of Mortality were British municipal death records.

30. Hopkins, *Princes and Peasants*, 75. Duffy, *Epidemics in Colonial America*, 20-2 cite reports by French mathematician Comte de La Condamine and English Royal Society secretary Dr. James Jurin, among others, giving similar cause-of-death ratios for the eighteenth century.

31. James Axtell, *The Invasion Within: The Contest of Cultures in Colonial North America* (New York: Oxford University Press, 1985), 228; and *The Spirit World* (Alexandria, Virginia: Time-Life Books, 1992), 135-6, 141.

32. John F. Taylor, "Sociocultural Effects of Epidemics on the Northern Plains: 1734-1850," reprint, *The Western Canadian Journal of Anthropology* 7, no. 4 (1977): 58.

33. Shurkin, *Invisible Fire*, 113; *The Spirit World*, 33, 128; and Stearn and Stearn, *Effect of Smallpox*, 16.

34. Stearn and Stearn, *Effect of Smallpox*, 16.

35. Shurkin, *Invisible Fire*, 155-7. Some historians incorrectly report that Dr. Boylston learned about inoculation from his own slave, instead of indirectly from Cotton Mather's slave, Onesimus.

36. Ibid., 145.

37. Duffy, *Epidemics in Colonial America*, 29.

38. Shurkin, *Invisible Fire*, 163, 165. Differing from Shurkin, Giblin, *When Plague Strikes*, 85 reports 280 inoculees and 5,800 Bostonians who caught the disease naturally.

39. Duffy, *Epidemics in Colonial America*, 33-4. On pages 36-7, Duffy notes that in the second half of the eighteenth century, Boston's inoculators enjoyed better success.

40. Ibid., 37-40.

41. Hopkins, *Princes and Peasants*, 255-6.

42. Richard Wolkomir, "In Vermont, A Valiant Stand for Freedom," *Smithsonian* 29, no. 4 (July 1998): 60.

43. Hopkins, *Princes and Peasants*, 221, 261-2.

44. Cockburn, *Infectious Diseases*, 197. In America, cowpox was also known as kinepox.

45. Cartwright, *Disease and History*, 126.

46. According to Giblin, *When Plague Strikes*, 101, nineteenth-century British physicians advocated revaccination every seven to ten years in order to maintain immunity.

47. Cartwright, *Disease and History*, 128.

Chapter Three

Late Spring 1837

During the first three days of May 1837, the Arikaras traded another 430 buffalo robes at Fort Clark. Although the month had begun with a blustery, southeast wind, the weather soon turned warm and pleasant, infecting the trading post with spring fever. Francis Chardon and the other men at the fort found it a delightful change from April, when everyone had wondered if spring would ever arrive.

At Mitutanka Village, the Mandans had opened their lodges to the Arikaras, who had moved in and begun treating the town as their own. With double the number of mouths to feed, the Mandans quickly consumed their meager store of meat and corn. They were again starving, as were their Arikara guests. On Wednesday morning, May 3, a combined hunting party from the two tribes crossed the Missouri in search of buffalo. Shamans prayed to the Manitou, entreating the spirit to lead the hunters to the herds rather than into a Lakota ambush.

Later in the day after the Indian hunters had disappeared on the plain, the western sky darkened. Clouds piled atop clouds, bridging the prairie to the heavens. For the first time that year, thunder rumbled across the expanse, its gravelly voice resonating like the sound of stampeding buffalo. Perhaps the shamans took it as an omen, a sign from the Manitou that their men would have a successful hunt. As the storm approached Mitutanka Village, Indians dashed into their lodges, anticipating a downpour. But instead of a cloudburst, the thunderheads produced only a light shower. The squall soon passed, swept eastward by a freshening breeze that also carried away the summerlike air. In its stead, a slate-gray sky loomed over the prairie, and a raw wind bit to the bone. At Fort Clark, weather prognosticators predicted more rain by morning. A cold drizzle would be bad enough; everyone hoped it would not be snow.

That night, a rooster at the trading post pierced the quiet. Five times its cock-a-doodle-doo echoed throughout the stockade, awakening everyone from the *bourgeois* to the lowest *engagé*. At breakfast the next morning, the crowing consumed the conversations. Every man in the fort viewed the event with foreboding. All agreed the rooster's call portended disaster. Meanwhile, rain tattooed against the roofs, adding a damp chill to the gloom.

Far downriver, the *St. Peter's* had reached the Blacksnake Hills Trading Post of Joseph Robidoux III. Robidoux's post was about twelve years old. Already, a number of families had staked out homesteads in its shadow, and there was talk that the Blacksnake Hills landing would someday evolve into a town.[1]

Aboard the steamboat, the sick black deckhand lay moaning beneath his blanket. His fever again hovered above 100 degrees. An itchy rash had spread over his cheeks and the undersides of his arms, and was now inching its way across his stomach and chest. Although his messmates had tried to feed him and give him water, his raw, burning throat pained him to swallow. His muscles ached, and his head throbbed. Delirious, he mumbled incoherently, oblivious to those who stopped by to check on his condition.

Indian agent William Fulkerson pressed Captain Pratte with his conviction that the man had smallpox. Fulkerson urged Pratte to put him ashore at Robidoux's post, arguing that if the diagnosis was correct, the deckhand would be better off where there were people to offer him care.[2] The captain was far less certain that the illness was smallpox. Pratte still thought the

George Catlin painting, Smithsonian American Art Museum; Gift of Mrs. Joseph Harrison, Jr.
Mitutanka, the Mandan village next to Fort Clark.

disease could be simple ague. At worst, it was chickenpox or scarlet fever. He saw no reason to deprive the *St. Peter's* of a good hand, one who would no doubt be well enough to return to his duties within another few days.

After the steamer's crew finished unloading supplies for the Blacksnake Hills Trading Post, the pilot signaled that it was time to leave. The passengers quickly filed across the gangplank, and within minutes the *St. Peter's* backed away from the bank, swung its bow into the Missouri's current, and continued upriver. The black crewman remained aboard.

As the boat churned toward Fort Bellevue and the Council Bluffs Indian Agency for the Otoes, Omahas, and Pawnees, the deckhand's rash elevated into small, circular bumps. Three days later, the bumps filled with a clear fluid, blotching his cheeks, arms, legs, and stomach with a rotating pattern of blisters. More blisters ulcerated his throat, making every swallow a torture. As the hours passed, the liquid in the blisters slowly turned to pus. Now highly contagious, the deckhand writhed beneath his blanket, exhaling the deadly *Variola* virus with every breath. All those on the steamer who had neither had the disease nor been recently vaccinated were at risk. Soon, small-pox began incubating in the lungs of several passengers and other members of the crew.[3]

On the upper Missouri beyond the *St. Peter's* and its lethal cargo, a bitter west wind numbed the prairie as though it were still winter. Nearly every other day, chilling rain drenched Fort Clark and Mitutanka Village. *Engagés* within the trading post kept the fireplaces stoked, but the fires were no match for the damp cold. Inside the trade room, warehouse, and other buildings, men worked with their clothes snugged tight and their shoulders hunched.

At the Mandans' town, rain soaked the earth. Hooves, paws, and moccasins kneaded mud, horse droppings, dog feces, and human waste into a dark goo that clung to the Indians' leggings like plaster. The Mandans lived in large, conical-shaped, earth-en lodges—as did many Missouri River tribes—that were bunched together at random. The spaces between some lodges barely permitted people to walk single file. Mandan warriors often stabled their favorite horses inside their homes to ensure the animals would be safe from Lakota raiders. In addition to a horse or two, each lodge also housed an extended Mandan fam-ily that could number thirty individuals. With the arrival of the Arikaras, the Mandans' homes were ready to burst. Crowding was so bad, twenty Arikara families had moved to the Hidatsas' summer village on the Knife River. Their absence barely made a dent in the crush of bodies. Now the raw, wet weather drove the Indians inside. Musty during an August drought, the lodge interiors became cramped, dank caverns. The pit fire at the cen-ter of each lodge gave off more smoke than warmth. For Indians coming in from the rain, their buckskin tunics and muddy leg-gings dried slowly, keeping their skin as clammy as the air.

Despite the stormy weather, the robe trade continued. Each day the Missouri rose a bit more, evidencing the mountain snowmelt farther upcountry. Pratte & Chouteau's annual steamboat needed high water if it was to have a prayer of reach-ing the Missouri-Yellowstone confluence and Fort Union.

Eighteen years had passed since the first steamboat

penetrated the mouth of the Missouri River. Shortly after its voyage, the steamer *Western Engineer* had made it to Council Bluffs. During the next decade, steam traffic expanded slowly on the lower Missouri, most of it confined below the mouth of the Kansas River. Although steam packets occasionally went to Council Bluffs, none went higher.

In 1830, Pratte & Chouteau's forerunner, the American Fur Company, decided to gamble on steam transportation, hoping to cut the time and expense of supplying its upper Missouri trading posts via keelboats. That winter a boatyard in Louisville, Kentucky, constructed the side-wheeler *Yellow Stone* for the firm. In April 1831, the *Yellow Stone* powered up the Missouri to Fort Tecumseh (across from Pierre, South Dakota), making it the first steamer to go beyond Council Bluffs. The following year, the *Yellow Stone* reached Fort Union, persuading Pierre Chouteau Jr. that the future lay in steam. In 1834, after buying the American Fur Company's Western Department and Upper Missouri Outfit, Pierre Chouteau Jr. and his partners sought to extend the steamboat's range beyond the mouth of the Yellowstone. That summer, the *Assiniboine* chugged past Fort Union, pushing the limits of steam navigation on the upper Missouri.

The experiment nearly ended in disaster at the mouth of the Poplar River (near Poplar, Montana) when the boat ran aground in low water. The *Assiniboine's* crew tried to free the vessel, but it refused to budge, leaving the men no choice but to wait for the spring snowmelt.

That fall traders from Fort Union came upriver to guard the steamer and barter with the nearby tribes. The following March, the Missouri's runoff refloated the steamboat and permitted its crew to head downstream with the buffalo robes that had been acquired during the winter. Pausing at Fort Union, the *Assiniboine* took on more robes. At the mouth of the White Earth River (in western North Dakota), the boat again ran aground and had to wait for the river to rise before continuing. Near the Missouri's confluence with the Heart River (near Bismarck, North Dakota), bad luck again struck—this time permanently. The *Assiniboine* caught fire and burned to the waterline. In addition to the boat, the blaze consumed its cargo of buffalo robes, valued between $60,000 and $80,000.[4]

Although the disaster was costly, Pierre Chouteau Jr. had no intention of abandoning steam. Because of a steamboat's speed and lower labor costs, he realized that steamers held a competitive advantage over every other form of riverine transportation.

This year the *St. Peter's* had orders to go no farther than Fort Union. Pratte & Chouteau's most distant trading post, Fort McKenzie (located about thirteen miles below present-day Fort Benton, Montana) would continue to be supplied by keelboat. Rivermen delighted debating whether shipwrights would ever have the know-how to construct a steamer that could reach the Falls of the Missouri (at Great Falls, Montana). If a boat ever did make it that far, one thing was certain: it would belong to Pierre Chouteau Jr.

As May entered its second week, a number of Arikaras performed a spirited dance for the traders at Fort Clark. Chardon watched, but without enjoyment. Although he smoked and treated with the Arikaras because he needed their buffalo robes, in truth, he detested them more than he did the Mandans. Later that day, he confided to his journal that he hoped the Arikaras' dance would be the last performance he would have to endure.

Before ending his record of the day's events, Chardon noted having seen a gray horse that carried the Pratte & Chouteau brand. The animal belonged to an Arikara warrior who had stolen it during a raid on the Yankton Lakotas. A Yankton had no doubt pirated the horse from Fort Pierre. For Indian men, poaching horses was as much a game as it was a way for them to increase their herds. The Arikaras robbed the Lakotas, who robbed the Mandans, who robbed the Assiniboines, who robbed the Crows. . . . The circle was endless. Pratte & Chouteau lost its share of horses to Indian bandits, but far fewer than it would have if the tribes spent less time stealing from one another.

On May 8, three horses from the Fort Clark remuda disappeared. Although Chardon did not venture a hunch concerning their whereabouts when he recorded the event in his journal, he no doubt suspected they had been run off by Arikaras.

George Catlin painting, Smithsonian American Art Museum

Many native hunters preferred the bow to the single shot rifle when hunting buffalo because it was easier to take multiple shots.

The following night, the Yankton woman who had been taken captive by the Mandans in mid January escaped with a fellow female prisoner.[5] The Indian gossip mill pointed its finger at Chardon, alleging that he had aided their getaway. But other than giving the *bourgeois* an occasional furtive glance, the Mandans chose not to confront him or do anything else to challenge the merit of the rumor. Despite the suspicion that Chardon had helped the women escape, the Arikaras continued trading at Fort Clark, swelling its inventory of robes.

Spring had not heralded a return of the buffalo herds. The Indians at Mitutanka Village as well as the personnel at Fort Clark craved fresh meat. The foul weather had combined with short rations, dampening the spirits of both Indians and whites. On May 11, a mixed party of Mandans and Arikaras rode onto the prairie in search of game. With Chardon's blessing, two hunters from Fort Clark went along. If the Manitou answered the tribal prayers and led the Indians to buffalo, they intended remaining away for some time, drying their kill into jerky.

On Friday, May 12, a brisk north wind ushered away the clouds, but in their place it carried smoke from the numerous fires that scorched the upper prairie. Some had probably been set by the recently-departed hunters, who hoped to drive any buffalo they found into a surround where they could be more easily killed. That night the temperature at Fort Clark and Mitutanka Village plunged below freezing, leaving the grass, shrubs, and trees rimed in white. Ignoring the cold, the Mandan women turned out at daylight and began planting their corn-fields in the Missouri bottomland.

While the Mandan women put in their corn crop, the *St. Peter's* passed the mouth of the Platte River. Boatmen joked about the Platte, saying it was too thick to drink and too thin to plow. Spring thunderstorms on the plains and snowmelt in the western mountains had flooded the lower Platte, spread-ing its mouth across a mile of river bottom. Once the runoff was finished, the water would recede and enter the Missouri through three channels.

On May 14, the steamer reached Council Bluffs, home of Fort Bellevue and the Otoe, Omaha, and Pawnee Indian Agency.[6] The name Council Bluffs stemmed from 1804 when Lewis and Clark had parleyed with a group of Otoe and Missouri Indians at a bluff overlooking the Missouri River. Although the meeting took place thirty-nine miles above the mouth of the Platte, con-vention soon named the entire region Council Bluffs. The Missouri Fur Company opened Fort Bellevue for the Omaha trade in the spring or summer of 1823, locating it on the west side of the Missouri, about nine miles north of its confluence with the Platte. Following the demise of the Missouri Fur Company, Fort Bellevue eventually passed to the American Fur Company, and then to Pratte & Chouteau.

After the *St. Peter's* deck crew extended the gangway onto the riverbank at Fort Bellevue, Indian agents Pilcher and Fulkerson were probably among the first passengers to disem-bark. Because both men answered to senior agent John Dougherty, they no doubt hurried to his office to make their reports. Out of necessity, their visit would be short, since the *St. Peter's* was scheduled to leave in a few hours.

While the two agents passed along greetings from Superintendent William Clark and caught up on news, the steamboat's deckhands and the passengers working their way upriver off-loaded the stores and Indian annuities slated for Fort Bellevue and the neighboring tribes. After finishing with the supplies, the laborers carried aboard numerous sticks of wood. Indians at the agency cut and sold firewood to visiting steamers. Their payment for three or four dozen cords was a few cups of sugar and a half pound of coffee beans, goods which cost only twenty-five cents in St. Louis.[7]

Although the *St. Peter's* would carry some robes during the return leg of its voyage, most of the upper and middle Missouri fur inventory was freighted downriver in mackinaw flotillas. Mackinaws were cheap, flat-bottomed boats that carpenters nailed together from two-inch cottonwood planks at trading post boatyards, or *chantiers* as they were called. Drawing twenty to thirty inches of water, most mackinaws had pointed bows and sterns and were fifty feet long, with beams of nine to twelve feet. Their cargo holds ranged from three to five feet deep and held over twelve tons of buffalo robes—upwards of 300 pressed bales.

In addition to a steersman, who controlled a stern-mounted tiller, each vessel was crewed by four oarsmen. Going downstream, the boats averaged 100 miles per day. Most mackinaws ended their journeys in St. Louis, where they were burned for firewood. Pratte & Chouteau found it less costly to build new boats than to haul the old ones back upriver. Of late, there was talk of off-loading the mackinaws at Fort Bellevue and transferring their cargoes to packet steamers for the final run to St. Louis.

The packets, which were much faster than drift boats, regularly operated between Fort Leavenworth and the Mississippi, so it would be simple to increase their range to Council Bluffs. Mackinaws and keelboats were products of the past. Nowadays, everyone wanted speed, and nothing could ply the lower Missouri faster than a packet steamer. But mackinaws still had their use. Most steamboats heading to the upper Missouri towed two or three, and the *St. Peter's* was no exception. They were invaluable if a steamer needed to lighten its load in order to pass through a shallow stretch of water, something that happened all too often above Council Bluffs. The *St. Peter's* had two mackinaws tied to its stern, but whether it had towed them from St. Louis or picked them up at Fort Bellevue is unknown. Captain Pratte intended taking them at least as far as Fort Clark.[8]

By now most of the black deckhand's pus-filled blisters had scabbed to a dark crust. His fever continued to rage, and his lower back still ached. During the daytime, the sunlight seared his eyes. His heartbeats reverberated in his brain, and his breath and sneezes flooded the air with the deadly *Variola* virus. Meanwhile, among the *St. Peter's* passengers and other crewmen who had been infected, the disease was nearing the end of its incubation.[9]

Once the work gang finished loading all the firewood the *St. Peter's* could hold, Captain Pratte ordered his pilot to ring the steamer's bell, signaling departure. Pilcher and Fulkerson said their good-byes and hurried to the riverbank, where they queued up with the boat's other travelers who had gone ashore to stretch their legs.

Awaiting their turn to file onto the loading plank were a few new passengers, including three Arikara women and their children.[10] The Arikaras had been visiting their Pawnee friends—and distant relatives—and now sought passage to Fort Clark so they could join their families at Mitutanka Village. As soon as the last passenger came on deck, crewmen pulled in the gangway, and the side-wheeler backed into the current. Following what had now become a farewell tradition, the trappers and *engagés* fired their rifles, while on shore, clusters of Indians and a sprinkling of whites shouted and waved.

Within three days of the *St. Peter's* leaving Fort Bellevue, the first victims infected by the black deckhand developed high fevers and aching backs. Now having to admit that his steamboat carried the dreaded pestilence, Captain Pratte most likely ordered the newly sick crewmen and steerage passengers placed alongside the black deckhand in the cargo hold or someplace else that offered a measure of protection from the weather. Ailing first-class passengers were probably confined to their berths. Those passengers and crew who were at risk of catching smallpox were no doubt cautioned to stay away from those who were sick, but beyond that, nothing was done to keep the virus contained.

Joshua Pilcher and William Fulkerson recognized the danger of transporting such a contagious disease among the tribes of the upper Missouri, but they had no authority to interfere with the *St. Peter's* operation. Perhaps they tried persuading Captain Pratte to return to St. Louis or at least to stop until the virus had run its course. The record is silent. If they did put forth such arguments, Pratte probably reminded them that the steamer had to complete its journey, or the Indians waiting at their agencies would receive no annuities.

Pilcher and Fulkerson were fully aware that such an occurrence could turn the upper Missouri into a battleground. Besides, the captain is sure to have added, Pratte & Chouteau's trading posts needed to be resupplied. Pilcher and Fulkerson could object all they wanted, but the voyage would continue. As a sop, Captain Pratte may have promised that he would try keeping Indians off the boat when it put in to shore. Beyond that, he could do nothing.

Because of the steamer's cramped quarters and numerous occupants, the quarantine—such as it was—leaked like a colander. The Arikara women and children who had boarded at Council Bluffs inhaled the smallpox-infected air before the boat reached the mouth of the Little Sioux River (near River Sioux, Iowa). As the *St. Peter's* labored toward Pratte & Chouteau's Big Sioux Post at the Missouri-Big Sioux River confluence, the *Variola* virus started incubating within another set of victims.

In this country timber was scarce. After the steamer's fireboxes had consumed the last of the fuel acquired at Fort Bellevue, the crew and working passengers began gathering driftwood, though much of it was damp and burned grudgingly. When possible, the men also salvaged logs from abandoned trading posts. It was always a contest to see which could destroy a deserted structure first: the weather or passing steamboats.

This time of year, the Missouri carried down not only uprooted trees but also the bloated bodies of drowned buffalo, often so many, their numbers defied counting. Some had washed into *embarras* at the head of the river's numerous islands and sand-bars. Their decaying carcasses would remain in these tangled cages until a flood surge tore them loose or scavengers and rot reduced them to bones. Other buffalo had become marooned in the quicksand and muck that collected beneath shallow eddies.

It was one of nature's ironies that a buffalo could survive a swim across the Missouri only to become trapped within spitting distance of shore. With their legs stuck fast in the soft riverbed, big, powerful bulls as well as smaller cows and calves starved to death while ravens sat on their backs and pecked their flesh. For the bored passengers on the *St. Peter's,* these helpless beasts made tempting targets for their rifles.

As the steamer continued upriver, it passed the occasional Indian camp and village. Iowa, Omaha, and Ponca men, women, and children watched from the banks as the boat belched black smoke from its tall stacks and its paddle wheels thrashed the water into foam. Expressing their awe, many natives covered their mouths with their hands. Some beckoned the pilot to put in to shore so they could trade.

Steamboats still generated excitement among the tribes, but less than in years past. In 1832, when the *Yellow Stone* made the first steamed voyage this far up the Missouri, most of the Indians were frightened, having never before seen a steam-powered boat. When the *Yellow Stone's* crew discharged cannons in salute, many tribesmen fled their villages in terror. Others dropped to the ground and prayed for protection from "the thunder canoe that walked on water."[11]

When the side-wheeler stopped at native villages, its engineer delighted in startling Indians who had lined the banks to gape. Crewmen and passengers clutched their sides with laughter as the engineer discharged steam from the boilers' escape valves. The clouds of scalding water vapor sent the natives clawing over the backs of their fellow spectators as each sought to flee from such frightening *medicine.* Since then, the novelty of steamboats had waned. Yet, at every encampment there were always a few Indians who could be made to jump.

A bit below the mouth of the Big Sioux River and Pratte, Chouteau & Company's Big Sioux Trading Post (now Sioux City, Iowa), the *St. Peter's* passed Floyd's Bluff. Passengers such as

Joshua Pilcher, who had been upcountry before, no doubt pointed out the famous burial site to first-time travelers. Sergeant Charles Floyd had died near here on August 20, 1804, during the initial year of Lewis and Clark's exploration of the Louisiana and Oregon territories. A member of the Corps of Discovery, Floyd was the expedition's only casualty.

Just upstream from Floyd's Bluff, the *St. Peter's* stopped at Pratte & Chouteau's southern-most trading house for the Lakotas. A French Canadian named Joseph LaFramboise is thought to have established the post in the mid 1820s. In 1827, the American Fur Company acquired it, followed by Pierre Chouteau Jr. and his partners in 1834. As did other trading posts, Big Sioux Post had its complement of Indian women who were married to the post's *engagés* and traders. In addition, it no doubt attracted a number of native hangers-on who had been corrupted by liquor and now found it easier to beg than to join their kin, hunting buffalo. Unless the steamer arrived in the early evening—when it would have been tied up for the night—its stay was short, an hour or two at most. Captain Pratte probably cautioned his crew to keep any curious Lakotas off the boat, lest they become infected by the smallpox.

By now the black deckhand had shed his scabs, and he was no longer contagious. His fever was gone as were his aching muscles and malaise. It is likely that he had already returned to work, or at least light duty. The spinning pattern of pockmarks that marred his cheeks, trunk, upper legs, and the undersides of his forearms were the only permanent record of his illness. He would carry the scars for the rest of his life.

While the crew hurried to off-load supplies intended for the post, and Pilcher and Fulkerson chatted with its *bourgeois,* the steamboat's latest smallpox patients writhed beneath their blankets, burning with fever one minute and the next shivering with chills. On some, the rash had barely started, whereas on others, it had elevated and matured into pus-filled blisters. It is probable the disease did not impact them all equally. To the medically ignorant, smallpox seemed as arbitrary as luck. Through their eyes, it attacked at random, killing the strong as well as the infirm, disfiguring the comely while leaving the plain without a mark. It was no wonder the disease generated so much superstition and fear. Within a couple of days, it would visit the three Arikara women and their children who had boarded at Fort Bellevue. When the *St. Peter's* pulled away from Big Sioux Post, they still felt fine. They had no idea that within their lungs, the virus had nearly finished its incubation.

About fifty miles or so above Big Sioux Post, the *St. Peter's* reached Vermilion Post, which sat immediately below the Missouri's confluence with the Vermillion River. The fort's *bourgeois,* William Dickson, had traded along this stretch of the Missouri since the early 1820s, when he worked for the Columbia Fur Company. In those days, he focused his efforts near the mouth of the James River, about twenty miles west of his current location. Known by French Canadians as *Riviére à Jacques,* the James had for several generations witnessed an annual Lakota trade fair.

Each summer, bands of Yanktons, Tetons, Yanktonais, and Santees gathered on the upper James, swapping furs for the lead, gunpowder, muskets, and copper kettles that the Santees had obtained from British traders on the St. Peters River (now the Minnesota River). Dickson had succeeded in siphoning off much of the British trade, to the delight of the Columbia Fur Company's partners in St. Louis. Seeing his success, Bernard Pratte & Company (the forerunner of Pratte & Chouteau) opened a competing fort nearby. Captain Pratte's older brother, Sylvestre, ran the operation during the winter of 1824 and 1825. In 1827, when the American Fur Company absorbed the Columbia Fur Company, Dickson retained responsibility for commerce between the James and Vermillion rivers. Over the ensuing years, he relocated his trading house several times as he followed the nomadic Lakotas. After Pratte & Chouteau bought the American Fur Company's Missouri River operations in 1834, Dickson positioned his trade at Vermilion Post.[12]

When the *St. Peter's* stopped at Vermilion Post, the crew had to keep careful watch to prevent inquisitive Lakotas from sneaking aboard and accidentally contracting the deadly virus. Again, unless it was close to nightfall, the visit was short, perhaps an hour, certainly no longer than two. After hearing about the lethal cargo the steamboat was carrying, Dickson probably breathed a sigh of relief when Captain Pratte gave the order to depart.

Past Vermilion Post, the next landmark of note was the James River. Above here, the *St. Peter's* entered the land of the Poncas, a tribe that numbered between seventy-five and eighty lodges. Most of the Poncas lived on the right side of the Missouri River near its confluence with the Niobrara, about 1,000 miles above St. Louis. Also known as Running Water River, Rapid River, and Spreading Water River, the Niobrara was notorious for the sandbars it deposited immediately below its mouth.[13] A few old French-Canadian trappers continued calling the river *L'Eau qui Court,* a name they had used when the Poncas were still a mighty nation. But that was long ago, in the days before disease and whiskey had reduced them from a proud, village culture to a semi-nomadic band that trailed the buffalo herds and lived in the shadow of the more powerful Lakotas.

By the time the Poncas' lodges came into view from the *St. Peter's* decks, the *Variola* virus had completed its incubation within the Arikara passengers. The three women and their children lay huddled together, their bodies inflamed with fever, the muscles in their lower backs in spasm, and their heads pounding like the thump of the steamer's engines. Agents Pilcher and Fulkerson knew if the Arikaras lived to see their families at Mitutanka Village, it would be a miracle.

At Fort Clark, Francis Chardon grew tired of sleeping alone. He had cared for his Lakota wife, Tchon-su-mons-ka, but she was dead. Despite having lived among Indians most of his adult life, he disliked them as a people, to which the entries in his journal testify. But Tchon-su-mons-ka had been different. Her loss left a void. Out of respect, he had sent her body downriver to Fort Pierre so she could be buried among her kin. It was little enough to do for a faithful wife, who had borne him two sons. Their youngest boy, Andrew Jackson, had accompanied her body and would return to Fort Clark aboard the company's annual steamboat. Chardon missed the lad and looked forward to seeing him. Chardon also missed Tchon-su-mons-ka. He had mourned her death for a month, not long by the standards of Philadelphia and New York, but long enough on the upper

Missouri. Her memory could not warm his bed. Closing the chapter of his life in which Tchon-su-mons-ka had played a key role, Chardon went to Mitutanka Village and acquired a new wife among the Arikaras.[14]

Apart from the presence of Chardon's new bride at Fort Clark, the daily routine at the trading post continued in its usual humdrum fashion. For all of May, *engagés* had pressed over twelve dozen packs of buffalo robes, bringing the total for the season to 300—roughly thirteen and a half tons of dressed hides. The 400 pounds of beaver pelts the workmen had also baled put Chardon well on his way to making his fur quota for the year. But robes and pelts could do nothing to relieve hunger. At Mitutanka and Ruhptare villages, food remained scarce. Most of the Indians had nothing to eat except roots. Fort Clark's larder was nearly as bare as those of the Mandans, and its supply of corn was almost exhausted. If the post hunters did not return soon, Chardon and his men would probably be compelled to dig roots alongside the Mandan women—either that or starve.

On May 21, the hunters who had left Fort Clark in company with the Mandans and Arikaras a week and a half before finally came back to the stockade. Although their five pack horses were piled high with the remains of four butchered buffalo, the meat would make tough chewing. All the hunters had been able to kill were emaciated bulls.

The Mandans and Arikaras had also found the hunting lean. A few Indians had given up and were trickling back to their homes, but most of their party had chosen to remain on the prairie, hoping to change their luck by shifting their camp to a different locale. Until the native hunters tracked down a herd, their families had no choice but to tighten their belts and keep to their diet of roots.

For much of the month, the air at Fort Clark had smelled of smoke. Assiniboine, Hidatsa, and Lakota war parties were continually setting fire to the prairie north and east of the Missouri River, then using the smoke and flames to hide their movements. This coming summer, if the tribes did not starve to death first, Chardon expected the upper Missouri plain to run red with blood.

On May 23, the shamans' prayers were answered. Several Arikaras returned to Mitutanka Village with a few haunches of fresh meat. The news they brought was as welcome as the food. The Indians hunters had jumped a small herd of buffalo and killed a goodly number. As soon as their wives finished butchering and drying the meat, the hunters would bring it back to Mitutanka Village so everyone could eat. The next day, the main body of hunters arrived, their travois and horses loaded with jerky, hump ribs, and tongues. Every mouth in the town salivated in anticipation of the feast the two tribes would hold, celebrating the Manitou's kindness. The buffalo spirit had not allowed the Mandans and Arikaras to perish.

The following morning, a cold northeast wind greeted the Mitutanka revelers as they devoured their gift from the Manitou. The meat brought in by their hunters was quickly consumed amid an air of jubilation. The villagers' hunger pangs could return tomorrow, but today the Indians gorged themselves until their bellies were stuffed as plump as vine-ripened melons.

On May 27, a Hidatsa war party took to the Missouri in buffalo-hide bull boats and began paddling downriver toward Fort Pierre in search of Lakota scalps.[15] The next day, a number of Mandans and Arikaras from Mitutanka Village moved down the Missouri in a renewed quest for buffalo. The tribes had eaten most of their meat during the recent celebration and were once again on the verge of starving. Meanwhile, four horses disappeared from Fort Clark's remuda, prompting Chardon to think they had been stolen. If he suspected the departing Mandans or Arikaras of the theft, he failed to note it in his journal.

On May 29, Toussaint Charbonneau, a French-Canadian trader working for Pratte & Chouteau, arrived at Fort Clark from the Knife River, reporting that the Hidatsas, too, were out of food. Like the Mandans and Arikaras, the Hidatsas had also found few buffalo. Since the post's hunters had fared no better, Chardon could offer the weathered trader nothing to carry back to the hungry tribe. Hidatsa children would have to satisfy their empty stomachs by sucking on strips of rawhide.

A former employee of the defunct North West Company,

Charbonneau had wintered on Canada's Assiniboine River between 1793 and 1794, at the firm's Pine Fort trading house.[16] In 1795, when he was about thirty-six years old, he came to the lower Knife River and settled among the Hidatsas, acquiring a Shoshoni wife, who was probably a Hidatsa captive. Following in the footsteps of fellow French Canadians René Jusseaume— who had moved in with the Mandans in the early 1790s—and Joseph Garreau—who had taken up residence with the Arikaras in 1793—Charbonneau adopted Indian ways and was accepted by the tribe.[17] Over the years, he trapped, traded, and interpreted for other Europeans who sought to do business on the upper Missouri.

In the early 1800s, Charbonneau wagered with a Hidatsa warrior, winning a teenage Shoshoni girl who had been captured by a Hidatsa war party around the Three Forks of the Missouri, an area where the Gallatin, Madison, and Jefferson rivers converge, forming the Missouri (in west-central Montana). Charbonneau took the girl as his wife, unaware that she would soon make him famous as a member of Lewis and Clark's Corps of Discovery. Her name was Sacajawea.[18]

In 1806, during the return from their exploration of the Missouri headwaters and Oregon coast, Lewis and Clark stopped at the Knife River villages. Charbonneau, Sacajawea, and their son remained on the upper Missouri, while the captains continued downstream to their hero's welcome and their place in history. At Clark's behest, Charbonneau and his family eventually purchased a farm on the lower Missouri, but Charbonneau had lived too long among Indians to find comfort near the settlements. In 1811, he and Sacajawea headed back to the Knife River, journeying aboard a Missouri Fur Company keelboat. By some accounts, Sacajawea died of fever late the following year.[19]

In the seasons that followed, Charbonneau reverted to the trading life he had known before Lewis and Clark. Eventually, he became a Hidatsa trader for the American Fur Company and then for its successor, Pratte & Chouteau.

May 1837 ended with Chardon's dead-rat tally increased by 108. If he ate any of them to ease his hunger, he failed to mention it in his journal. On the final night of the month, 100

Arikara warriors departed Mitutanka Village, intending to count coup on the Yankton Lakotas. It certainly looked as if Chardon's prediction about the summer would be accurate; it was going to be bloody.

The second day of June brought welcomed news to the upper Missouri. Overnight the river had risen two feet, ensuring the speedy arrival of Pratte & Chouteau's annual steamboat. That morning at Mitutanka Village, Mandan warriors purified themselves in sweat lodges, praying to their spirits for protection on their upcoming raid against the Yanktons. Chief Ball dans Le Coup had stirred the blood of the Mandan young men, entreating them with eloquent speeches to ride with him against their Lakota enemy.

The previous summer, the Yanktons had scalped twenty-eight Mandans, and now Ball dans Le Coup was determined to repay those deaths in kind. As the noon hour approached, a couple of villagers spotted a small buffalo herd grazing on the prairie. Temporarily abandoning their preparations for battle, members of the war party ran for their horses, joining the other village men in a buffalo chase. Almost immediately, word of the buffalo filtered into Fort Clark, prompting the entire garrison to grab a piece of the fun.[20] At three o'clock that afternoon, the Indian and white hunters returned victorious, their horses loaded with fresh meat from sixteen cows and two bulls. The hunters had slaughtered every animal in the herd.

That evening the Mandans and Arikaras at Mitutanka Village again feasted on hump ribs and tongues. No doubt the confidence of Ball dans Le Coup's war party soared. The Manitou had sent the buffalo, so it was natural that the spirit would also lead the Yanktons into a Mandan trap. As the night wore on, a number of Mandan warriors probably lay awake in their earthen lodges, contemplating their coming coups.

June 4 was the Sabbath, but at Fort Clark as at other trading posts on the upper Missouri, it was a day of work instead of worship and rest. For Francis Chardon, this Sunday brought a measure of disappointment. The Missouri had fallen two feet since the previous night. Unless the river quickly rose, the company's steamboat would probably end its trip at Fort Pierre. If that happened, Fort Pierre's *engagés* would have to haul the supplies to forts Clark and Union in a keelboat or mackinaw. It would also be that much longer before Chardon could reunite with his son, Andrew Jackson. The *bourgeois's* new Arikara wife warmed his bed, but she could not end his longing to see his boy.

That night Chief Ball dans Le Coup led his war party east from Mitutanka Village. During the absence of the warriors, their wives and children would take care to observe all tribal taboos. Breaking one was the surest way for them to see their husbands and fathers come to harm.

Sometime after dawn, most of the Mandans and Arikaras who were still in the village departed. They planned being gone for several weeks, hunting buffalo and drying meat for storage and pemmican—a nutritious mixture of powdered buffalo jerky, buffalo fat, and occasionally fresh or dried berries. Only the tribes' grandfathers and grandmothers stayed behind. Too old to hunt and too feeble to perform the heavy labor of skinning and butchering, the elders had nothing to do but await the return of their families.

On June 5, while the old people at Mitutanka Village sat in their earthen lodges and the *engagés* at Fort Clark pressed twenty-nine packs of buffalo robes, many miles down the Missouri River, the *St. Peter's* edged against the right shore, and crewmen laid the gangplank in front of Fort Kiowa. Aware that the steamboat was bringing their government annuities, several hundred Yankton and Santee Lakotas lined the riverbank, eagerly awaiting their presents.[21]

Fort Kiowa sat on the Missouri's west side, about twenty-five miles above the mouth of the White River (a bit south of South Dakota's Crow-Creek Indian Reservation and about ten miles northwest of present-day Chamberlain). In the fall of 1822, Joseph Brazeau (or Brassaux) had built the trading post for an early forerunner of Pratte & Chouteau. Intended for the Lakota trade, the post was also called Fort Lookout as well as Brazeau's Fort.[22]

When the *St. Peter's* reached Fort Kiowa, the Arikara women and children who had boarded the boat at Council Bluffs were deathly ill, their faces a mass of oozing sores. Consumed with fever, their bodies ached. When not delirious, they longed for a sip of cool water, then felt as if they were swallowing fire when someone gave them a drink. Eating was out of the question. Shutting their eyes against the painful daylight, they moaned and twisted beneath their blankets. Death would have been a relief.[23]

By now, the black crewman who had brought smallpox aboard the *St. Peter's* was completely well. Among the non-Indians he had infected, many had already shed their scabs and were nearly recovered. Their fevers had passed, and they were slowly regaining their vigor. Exercise, including walking, quickly tired them, so they likely rested on deck, absorbing the weak June sun. Most of those convalescing probably wrapped in blankets to cut the wind. This spring it had been particularly strong, a chilly reminder that on the upper Missouri, winter was never far away.

Although the majority of the non-Arikara patients had mended, several were still molting their scabs and remained contagious. Thus far, the disease had been held to a few cases and appeared under control. Captain Pratte probably congratulated himself on his decision to keep the black deckhand on board. Agent Fulkerson's fears about starting an epidemic among the tribes had proved groundless. All the captain needed now was for the snowmelt in the Rocky Mountains to raise the Missouri another couple of feet. If that happened, the *St. Peter's* should be able to reach Fort Union. Counting every minute on the river as precious, Pratte urged his crew to hurry unloading the supplies for the trading post and the government rations for the waiting Lakotas.

In contrast with Captain Pratte, Joshua Pilcher was far less confident about the risk of the smallpox spreading to the Indians.[24] Pilcher—who intended remaining at Fort Kiowa— had spent most of his adult life on the Missouri and knew well the danger of smallpox to the tribes. During his years as a trader at Council Bluffs, he undoubtedly heard stories about how the *Variola* epidemic of 1801 and 1802 had nearly annihilated the powerful Omahas.

Despite any assurance by Captain Pratte that the disease was contained, Pilcher understood the hazard. Yet, as he pondered whether to release the annuities to the waiting Lakotas, he recognized the peril of withholding them. He knew that if he urged the Indians to leave without their subsidy, they would take his warning as a trick. Although they trusted Pilcher better than most white men, the Lakotas had been swindled enough over the years to be wary of any white promise. Seeing no way to avoid doing so, Pilcher arranged for the annuities to be distributed.

Perhaps smallpox scabs had inadvertently contaminated one of the annuity blankets or a bolt of cloth, or maybe one of the Lakotas sneaked aboard the steamboat and encountered the sick Arikara women. Then again, a contagious white passenger or deckhand may have gone ashore and mingled with the waterfront crowd. The way it happened will probably never be known, but somehow, at least one Yankton or Santee tribesman inhaled the deadly *Variola* virus. Once more, the incubation clock began to tick.

As the *St. Peter's* steamed away from Fort Kiowa and headed toward the Missouri's Grand Detour and Fort Pierre, Pilcher began to worry that the Lakotas at his agency had become infected.[25] Hoping to prevent an epidemic, he dispatched interpreters to the outlying Lakota bands, imploring them to stay away from the Missouri and all fur company trading posts until autumn. He prayed they would heed the warning. Meanwhile, the Yanktons and Santees who had met the *St. Peter's* gathered around their campfires, celebrating their annuities, unaware that the smallpox virus was multiplying inside the lungs of one or more of their members.

About twenty miles above Fort Kiowa, the *St. Peter's* entered the Missouri's Grand Detour. Here, the river looped back on itself, forming a nearly thirty-mile bend. At its narrowest stretch, the enclosed land was barely 2,000 feet wide. Although a man could hike across this neck in less than an hour, a steamboat needed most of a day to arrive at the same place.

Upstream from the Grand Detour, the Missouri braided around numerous sandbars, its channel playing hide-and-seek with the *St. Peter's* pilot and lookouts. Becoming exasperated with the loss of time, Captain Pratte may have been tempted to launch the steamer's yawl and have a sounding crew negotiate a route through the riverine labyrinth.[26] Steamboat captains too proud to do so often regretted their decisions.

Eventually, the *St. Peter's* reached Farm Island, located about seven miles below Fort Pierre. *Engagés* from the trading post cultivated fifteen acres of the island, growing potatoes, cucumbers, turnips, beets, onions, melons, and corn. A small cabin provided shelter for the farm crew, which not only needed to sow and harvest the crops, but also protect them from pilfering by the Lakotas. The garden and cornfields had been hacked from a stand of timber. *Engagés* piled cords of wood near the main river channel for use by Pratte & Chouteau's steamboats.[27] Continually in need of fuel for its boilers, the *St. Peter's* likely stopped at the island so work gangs could replenish its supply.

The *St. Peter's* may have arrived at Fort Pierre on the afternoon of June 6, but it was more likely sometime the following day.[28] The 100,000-square-foot trading facility was officially named Fort Pierre Chouteau—in honor of Pierre Chouteau Jr.—although most everyone shortened it to Fort Pierre (pronounced pier). It had been constructed between 1831 and 1833, replacing nearby Fort Tecumseh, which was being undercut by the Missouri River. As usual, the steamboat's crew rushed to unload supplies intended for the fort. Meanwhile, William Fulkerson and a number of other passengers headed inside the post stockade to look around. Those Pratte & Chouteau employees who had been hired for Fort Pierre disembarked, ready to fulfill the terms of their enlistments.

By now the pus-filled blisters on the sick Arikaras had begun drying into scabby crusts.[29] Their fevers and muscle-aches continued, but with less intensity than in days past. Although they still risked catching pneumonia or going blind, their chances for recovery appeared better than they had been in a couple of weeks. The other passengers and crew who had caught the disease were either completely well or nearly so. The complexions of those who had suffered only a few scabs appeared almost normal. In contrast, those whose faces had been heavily scabbed now bore cheeks that looked as raw as a side of meat. Their skin would eventually regain its natural color, but their pockmarks would accompany them to the grave.

When the *St. Peter's* pilot rang the signal bell, calling everyone back to the boat, a few new travelers joined William Fulkerson and the other passengers as they filed across the gangway. Probably the most excited to be going was Jacob Halsey, until now, Fort Pierre's senior clerk and a junior partner in the Upper Missouri Outfit. Pratte & Chouteau had appointed him temporary *bourgeois* of Fort Union, and Halsey was heading upriver to take command. If he did a good job, the position could be made permanent.

Halsey had joined the American Fur Company in 1826 and spent the past eleven years on the upper Missouri. Since the spring of 1829, he had been stationed at Fort Tecumseh and its replacement, Fort Pierre. Traveling with him were his pregnant, mixed-blood wife and their three-year-old son.[30] Francis Chardon's son, Andrew Jackson, also boarded the *St. Peter's,* having finished seeing to the burial of his mother, Tchon-su-mons-ka. Still mourning her death, the boy looked forward to reuniting with his father. Fort Pierre's *bourgeois,* Pierre Papin, was also making the trip, perhaps as a chaperon for young Andrew Jackson and as a favor to the lad's father.

June 8 found the *St. Peter's* bucking a strong head wind that quartered from the northwest.[31] Powerful gusts hurled the clouds across the prairie like cottonballs. In the distance, thunderheads darkened the sky, threatening rain. Some miles above Fort Pierre, the steamboat passed the quarter-mile-wide mouth of the Cheyenne River, named for the Cheyenne Indians who lived near its headwaters in the Black Hills. A day or so later, the *St. Peter's* reached the Missouri's confluence with the Moreau, a river that took its name from a French trader who was unlucky in love. Many years earlier, Moreau had angered a Cheyenne woman—possibly his wife, perchance a mistress. Whatever their relationship, her fury became so intense, she plunged her knife between his ribs.[32]

Aboard the steamer, Jacob Halsey and his wife may have conversed with a passenger who was recovering from smallpox but still contagious, or perhaps they accidentally encountered the sick Arikara women or their children. Then again, the Halseys could have come in contact with some contaminated bedding. The record is silent about how it occurred, but within two or three days of joining the *St. Peter's,* Halsey and his wife inhaled the *Variola* virus.

If Captain Pratte or someone else had told Halsey about the presence of smallpox, he was probably not overly concerned, especially about his own health. He had been vaccinated with cowpox vaccine some years back and considered himself immune.[33] He was unaware that the effectiveness of a vaccination wears off over time. As the riverboat plowed relentlessly toward its next scheduled stop at Fort Clark, the deadly disease began to incubate within its new hosts—Jacob Halsey and his wife.

At Fort Clark a day earlier—June 7—Chardon had studied his ledgers, disappointed with the mediocre returns from this year's trade. The Hidatsas had bartered only 630 buffalo robes and 180 pounds of beaver pelts, a poor showing by any measure. The Mandans had done worse—almost fifty percent worse. It was the result of them cowering inside their lodges for most of the spring, too frightened of phantom Lakota war parties to hunt. No doubt Chardon felt it served the Mandans right that they had nearly starved for want of food. If the Arikaras had not stiffened their backbone by moving to Mitutanka Village, the Mandans could yet be hiding within their homes, paralyzed with fear. At least the Arikaras' robes had saved the trading season from total disaster. Closing his books, the *bourgeois* hoped conditions would improve in the fall when the trade started anew.

A bit after dawn the next day, a rain shower settled the dust. After a few minutes the storm was gone, whisked away by a brisk northwest wind that herded clouds like Indian riders running buffalo. Later that morning or sometime in the afternoon, five members of the Arikara war party that had left to raid the Yanktons the middle of the previous month limped into Mitutanka Village.[34] The Yanktons had been camped near the Cheyenne River. The returning Arikaras reported how they had attempted stealing the Yanktons' ponies under the cover of night, but had been discovered and compelled to disperse amid a hail of arrows and lead. At sunset, thirteen more Arikara stragglers filed into the village, among them two who were wounded. On foot and needing to travel light, they had tossed away their buffalo robes and tunics, and arrived wearing nothing but their breechclouts and moccasins. The news they brought was somber. Eighteen members of the war party were still unaccounted for, and two others were confirmed dead.

As the Mandans at Mitutanka Village (the old people who were not at the hunting camp with the rest of their tribe) listened to a recount of the disaster, they probably worried about their own warrior-sons who had gone for Lakota scalps. The Mandans had ridden off four nights earlier, confident of victory. But the failed Arikara raid now had the Yanktons stirred up like a nest of angry bees. Instead of earning a great coup, the Mandans were more apt to be heading into a Lakota ambush.

The following afternoon, four more Arikara warriors returned to Mitutanka Village. They too wore nothing but breechclouts and moccasins. Like their fellow warriors who had arrived the day before, the four Arikaras knew nothing about their members who were still missing.

The next day, Saturday, June 10, the Missouri began to rise, again giving hope that the company steamboat would be able to complete its journey. The old women of the village went to the upper plain, eager to dig the prairie turnips that had recently matured. Toward evening, they all scurried back to their lodges, barely outrunning a gathering storm. During the night, lightening and thunder rattled the countryside, while rain pummeled the village and Fort Clark. Warm and dry before a toasty fire, Francis Chardon could enjoy the charms of his Arikara wife. How different it was for the Arikara warriors still fleeing for their lives. Wet and cold, they lived in fear, not knowing if morning would find their hair decorating a Yankton lodgepole.

On Sunday, as the men at Fort Clark went about their duties, everyone eagerly anticipated the annual steamboat. Although the nearly continual thunderstorms had whetted the weather to a raw edge, they kept the Missouri River flowing full, giving the steamer a better than even chance of making it to Fort Union. On Sunday night, June 11, the last of the missing Arikaras trudged into Mitutanka Village, bringing with them three Yankton horses they had managed to steal before being routed. They also brought word of two more Arikara dead.[35] Displaying the elation of a second place finisher in a two-man race, the warriors brandished a single Yankton scalp. That and the horses were their war party's only trophies. All in all, it had been a bad raid.

On June 13, members of the Mandan and Arikara hunting camp that had departed near the end of May returned. Their travois carried a respectable store of dried meat, but less than had been hoped. The following day, a Hidatsa war party rode past Fort Clark, showing off ten horses and two mules it had pirated from a Lakota camp on the Bad River. On May 27, the Hidatsas had paddled down the Missouri in bull boats, full of bravado and anticipating many coups. Compared with the disastrous raid of the Arikaras, the Hidatsas had won a great victory. As Chardon watched the warriors parade by the post stockade, he noticed that two of their captured horses carried the Pratte & Chouteau brand. No doubt the Lakotas had stolen them from Fort Pierre.

Sometime after the latest war party's triumphant return, Toussaint Charbonneau arrived at the trading post, having come from the Hidatsas' village on the Knife River. The trader reported that eight company mackinaws loaded with robes and furs were on their way downstream from Fort Union and were expected on the morrow.

All the next day, Chardon watched for the mackinaws, but a strong, southerly chinook held the boats wind-bound between the Little Missouri and Knife rivers. The following morning the wind abated, and at ten o'clock the mackinaws hove to before the trading post. Knowing that his son, Andrew Jackson, was coming upriver from Fort Pierre aboard the company's steamboat, Chardon decided to float downstream with the mackinaws, intercept the steamer, and join his boy for a relaxing return-voyage to Fort Clark.

Just after sunrise on June 17, Chardon boarded one of the flat-bottomed barges as their voyageurs prepared to pole the flotilla into the Missouri's main channel. The river roiled with downed trees that had been torn loose by the spring runoff and upcountry thunderstorms. Some of the debris had drifted from as far away as the headwaters of the Yellowstone and Milk. The same south wind that had plagued the mackinaws for the past couple of days persisted, making for slow going. Despite the strong current, the wind gave ground grudgingly. At times the mackinaws sat stationary, held prisoner by the gusts, while beneath their hulls the river continued to flow.

Late that afternoon, Chardon and the voyageurs made camp, nowhere near as far downstream as they had expected to be. Then sometime after dark, the wind ushered in a thunderstorm. Rain and waves lashed the mackinaws as the men squatted cold and wet beneath whatever shelter they could find. When it seemed they had seen the worst, one of the mackinaws sprang a leak and began to sink. Frantic to save its cargo, Chardon and the boatmen transferred the craft's ninety-pound packs of buffalo robes to the other boats, a labor that occupied much of the night. Despite the effort, water soaked a good many robes. By morning, the rain had stopped, allowing the men to spread the robes to dry. Not doing so meant they would rot.

That day, the wind turned from villain to savior. By early afternoon, it had dried those robes that had not been sopped. The rest would take longer, assuming there was no more rain. At two o'clock, Chardon or one of the voyageurs spotted the *St. Peter's* with its two mackinaws in tow.[36] Seeing their camp— and no doubt Chardon's waving arms—the steamer's pilot nudged the bow close to shore and ordered a crewman to run out the gangway. After bidding the voyageurs good-bye, the *bourgeois* boarded the steamboat and, one would guess, lifted his son in his arms, giving the boy a big hug.

The daily journal of Francis Chardon contains few details about his time on the *St. Peter's,* but it seems reasonable that his longtime friends, Jacob Halsey and Pierre Papin, caught him up on all the news and gossip from Fort Pierre, including details about the burial of Andrew Jackson's mother, Tchon-su-mons-ka. It is also likely that subagent William Fulkerson questioned Chardon about events at Mitutanka and Ruhptare villages as well as those of the Hidatsas. Fulkerson is certain to have shown interest in the Arikaras and how the Mandans were adjusting to their oft fickle lodge-guests. At nightfall, the steamboat stopped about thirty miles below Fort Clark.

By now it had been eight or nine days since Halsey and his wife had inhaled the *Variola* virus. Neither exhibited any sign of being sick, though within their lungs the disease was fast approaching critical mass. The crew and white passengers who had caught smallpox from the black deckhand were well or close to it, though possibly one or two of them were still capable of spreading the affliction despite feeling much improved. The Arikara women and children had survived their illnesses and were recovering. Most of their scabs had fallen off, leaving their cheeks raw and scarred. No one guessed that they remained highly contagious.

At dawn the following day, June 19, the *St. Peter's* resumed its voyage, reaching Fort Clark at three o'clock that afternoon. As usual, the crew rushed to unload supplies for the trading post. This time they had more reason to hurry than concern that the Missouri would drop, preventing the steamer from continuing to Fort Union. Captain Pratte had decided to spend the night at Fort Clark and allow his boatmen an evening of fun. Although many of the Mandans and Arikaras were still in hunting camps on the prairie, enough young women had returned to Mitutanka Village to satisfy the crew's lust. Mandan and Arikara husbands and fathers eagerly sold the sexual favors of their wives and daughters. For a few fishhooks, a half dozen loads of ammunition, or a cup or two of watered-down alcohol, a white man could purchase a night of carnal bliss.

While the *St. Peter's* crewmen sped through their chores, Chardon most likely invited Pratte, Halsey, Fulkerson, and Papin to his home for a drink. Papin intended waiting at Fort Clark until the *St. Peter's* returned from Fort Union, then reboarding and going back to Fort Pierre.[37] The craftsmen, *engagés,* and other employees who were assigned to Fort Clark also disembarked and took up their new lodgings within the stockade. Infectious and still posing a danger, the three Arikara women passengers and their children hastened to join their families at Mitutanka Village. Meanwhile, a number of Mandans lined the riverbank, gawking at the steamer and wealth of merchandise that was being carried ashore. Unfortunately for the Indians, subagent Fulkerson had brought them no annuities.[38] Despite any quarantine that Captain Pratte may yet have had in place, the bolder Indian onlookers probably took advantage of the commotion and thronged over the steamer's decks, ignoring shouts from the crew that they ought to keep off for their own good. Every time a steamboat landed at Fort Clark, Mandans clambered aboard, and doubtless, they saw no reason to alter their behavior for the *St. Peter's.*[39]

By dusk the fort's supplies had been stored in a warehouse. Workmen had also untethered the two mackinaws from the *St. Peter's* and secured them to the riverbank. Their work finished, the steamer's crew and most of the personnel from the fort went to Mitutanka Village for a "frolic." A few of the younger boatmen may have felt embarrassed about buying a woman for the night, but the seasoned hands made their purchases quickly and often with less thought than if they had been acquiring a horse. The upper Missouri was no place for prudish morality.

That evening Mitutanka Village reverberated with drums and dancing. Whiskey flowed freely, burning its way down Indian and white gullets alike. Passengers and crew from the *St. Peter's,* including those who had recently left their sickbeds, caroused with abandon. The Arikara women who had come aboard the steamboat from Fort Bellevue may too have joined the revelry. Mandans, Arikaras, and the mishmash of Virginians, Kentuckians, Spaniards, free blacks, Creoles, mixed-bloods, and French Canadians who had been lured to the upper Missouri by the fur trade cavorted as though they were brothers. As the celebration wore on, men and young women slipped away to the earthen lodges or to the riverbank for their bartered trysts. In the midst of all the merriment, no one knew that a killer had also come to party.

That night, at least one of the Mandans inhaled the *Variola* virus. The unwitting carrier could have been the female Arikara passengers or their children, or perhaps a recovering crewman, or merely someone with a spore-infected blanket or shirt. How the disease was passed may never be known, but during the night of June 19, 1837, smallpox invaded its newest host—the Mandans of Mitutanka Village.

Chapter three notes

1. In 1843, Joseph Robidoux III platted a town around his Blacksnake Hills Trading Post, naming it St. Joseph, Missouri.

2. Clyde D. Dollar, "The High Plains Smallpox Epidemic of 1837-38," reprint, *The Western Historical Quarterly* 8, no. 1 (January 1977): 20.

3. In contrast with my description of how the *St. Peter's* became infected with smallpox, Alexander Culbertson, *bourgeois* of Fort McKenzie, stated that a trapper named Bill May hid some smallpox-infected clothing aboard the steamboat because Pratte & Chouteau had refused him passage. Bernard DeVoto, *Across the Wide Missouri* (Boston: Houghton Mifflin, 1947), 417-18 n. 1 pokes a hole in Culbertson's story.

4. Hiram Martin Chittenden, *The American Fur Trade of the Far West*, 3 vols. (New York: Francis Harper, 1902; reprint, 3 vols. in 2, New York: Press of the Pioneers, 1935; 2 vols., Lincoln: University of Nebraska Press, Bison Book Edition, 1986), 1:337-9; and Robertson, *Competitive Struggle*, 59-60.

5. Chardon's journal entry for January 18, 1837 (Chardon, *Journal*, 94-5), reports that the Mandans killed five Yankton ambassadors and captured one Yankton woman. The entry for May 10 (page 111) says that two Yankton women escaped the previous night, adding that they had been taken captive during the Yanktons' January massacre. My narrative assumes that the first entry is correct and only one woman was captured on January 18. If so, the second woman must have been taken at a different time.

6. Trimble, "Spread of Smallpox," 40 reports that the *St. Peter's* voyage from St. Louis to Council Bluffs took twenty-eight days. Assuming it left St. Louis on April 17 and counting its departure and arrival dates, it would have arrived at Fort Bellevue on May 14. On page 41, Trimble states that the steamer reached the Sioux (Lakota) Agency—Fort Kiowa—on June 5 (one of the few known dates from the *St. Peter's* 1837 voyage), adding that the Arikara women who boarded at Fort Bellevue had been on the boat for twenty-three days; June 5 and the twenty-three days are supported by Dollar, "High Plains Smallpox Epidemic," 20. Including June 5 and counting back twenty-three days puts the *St. Peter's* departure from Fort Bellevue on May 14. This assumes the steamboat arrived and departed Council Bluffs the same day, certainly probable given the urgency of completing its voyage before the Missouri fell too low to navigate.

7. Audubon, *Journals*, 1:477.

8. Chardon, *Journal*, 118. I have found no record of where the *St. Peter's* acquired its two mackinaws. Although the steamer may have started with them from St. Louis, it seems unlikely. Because the lower Missouri was generally wide and deep, it appears more probable that the mackinaws were picked up at Fort Bellevue. According to Lass, *Steamboating*, 13, steamboats typically towed between two and four mackinaws on the upper stretches of the Missouri in case they were needed as lighters.

9. My calendar for the progression of the black deckhand's case hinges on reports that he became sick as the *St. Peter's* neared Fort Leavenworth. Dollar, "High Plains Smallpox Epidemic," 20 states that the crew members and passengers who were the first to be infected by him ended their incubation before the *St. Peter's* reached Fort Bellevue. Because smallpox is normally most infectious after its skin rash begins to elevate, the black crewman was probably not highly contagious until a couple of days after the steamboat departed the Blacksnake Hills. The incubation

period for smallpox is typically twelve days, although it can be as short as eight days or as long as fourteen. Accordingly, the soonest the passengers and other crewmen could have ended their incubations was May 14. My narrative assumes a twelve-day incubation. Since few dates from the *St. Peter's* 1837 voyage are known with certainty, it is possible that Dollar's timetable, instead of mine, is closer to the mark.

10. Most accounts of these women make no mention of their having children; for example, see Dollar, "High Plains Smallpox Epidemic," 20. In his journal entry for June 23 (Chardon, *Journal*, 118-19), Francis Chardon mentioned seeing one of the Arikara women who had arrived on the *St. Peter's,* noting that her children had come with her. It is likely that the other women had children, as well.

11. Catlin, *Letters*, 1:20.

12. Robertson, *Competitive Struggle*, 106-7. William Dickson remained *bourgeois* of Vermilion Post until committing suicide in 1838.

13. Lass, *Steamboating*, 13.

14. Chardon made no mention of this marriage in his journal entries for May 1837, but on May 18, 1838 (Chardon, *Journal*, 160), he wrote that he "Separated from My [his] dear Ree Wife, after a Marriage of one Year." On page 319 n. 506, editor Annie Abel concludes that he acquired his Arikara bride within a month of Tchon-su-mons-ka's death.

15. On May 27, 1837 (Chardon, *Journal*, 114), Chardon wrote that "A War Party of Gros Ventres left here [Fort Clark] to day [*sic*] for the Little Misso in skin canoes." Chardon called the Hidatsas the Gros Ventres. Other white men called them Minetarees (spelled various ways). Early French traders learned the names from the Mandans. Loosely translated, Gros Ventre meant that the Hidatsas were always hungry, and Minetaree signified the ones who lived across the river. Adding to the confusion, French traders also called the Atsinas the Gros Ventres, because of the tribe's propensity to visit—and sponge off—their Arapaho cousins as well as their Blackfoot allies. The Atsinas' hosts often resented their guests' hearty appetites. Historians who use the Gros Ventre name for both the Hidatsas and Atsinas typically designate the Atsinas the Gros Ventres of the Prairie.

Addressing another point of confusion, at one time, South Dakota's Bad River was also known as the Teton River (so named by Lewis and Clark because they first met the Teton Lakotas on it) and the Little Missouri River; the Lakotas called it the *Wakpa Seecha*. The Little Missouri name is misleading because the modern Little Missouri River enters the main Missouri on North Dakota's Fort Berthold Indian Reservation. For a reference showing that the Hidatsa war party was indeed heading toward the Bad River and not North Dakota's Little Missouri, see the index entry for Bad River in Chardon, *Journal*, 414. Finally, an Indian bull boat was a small, tub-shaped craft built by stretching a fresh buffalo hide over a willow frame. It carried two or three passengers.

16. Elliott Coues, ed., *The Manuscript Journals of Alexander Henry, Fur Trader of the Northwest Company, and of David Thompson, Official Geographer and Explorer of the same Company*, 2 vols. (Minneapolis: Ross & Haines, 1897; reprint, 1965), 1:50 n. 3.

17. John C. Ewers, *Indian Life on the Upper Missouri* (Norman: University of Oklahoma Press, 1968), 59.

18. Oral tradition says that Charbonneau had an older wife when he acquired Sacajawea. Some sources say that he also won a second young Shoshoni captive at the same time he wagered for Sacajawea, which, if true, would have given him three wives. Stephen E. Ambrose, *Undaunted Courage: Meriwether Lewis, Thomas Jefferson, and the Opening of the American West* (New York: Simon & Schuster,

1996), 187 asserts that his bet netted him two young Shoshoni girls and makes no mention of an older wife. Although he may have had an older wife, logic dictates that he won only Sacajawea. If he had had another young Shoshoni wife, Lewis and Clark would have probably taken her up the Missouri in addition to or in place of Sacajawea, especially since Sacajawea had undergone a difficult childbirth during the expedition's winter encampment among the Mandans and was encumbered with a baby.

19. Ewers, *Indian Life*, 60-1. Arguing against her untimely death, some oral traditions say that Sacajawea lived to be an old woman.

20. Chardon's entry for June 2, 1837 (Chardon, *Journal*, 115), states that after the Indians spotted the buffalo, "all hands [went] out to run them." I assume "all hands" means the personnel at Fort Clark. Indian scouts had discovered the herd, so it seems likely they would have alerted Mitutanka Village, especially since their families were starving. The men at Fort Clark probably heard about the buffalo from the villagers as they were preparing for the chase.

21. Trimble, "Spread of Smallpox," 41.

22. Morgan, *Jedediah Smith*, 376-7 n. 22; Robertson, *Competitive Struggle*, 138-9, 279 n. 12; and Sunder, *Joshua Pilcher*, 37, 110-11. The trading post may have derived its Kiowa name from its founder, who was referred to as Young Cayewa.

23. Joshua Pilcher, an eye witness, stated that the Arikaras "were much afflicted" when the *St. Peter's* landed at the Lakota Agency; see Dollar, "High Plains Smallpox Epidemic," 20. My description of the Indians' condition is based on the symptoms of the disease. I take "much afflicted" to mean they were extremely sick.

24. I base this opinion on Joshua Pilcher to William Clark, June 10, 1837, reprinted in "Spread of Smallpox," by Trimble, 63-5, which was written five days after Pilcher arrived at his agency. Soon after leaving the *St. Peter's,* Pilcher dispatched interpreters to warn the outlying Lakota bands about the danger of smallpox at the trading posts, urging them to stay away. Assuming an Indian at Fort Kiowa had caught smallpox the day the steamboat arrived, the virus would have been incubating when Pilcher issued his warning and penned his letter. Until the disease showed itself, Pilcher had no proof any Lakotas were infected. Therefore, his letter clearly demonstrates that he suspected the tribe would become sick.

25. In Joshua Pilcher to William Clark, June 10, 1837, "Spread of Smallpox," by Trimble, 63-5, Pilcher wrote "I can scarcely consieve [*sic*] it possible for them to escape it."

26. Audubon, *Journals*, 1:518 reports that this stretch of the Missouri was exceedingly difficult. During John James Audubon's journey up the Missouri in 1843, Joseph Sire, captain of the steamer *Omega,* resorted to a yawl and sounding crew in order to find a path among the many sandbars. Occasionally, steamer crews found it necessary to warp their boats through shallow stretches of river. To do so, crewmen fastened a line to a tree or stump that was securely anchored in the sand, then winched the craft forward using a steam-powered windlass located near the bow. If the water was too shallow for warping, captains often resorted to sparring. In this procedure, two log spars were secured just aft of the bow and angled forward so they touched the riverbottom. Ropes were then run from the spars to a windlass, which tightened the lines and levered the boat onto the log "grasshopper poles" and over the obstruction. By repeating the operation—known as grasshoppering—deckhands walked the steamboat upstream. Where rocky shoals prevented warping and sparring, captains resorted to double-tripping, using the mackinaws they usually towed behind as lighters. The mackinaws would carry enough cargo to shore so the steamer could pass over the obstacle and deposit its remaining cargo upriver. Afterward, it dropped downstream and retrieved the stores it had left behind.

Compared with warping and sparring, double-tripping took the longest amount of time and demanded the most labor from the crew.

27. Harold H. Schuler, *Fort Pierre Chouteau* (Vermillion: University of South Dakota Press, 1990), 62, 68-9.

28. The logic for assuming the *St. Peter's* arrived at Fort Pierre on June 7 instead of June 6 stems from the distance between it and Fort Kiowa—which the steamer had departed on June 5—and the difficulty the boat probably had negotiating the river above the Grand Detour, a stretch that gave trouble to the steamboats *Yellow Stone* and *Omega*. Further, the *St. Peter's* remained at Fort Pierre only a short time; see Dollar, "High Plains Smallpox Epidemic," 21. If it had arrived in the late afternoon of June 6, which is the earliest it could have made it from Fort Kiowa, Captain Pratte would have most likely spent the night. On the upper Missouri, steamboats rarely traveled at night because of the river's hidden obstacles.

29. Assuming the Arikara women and children boarded the *St. Peter's* at Fort Bellevue on May 14, they would have been on the steamer twenty-five days as of June 7. If they inhaled the virus a day or two after the boat left Council Bluffs and their incubations lasted the normal twelve days, they would have been in their eleventh or twelfth day of sickness when they reached Fort Pierre. As a result, they were highly contagious.

30. Chardon, *Journal*, 211 n. 50; DeLand, abst., "Fort Tecumseh and Fort Pierre Journal and Letter Books," 9:101-03; and Charles Larpenteur, "White Man Bear (Mato Washejoe), Upper Missouri Trader: Journals and Notes of Charles Larpenteur between 1834 and 1872," transcrb. Edwin T. Thompson (National Park Service Library, Denver, photocopied), 159. Larpenteur wrote that Halsey's son was three years old, but he may have been five. The Fort Pierre Journal entry for April 19, 1832 (page 155), reads "Halsey's child born." Whether or not that was the same child who boarded the *St. Peter's* is unknown.

31. Chardon, *Journal*, 116 reports that a strong, northwest wind buffeted Fort Clark on June 8. I assume such a wind would carry into South Dakota, as well.

32. Bradbury, *Travels*, 127, n. 82.

33. Charles Larpenteur, *Forty Years a Fur Trader on the Upper Missouri: The Personal Narrative of Charles Larpenteur, 1833-1872*, ed. Elliott Coues, 2 vols. (New York, 1898; re-ed. Milo M. Quaife, 2 vols. in 1, Chicago: R. R. Donnelley & Sons, Lakeside Classic, 1933; Lincoln: University of Nebraska Press, Bison Book Edition, 1989), 109.

34. Chardon wrote that the returning warriors had left on May 15; see Chardon, *Journal*, 116. His journal entry for that day (page 112) says they were Arikaras. DeVoto, *Across the Wide Missouri*, 279-80 err by calling them Mandans. Perhaps the war party included Mandans, but I conclude that most of its members were Arikaras, since Chardon labeled them such.

35. I assume the two deaths that Chardon chronicled on June 12 are in addition to the two he had mentioned on June 8; see Chardon, *Journal*, 116-17.

36. In his journal entry for June 18, 1837 (ibid., 118), Chardon wrote that a number of buffalo robes on one of the mackinaws had become soaked. Since wet robes would mildew and rot, it seems probable that Chardon, as an officer of Pratte & Chouteau, would insist that they be dried before continuing downstream—though he made no mention of it in his journal. Because drying would take several hours, I assume he and the voyageurs were still in camp when the *St. Peter's* appeared at two o'clock that afternoon. The journal entry is ambiguous. It is possible that it took only a short time to dry the robes, allowing Chardon and the voyageurs to resume their descent late that morning. If so, they probably met the steamboat while floating the river.

37. Ibid., 316 n. 481 states that Papin stayed at Fort Clark while the *St. Peter's* continued upriver. By July 1837, Papin was back at Fort Pierre, where he penned a letter to Colin Campbell, appointing him temporary *bourgeois* while Papin made a trip to St. Louis; see Schuler, *Fort Pierre Chouteau*, 48, 148 n. 3. I have found no record of how Papin went down to Fort Pierre, but it seems logical that he would have gone aboard the *St. Peter's*.

38. Chardon, *Journal*, 118.

39. Indians clambered aboard steamboats whenever they could, as indicated by Audubon, *Journals*, 2:15, which reports Arikaras crowding onto the *Omega* during a stop at Fort Clark in 1843.

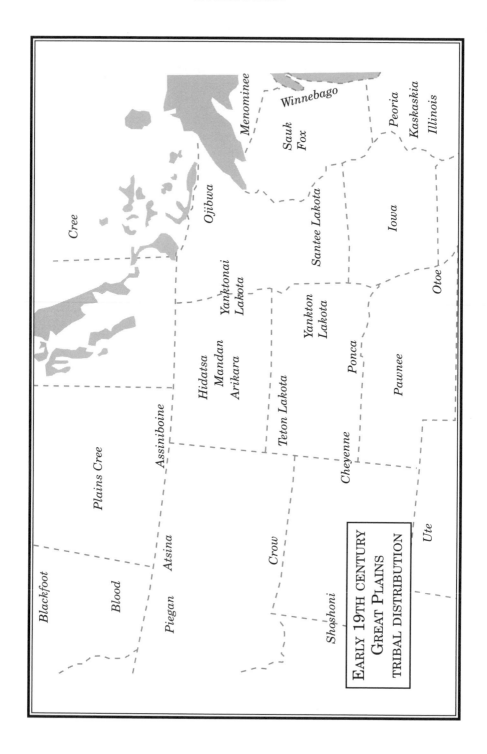

Menominee

Winnebago

Peoria

Kaskaskia

Illinois

Sauk
Fox

Ojibwa

Cree

Santee Lakota

Iowa

Yanktonai
Lakota

Otoe

Yankton
Lakota

Hidatsa
Mandan
Arikara

Ponca

Teton Lakota

Pawnee

Assiniboine

Cheyenne

Plains Cree

Crow

Ute

Atsina

Blackfoot

Piegan

Blood

Shoshoni

EARLY 19TH CENTURY
GREAT PLAINS
TRIBAL DISTRIBUTION

Chapter Four

Smallpox in the New World

Two hours past midnight on October 12, 1492, a gunner on the Spanish caravel *Pinta* fired a cannon, signaling the fleet flagship that a lookout had sighted land. Aboard the *Santa Maria,* the fleet commander and navigator, Cristóbal Colón—a Genoese mapmaker in the employ of Spain—no doubt uttered a silent prayer of gratitude, relieved that he had been proven correct. He had disputed Europe's most noted geographers and won. He had not sailed off the edge of the Atlantic Ocean into an abyss. The earth was not flat. Instead of sending him into historical oblivion, the North Atlantic's west-blowing trade winds had earned him immortality.

Soon after dawn, Colón—or as he is more popularly known, Christopher Columbus—stepped onto the sandy atoll of San Salvador in the Bahamas. While the local Taino natives stood awestruck before the admiral and his retinue of soldiers, Columbus claimed their island and the rest of the western hemisphere for Queen Isabella and her husband, King Ferdinand.[1]

From the Bahamas, Columbus explored the other islands of the Caribbean, certain that they lay just off the mainland of Asia. Thinking that the Caribbean natives were descended from the Hindus of India, he called them Indians. The friendly

Arawaks, Caribs,[2] and Ciboneys welcomed the bearded Europeans, never guessing the horrors their invasion would bring.

When word of Columbus's discovery reached Pope Alexander VI in 1493, the Spanish-born pontiff legalized Columbus's claim and awarded Spain the entire New World. The Pope thought the famed mariner had found a handful of islands on the route to Cathay. Portugal protested the papal ruling, so a year later, Spain and Portugal signed the Treaty of Tordesillas, dividing the Americas along a north-south meridian 370 leagues (about 1,000 miles) west of the Azores. The partition gave Portugal a large eastern bulge in South America (Brazil), leaving the bulk of Columbus's discovery for Spain. Spanish clerics, eager to see the natives of the New World Christianized, soon persuaded the Spanish crown to issue the *requerimiento*. By law conquistadors were required to exhort the Indians to obey the Pope and the rule of Spain. Any Indian who resisted Catholicism and Spanish dictates risked enslavement and death.

Columbus and Spanish explorers such as Amerigo Vespucci and Alonso de Ojeda, who followed in his wake, found the Indians of the New World peaceful. They were awed by European horses and technology, which native religion deemed to have been given the whites by the gods. Because of this belief, the Indians initially viewed the Spanish themselves as godlike, an illusion that quickly faded. Spanish cruelty soon made the Indians think that if these white men were sent by the gods, they must have been gods from hell.

Lusting for gold and silver, Spanish conquistadors enslaved the natives, killing them with brutal labor and maiming those who failed to do their bidding. Viewing the Indians as wanton idolaters, the Spaniards enforced their will by chopping off hands, gouging out eyes, and ripping unborn babies from the wombs of their mothers. Yet, the horror of such butchery pales in comparison with the devastation the Spanish wreaked by unwittingly infecting the New World tribes with diseases for which they had no immunity.

Of all the pestilences the conquistadors introduced, none was more deadly than smallpox. History has forgotten if smallpox was brought to the New World by Spanish seamen or by the

West African slaves the conquistadors began importing to the Caribbean by 1503. But within a quarter century of Columbus first setting foot on Hispaniola, *Variola major* was exterminating the natives whole villages at a time.[3] As the Spanish subjugated one Caribbean island after another, smallpox accompanied them, annihilating the natives of Jamaica, Puerto Rico, Antigua, Martinique, Barbados, and Cuba before eventually reaching Central America.

Like a tiny flame set in a field of tinder-dry grass, *Variola major* kindled a virgin-soil epidemic each time it touched a tribe that had never before been infected. In village after village, nearly every native who inhaled the poisonous virus became ill. Death rates among the afflicted surpassed one in two, often reaching three in four or higher. Within each virgin population, the disease spread so fast there was no one to nurse and feed the sick, let alone tend the crops or hunt and fish. Many bedridden Indians died from starvation when they could have recovered had they been given only a small measure of care.

All across the Caribbean, Spanish land grantees cloaked their enslavement of the natives within the Laws of Burgos and its infamous *encomienda*. This statute had been enacted in 1512 to end the abuses of the *requerimiento*. Under the guise of converting the Indians to Christianity, Spanish overlords compelled their native charges to labor year-round instead of nine months out of every twelve as dictated by the new clerical decree. The Indians saw no difference in their treatment after the *encomienda* replaced the *requerimiento*. Any Indian who refused to work still risked maiming or death. Caribbean natives toiled away their lives on ranches—many of which were large horse-breeding depots—farms, and in mines, enriching their masters as well as the Spanish crown, which received a head tax on every Indian slave.[4] To the natives, it mattered not when Pope Julius II finally pronounced them human, proclaiming that they were indeed descended from Adam and Eve. Their extermination continued.

In December 1518 or January 1519, smallpox erupted on Hispaniola and quickly spread to Puerto Rico. Within weeks, the disease reached Cuba.[5] In early 1519, Hernán Cortéz invaded Mexico, intending to capture native slaves for use on Cuba,

Hispaniola, and other islands of the Caribbean. Hearing rumors that the Aztec empire contained wealth beyond belief, Cortéz abandoned his quest for slaves, opting instead to conquer the Aztecs. With fewer than 600 soldiers, his *entrada* pushed inland to the capital city of Tenochtitlán, thought by Cortéz to be the "most beautiful city in the world." Believing that the Spaniards were descended from the legendary god Quetzalcoatl—the Plumed Serpent—and fearing their harquebuses and horses, the Aztecs fell into disarray. Cortéz gained favor with their ruler, Moctezuma II, and quickly brought Tenochtitlán and the Aztec empire under Spanish control.

Meantime, in May 1519, while Moctezuma was inviting the Spaniards into Tenochtitlán, the governor of Cuba, Diego Velázquez (or Velasquez), dispatched the conquistador Pánfilo de Narváez to arrest Cortéz and take over his command. Narváez and his soldiers sailed from Cuba, where smallpox was raging, and landed at Cempoala (near modern-day Vera Cruz, Mexico).

An African slave accompanied Narváez's force, unaware that he was to be the instrument that would bring about the Aztecs' near annihilation. Sick with smallpox, the slave infected a number of Indians with whom he had contact.[6] With Tenochtitlán seemingly within his grasp, Cortéz left his lieutenant, Pedro de Alvarado, in charge of the capital while he returned to the coast to confront Narváez. A sadistic monster, Alvarado unleashed his soldiers in a wave of terror that galvanized the native leadership and enabled the Aztecs to regain control of Tenochtitlán. Tragically, the rebellion led to the death of Moctezuma.

Cortéz soon foiled Narváez's attempt to escort him to Cuba in irons. His authority at last undisputed, Cortéz rushed back to Tenochtitlán to repair the damage done by Alvarado. But Cortéz was too late; the city was lost. During the night of June 30, he and what remained of his men had to fight their way out of the Aztec capital. Cortéz now turned his energy toward the city's recapture. Relying on ancient hatreds, he recruited the Totonacs and other native enemies of the Aztecs to his army and prepared to invade Tenochtitlán for a second time.

While Cortéz was assembling his forces, the smallpox imported by Narváez's black slave ignited like a grass fire in

Historia de Las Cosas de Nueva Espana, Vol. IV, Library of Congress

early September. The virus enveloped the native population along the coast—including many of Cortéz's Indian recruits— then spread inland to central Mexico, destroying the Aztecs ahead of Cortéz's advancing horde. At Tenochtitlán the Aztecs stood their ground, forcing the Spanish into a multi-week battle for control of the city.

When the Aztec commander Guatemozin, a nephew of the deceased Moctezuma, finally surrendered Tenochtitlán on August 13, 1521, its streets were littered with the rotting bodies of the dead, most of them victims of smallpox. As Cortéz inspected what he had once thought to be the loveliest city in the world, the merciless conquistador fell ill from the stench.[7] Aztec survivors pulled down countless houses, using the rubble to cover the dead. Cortéz had won, but it is doubtful he would have won so handily without the assistance of the deadly *Variola* virus. By some estimates, the epidemic eventually exterminated between two million and fifteen million Indians across all of Mexico.[8]

Many surviving Aztecs blamed their defeat on the superiority of the Christian God. Some hitherto unknown disease had devastated the Aztec army, while leaving Spanish soldiers hale. Surely, that evidenced that the God of Cortéz was more powerful than those of the Aztecs. The Aztecs were unaware that most of the Spaniards had survived smallpox as children and were thereafter immune. Turning their backs on their traditional priesthood, Indians across the Tenochtitlán empire docilely embraced Catholicism and yielded to Spanish rule.

In the mid 1520s smallpox reached the Incas of South America, annihilating them by the tens of thousands and possibly killing their ruler, Wayna Qhapac (or Huayna Capac).[9] By the time Francisco Pizarro invaded the mountain kingdom in 1532, Inca leadership was in shambles. Pizarro captured Atahualpa, the current Inca chieftain (Atahualpa had recently consolidated his authority by executing his brother, Huáscar), toppling his shaky domain and opening the Peruvian empire and its golden riches to Spanish pillage.[10]

Spanish harquebuses and pikestaffs slaughtered countless New World natives, but nowhere near as many as did smallpox. During the century following Cortéz's initial invasion, the population of central Mexico plunged from between five million and ten million (or higher) to approximately 1.4 million. As in Mexico, the native populace of Peru declined possibly as much as eighty-five percent. Although Spanish gunfire and diseases such as scarlet fever and measles accounted for many of the deaths, most were caused by smallpox.[11]

Incensed that the illnesses had no effect on their Spanish masters, some native servants submerged disease-ridden corpses in Spanish wells and mixed infected blood into the food they prepared for Spanish tables. To the Indians' frustration and bewilderment, the Spaniards refused to sicken and die.[12]

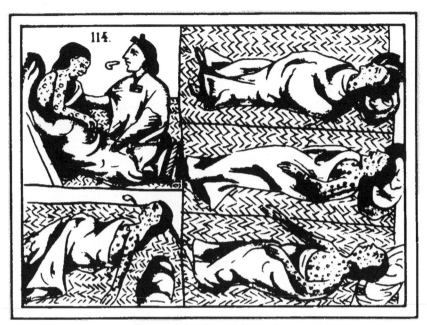

Historia de Las Cosas de Nueva Espana, Vol. IV, Library of Congress

Around the time Cortéz was conquering Mexico, French, English, and Portuguese fisherman began plying the Gulf of St. Lawrence and the waters south of Nova Scotia, harvesting shiploads of cod. Basque whalers came, too, hunting the Labrador Sea south past the Strait of Belle Isle and on to Newfoundland's Conception Bay. Needing to construct tryworks for rendering whale blubber into lamp oil and drying racks to preserve their catches of cod,[13] the European whalers and fishermen erected seasonal camps along the North American coast. From Hudson Strait to Cape Cod, Indians flocked to these camps to barter animal skins for European riches. Although the tribes prized glass beads, ceramic pipes, and buttons, they were fascinated by the utility of metal products such as kettles, knives, nails, and fire steels. Of all the metal goods the Europeans offered, matchlock muskets fetched the most pelts.

During the early part of the sixteenth century, this commercial activity was far more important to the coastal natives than to the whites. Whaling and fishing captains earned supplemental profits from Indian furs, but they considered such items secondary to their more lucrative cargoes of whale oil and dried cod.

Initially, the Europeans valued the furs for their warmth and beauty. Then around 1540, French hatters discovered that beaver underhair made a superior quality felt, the material from which hats were fashioned.[14] Soon, Parisian hatters were clamoring for the rodent's fur, causing the market for beaver pelts to outstrip those of other animal skins. Before long, English and Dutch hatters also learned the benefits of making felt from beaver, adding to its demand.

In 1582, French investors from the Brittany port of Saint-Malo earned nearly a 1,500 percent return on a shipload of beaver. The following year, these and other Frenchmen dispatched at least four ships, directing their crews to fill their holds not only with beaver skins but also with those of otter, mink, deer, and lynx. Carrying a cargo of trade goods that had cost forty livres, the trader-captain Étienne Bellenger sailed to Nova Scotia, then returned home with furs that brought him 440 crowns, a profit of 3,250 percent.[15]

In the early days of the beaver trade, Europeans placed a higher value on Indian garments made from beaver pelts that had been worn for a year or two than they did on freshly cured skins. Before hatters learned to separate the long guard hairs from the barbed underhair that was used in felting, hard usage as Indian clothing (the garments were worn fur-side-in) was the preferred method of ridding beaver pelts of their undesirable hairs. That the fur from such garments would eventually adorn the heads of European aristocracy is one of history's better ironies.

After hearing about the success of ventures such as Bellenger's, whalers and fishermen upped the quantity of trade goods they gave the Indians for each dressed beaver pelt. Inflation had now reached America. The higher returns spurred one coastal tribe after another to deplete the beaver within its respective territory. When a tribe could no longer harvest beaver from its own ponds, it turned middleman and brokered fur and European merchandise between its outlying neighbors—who had not yet killed off their beaver—and the white traders.

Over the years as the value and volume of this commerce between Indians and Europeans grew, inter-tribal warfare increased as each tribe sought to monopolize the trade and control the distribution of manufactured goods to rival bands. The Indian response was rational, since by restricting the number of furs that were going to the traders, a tribe could bid down the price of the traders' wares. In other words, tribes sought to make furs scarce relative to the supply of trade goods, thereby increasing a given amount of merchandise that could be purchased with a fixed quantity of pelts. By far the most important reason Indians sought to monopolize trade was that no tribe wished to see its enemies gain access to wealth and advanced technology—meaning guns.

Wanting to maximize their profits, European traders sought to obtain their furs at the lowest cost. To do so required them to bypass tribes that had exhausted their stock of fur-bearing animals—and by necessity had become brokers—and trade directly with Indians who could produce their own pelts, thereby cutting out the native middlemen. Over the entire three-and-one-half-century span of the fur trade, this most basic tenet of economics—each side, Indian and white, striving to buy what it wanted at the cheapest price—fueled European expansion and inter-tribal rivalry.

Although European contact with the Atlantic coast Indians may have introduced smallpox to the region as early as the 1520s, the record is hazy.[16] By 1600, an estimated 144,000 natives lived between southern Maine and western Connecticut. In 1602, English adventurer Bartholomew Gosnald (or Gosnold) made his first voyage to Cape Cod and traded with the Wampanoags, who he found in good health.[17] A year later another Englishman, Martin Pring, visited Maine and Massachusetts, followed in 1605 by George Waymouth, who bought furs from the Abnakis and Penobscots. The next season George Popham added his name to the list of English seamen who had set foot on North American soil. And so the mariners continued coming, some carrying with them the deadly *Variola* virus.

In 1609, English-born explorer Henry Hudson—sailing aboard the *Haelf Maen* (the *Half Moon*)—discovered and named the Hudson River, allowing its fertile valley to be claimed by his current employer, the Netherlands. In the seasons that followed, Dutch traders pushed inland along Hudson's river and in 1614 built Fort Nassau (at the future site of Albany, New York) in order to corner the burgeoning beaver market.

In 1612 and 1613, a disease that may have been smallpox eradicated the Pawtucketts of Massachusetts. Between 1617 and 1619, another epidemic devastated the other natives of coastal New England, killing nine out of every ten. Whether this disease was smallpox or plague is unclear, although consensus places the blame on either bubonic or pneumonic plague.[18] Entire tribes were exterminated, leaving vast tracts of seaboard countryside open for settlement when the Pilgrims came ashore at Plymouth Rock in 1620. In some native villages so many Indians had died, their bones littered the ground, making at least one Pilgrim think that he had stumbled on a New World "Golgotha."[19] Fortunately for the Pilgrims, a few Indians still lived in the vicinity, including the English-speaking Squanto (or Tisquantum).

In 1614, Squanto and twenty-six other Indians had been captured by English Captain Thomas Hunt and sold into slavery in Malága, Spain. A member of the Wampanoag tribe, Squanto slipped his Spanish bonds and made his way to England, where he learned to speak English. After returning to the New World with the Newfoundland Company, he found life disappointing and retired to England with Captain Thomas Dermer. In 1619, Squanto sailed with Dermer to Cape Cod. Searching for his Wampanoag people, he learned they had died in an epidemic.

The following year when the Pilgrims landed, Squanto went to their aid. Had he not taught them to fish and grow corn, their colony may have starved. As they did Squanto's help, the religious separatists viewed the lack of Indians and the resulting vacant land as a gift from God.[20] It was a belief that other, later whites would also have as they too took up plows on Indian fields made empty by smallpox.

Toward the few Indians still living in the vicinity of Cape Cod, Squanto showed far less magnanimity than he did to the Pilgrims. He extracted presents from his countrymen by warning that the Pilgrims had hidden a deadly pestilence in the ground and if the neighboring tribes refused to do his bidding, he would direct his English friends to unleash it as a punishment. Many of the Pilgrims were equally cruel. In addition to stealing native land, the Pilgrims also rifled Indian graves, looting the furs, axes, muskets, and other wealth the Indian dead were taking to their afterlives.[21]

In 1633, smallpox ravaged the *Mayflower* colony, killing twenty of its members and scarring many more. Infecting the Pilgrims' Native American neighbors, the disease touched off a full-blown epidemic, destroying entire villages and opening up additional countryside for white cultivation. Clergymen such as Increase Mather found the pestilence a godsend, since it annihilated most of the Saugust Indians who had been disputing the sale of their land.[22]

Soon the epidemic invaded the Connecticuts and Narragansetts, prompting the New England governor, William Bradford, to remark that the Indians were dying "like rotten sheep." Striking west, *Variola major* tore into the tribes along the St. Lawrence River and around the eastern Great Lakes. Among the Hurons, the virus was especially deadly. During the decade and a half before the epidemic, the Hurons had dominated the fur trade north of the St. Lawrence River, furnishing New France two-thirds of its annual beaver harvest. Operating as middlemen as well as hunters, the Hurons brokered pelts from tribes as far away as the Ojibwas, who lived west of Lake Superior.[23] Totaling about 20,000 people, the Huron Confederation was composed of four woodland tribes that were concentrated around Lake Simcoe (in modern Ontario), a territory known as Huronia.

French traders used every ploy imaginable to keep the Indians focused on the fur trade, often recruiting priests to the effort. At the traders' behest, Jesuit missionaries urged the Hurons to leave their children at French settlements for religious training while the parents went inland seeking furs. Parents who did so were less likely to trade their pelts to the Dutch.[24] Each year Huron canoe-flotillas plied the rivers and lakes of New France, collecting furs from the outlying tribes and brokering them to the French in Quebec City, Trois Rivières, and (after its founding in 1642) Montreal. With the advent of smallpox, the economic supremacy of the Hurons vanished.

Unlike the English and Dutch, the French made halfhearted attempts to care for the sick. In 1639, French nuns in Quebec City opened *l'Hôtel-Dieu* as an Indian smallpox hospital, but the effort barely made a dent in the overall Huron death rate. By 1641, the disease had claimed over half the Huron population, leaving the survivors vulnerable to attacks by the Iroquois.[25]

The Iroquois League occupied the Finger Lake region south of Lake Ontario (in west-central New York State). Composed of five separate nations, the league included—from east to west—the Mohawks, Oneidas, Onondagas, Cayugas, and Senecas.[26] The Iroquois and Hurons had been at each other's throats long before Europeans penetrated the St. Lawrence River. Early French traders were friendly with both nations, but that changed in 1609 when Samuel de Champlain supported a Huron attack on the Iroquois near Lake Champlain. Thereafter, the Iroquois counted the French among their enemies.[27]

In the late 1630s and early 1640s, Iroquois warriors, armed with Dutch matchlocks, gained many lopsided victories over their northern foe, but the price of their success included *Variola major*. In 1637, smallpox swept the Iroquois, although they fared better than the Hurons, from whom they may have caught the disease.

In March 1649, Iroquois war parties sought to finish the work begun by smallpox and eliminate a competitor in the fur trade. Nearly 1,000 Seneca and Mohawk warriors invaded the Huron lands south of Georgian Bay (near modern Toronto), burning the Hurons' main towns and butchering many Huron men, women, and children. Within a few months, the Iroquois League nearly succeeded wiping out that portion of the southern Huron tribes that had survived smallpox; nevertheless, the Hurons ultimately had their revenge. Later in 1649, the *Variola* virus once again ravaged several Iroquois villages.[28]

Enough Iroquois remained after this latest bout of smallpox to continue the league's drive to corner the fur trade. As with many other inter-tribal conflicts, the basis for Iroquois' aggression was beaver pelts, or in the case of the Iroquois, their absence. Iroquois hunters had emptied their streams and ponds of beaver by the 1640s.[29] Having become dependent on European weapons and other manufactured goods, the confederacy had begun brokering furs from western tribes to the Dutch and English. The determination to eliminate all competition had led the Iroquois to plunder the Hurons.

After the Hurons' defeat, the Iroquois League focused its aggression on its other neighbors, launching the Beaver Wars. In late 1649, the Iroquois routed the Tobacco Indians, Huron allies who lived between Lake Huron and Lake Ontario. From 1650 to 1651, the Senecas carried the fight to the Neutrals, who dwelled north of Lake Erie. Then between 1653 and 1656, the Senecas attacked their western neighbor, the Eries, and in 1660, league warriors sacked the Ottawas north of Lake Huron. Less numerous than the Iroquois, especially after having been hit by repeated bouts of smallpox, these Great Lakes tribes were an easy mark. With each victory, the Iroquois' stranglehold on the fur trade grew tighter.

During the seventeenth century, competition for the St. Lawrence and lower Great Lakes fur trade not only ignited deep-seated hostilities between the Iroquois and their Huron and Algonquian neighbors but also between England, France, and the Netherlands. Dutch traders of the United New Netherland Company had penetrated the Hudson River and established Fort Nassau by 1614, but their government saw scant value in the New World beyond trade. In September 1664, Peter Stuyvesant, governor of the Dutch colony, surrendered to Richard Nicholls and 400 English soldiers. With a few strokes of a quill pen, New Netherland became New York. At the time of its capitulation, New Netherland held only a fraction of the estimated 80,000 men, women, and children who populated the English settlements of North America.[30]

In contrast with England, which held sway over her colonial territory by sheer numbers, France, with fewer colonists, maintained control of New France by making a partner of the Indians. Frenchmen, unlike their Dutch and English counterparts, readily married into Indian families, gaining tribal loyalty for the French crown. Another difference between the French and English concerned their policy toward Indian land. For the most part, French settlements in Newfoundland, Nova Scotia, and along the St. Lawrence River occupied territory that the Indians had vacated. Granted, most of the former native inhabitants had perished from white-introduced smallpox, but the land was empty, nonetheless.

Only after absorbing New Netherland did the English fully appreciate the value of the fur trade. Until then, England had viewed the expansion of its agrarian colonies as the best way to control North America. Indian-produced furs were secondary to the wealth generated by a host of energetic farmers. As a result of the English colonists' continual lust for tillage, thousands of Indians were dispossessed of their birthright. Having no understanding of property rights, Native Americans signed countless treaties, thinking they were licensing the English to work their land while maintaining their own claim of usage. But such beliefs were no match for lead and gunpowder. Indians attempting to trespass on what they viewed as tribal territory were shot. With each succeeding season, English settlements pressed inland from the Atlantic coast, relentlessly driving America's Indians farther from their ancestral homes.

After acquiring New Netherland, the English wasted no time taking over their former adversary's Indian trading alliances. Meanwhile, Iroquois war parties continued their campaign to dominate the fur trade. Wanting to keep the Iroquois from dealing with the French, the English supplied the confederation with muskets and ammunition.

During the 1660s, smallpox again invaded the Iroquois. Throughout the decade, the disease spread from one village to another, subsided, then flared again, eventually crossing to the enemy tribes living north of Lake Ontario. Some historians have speculated that the virus was introduced by seamen on the St. Lawrence waterway. Others have argued that it more likely came from one of the white settlements. Either cause is possible.

In a pattern that continually repeated itself, a family or two of colonial children would catch a mild form of smallpox and recover. Despite attempts at quarantining the sick, the disease would spread to a visiting Indian, who would infect his village. Gaining fury exponentially among the tribes, the pestilence would ignite a raging inferno that often returned to the same white settlement where it had begun—this time with increased virulence.[31]

As smallpox continued to winnow the tribes of eastern North America, the colonists reaped its bounty—empty Indian land. Smallpox-ravaged native villages consolidated. Smaller tribes that had been able to hold their stronger neighbors at bay capitulated and fled. Although a few whites were sympathetic to the Indians' plight, most rationalized that their Christian God had willed the Indians' removal. Calvinists and fellow Protestants believed that disease was a divine punishment for sin. Viewing the "heathen" red man as the greatest sinner of all, colonists thought it natural that their God should destroy the Indians with smallpox. Some natives who heard such dogma converted to Christianity. Many others shook their fists at the whites, rightfully blaming them for the epidemics.

By the late 1660s, the New England colonies were shrugging off their latest *Variola* onslaught. Then in 1669, as the traders at Fort Orange—the renamed Fort Nassau—looked forward to a bountiful harvest of pelts, smallpox wiped out so many Mohawks the English beaver trade nearly ground to a halt.[32] Hoping to keep the English from bypassing it and subverting its role as a broker, the Iroquois League boldly expanded its economic warfare. During the next two decades, Iroquois war parties raided the Delawares (between the Delaware and Hudson rivers), the Susquehannocks (between the Allegheny and Susquehanna rivers), the Nipissings (northeast of Lake Huron's Georgian Bay), the Potawatomis (in the Michigan lower peninsula), the Miamis (southeast of Lake Michigan), and the Illinois (along the Illinois River).[33] In 1684, after being repelled in their attempt to capture Fort St. Louis on the central Illinois River (in north-central Illinois), the Iroquois ended their wars of expansion and consolidated their role as middlemen.

In 1659 and 1660, a few years before Holland forfeited New Netherland to England, French traders Médard Chouart, La Sieur des Groseilliers, and his brother-in-law, Pierre Esprit Radisson, journeyed to the northwest shore of Lake Superior, seeking to bypass the Hurons and open trade directly with the

Crees.[34] Despite having been reduced by smallpox in the 1630s and defeated by the Iroquois in the late 1640s, the Hurons—especially the northern Hurons—had continued brokering high quality Cree furs to the French. At the time, the Crees occupied the subarctic lake country that was bounded by the south side of Hudson and James bays, the Churchill River and the north shore of Lake Winnipeg (in Ontario and eastern Manitoba).

Although Groseilliers and Radisson never sighted Hudson Bay, they crossed numerous rivers that drained into the Crees' so-called "Bay of the North" and procured a substantial load of pelts. With their knowledge of the region's topography, they realized that traders could carry the Crees' fur to Hudson Bay via these north-flowing waterways. If oceangoing ships met the traders at the south end of the bay, their cargo could be sent directly to France at a fraction of what it cost traversing the Great Lakes and St. Lawrence River. As an added benefit, French traders could avoid the Iroquois, who patrolled the St. Lawrence waterway.

The government of New France gave Groseilliers and Radisson a hearing but failed to see merit in their plan. Undeterred, the two visionaries sailed to England and sought an audience with the court of King Charles II. Recognizing the value of the Frenchmen's scheme, a few wealthy Englishmen—including the king's cousin, Prince Rupert—financed a trading venture to Hudson and James bays.

On June 3, 1668, Groseilliers set out for North America aboard the fifty-three-foot *Nonsuch,* while Radisson sailed on the larger *Eaglet.* Heavy seas soon damaged the *Eaglet,* forcing it to return to port. Despite the storm, the *Nonsuch* and its eleven-man crew continued across the Atlantic Ocean and into Hudson Bay. Groseilliers established a wintering post at the south end of James Bay, traded with the Crees, and in the fall of 1669, returned to England with a cargo of pelts. The *Nonsuch's* trade goods that had cost £650 fetched £1,379 from the London fur buyers, but wages and other expenses consumed the fifty percent operating profit, turning the voyage into a financial loss. Still, Groseilliers had proved that his and Radisson's plan would work.[35]

The following year, the English crown granted a royal

charter to the *Nonsuch's* investors, incorporating the "Governor and Company of Adventurers of England tradeing [*sic*] into Hudsons Bay," more commonly called the Hudson's Bay Company. The charter gave the firm an entrée to the northern Indian tribes that produced New France's finest beaver.

While the Hudson's Bay Company began to exploit its franchise, English traders south of the St. Lawrence River inflated the ratio of trade goods they paid for furs, bettering French prices by four to one.[36] Unwilling to match the English exchange rate, French traders penetrated the Great Lakes beyond the reach of England's Iroquois trading partners. Seeing their role as middlemen being eroded by French *coureurs de bois*[37]—roving traders—the Iroquois strengthened their alliance with England, forming a bond that lasted through the American Revolution.

As profits from fur expanded vis-à-vis those generated by colonial farmers, English policy did an about-face. Because Indians were needed to trap and dress pelts, it was uneconomical to allow increasing numbers of colonists to drive them from their homeland and into the arms of the French. Accordingly, the crown put the brakes on colonial expansion, halting it east of the Appalachian Mountains. Denied permission to develop land they viewed as being wasted by "ignorant savages," the colonials seethed.[38]

Along the St. Lawrence and other waterways of northeastern New France, smallpox and the fur trade were inseparable. Infestations of *Variola major* arrived at the Atlantic seaboard with European emigrants and African slaves, then spread inland with the commerce in metal trade goods and animal skins. Introduced by *coureurs de bois* and the Jesuit and Recollect priests who followed in their wake, smallpox diffused along the Indian trading networks, often far in advance of any European carrier.

One of the sad ironies of this era was that North American natives who accepted Christianity suffered more from smallpox than did those Indians who rejected the white man's religion. Jesuit and Recollect missionaries among the infected tribes unknowingly spread the virus by having the sick and healthy alike touch their lips to the crucifix and drink from a common

Communion cup.[39] At first Indians suspected the priests used some demonic power to unleash the *Variola* epidemics, but as the tribes grew more accustomed to the Black Robes, they viewed the priests' lack of susceptibility to smallpox as a sign of moral and spiritual alignment. Unable to comprehend that most of the priests had become immune to the disease by having caught it as children, the Indians came to see them as superior to their own shamans, who along with the rest of the tribes sickened and often died. The Black Robes gained further acceptance among the stricken by nursing those who were ill and by distributing water and firewood when no one else in a village could lift his head, let alone work.

Although the priests had no cure for smallpox, they administered placebos that occasionally gave the sick temporary relief. Usually these were as benign as sugar-water, but the Indians readily accepted them, having witnessed the healing failure of their shamans. Bleeding was also used. During an epidemic among the Huron in 1636 and 1637, Jesuit Simon Baron bled over 200 members of the tribe, a practice that was performed on the sick and well alike.[40] Having no antidote that could stem the virus, the Black Robes gave the Extreme Unction to Indians who were on the verge of death. Natives witnessing the rites and the subsequent passing of their brethren often concluded that the missionaries had used magic in order to kill. It was a belief the priests had difficulty dispelling.

Eager for Catholic converts, the priests typically attributed diseases such as smallpox to tribal sin, especially the cardinal sin of refusing to believe in Christ. Calling the *rotting face* a punishment from God, priests sought to weaken the influence of native shamans and thereby draw the tribes within the Catholic orbit.

For those Indians who survived their bouts of smallpox, the Black Robes ascribed their recovery to the power of the Almighty. In contrast, shamans personalized their results, taking credit for their healing successes and blaming only their failures on demons and evil spirits. Priests, on the other hand, claimed that both the gift of life and the penalty of death stemmed from divine intervention, a logic that gradually eroded the power of the shamans and added more Indians to the list of Catholic converts. Such a result happened to the Huron shaman Tonneraouanont during the winter of 1637. Unable to cure his tribe of smallpox and having seen his prophecies about the disease proved false, Tonneraouanont lost face to the resident Jesuit, Jean de Brébeuf. After the shaman accidentally broke his leg and then died from infection, Father Brébeuf donned the shaman's mantle of authority by assigning the calamity to the omnipotence of Almighty Justice.[41]

The lower Mississippi Valley and lower Ohio River Valley had been home to an ancient agrarian culture that began erecting earthen mounds around A.D. 700. Built over several centuries, the largest of these religious monuments covered a dozen or more acres and stood 100 feet tall. By the time Columbus made his first voyage to the New World, Mississippian villages with their ceremonial temple mounds stretched from the Arkansas River (in eastern Oklahoma) to the Savannah River (on the Georgia-South Carolina border). One large trading center located on the east side of the Mississippi, below the mouth of the Missouri (near Cahokia, Illinois), supported a population that may have been 75,000 members strong.[42]

Such dense concentrations of people offered prime breeding grounds for European viruses such as *Variola major*. By the time Spanish explorer Hernando de Soto first entered the Mississippi Valley in 1541, the mound-building tribes had vanished, as if swallowed by the earth. Although no one knows the reason for their disappearance, some archaeologists think they were destroyed by smallpox, which may have dispersed north from the Aztecs ahead of the first European visitor. Near the mouth of the Arkansas River and along the lower Mississippi, de Soto did see over two dozen large Indian towns, but these too were soon absorbed by the land. By the time French explorers penetrated the region in the 1600s, the towns had all but disappeared.[43]

The only living descendants of the mound builders, the Natchez, survived with their civilization intact—at least for a while. When René-Robert Cavelier, Sieur de La Salle reached the mouth of the Mississippi River in 1682, the tribe numbered about 4,000 people, who occupied nine villages. By 1704, so many Natchez had perished from war and disease, it prompted the French missionary Henri Roulleaux de La Vente to write "that it seem[ed] God wish[ed] to make them give place to others."[44]

During the seventeenth century, the Quapaws migrated to the country vacated by the mound builders, eventually settling in four large towns near the confluence of the Arkansas and Mississippi rivers. Then in 1698, smallpox again struck the lower Mississippi Valley. Shortly after the Quapaws were infected, the French missionary Jean François Buisson de Saint-Cosme visited the tribe, finding only grown men—fewer than 100—and women among the living. The degree of grief that Saint-Cosme witnessed is impossible to imagine. Smallpox had destroyed the tribe's future, killing not only numerous adults but also every child down to the tiniest baby.[45]

West of the Mississippi River, one of the most sophisticated inter-tribal trading systems in North America had its hub beside the confluence of the Missouri and Heart rivers (near today's Bismarck, North Dakota).

The village-dwelling Mandans had capitalized on their location in the midst of the Great Plains by becoming traders to the prairie's many nomadic tribes. To a lesser degree the Hidatsas, whose towns along the Knife River (near Stanton, North Dakota) were a bit north of the Mandans, and the Arikaras, who at the time lived in villages around the mouth of the Bad River (near Pierre, South Dakota), also worked as brokers, exploiting their strategic position on the central Missouri.

For generations before the arrival of the Europeans, the three tribes had perfected their role as middlemen, bartering the excess corn, melons, beans, and squashes from their gardens for dried meat, prairie-turnip flour, buffalo robes, pemmican, quill-decorated shirts and leggings, and the other output of their nomadic neighbors.

Each June witnessed a vast Indian gathering at the mouth of the Heart River. Putting aside their tribal differences, the Lakotas,[46] Pawnees, Poncas, Crows, Assiniboines, and other nations of the central prairie traded with one another and with the Mandans, Hidatsas, and Arikaras. In addition to the bounty of the plains, trade goods included sea shells from the Gulf of Mexico, arrowhead obsidian from central Oregon and the upper Yellowstone, copper from the country around Lake Superior, and catlinite stone from the Red Pipestone Quarry (now Pipestone National Monument in southwestern Minnesota) on the southeastern end of the Côteau Des Prairies.[47] Many of these items had passed through the hands of multiple Indian owners before reaching the upper Missouri.

With the Spanish settlement of the upper Rio Grande Valley, horses also entered the Mandan-dominated trading scheme. In 1610, the Spanish founded Santa Fe as the capital of their New Mexico colony. Former Spanish soldiers joined the land rush, building *haciendas* beside the Rio Grande and pressing natives from nearby pueblos into their service. The Pueblo Indians planted corn for their Spanish lords and tended vast herds of sheep, cattle, and horses. Tempted by such easy pickings, Jicarilla and Mescalero Apaches stole Spanish horses and mules from the new settlements. The Apaches butchered and ate many of these animals, but some of them and their offspring entered the Indian trading network, passing from the Apaches to the Kiowas, Arapahos, and other tribes.

Instead of chasing the Apaches, the Spanish found it more expedient to replace the stolen animals by importing additional stock from central Mexico. By the start of the seventeenth century, rancheros dotted the plains of Mexico, a *small* one typically boasting over 150,000 cattle and 20,000 horses.[48]

The Pueblo Indians soon learned that their Spanish masters had brought them more than livestock to tend and Franciscan friars to convert them to Catholicism. The Spanish had also brought smallpox. In 1638, 20,000 New Mexican natives—one-third of all Pueblos—perished. While many probably died from measles, diphtheria, typhus, and other European diseases for which they had no immunity, the largest number most likely succumbed to *Variola major*. Two years later another epidemic claimed 10,000 more Indian lives.[49] Through it all, the Apaches continued their thefts, no doubt acquiring smallpox as well as Spanish horses.

In the summer of 1680, the Pueblos rebelled, expelling their Spanish masters. Nine years would pass before the Spanish reclaimed their New Mexican holdings. During that time, the Pueblos traded off the vast herds of Spanish horses, bartering them to the Apaches and Navajos. Having more animals than they could possibly eat, the Apaches and Navajos flooded the Indian trading network with horses and mules.

The Navajos swapped horses to the Utes, who passed them to the Shoshonis, who sent them to the Cayuses, Palouses, and Nez Perce. From the Apaches, horses filtered to the Wichitas, Kiowas, Arapahos and Pawnees, until they eventually reached the Mandans. Mandan traders then swapped them to the Cheyennes, Assiniboines, Lakotas, and other tribes of the middle and upper Missouri. In time, horses spread to the Crees living along Canada's Saskatchewan River. According to most historians, the Plains Indian renaissance of the eighteenth century had its genesis in the Pueblo uprising of 1680.

At the same time Spanish horses were gaining importance in the Mandan-dominated trading scheme, muskets, metal knives and arrowpoints, and iron cooking kettles also made their appearance at the upper Missouri trade fairs. Introduced by *coureurs de bois* who had penetrated the Great Lakes, these mostly French-manufactured products percolated west via Indian intermediaries. Beyond making it easier for Indians to provide their food and basic clothing and shelter, metal trade goods also enabled them to produce more of the furs that were so coveted by the white traders. This excess production then allowed the Indians to purchase goods that were unnecessary to their subsistence survival, luxuries such as Chinese vermilion, muslin and flannel, colored beads, finger rings, tobacco, and liquor.

Although trade items such as bells, mirrors, and the like were new to Native Americans, others such as blankets, fire steels, metal arrowpoints, metal knives, and metal axes replaced less efficient products that the Indians had been making for themselves. A similar substitution also happened with tobacco. Most tribes smoked tobacco, growing their own or bartering for it from other Indians who did. Soon after its introduction, plantation tobacco from Virginia and Brazil edged aside the native variety.

Of all the metal goods introduced by white traders, none had such a profound effect on the Indians as did firearms. In the woodland country east of the Mississippi River and in eastern Canada, gunshots so frightened the game that it became nearly impossible for Indians to furnish meat for their families with bows and arrows. As more eastern native hunters out of necessity abandoned bows for muskets, the skill needed to bring down deer and moose with traditional weapons disappeared.[50]

Continually requiring lead, gunpowder, and new muskets as well as the services of gunsmiths to replace frizzens, springs, and other broken parts, the eastern tribes became wholly dependent on the fur trade. Originally prized as a weapon of war, the gun had evolved into an essential for everyday living. Knowing this, territorial governors tried bringing tribes to heel by forbidding traders from furnishing them with shot and powder. Indian leaders usually capitulated to white demands rather than see their people starve.

Such a case occurred following the defeat of France in the French and Indian War. With the surrender of New France to Great Britain, command of the English North American military forces fell to Lord Jeffrey Amherst. An arrogant aristocrat who despised all Indians, Amherst withheld gunpowder and lead from France's former native allies, stating that England's enemies ought to be punished, not rewarded. When informed that the tribes depended on their muskets for taking game and would starve without ammunition, he remained unswayed, callously informing his aides that they should seed the complaining bands with smallpox so as to lend starvation a speedy hand.[51]

East of the Continental Divide, on the vast plains drained by the Missouri and North and South Saskatchewan rivers (Montana and southern Alberta), horses, guns, and other metal trade goods eventually reached the Blackfeet. The Blackfeet were a confederation of three related but politically independent tribes: the *Pikuni* (dubbed Piegans by French traders), *Kainai* (known by the whites as Bloods), and *Siksika* (called the

Northern Blackfeet or Blackfeet proper). Collectively, they called themselves the *Nitzitapi*. Speaking the same language, the tribes had a common heritage and similar customs. They intermarried and fought shared enemies. Although their territories overlapped, the *Siksika* usually ranged farthest north and the *Pikuni* farthest south.

In all likelihood, the Blackfeet had heard about the strange, bearded men with white skin who traded with the Crees several decades before they saw their first French trader. The Blackfeet had migrated to the western prairie generations before their Algonquian relatives—the Atsinas, Arapahos, Cheyennes, Plains Crees, and Plains Ojibwas—also abandoned their eastern woodland cultures and adopted a life that centered on buffalo. Perhaps 30,000 to 40,000 members strong,[52] the Blackfeet were pedestrian nomads, trailing after the vast bison herds that provided their food and shelter. Having no knowledge of horses, they used dogs as their beasts of burden, either packing them with saddlelike frames or harnessing them to A-framed travois and weighting them down with loads that often reached 100 pounds.[53]

Around 1730, a mounted Shoshoni war party attacked a band of Piegans living above the forty-ninth parallel. Having never before seen horses, the Piegans were terrified and fell back in disarray, granting the Shoshonis an easy victory. Not knowing what sort of animal the Shoshonis had ridden, the Piegans named it *ponokamita,* meaning elk dog.[54]

Soon thereafter, the Piegans learned from their eastern Cree and Assiniboine neighbors about another marvel of warfare, the smoothbore musket. Eager to possess these new technologies, the Blackfeet began to procure them the only way they could— through trade and theft. The confederation probably obtained horses from the Flatheads and Kutenais, who lived at the western margin of the plains where the prairie uplifted toward the Rocky Mountains. These most eastern of the plateau tribes had acquired horses shortly after the Shoshonis, no doubt bartering for them at the Shoshonis' annual trade fairs.[55]

Horses not only allowed Indians to travel faster and farther, but they also permitted them to kill buffalo cows or bulls selectively, instead of at random at buffalo jumps. Since a cow's meat was more tender than a bull's and its hide easier to tan, mounted Indian hunters harvested far more cows than bulls, eventually altering the sexual composition of the herds.

The horse also changed traditional trading patterns. By enabling tribes such as the Nez Perce and Coeur d'Alenes to journey rapidly across the Continental Divide while packing equipment and stores that exceeded their immediate needs, the horse stimulated trade between the plateau country and plains. Horses allowed the Blackfeet, Crows, and Assiniboines to acquire salmon oil, fishskin bags of salmon pemmican, camas bread, hemp twine, and compound bows made from the horns of bighorn sheep. At the same time, horses permitted the Nez Perce and Coeur d'Alenes to satisfy their desire for feathered warbonnets and catlinite pipes. By making these exchanges possible, horses increased the living standard of all trading-oriented tribes. And because horses facilitated trade—as well as warfare—Indians naturally sought to acquire ever larger herds.[56]

Northeast of the Blackfeet lived the Plains Crees, members of the vast Cree nation, whose territory extended to Hudson and James bays. The Crees had begun expanding west from their traditional subarctic homeland below the bays soon after acquiring French matchlock muskets in the early 1600s. The Cree expansion eventually brought the tribe into conflict with the Ojibwas, who lived north and west of Lake Superior.

In addition to outfitting the Crees, the Ottawa-Huron-French trading combine also supplied the Ojibwas with guns and ammunition. Having firearms enabled the Ojibwas to keep the Crees from overrunning their territory. Instead of confronting the Ojibwas head-on, the Crees spread into the country west of Hudson Bay and built their villages north to the Churchill River. Facing west, the tribe then fanned into the region between the Churchill and the north side of Lake Winnipeg, driving the indigenous Chipewyans—who had few guns—farther into the subarctic. In time, the western-most Cree bands reached the Saskatchewan Plain, where they adopted the buffalo culture of the Atsinas and Blackfeet.

Because of their familiarity with canoes and the lakes and

rivers of their historical homeland, the Plains Crees readily traveled long distances to trade. Following the establishment of the Hudson's Bay Company's York Factory trading house at the mouth of the Hayes River in 1684, the Plains Crees switched their trading allegiance from the Ottawa-Huron-French combine to the English at Hudson Bay.[57] The distance was shorter, and the Crees could avoid the Ojibwas, who roamed from Lake of the Woods to the northern reaches of Lake Superior.

Around 1660 or 1670, the Assiniboines migrated north from the upper Mississippi River (Minnesota), and by the 1690s had settled on the prairie south and west of Lakes Winnipegosis and Manitoba (in southern Manitoba and southeastern Saskatchewan), where they formed an alliance with the Plains Crees. The Assiniboines had fled their homeland after the Ojibwas obtained firearms and began turning the upper Mississippi into a battleground.[58] The Assiniboines occasionally joined Cree canoe convoys—some 300 canoes strong—on trading missions to York Factory and Fort Prince of Wales (eventually renamed Fort Churchill), after it opened near the mouth of the Churchill River in 1717.

In the early 1730s, the Blackfeet—who were in need of firearms in order to repel the Shoshonis—began trading with the Plains Crees for guns. The Blackfeet paid for the weapons with fur, which the Crees brokered to the English on Hudson Bay. Other than tobacco, most of the European trade goods acquired by the Crees were intended for their own service instead of immediate barter to the Blackfeet. The Crees typically used their guns, metal knives, and other trade items for a year or two before brokering them secondhand.

In the mid 1700s, the French siphoned off the lion's share of this traffic to Hudson Bay by constructing Fort à La Corne fifteen miles below the confluence of the North and South Saskatchewan rivers (a bit east of Prince Albert, Saskatchewan). This also allowed the Assiniboines, who ranged south of the Crees, to don a middleman's cloak and carve out a piece of the Blackfoot trade. As the seasons passed, the Plains Crees and Assiniboines honed their trading skills and allowed their trapping skills to wane. Because Fort à La Corne was closer to their territory than were the English trading factories, the

Crees and Assiniboines began swapping the best of the Blackfoot furs to the French, leaving only the less-than-prime pelts and heavy bearskins to be sold at Hudson Bay.

Seeing the thick pelts the Blackfeet produced, the French made plans to bypass the Cree and Assiniboine middlemen and initiate trade directly with the confederation. Although the French traders knew that such action would threaten the Cree and Assiniboine role as brokers—and perhaps turn the two tribes against them—they figured the reward was worth the risk. Alarmed that the Crees and Assiniboines were bartering the best Blackfoot pelts at Fort à La Corne, English traders at Hudson Bay also resolved to tap the Blackfoot trade directly and preempt the French.

While the French and English plotted how to directly access the Blackfoot trade, the three tribes of the confederation incorporated the horse into their nomadic culture and became adept with their newly acquired muskets. Having the mobility of their Shoshoni enemies and now possessing guns, which the Shoshonis did not yet have, the Blackfeet expelled the interlopers from the Red Deer Valley (in Alberta). For the next thirty years, Shoshoni hunting parties that were brave enough to enter the southern Saskatchewan plains limited their excursions to the Bow River.

The North American contest between France and England culminated with the French and Indian War. During the conflict, smallpox occasionally determined the outcome of battles by ravaging the ranks of Indian warriors allied to either the French or English.

In 1757, after watching his soldiers die from French cannons as well as smallpox, the English commander of besieged Fort William Henry (on the south side of New York's Lake George) surrendered to Field Marshal Louis Joseph, Marquis de Montcalm-Gozon de Saint-Véran. After the English garrison had been marched away, French-supported Indians unearthed the smallpox-infected English corpses, lifted their hair, and unwittingly inhaled the *Variola* virus. Smallpox soon raged within Montcalm's Indian legions.[59]

In 1760, the disease reached the Santee Lakotas after a band of them became infected while parleying with the English in Quebec City.[60] That same year, smallpox also attacked the Menominees, who lived near the trading fort at Green Bay on the western edge of Lake Michigan. Probably carried by Santee war parties, the virus moved west, punishing the Arikaras. It is likely that this epidemic also touched the Mandans and Hidatsas.

In the spring of 1763, during the Indian uprising led by Ottawa Chief Pontiac, a party of Delawares ringed British-owned Fort Pitt (now Pittsburgh, Pennsylvania), calling for its surrender. Captain Simeon Ecuyer, a Swiss mercenary and the fort's senior officer, saved the garrison by giving the Delawares a gift—two blankets and a handkerchief. The Indians readily accepted the offering, but still demanded that Ecuyer vacate the stockade. They had no inkling that the blankets and kerchief were more deadly than a platoon of English sharpshooters. Ecuyer had ordered the presents deliberately infected with smallpox spores at the post hospital. By mid July, the Delawares were dying as though they had been raked by a grape cannonade. Fort Pitt remained firmly in English hands.[61]

The same year, British General Sir Jeffrey Amherst urged Colonel Henry Bouquet to figure some way of infecting France's Indian allies with smallpox. On July 13, the colonel wrote that he would attempt seeding some blankets with *Variola,* then send them to the warring tribes. Recognizing the risk of such a tactic, Bouquet expressed the hope that he would not catch the sickness himself. Whether the plan was ever carried out is unknown.[62]

The intentional infection of Indians was the exception, not the norm. Although Europeans such as Amherst wanted to give smallpox and other lethal diseases to their native enemies, they did not possess the knowledge to wage biological warfare. Smallpox scabs had a finite life—eighteen to twenty-four months. Anyone attempting to store them risked catching the disease (if he was not immune) or giving it to a friend. Using smallpox victims as weapons was more difficult. The mind-set of colonial America was to quarantine smallpox, not pass it to the Indians, who could spread it to their white neighbors.[63]

In 1763, the Treaty of Paris formally ended the French and

Indian War, requiring France to relinquish her North American property. All of Canada was now open to licensed British traders. Five years later the crown rescinded the licensing regulation, paving the way for unbridled competition.[64]

As far as the Blackfeet, Atsinas, Crees, and Assiniboines were concerned, little had changed after France surrendered New France. Scottish merchants stepped into the vacuum left by France's departure. Known derisively as Peddlers by their Hudson's Bay competitors, these savvy, Montreal-based businessmen absorbed the French trading system, employing experienced French-Canadian *coureurs de bois* who had been thrown out of work by France's defeat.

To the chagrin of the Hudson's Bay Company's directors, Cree and Assiniboine traders continued brokering the best quality Blackfoot furs at the forts on the lower Saskatchewan River—now owned by the Peddlers instead of the French. Indian middlemen still traded only their inferior, leftover furs at Hudson Bay.[65]

Realizing that it would have to go to the Blackfeet if it wanted their business, the Hudson's Bay Company constructed a trading post at Pine Island Lake (near Cumberland House, Saskatchewan; Pine Island Lake is now Cumberland Lake) in 1774. Located 700 canoe-miles from York Factory, this first Cumberland House was a dank log cabin, but it was closer to the western tribes than the competing Peddler trading posts at The Pas, sixty miles east. Six years after Cumberland House opened, the Hudson's Bay Company finally established a trading post in the midst of the Blackfoot Confederation. Set alongside the North Saskatchewan River, 550 miles above Cumberland House, Buckingham House at last brought the European fur trade directly to the Piegans, Bloods, and Northern Blackfeet, thereby cutting out the Cree and Assiniboine middlemen.

As happened in Canada, the fur trade south of the forty-ninth parallel improved the Indians' lot, particularly that of the Mandans, who reached their peak of power and wealth in the late 1770s.[66] But as it had done among the Hurons,

Iroquois, and other tribes of the northeast, the fur trade also greased the skids for smallpox.

In 1780, the fur trade ushered in one of the worst smallpox epidemics to strike North America since Cortéz invaded the Aztecs. It began in the Valley of Mexico in the late 1770s, killing upwards of 22,000 Indians before moving to the Pueblos of New Mexico in 1780, where it claimed another 5,000 victims. From the highlands around Santa Fe, the virus quickly spread north to the plains, ushered along the Indian trading network that radiated out from the Mandans.[67]

The wide use of horses enabled the disease to move rapidly between native bands. Mounted Indians who had recently been infected could cover hundreds of miles while the virus incubated, then come down sick while trading with a distant tribe.

The epidemic devastated the Pawnees, then struck the village tribes of the upper Missouri. Among the Mandans, Hidatsas, and Arikaras, the virus killed so many members, it disrupted the tribes' position as brokers and shattered their prosperity, leaving them vulnerable to their enemies.[68] The pestilence quickly spread to the Yankton Lakotas, and from them to the Poncas around the mouth of the Niobrara River. It blew across the grassy plains as though it were a fire running wild before the wind. Consuming Indians by the thousands, the epidemic waded into the Ojibwas, slaying half.

Native lore reports that in 1781 a combined Ojibwa, Cree, and Assiniboine war party attacked a Hidatsa village that was beset with the disease. So many Hidatsas were bedridden or dead, the tribe could field only a handful of warriors. The allied force quickly overwhelmed the defenders and lifted their scalps. But the victory was Pyrrhic. During their return march to their own villages, the conquerors began to sicken and die. Only a few made it home alive. Their kinsmen welcomed the survivors, unaware that the warriors had brought with them more than Hidatsa scalps. They had also brought the *rotting face*.[69]

Moving north into Canada, the disease destroyed a large Assiniboine camp[70] at the Assiniboine River's confluence with the Red (near Winnipeg, Manitoba) and laid waste to the Assiniboines living around Fort Dauphin near the south end of Lake Dauphin (west of Lake Manitoba). In 1782 and 1783, it touched the Sanpoils on the Columbia Plateau (north central Washington) and may have infected tribes around Puget Sound.

British explorer George Vancouver visited Puget Sound in 1783 and was met by Indians with pockmarked cheeks. At Point Discovery, he saw human bones littering the sand, giving more evidence of a recent catastrophe.[71]

Before running its course, the epidemic also engulfed tribes on the central Canadian prairie, dealing death and morbidity from the Saskatchewan River to Great Slave Lake. Among the powerful Crees, smallpox destroyed so much of the tribe that the Chipewyans, who the Crees had driven north over 100 years earlier, were able to reclaim their homeland. But the victory cost the Chipewyans dearly, for the epidemic soon consumed close to half of their members. On the upper North Saskatchewan River (just east of Edmonton, Alberta), *Variola major* killed so many Beaver Hills Cree hunters, the survivors were forced to eat their dogs and horses to keep from starving.[72]

At some of the Peddlers' and Hudson's Bay Company's outlying posts, the fur trade nearly ground to a halt. As was the custom, traders often outfitted native hunters with gunpowder, lead, tobacco, and other stores on credit. Many of the Indians who sickened and died had outstanding debts on the fur companies' ledgers. Wanting to stem their losses, a number of trading post factors (the British called their fort commanders factors instead of *bourgeois*) ordered their *engagés* to pillage furs from the lodges of the dead. In their eagerness to do the factors' bidding, *engagés* occasionally stripped beaver tunics and robes from Indian corpses, unwittingly helping the epidemic spread. The fur company men usually covered the naked bodies with wood or coarse woolen duffel, but such shrouds offered no protection. As soon as the *engagés* departed, wolves, dogs, and rats feasted on the human remains.[73]

In addition to watching their kinsmen die from the *rotting face,* the surviving Crees, Chipewyans, and northern Assiniboines also faced starvation. For some unexplained reason, game disappeared from the north-central Canadian plains and lake country in the early 1780s. Believing that smallpox was punishment for a religious transgression, the tribes saw the absence of buffalo, deer, and waterfowl in spiritual terms, as well. Native logic held that because so many Canadian Indians had died, the Manitou sent the animals to tribes that still had hunters.

The epidemic reached the Blackfeet via a large band of Piegans camped beside the Red Deer River (in southern Alberta). Southwest of the Piegans, the tribe's Shoshoni enemies harvested buffalo along Canada's Bow River, often occupying their hunting camps for months at a time.

In 1781, a Piegan scouting party slipped undetected into the Bow River Valley and sighted a large tipi village. For several hours the Piegans watched the encampment, concealing themselves lest they be discovered. They saw Shoshoni horses cropping the summer grass; they heard Shoshoni dogs yelping as they tussled for bones; but they saw no people. The Shoshoni tipis appeared as deserted as if they were inhabited by ghosts. Fearing a trap, the Piegans returned home and reported what they had seen. After listening to the story, the Piegan elders sent the scouting party back to the Bow River to search for additional signs. A few days later the scouts brought word that they could find only the one camp.

Eager to steal Shoshoni horses and pilfer the lodges their enemies had seemingly abandoned, a Piegan war party rode to the Bow River camp. The warrior Saukamappee—who later related details of the attack to the North West Fur Company trader, David Thompson—claimed to have participated in the raid.[74]

Still wary of a trick, the Piegans slowly entered the tipi village, their war clubs and muskets at the ready. Shoshoni dogs snarled and snapped, but no Shoshoni warriors rushed forth to defend their families. When the Piegans entered a tipi at the outermost edge of the camp, they recoiled as the stench of rotting flesh scalded the air. Inside lay a family of Shoshonis, their naked forms swollen with decay. In every lodge the scene repeated its grisly horror: Shoshoni men, women, and children lying dead or barely alive, their bodies putrefied by smallpox.

Believing that the Shoshonis had been delivered to them by their Blackfoot gods, the Piegans looted the camp, carrying home their enemies' belongings, horses, and scalps. But unbeknownst to the Piegan warriors, they also carried home the deadly *Variola* virus.

Following its incubation, the *rotting face* attacked the Red Deer Piegans, eventually spreading to all three tribes of the Blackfoot Confederation. Before the epidemic exhausted its reservoir of human grist, over half of the Blackfeet entered the spirit world, believed to be located in the Great Sand Hills southeast of the confluence of the Red Deer and South Saskatchewan rivers. Here in this bleak, alkali wasteland, the Blackfeet held that the ghosts of people and animals entered a netherworld invisible to the living but similar to the one they had known while alive.[75]

Having been hit harder by the disease than had the Blackfoot Confederation, the surviving Shoshonis sought to keep distance between themselves and their northern enemy. After the pestilence ended, the Shoshonis abandoned the Bow River hunting grounds to the Piegans and their Blackfoot brothers.[76] When the Shoshonis ventured that far north again, it would be for one purpose only, Blackfoot captives and scalps.

Chapter four notes

1. Also called Watling or Watlings Island, San Salvador was known as *Guanahani* by its natives.

2. According to Herman J. Viola, *After Columbus: The Smithsonian Chronicle of the North American Indians* (Washington: Smithsonian Books, 1990; distributed by Orion Books), 43, the Arawaks and Caribs may have been members of the same tribe. Columbus categorized the Caribbean Indians as either friendly or unfriendly, labeling the compliant ones Arawaks and those who preferred to fight rather than be enslaved Caribs.

3. Henry F. Dobyns, *Their Number Become Thinned: Native American Population Dynamics in Eastern North America* (Knoxville: University of Tennessee Press, 1983), 257; and Hopkins, *Princes and Peasants*, 204 lean toward an early date for the initial introduction of smallpox in the New World. The disease may have arrived on Columbus's second voyage in 1493—his fleet numbered seventeen ships and carried between 1,200 and 1,500 men—since Stearn and Stearn, *Effect of Smallpox*, 13 estimates that two-thirds of the Indians on Hispaniola (originally called *La Isla Española,* the island is now divided into Haiti and the Dominican Republic) had died by 1495. Henige, *Numbers from Nowhere*, 169 asserts that smallpox could not have been introduced during Columbus's first voyage, since the Spanish crew was reported to be enjoying good health. During his second voyage, Columbus noted that a number of his sailors and soldiers were sick, although the exact diagnosis of their illness has never been confirmed. On page 173, Henige discounts that the disorder was swine influenza, as proposed by some sources, adding that there is no evidence that the sickness was smallpox, either. Crosby, *Ecological Imperialism*, 200 states that smallpox did not reach the New World until late 1518 or early 1519. Alfred W. Crosby, Jr., *The Columbian Exchange: Biological and Cultural Consequences of 1492* (Westport, Connecticut: Greenwood Press, 1972), 47 reports that most of the deaths on Hispaniola occurred during the epidemic of 1519. On pages 45-6, Crosby argues that the early trans-Atlantic crossings were too long for the *Variola* virus to have survived, including instances where a carrier was infected the day he set sail from Spain. Although the long voyage meant that the man would have died or become well while at sea, Crosby admits that his scabs could have contaminated his clothes, bedding, or some other cloth aboard the ship. If so, there is a chance that a Caribbean Indian could have come in contact with the infected material and caught the disease. All we know for certain is that while smallpox may have been brought to the Caribbean in the initial years of Spanish exploration, it definitely arrived no later than January 1519.

4. Waldman, *Atlas of the North American Indian*, 169.

5. Crosby, *Columbian Exchange*, 47; and Dobyns, *Their Number Become Thinned*, 259.

6. M. Ashburn, *The Ranks of Death: A Medical History of the Conquest of America,* edited by Frank D. Ashburn (New York: Coward-McCann, 1947), 85; and Hopkins, *Princes and Peasants*, 205 call the black smallpox carrier a slave. Dobyns, *Their Number Become Thinned*, 259 says he was one of Narváez's soldiers, as does Crosby, *Ecological Imperialism*, 200. McCaa, "Spanish and Nahuatl Views," 4 argues that the story about a black slave introducing smallpox to the Aztecs could be a myth and that the disease may have been brought by Narváez's Cuban soldiers.

Pánfilo de Narváez, who lost an eye while fighting Cortéz in Mexico, is better known for his incompetent command during an ill-fated expedition to conquer the Gulf coast from Florida to Texas in 1527. Only four men from Narváez's 400-man party survived the nearly nine-year ordeal and made their way to Mexico's Sonora Valley, where they were rescued by a Spanish slaver named Diego de Alcaraz.

7. Ashburn, *Ranks of Death*, 84; and Crosby, *Columbian Exchange*, 49-50.

8. Hopkins, *Princes and Peasants*, 207 suggests that the disease claimed one-half of the Aztecs, whatever their population. High Counters, such as ethnohistorian Henry F. Dobyns, lean toward bigger death tolls than do the Low Counters. For more, see Henige, *Numbers from Nowhere*, 82-3; and McCaa, "Spanish and Nahuatl Views," 1-21.

Although the actual number of deaths may have been millions fewer than those expounded by the High Counters, they were no less terrible. Scholars continue to debate the native population figures for North and South America, as they have done for years. For North America, the number of natives at the time of first European contact ranges from a few million to sixty million. The one thing the "experts" do agree on is that whatever total the Indian population of North and South America reached, the majority of western hemisphere natives lived in southern Mexico and northern Central America—an area often called Mesoamerica—and in the South American Andes.

In contrast with the High Counters, historian Rudolph A. Zambardino puts the 1519 population of central Mexico between five million and ten million people—versus the twenty-five million proposed by Sherburne F. Cook and Woodrow W. Borah, and the thirty million suggested by Henry F. Dobyns. Zambardino estimates that Mexico's population fell approximately fifty percent by 1548, to between 2.7 million and 4.5 million. By 1595, he calculates that it declined further to between 1.1 million and 1.7 million people (these figures appear in Henige, *Numbers from Nowhere*, 44, 58, table 1). From their estimate of twenty-five million Mesoamerican Indians in 1519, Cook and Borah argue that the population dropped to 16.8 million in 1532; 7.3 million in 1548; 1.9 million in 1585; and 1.275 million in 1595; see Henry F. Dobyns, *Native American Historical Demography: A Critical Bibliography* (Bloomington: Indiana University Press, 1976), 40. Medical-historian Carlos Camargo puts the death rate for the 1520 Mexican smallpox epidemic at thirty percent, giving the region a pre-contact population of between five million and twenty-five million people; see Henige, *Numbers from Nowhere*, 210.

Most pre-Columbus Indian population estimates for America north of Mexico range from one million to twelve million (inflated to eighteen million by Dobyns, as reported in Henige, *Numbers from Nowhere*, 83). Three-quarters of the people lived in what is now the United States and the rest in Canada. These figures gain importance when considering the effect of white impact on Native Americans. Indian-white warfare accounted for slightly more than a ten percent decline in North America's native population. In contrast, disease, particularly smallpox, was far more devastating. In the United States, the Indian population reached its lowest point—237,000—in 1900. (Although it is no doubt off by several thousand, 237,000 is probably closer to the actual number of Indians at that time—because of the 1900 U.S. Census—than are the academic "guesstimates" about native population levels in the four centuries following European contact.) A decline from 750,000 (the Low Counters' Indian population estimate for the United States at first European contact) to 237,000 is a drop of sixty-eight percent, tragic certainly, but no where near as horrific as would be a decline from nine million (the High Counters' Indian population estimate for the United States at first European contact) to 237,000, an attrition of ninety-seven percent. For more, see Waldman, *Atlas of the North American Indian*, 29, 166. The 237,000 figure comes from Geoffrey C. Ward, *The West: An Illustrated History* (New York: Little, Brown, 1996), 416.

Waldman rounds the number off to a quarter of a million. For a more complete discussion of the pre-contact population debate, read Henige, *Numbers from Nowhere*.

Readers who are skeptical that smallpox could kill virgin populations in such numbers should examine modern epidemics. According to Crosby, *Columbian Exchange*, 44, between 1707 and 1709 during Iceland's first smallpox outbreak, thirty-six percent of the island's inhabitants died. Another example occurred on Mexico's Yucatan Peninsula a century and a half later. In the mid 1800s, the Cruzob Mayas cut off all intercourse with the outside world. For over two generations the tribe lived in isolation. When Mexican officials approached the Cruzobs about ending their self-imposed quarantine, smallpox struck. Raging like a fire in an overgrown forest, the virus killed between 3,000 and 5,000 Indians out of a total population of between 8,000 and 10,000—a death rate of between thirty and fifty percent. In a less tragic example, twentieth-century medicine was unable to prevent measles from infecting nearly every Indian and Eskimo of northern Quebec's Ungava Bay in 1952. Despite heroic efforts by Canadian doctors, the death rate hit seven percent. Two years later, this so-called childhood disease attacked a virgin population of Indians in Brazil's Xingu National Park. Crosby, *Ecological Imperialism*, 197, 287 report that among the Xingu natives who could not be reached by medical teams, the death count topped one in four.

9. Hopkins, *Princes and Peasants*, 209. Henige, *Numbers from Nowhere*, 148 points out that not all historians accept that Wayna Qhapac died from smallpox. Crosby, *Columbian Exchange*, 52 states that smallpox was the most likely cause, although it may have been measles; when Wayna Qhapac died, his face was reportedly covered with scabs.

10. Josephy, *Indian Heritage*, 288.

11. Henige, *Numbers from Nowhere*, 44; Hopkins, *Princes and Peasants*, 215, 221; Josephy, *Indian Heritage*, 284; and Stearn and Stearn, *Effect of Smallpox*, 13. Ethnohistorian Henry F. Dobyns argues that the smallpox introduced into Mexico by the slave of Pánfilo de Narváez in April 1520 eventually became a hemisphere-wide pandemic, killing Indians from Tierra del Fuego to Hudson Bay. Alvar Núñez Cabeza de Vaca, a surviving member of Pánfilo de Narváez's ill-fated expedition to Florida, visited an Indian village in Texas where many of the inhabitants were blind in one or both eyes. Because smallpox survivors are often blind, Dobyns cites that as evidence that the epidemic of 1520 moved north from Mexico and engulfed the rest of North America; see Dobyns, *Their Number Become Thinned*, 12-13. While admitting the possibility of Dobyns's theory, archaeologist and anthropologist Ann F. Ramenofsky thinks that smallpox was most likely introduced to the region immediately north of Mexico by Hernando de Soto, who first explored the lower Mississippi in 1541. In fewer than six generations, the native population of that region fell eighty percent, a decline that Ramenofsky attributes to smallpox; see Ramenofsky, *Vectors of Death*, 12, 44, 47, 58-9; and Ann F. Ramenofsky, *The Archaeology of Population Collapse: Native American Response to the Introduction of Infectious Disease* (Ann Arbor: University Microfilms International, 1982), 257. For a critical analysis of Dobyns's work, read Henige, *Numbers from Nowhere*, Chapter 5. On page 124 Henige questions Dobyns's theory that the smallpox pandemic of the 1520s extended from pole to pole, and on pages 162 and 177 he states that there is no evidence that de Soto infected the Indians of the southeast with smallpox, as claimed by Ramenofsky. Finally, on page 176 Henige disputes Dobyns's assertion that during the sixteenth century the western hemisphere underwent twelve epidemics, the majority of which Dobyns claims were smallpox.

12. Crosby, *Columbian Exchange*, 38.

13. The European demand for seafood, particularly cod that was dried and lightly salt-

ed, stemmed from the Catholic calendar, which required the sixteenth-century
faithful to avoid meat 165 days of the year; see Axtell, *Invasion Within*, 30, 339 n.
18.

14. Josephy, *Indian Heritage*, 299.

15. Axtell, *Invasion Within*, 30.

16. Duffy, *Epidemics in Colonial America*, 43 says that there is no evidence that smallpox reached New England—and by association, eastern Canada—until 1630.
Ashburn, *Ranks of Death*, 88 disagrees.

17. Duffy, "Smallpox and the Indians in the American Colonies," 324. Bartholomew
Gosnald is most famous for naming Martha's Vineyard.

18. Axtell, *Invasion Within*, 219-20; Hopkins, *Princes and Peasants*, 234; Josephy,
Indian Heritage, 302; Calvin Martin, "Wildlife Diseases as a Factor in the
Depopulation of the North American Indian," *The Western Historical Quarterly* 7,
no. 1 (January 1976): 50-1; and Ramenofsky, *Vectors of Death*, 99-100 state that
plague was the probable cause. Shurkin, *Invisible Fire*, 146 insists the epidemic of
1617 through 1619 was smallpox. Duffy, *Epidemics in Colonial America*, 43 states
that the Pawtuckett epidemic of 1612 and 1613 was not *Variola major,* arguing
that there is no historical evidence that smallpox infected New England before
1630.

19. Crosby, *Columbian Exchange*, 42.

20. Robert M. Utley and Wilcomb E. Washburn, *Indian Wars* (American Heritage,
1977; Boston: Houghton Mifflin, 1987), 33; and Edwin C. Rozwenc, *The Making of
American Society*, vol. 1 to 1877 (Boston: Allyn and Bacon, 1972), 26-8. James
Axtell, *The European and the Indian: Essays in the Ethnohistory of Colonial North
America* (New York: Oxford University Press, 1981), 248 reports that from the
arrival of the Pilgrims until the mid 1700s, disease annually killed an average of
one and a half percent of New England's Native Americans, eventually decreasing
their overall number eightfold.

21. Axtell, *European and the Indian*, 118-19, 252-3.

22. Duffy, "Smallpox and the Indians in the American Colonies," 327.

23. Axtell, *Invasion Within*, 46. White traders adulterated the Ojibwa name to
Chippewa.

24. Harold A. Innis, *The Fur Trade in Canada: An Introduction to Canadian Economic
History* (New Haven: Yale University Press, 1930; revised, 1956; Yale Western
Americana Special Contents Edition, 1962), 29-30.

25. Hopkins, *Princes and Peasants*, 235; Ramenofsky, *Vectors of Death*, 98; and
Shurkin, *Invisible Fire*, 110.

26. The Tuscaroras, who eventually joined the Iroquois League, lived in eastern
Virginia and eastern North Carolina. In 1713, they fled to New York after being
routed by a colonial and Indian army led by Colonel James Moore. In 1722, the
Iroquois allowed the Tuscaroras to become the sixth member of their confederation;
for more, see Josephy, *Indian Heritage*, 82; Viola, *After Columbus*, 86; and
Waldman, *Atlas of the North American Indian*, 93, 104.

27. French governor, Jacques René de Brisay, Marquis Denonville, intensified the
Franco-Iroquois enmity when he destroyed several Seneca villages in 1687.

28. Hopkins, *Princes and Peasants*, 236. According to Ramenofsky, *Vectors of Death*,
100, between 1613 and 1690, the Iroquois and other northeastern tribes suffered
through twenty-four epidemics, almost all caused by smallpox. Duffy, "Smallpox
and the Indians in the American Colonies," 329 disagrees, stating that there were
few smallpox outbreaks in Quebec from 1641 until the early 1660s; in note 17
(page 329), Duffy argues that the supposed epidemic of 1649 actually occurred in

1694.

29. Axtell, *European and the Indian*, 261.

30. Waldman, *Atlas of the North American Indian*, 186.

31. Duffy, "Smallpox and the Indians in American Colonies," 329.

32. Stearn and Stearn, *Effect of Smallpox*, 30-1.

33. Waldman, *Atlas of the North American Indian*, 94.

34. The Ojibwas called the Crees *Keethisteno,* which French traders corrupted into *Kristeno* and then shortened to Cree. The Crees called themselves *Nai ah yah' og;* see Denig, *Indian Tribes*, 100 and n. 3.

35. Peter C. Newman, *Empire of the Bay: An illustrated history of the Hudson's Bay Company* (Toronto: Viking Studio/Madison Press Books, 1989), 33-6, 40; and Glyndwr Williams, "The Hudson's Bay Company and the Fur Trade: 1670-1870," *The Beaver* 314, no. 2 (autumn 1983); reprinted (1991): 4-5.

36. Axtell, *Invasion Within*, 247; and Ramenofsky, *Vectors of Death*, 92.

37. The literal translation of *coureurs de bois* is runners of the woods. According to Coues, ed., *Alexander Henry*, 1:166, another term for these roving traders is *coureurs de derouine,* which means traders who traveled among Indian bands, bartering—that is, drumming—for furs. If a *coureur de derouine* had no trade goods with him and the Indians knew and trusted him, they would occasionally give him their pelts in exchange for a written voucher that they could present for payment in merchandise at the trader's home post. French traders called this *s'en aller en derouine* or *courir la derouine,* which in English means to go drumming.
Innis, *Fur Trade in Canada*, 70 reports that each year from 1675 through 1684, New France shipped an average of 89,588 pounds of beaver pelts to Europe, an amount that increased to 140,000 pounds in both 1685 and 1686. A pelt from an adult beaver typically weighs between one and one-half and one and three-quarter pounds.

38. Years later, England formalized her non-expansion policy by issuing the Royal Proclamation of 1763, legally baring colonists from venturing west of the Appalachian Divide. The resulting anger among the land-hungry colonists undoubtedly did as much to ignite the American Revolution as did "taxation without representation."

39. Stearn and Stearn, *Effect of Smallpox*, 24, 27. Recollect missionaries and their English Protestant rivals sought to "civilize" the native tribes in order to convert them. In contrast, Jesuit priests saw that tribal resistance to being "civilized" hindered the Indians' embrace of Christianity. Accordingly, after 1640 the Jesuits gave up trying to turn the Indians into proper Europeans and, instead, concentrated on winning their hearts to the "yoke of Christ." As a result, Jesuit missions gained acceptance among the Indians, whereas those of the Recollects and Protestants languished; see Axtell, *Invasion Within*, 272-3, 276.

40. Axtell, *Invasion Within*, 86, 97.

41. Ibid., 99.

42. Waldman, *Atlas of the North American Indian*, 21-2 use this figure, whereas Crosby, *Ecological Imperialism*, 210 puts the number at 40,000. Monks Mound, the grandest of Cahokia's 120 temple mounds, covers sixteen acres and contains over 814,000 cubic yards of dirt. As were the other mounds, Monks Mound was also built entirely by human labor.

43. Crosby, *Ecological Imperialism*, 212. In contrast with the theory that the mound builders were victims of smallpox and other diseases, Henige, *Numbers from Nowhere*, 363 n. 14 cites archaeologists who think the Indians vacated their homeland because of drought.

44. Ramenofsky, *Vectors of Death*, 64-5 intimate that most of the deaths resulted from smallpox, as does Josephy, *Indian Heritage*, 106. Henige, *Numbers from Nowhere*, 148-50 criticize Ramenofsky's use of sources—including that of La Vente—alleging that she ignores evidence that many of the deaths were caused by inter-tribal warfare. In support of Ramenofsky, Dobyns, *Their Number Become Thinned*, 305 notes that in 1699, smallpox struck the tribes of the lower Mississippi River.

45. Ramenofsky, *Population Collapse*, 259-60, 262. As she does with La Vente, Ramenofsky ignores Saint-Cosme's references to war as the cause for many of the deaths, argues Henige, *Numbers from Nowhere*, 149.

46. The Lakotas are often called by their French name, Sioux. French traders transformed the Ojibwa word for poisonous snake or enemy—*nâdowessi*—into *Nadowessioux*, then shortened it to Sioux; see Josephy, *Indian Heritage*, 116; and Roe, *Indian and the Horse*, 240. Modern historians tend to use either Lakotas or Dakotas, depending on their spelling preference.

47. Catlin, *Letters*, 2:160, 167, 169-70; Meyer, *Village Indians*, 15; and Viola, *After Columbus*, 56-7. Named for the nineteenth-century painter of Native American culture, George Catlin, catlinite is a soft reddish stone that Indians carved into pipe bowls. Indians considered the Red Pipestone Quarry, where it was mined, to be sacred ground, open to all tribes. By the mid 1830s, the Santee Lakotas were ignoring the quarry's neutrality and denying access to their enemies. The Côteau Des Prairies is a long, northwest-southeast-running ridge that separates the Missouri River drainage from that of the Minnesota River. Copper was used by Great Lakes Indians beginning as early as 4000 B.C. On the south side of Lake Superior and on Isle Royale, natives mined pure copper nuggets from the soil and metal sheets from rock fissures.

48. Crosby, *Columbian Exchange*, 88. According to Roe, *Indian and the Horse*, 33-7, the notion that America's wild horse herds evolved from animals that escaped or were stolen from Francisco Vásquez de Coronado and Hernando de Soto during their explorations is a myth.

49. Ward, *The West*, 25.

50. Innis, *Fur Trade in Canada*, 109-10.

51. Viola, *After Columbus*, 98.

52. Walter McClintock, *The Old North Trail: or Life, Legends and Religion of the Blackfeet Indians* (London: Macmillian, 1910; Lincoln: University of Nebraska Press, Bison Book Edition, 1968; reprint, 1992), 5 uses these numbers, probably taking them from Catlin, *Letters*, 1:52. Catlin actually cites three population estimates for the Blackfeet of the early 1830s: his own estimate of 16,500; the Fort Union traders' estimate of 40,000; and Joshua Pilcher's estimate of 60,000.

53. Roe, *Indian and the Horse*, 26-8 state that a loaded travois ranged from thirty to 100 pounds, depending on the size and willingness of the dog. Generally, northern Indians had larger dogs than did tribes from the southern plains. Arthur J. Ray, *Indians in the Fur Trade: their role as trappers, hunters, and middlemen in the lands southwest of Hudson Bay, 1660-1870* (Toronto: University of Toronto Press, 1974), 161, 165 n. 54 report that a band of Gens du Pied Assiniboines on the North Saskatchewan River averaged thirteen dogs per family and that each dog hauled between fifty and 100 pounds.

54. John C. Ewers, *The Blackfeet: Raiders on the Northwest Plains* (Norman: University of Oklahoma Press, 1958), 22. Roe, *Indian and the Horse*, 61 points out that the Blackfeet were not alone in naming horses after dogs. The Assiniboines called them *sho-a-thin-ga* and *thongatch-shonga*, meaning great dog. The Crees referred to them as *mistatim* or big dog, and the Lakotas named them *shonk-a-*

wakan, which signifies medicine dog.

55. Ewers, *Indian Life,* 17.

56. Joseph Jablow, *The Cheyenne in Plains Indian Trade Relations, 1795-1840* (published as "Monograph 19" of the American Ethnological Society, 1950; New York: J. J. Augustin, 1951; Lincoln: University of Nebraska Press, Bison Book Edition, 1994), 12-14.

57. Josephy, *Indian Heritage,* 66, 70.

58. North West Company trader David Thompson wrote that the Assiniboines migrated to the southern Saskatchewan Plain around 1750, following a bloody feud with their Lakota cousins. According to Ray, *Indians in the Fur Trade,* 4-6, 14, most historians dismiss the report as tribal lore and date their move about eighty or ninety years earlier.

59. Duffy, "Smallpox and the Indians in the American Colonies," 337; and Stearn and Stearn, *Effect of Smallpox,* 43.

60. Duffy, "Smallpox and the Indians in the American Colonies," 339; and Stearn and Stearn, *Effect of Smallpox,* 43.

61. Utley and Washburn, *Indian Wars,* 98.

62. Duffy, "Smallpox and the Indians in the American Colonies," 340.

63. Crosby, *Ecological Imperialism,* 345 n. 38. Stearn and Stearn, *Effect of Smallpox,* 29; and Hopkins, *Princes and Peasants,* 236 report that Europeans may have intentionally infected the Ottawas with smallpox in the 1680s. If so, a blacker mark on the European colonization of North America cannot be imagined.

64. Ray, *Indians in the Fur Trade,* 125.

65. Williams, "Hudson's Bay Company," 35. In 1783, the Montreal Peddlers formed the North West Company and began to compete in earnest with the Hudson's Bay Company.

66. Donald J. Lehmer, *Selected Writings of Donald J. Lehmer,* (Lincoln: J & L Reprint, *Reprints in Anthropology* 8, 1977), 93, 99.

67. Ramenofsky, *Vectors of Death,* 130; and Ramenofsky, *Population Collapse,* 328. Henige, *Numbers from Nowhere,* 79-80 debunk Henry Dobyns's assertion that this epidemic killed over 40,000 people in Mexico City alone.

68. Lehmer, *Selected Writings,* 100-01 estimate that the smallpox epidemic of 1780 and 1781 destroyed between seventy-five and eighty percent of the Indians in the upper Missouri village tribes, casting their culture into a headlong disintegration. According to Axtell, *European and the Indian,* 370 n. 21, the epidemic killed so many women potters among the natives of the middle Missouri Valley, their art was lost to future generations.

69. Shurkin, *Invisible Fire,* 116.

70. Denig, *Indian Tribes,* 115 asserts that this 230-lodge camp belonged to the Crees, but it is more likely that the majority of the Indians were Assiniboines, since the Crees generally lived farther north.

71. Crosby, *Ecological Imperialism,* 203.

72. Coues, ed., *Alexander Henry,* 1:46, 176 n. 40; Lehmer, *Selected Writings,* 106; Newman, *Empire of the Bay,* 98; Ray, *Indians in the Fur Trade,* 98, 105-07; Roe, *Indian and the Horse,* 31; and Stearn and Stearn, *Effect of Smallpox,* 46-7, 49. A few historians say that the Chipewyans avoided the worst of the epidemic until 1787.

73. Martin, "Wildlife Diseases," 54.

74. Ibid., 53 states that Saukamappee was a Blackfoot. Ewers, *Indian Life,* 35 spells the Indian's name Saukamaupee, saying he was Cree. At the time, the Plains

Crees and Blackfeet were still allies, so Saukamappee could have taken part in the raid if he was Cree. Arguing against him having done so is his age. The raid most likely took place in the fall of 1781 or early 1782, at the latest. Saukamappee is described by Ewers as an old man when he met David Thompson during the winter of 1786 and 1787.

75. Ewers, *The Blackfeet*, 184; and McClintock, *Old North Trail*, 148.

76. Ewers, *The Blackfeet*, 28-9.

Chapter Five

Early Summer 1837

A bit before dawn on June 20, the crew and passengers of the *St. Peter's* awakened. Many of those who had participated in the previous night's drunken revelry at Mitutanka Village felt as if their heads would burst. The ones who had spent the wee hours in the arms of Mandan or Arikara maidens, crawled from their sleeping robes and shuffled toward the steamer, already looking forward to the boat's next port of call—Fort Union.

As the deckhands and passengers filed across the *St. Peter's* landing plank, a stoker tossed wood into the engine-room fireboxes and stirred the banked coals to a roaring blaze. By the time steam came up in the boilers, the dawn light had transposed Fort Clark from a murky silhouette to a gray, log stockade. On Captain Pratte's command, the pilot rang the signal bell, alerting those still ashore that the *St. Peter's* would soon depart. Moments after the last stragglers scurried aboard, deckhands pulled in the gangway, and the pilot backed the steamboat out of the shallows.

Once in the Missouri's main channel, the captain pointed the bow upstream, and began steaming toward the mouth of the Yellowstone, over 200 miles away. Included among the passengers were Indian subagent William Fulkerson, Jacob Halsey,

Halsey's pregnant, mixed-blood wife, and the couple's young son.

Shortly after departing Fort Clark, the steamer passed Ruhptare Village—the smaller, sister town of Mitutanka. Just beyond here and on the opposite side of the channel, the Knife River discharged into Missouri. The Hidatsas' principal village was located a few miles up the Knife. Some distance above the Knife-Missouri confluence, the *St. Peter's* swung hard left. For the rest of its journey to Fort Union, the boat would generally travel west by north.

Soon after the steamer left Fort Clark, the *Variola* virus completed its incubation within the Halseys. Mrs. Halsey developed a high temperature and severe pain in her head and lower back. Jacob Halsey could do nothing to ease her suffering for he too lay prostrate with fever and a blinding headache. Although he had been vaccinated with cowpox vaccine earlier in life, Halsey's immunity had been diluted by the ensuing years.

It is likely that someone aboard the *St. Peter's* notified Captain Pratte and William Fulkerson that the Halseys were ill. Though Pratte had been skeptical about the presence of smallpox when the black deckhand became sick below Fort Leavenworth, the captain would have been hard-pressed to deny that Halsey and his wife now had the disease. All the same, Pratte decided to continue to Fort Union, probably hoping to contain the pestilence by keeping the Halseys quarantined.

At the mouth of the Little Missouri River, a member of the Blackfoot Confederation signaled the *St. Peter's* to stop.[1] The Indian (whether male or female is unknown) begged passage to Fort Union, intending to go on to Blackfoot country with one of Pratte & Chouteau's traders. Captain Pratte allowed the Indian to come aboard. Despite the Halseys' quarantine, the Blackfoot passenger soon inhaled the lethal virus.

As the steamboat forged ahead, it passed beneath terraced bluffs that hid the prairie from view. Sculpted by eons of wind, rain, and snowmelt, the clay hillsides captured the imagination, bringing to mind medieval castles and citadels, ancient ruins, lofty spires, and crumbling porticos. Along one stretch of river, the clay had been molded into huge domes. Named the Brick

Kilns by early voyageurs who had manhandled keelboats up the Missouri before the days of steam, these rounded bluffs were composed of multi-hued layers of sediment. Their sun-lit summits glistened as though they were painted with vermilion. Below the burnt-red tops, bands of color cascaded toward the river, fading from yellow to ash to brown to indigo.[2] Mountain sheep sought refuge and forage amid this tortured landscape, as did the occasional herd of pronghorns and a few grizzly bears.

At other places along this stretch of the Missouri, the high banks receded, revealing a tall-grass prairie splashed with violet, amber, cobalt, and pink from an endless variety of wildflowers. Closer to the water, plum trees competed for space with gooseberry shrubs and wild currants. Elsewhere, brambles of wild roses and serviceberries white with blossoms crowded the river's edge, creating an impenetrable barrier of briers and thorns that often ran for miles.

As the steamboat chugged toward the mouth of the Yellowstone River, the condition of Halsey's pregnant wife worsened. Running a temperature and often delirious himself, her husband probably never knew when she began her labor. A day or so below Fort Union, the young woman gave birth to a daughter. Tormented by fever, a pounding head, and the agonizing pain in her lower back, she thrashed among her bedclothes, unable to care for her newborn child. Then, in one of her convulsive fits, Mrs. Halsey fell on the cabin floor, rupturing an internal organ, and hemorrhaged to death.[3]

While the Halseys were undergoing their ordeal, downstream at Mitutanka Village, the smallpox virus incubated within the unsuspecting Mandans. At Fort Clark, *engagés* loaded 320 packs of buffalo robes and five bundles of beaver pelts aboard the two mackinaws that had been left behind by the *St. Peter's*. On Wednesday afternoon, June 21, voyageurs poled the flat-bottomed boats into the Missouri's current and began their long float to St. Louis. The next day, the Mandans and Arikaras who had left Mitutanka Village on June 5 to establish a hunting camp returned, loaded with dried meat. A bit later, four Mandan warriors who were part of Ball dans Le Coup's war party—which had also departed on June 5—came home, as well.

The warriors thought the rest of their force would be back in a day or two. Although the war party had suffered no casualties, the Mandans had scant reason to celebrate. The warriors had reached the Yankton camp without being detected, but when the moment came to attack, their courage flagged. Chief Ball dans Le Coup and his band had turned tail and fled like a pack of whipped dogs. They had taken no Yankton scalps and had earned no victory.

Following a thundershower the next morning, Chardon met with several Mandan and Arikara chiefs to discuss trade and ensure that relations between the two tribes and Fort Clark remained cordial. Except for one sullen Arikara, the other Indian leaders professed friendship and looked forward to selling many robes during the coming trading season. In contrast, the disgruntled Arikara vowed to make war on Fort Clark in retaliation for a relative who had been killed by white men at Fort Bellevue. The wife of the angry chief was one of the three Arikara women who had caught smallpox after boarding the *St. Peter's* at Council Bluffs. Her story about the relative's murder had incensed her husband. Now, he assured Chardon that unless subagent Fulkerson paid him for the dead man, he would spill white blood for red.

On June 24, the remainder of Ball dans Le Coup's faint-hearted war party returned to Mitutanka Village. That same day a couple of miles above the Missouri-Yellowstone confluence, the *St. Peter's* pilot caught sight of Fort Union. Towering above the bottomland, the cottonwood and stone-bastioned trading post had all the trappings of a feudal castle.

Fort Union traced its history back to September 1828, when a party of American Fur Company traders had come up the Missouri from the Mandan villages, intending to establish a post for the Assiniboines near the mouth of the Yellowstone River. The traders continued about five river-miles past the Yellowstone, halting at a gravel bench that overlooked the north bank of the Missouri (in western North Dakota, a few dozen yards from the Montana state line). Deeming the location to be above the floodplain, the traders constructed a log cabin and settled in for a winter of barter with the neighboring tribes.

At the time, Kenneth McKenzie managed the American Fur Company's Upper Missouri Outfit from his headquarters at Fort Tecumseh. Wanting to expand his trading sphere to the Continental Divide, McKenzie decided to move his base from Fort Tecumseh to the mouth of the Yellowstone. In the fall of 1829, American Fur Company carpenters started building a large trading fort near the 1828 wintering house. The new post was named Fort Union.

When completed in 1830, the fort's cottonwood stockade measured 240 by 220 feet, making it larger than any other trading post on the upper Missouri, a distinction it held until the construction of Fort Pierre. Two, double-story, whitewashed, stone bastions protected the diagonal corners of Fort Union's stockade. Their armament consisted of a twelve-pounder and a couple of smaller brass swivel cannons. Inside the palisades, a wooden catwalk offered sharpshooters a firing platform in case of an Indian attack, a precaution that had yet to be needed. Instead, the elevated walkway primarily served as a promenade, providing an airy balcony from which to catch a breeze on a hot summer evening. It also gave fort personnel a scaffold from which to shoot wolves that lurked at night outside the fort wall. Such pastimes offered bored minds an alternative to the whiskey bottle.

The post's clerks, traders, craftsmen, hunters, and *engagés* lived in a long, partitioned building on the west side of the enclosed stockade. The east side was occupied by a similar structure, which contained warehouses and a company store for the fort's employees. The Indian trade room was located just inside the front gate, which opened toward the Missouri River. The post kitchen sat near the north palisade and was somewhat hidden by the *bourgeois's* long, single-story house, which faced the stockade's main entrance. The commander's home was white with green shutters and boasted eight glass windows. Had it been located in St. Louis atop the hill, where the town's fur merchants and gentry lived, the Fort Union residence would have blended in perfectly.

In addition to warehouses and trading rooms, Fort Union also contained a meat locker, icehouse, chicken coop, gunpowder magazine, cooperage, blacksmith shop, and dairy. Its stables accommodated a 150-horse remuda and included a special pen for buffalo calves. Most calves were captured during the winter, when the wind drove their mothers to seek shelter in the lee of the stockade walls. The main entrance to the trading post was capped by a painting that depicted friendship between the traders and Indians. Looking in from the front gate, the *bourgeois's* home could be seen across a large courtyard.

At the center of the courtyard, an iron four-pounder stood beside a sixty-three-foot-high flagpole. The cannon's muzzle pointed toward the trade room, reminding Indians who came in to barter that they had better behave. As an added precaution, native visitors to the fort had to give up their guns so the weapons could be locked in the armory. The Indians retained their knives and tomahawks, so the traders were still in danger of being stabbed, especially when the warriors imbibed too much whiskey. Traders accepted the risk, knowing that if they did not offer their customers liquor, the Assiniboines would take their buffalo robes to a Hudson's Bay Company trading post above the forty-ninth parallel. Because it was illegal to serve alcohol to Indians, Fort Union's *bourgeois* insisted that the whiskey be served at night. Despite the ruse, it is doubtful that Indian subagent Fulkerson was fooled. But he came to Fort Union so infrequently, his authority had atrophied like an unused leg.

As the *St. Peter's* approached the trading post landing, *engagés* within the stockade hoisted a large American flag atop the tall staff that marked the center of the courtyard. Other personnel fired welcoming salutes from one of the fort's cannons. Meanwhile, a throng of Assiniboine women lined the riverbank. Many covered their mouths with their hands as they excitedly watched the steamer turn bow-first into the slack water that bordered the landing. Most of the women were married to company employees and lived in a tipi camp outside the palisade. Clustered on the steamboat's main and hurricane decks, trappers and first-class passengers returned the cannon salutes by shouting, waving their hats, and firing repeated volleys from their rifles.

Oblivious to the commotion, Jacob Halsey lay shivering in his bed, his body consumed by fever, his cheeks, arms, and chest blotched by a red, itchy rash. Now infectious, Halsey exhaled the *Variola* virus with every breath.

As the *St. Peter's* crew began unloading trade goods and supplies, word of the illness quickly spread throughout the fort. To Captain Pratte's relief, Halsey's was the only known case of smallpox still on board. If the husbands of the Assiniboine onlookers mentioned the danger to them, it is doubtful the women understood. Although *Variola major* had swept their tribe in years past, the Assiniboines had no grasp of communicable disease. The sight of the new *bourgeois* being carried into the trading post on a litter failed to alert them to their risk.[4]

A couple of *engagés* took Halsey to the *bourgeois's* home and put him to bed. It is likely that Edwin Denig, one of the Fort Union clerks, ordered Halsey's room quarantined. A native of Pennsylvania, Denig had joined the American Fur Company in 1833, at the age of twenty-one. After trading among the Lakotas for about three years, he was transferred to Fort Union in the late fall or winter of 1836. As a young man, he had picked up a bit of medical insight from his physician-father, so the Fort Union personnel looked to Denig to treat their illnesses and accidents.[5]

Among those awaiting the arrival of the *St. Peter's* was the trader Alexander Harvey. He had keelboated down the Missouri from Fort McKenzie to collect stores for the Blackfoot Confederation. Located seven miles up the Missouri from its confluence with the Marias River (thirteen miles below modern-day Fort Benton, Montana), Fort McKenzie had replaced Fort Piegan (at the mouth of the Marias), which had been burned by the Blackfeet in the spring of 1832. That summer, American Fur Company clerk David Mitchell had journeyed up the Missouri, intending to trade with the confederation. Finding Fort Piegan reduced to ashes, he continued upriver a few miles and constructed a temporary trading post on the Missouri's left bank, naming it Fort McKenzie after the senior partner of the American Fur Company's Upper Missouri Outfit, Kenneth McKenzie. A year later, carpenters erected a more substantial post nearby, which was also given the Fort McKenzie name.

Because of the combative and unpredictable nature of the Blackfeet, Fort McKenzie was the firm's most dangerous posting.

A native of St. Louis, Alexander Harvey had developed an early reputation as a scrapper. As a young man, he had been apprenticed to a saddler, but his temper soon put him at odds with his employer. Determined to seek his fortune beyond the societal constrictions of the settlements, Harvey hired on with the American Fur Company in the early 1830s and was assigned to Fort McKenzie a short time after its completion. Despite his tendency to fight at the slightest insult—real or imagined—he became an adept trader. But his success did nothing to soften his disruptive influence among the rest of Fort McKenzie's personnel. Nearly everyone at the trading post thought it would be best if Pratte, Chouteau & Company expelled him from the upper Missouri. Most figured it was merely a matter of time before Harvey's shenanigans spelled his doom.[6]

As soon as Fort Union's clerks and *engagés* segregated the supplies for Fort McKenzie, Alexander Harvey ordered his voyageurs to stow the cargo aboard their keelboat so they could leave and reduce their chances of contracting smallpox. The Blackfoot who had boarded the *St. Peter's* at the mouth of the Little Missouri River prepared to travel with them. Unbeknownst to anyone, the *Variola* virus was multiplying within the Indian's lungs.[7]

Meanwhile, William Fulkerson made a brief survey of his upcountry agency—that is, he strolled around the trading post stockade—no doubt relieved that most of the Assiniboines were on the prairie, hunting buffalo. In any case, had they been present, he had nothing to give them besides one of his canned speeches urging them to keep the peace. After the *St. Peter's* was unloaded, Captain Pratte ordered its departure, eager to start downstream before the river fell and marooned him until the following year.

At six a.m., Wednesday, June 28, the *St. Peter's* again stopped at Fort Clark as it raced to descend the Missouri before the end of the mountain snowmelt. Subagent Fulkerson gave a few presents to the Mitutanka villagers and harangued them to stop raiding the Lakotas and Assiniboines. The gifts must have mollified the Arikara chief who wanted reimbursement for the death of his relative at Fort Bellevue, since Chardon made no mention in his journal of the Indian trying to exact further tribute. Fulkerson's audience was smaller than the agent probably expected. Two days earlier, a smattering of Arikaras had gone to steal horses from the Pawnees. And a day later, a larger Mandan and Arikara war party had ridden off hoping to lift some Yankton scalps. True to his nature, Francis Chardon had wished them good riddance.

After Fulkerson concluded his talk, the *St. Peter's* pilot signaled departure. Its stay had lasted only an hour. The Indian agent scurried aboard, happy to be heading downstream to the comforts of civilization. As the riverboat steamed out of sight, no one at Fort Clark had an inkling about the tragic consequences of its visit. At Mitutanka Village, the smallpox virus entered the ninth day of its incubation.

Sometime after the *St. Peter's* departure, Toussaint Charbonneau arrived at Fort Clark, bringing word that everything was quiet among the Hidatsas. Later in the day, a thunderstorm rumbled across the prairie, producing a mighty display of lightning and hail. The squall's fury produced a sharp contrast to the muted entrance of a large Arikara war party, which had departed Mitutanka Village on May 31. The warriors had intended ambushing the Yanktons, but the Arikaras returned home with the zeal of a deposed politician. They had failed to count a single coup.

On June 30, Chardon sent out a wood-cutting detail, later remarking in his journal that the month was ending on a cold and rainy note. Perhaps the raw weather had prompted Fort Clark's rat population to remain within its nests instead of running amok in the stockade. The *bourgeois's* monthly tally of dead rats topped out at a paltry thirty-one.

The same day Chardon recorded his monthly count of dead vermin, downriver near Fort Kiowa, the Yankton and Santee Lakotas underwent their own death count. Smallpox had broken out among the Lakota tribes two weeks earlier and was now racing through their tipi villages like water from a ruptured dam.[8] The disease seemed intent on destroying the entire Lakota nation. Still in residence at his agency within Fort Kiowa, Joshua Pilcher gave his native charges doses of salts and castor oil, but the drugs did nothing to stem the widening epidemic.[9] Every day the *rotting face* added new victims to its rolls.

Earlier in the month, while the virus was incubating, Pilcher had persuaded a number of Santee chiefs to accompany him to Washington, D.C. For decades the War Department had paraded Indian leaders through the halls of Congress, thinking the delegations would be awed by the power of the United States. The government hoped the Indians would see the futility of resisting white migration. Although the policy enjoyed only modest success, officials at the War Department continued its practice.

Eastern politicians and bureaucrats figured the stories told by the returning Indians would so impress their countrymen, no tribe would dare make war on the encroaching whites. With smallpox now spreading exponentially, Pilcher watched his Santee envoys sicken and die. Eventually, those who had not taken ill rallied their bands and fled to the prairie, correctly deeming Fort Kiowa to be a crucible of death. Knowing that his superiors were counting on him to provide native representatives, Pilcher cajoled other Lakotas to fill the quota, no longer concerned if they were Santees.[10]

In early July, Pilcher pasted together a substitute delegation and escorted them downriver to Fort Leavenworth. The effort went for naught. Before leaving Fort Kiowa, the Indian ambassadors had inhaled the *Variola* virus. By the middle of the month, all were dead. Desperate to assemble a fresh party, Pilcher dashed upstream to Joseph Robidoux's trading post at the Blacksnake Hills and persuaded a few Yanktons to join his mission. Try as he could, he found no other Santees willing to make the trip.

Unable to enlist any more Lakotas in the venture, Pilcher rounded out his commission with Fox and Sauk Indians. That summer, while Joshua Pilcher and his Indian representatives toured the nation's capital, the Santee, Yankton, Yanktonai, and Teton Lakotas deserted their dying kin and dispersed in small familial units on the upper Missouri and central prairie. Although infected bands spread the virus further, parties in whom the pestilence was not incubating safeguarded themselves, ensuring the survival of the Lakota nation and with it, the expansion of Lakota power. No one—neither Indian nor white—suspected that the burgeoning epidemic would forever change the tribal hegemony of the western plains.

On the Fourth of July, before the Lakotas had begun to recoil from a sickness they could not comprehend, upriver at Fort Clark, Francis Chardon celebrated the country's birthday with a glass of "old Monongahela." Raising his tumbler in salute, the *bourgeois* toasted former President Andrew Jackson, the namesake of Chardon's second son. Around noon, Toussaint Charbonneau added to the holiday festivities by preparing a sumptuous dinner, one that no doubt featured salted buffalo tongue and roasted hump. The personnel at the trading post feasted on Charbonneau's delicious fare, unaware that at Mitutanka Village the flame of smallpox had begun to burn.

For the past two days, a Mandan had lain amid his (or her) robes, his body seared by an internal fire, his speech a babble of delirium.[11] Reacting as they always did to illness, the family of the sickened Mandan probably summoned a shaman, hoping he could provide a magical cure. Employing the fanfare of a medicine-show barker, the shaman prayed to the spirits, recited incantations, shook rattles, and boasted about his power as a healer. Meanwhile, his patient writhed in pain. Captivated by the shaman's pompous performance, family members crowded around the victim, trusting that the cause of his suffering would soon disappear. They had no clue that each breath exhaled by their stricken kinsman saturated the air with *Variola major*.

As the Mandans waited for the shaman to extract a pebble or other token from the patient's body—demonstrating that he had removed the cause of the illness—they unwittingly inhaled the lethal canker. Settling into its new hosts, the smallpox virus began another round of incubation.

During the evening, the mixed Mandan and Arikara war party that had departed Mitutanka Village on May 27 returned. The warriors had spotted a solitary Lakota but had been unable to catch him. It was another missed chance to count coup. Wanting to make up for their tribesmen's failure, more Arikaras painted their bodies for war and trooped east toward their Lakota foes.

On July 5, the Missouri River began to fall, dropping two feet by the following day. Had the *St. Peter's* still been at Fort Clark, it might have been stranded. Over the next week, life at the trading post settled into its summer lethargy. Thunderstorms swept across the prairie like clockwork, keeping temperatures comfortably cool. The searing heat of August and early September was still several weeks away. A few Indians trickled into the stockade to trade buffalo robes, but by and large the traders had little to do. One day a bevy of Hidatsas broke the monotony by trooping down from the Knife River and entertaining Chardon and his men with a spirited dance. If the *bourgeois* rewarded the dancers with a gift of food, he failed to record it in his journal.

At Mitutanka Village another Arikara war party rode east to count coup on the Lakotas. As always, the families of the departing warriors prayed for their safe return. Mothers, wives, and sweethearts focused on their daily routines, being careful to do nothing that would anger the spirits. Tribal beliefs warned that botched ceremonies and muffed rituals were a sure way for the women to bring disaster to their husbands and sons.

Many of the Indians at Mitutanka Village headed to the prairie to hunt buffalo and make dried meat. About the only ones remaining behind were the elderly who were too feeble to work and a small but increasing number of Mandans who were beset by a mysterious illness. Although shamans had repeatedly tried to heal them, so far the medicine men had been unable to find a cure.

A few white-haired grandmothers and grandfathers may have remembered a similar sickness that had battered their tribe fifty-seven years before. They would have been children then, perhaps too young for the disease to have etched emotional scars in their hearts to match the physical scars it had branded on their cheeks. Many Mandan elders wore pockmarks on their time-chiseled faces. They had seen their tribe mowed down like hay during the smallpox epidemic of 1780 and 1781.

Twenty years later, another bout of *Variola major* had swept the plains, though it was nowhere near as bad as the epidemic of their childhood. Now as the elders listened to the high-pitched trill of the shamans' medicine whistles, they feared that the *rotting face* had again descended on the upper Missouri.

Friday, July 14, dawned hot and sultry. Smoke from numerous grass fires on the prairie veiled the sun behind a brownish-gray screen. Most had probably been set by Mandan and Arikara hunters, who were using the flames to drive the buffalo. To the men at Fort Clark the smoky air did not matter, for they relished the warmth. They were weary of the chill and rain that had made their spring and early summer a misery.

At first blush, the day showed nothing to distinguish it from other mid-July days. The post's traders, carpenters, and *engagés* went about their chores; the cooks rendered up a tasty meal from the three buffalo bulls that hunters had brought in the previous afternoon. At their dried meat camps on the plains, Mandan and Arikara women skinned and butchered the buffalo killed by their husbands; and to the east, Mandan and Arikara warriors continued to search for unwary Lakotas, hoping to end their dearth of coups. But within Mitutanka Village, July 14 heralded disaster. A young Mandan died of *Variola major*. For the Mandans, this initial smallpox fatality marked the beginning of their doom.

Within the lodge of the deceased, relatives mourned his passing by cropping their hair.[12] Driven by their grief, some of his family no doubt severed the last joint from one of their little fingers. Such public displays of bereavement were common among the tribes of the upper Missouri. That afternoon, while the boy's family wrapped his body in the raw skin of a freshly killed buffalo,[13] Chardon noted in his journal that a number of other Mandans in Mitutanka Village also had smallpox. The majority of the Arikaras and Mandans were still on the prairie, hunting. Although this unplanned quarantine afforded the tribes a measure of protection, the continual comings and goings between the village and dried meat camp made the buffer as porous as a spider's web.

On July 8 or 9, a few days before the first Mandan died at Mitutanka Village, Jacob Halsey's young son and the clerk Edwin Denig had come down with smallpox at Fort Union.[14] Clerk Charles Larpenteur recognized the peril to the Assiniboines, once they returned to the fort for the fall trading season. At present, the tribe was safely scattered across the prairie, chasing buffalo.

In more immediate danger were a number of fur company employees who had neither had the disease as children nor been recently vaccinated. Adding to the risk of the virus dispersing were a number of Indian women and their mixed-blood children who lived full-time near the stockade. The women were married to fort personnel, and one was Larpenteur's wife. The clerk realized that if the smallpox gradually spread to the non-immune employees and Indian women and their children, the post would still be infectious when the Assiniboines came to trade in September. If the disease carried to the tribe, it could launch an epidemic that might imperil the entire trading season.

Wanting to be rid of the disease before the Assiniboines arrived, Larpenteur and the other clerks decided to inoculate everyone at the fort who was in danger of becoming sick. The clerks understood that vaccination was safer than inoculation, but they had no cowpox vaccine. If they were to carry out their plan, they would need to improvise.

In a bookcase in the *bourgeois's* office, they found a medical book by Dr. Robert Thomas,[15] which explained the procedure for inoculation. For serum, the clerks scraped pus from Halsey's ripened blisters.

To prevent the women and their children from fleeing to their tribes after the inoculation began to take effect, the clerks locked them in a makeshift prison, possibly a small storeroom or one of the fort's stone bastions.[16] Among the women was Larpenteur's Indian wife. On July 12, after collecting a vial of Halsey's pus, Larpenteur and one or two other clerks made tiny cuts on the inoculees' arms, using a lancet. Afterward, they dipped the tip of the lancet in the vial and rubbed a small amount of pus in each wound. The company men who were inoculated may have understood the danger, but the Indian women and their children no doubt thought the thick, yellow fluid was a magic elixir that would keep them safe.[17] They could not have been more wrong.

Chapter five notes

1. In Jacob Halsey to Pratte, Chouteau & Company, November 2, 1837, reprinted in Chardon, *Journal*, 394-6, Halsey wrote that a "Pied noirs" boarded the *St. Peter's* at the mouth of the Little Missouri River. Ewers, *The Blackfeet*, 65 asserts that the Blackfoot became infected en route to Fort Union.

2. Catlin, *Letters*, 1:69-70.

3. Larpenteur, "Journals and Notes," 159.

4. I have found no reference about Jacob Halsey being carried into Fort Union on a stretcher, but in light of his condition, it seems logical.

5. Denig, *Indian Tribes*, xxiv.

6. Larpenteur, *Forty Years*, 142-3. In the fall of 1839, Pierre Chouteau Jr. finally dismissed the troublesome trader, ordering him to report in person to company headquarters. Using a pack dog to carry his kit, Alexander Harvey made a solo trek down the Missouri River during the winter, reaching St. Louis in early March 1840. Harvey's tenacity so impressed Chouteau, the managing partner canceled his discharge and reassigned him to Fort McKenzie.

7. Ewers, *The Blackfeet*, 65. DeVoto, *Across the Wide Missouri*, 290 makes no mention of a Blackfoot joining the *St. Peter's* below Fort Union. DeVoto says that Harvey's keelboat carried an "Indian girl." Perhaps the Blackfoot passenger and the Indian girl were the same person, or perhaps not. The record is silent.

8. Assuming the smallpox virus among the Santees and Yanktons went through a typical twelve-day incubation, the first cases of the disease would have appeared June 17.

9. Sunder, *Joshua Pilcher*, 123.

10. Ibid., 124-6; and Joshua Pilcher to William Clark, July 1, 1837, reprinted in "Spread of Smallpox," by Trimble, 65-6.

11. No one knows when the first Mandan became sick. July 1, 1837, marked the twelfth full day since the *St. Peter's* upstream arrival at Fort Clark. Although Chardon did not write about smallpox until July 14, when he recorded the first death, an initial illness or two may have appeared as early as July 2. On the other hand, if a Mandan did not inhale the virus until the steamboat's downriver stop at Fort Clark on June 28, the twelve-day incubation would have ended around dawn July 10, four days before Chardon noted the first fatality. Either scenario is feasible. Because the three contagious Arikara women and their children disembarked from the *St. Peter's* on June 19—during the upriver leg of the steamer's journey—I assume that at least one Mandan became infected that evening. Although the Mandan probably caught the virus from the Arikara passengers, it is possible the victim contracted the disease from a contagious white passenger or member of the crew, or from contact with a contaminated blanket or bolt of cloth. I assume the disease underwent a typical twelve-day incubation. If it had a longer or shorter incubation (anywhere from eight to fourteen days is possible), then my timetable is off. Only the days the *St. Peter's* landed at Fort Clark and the date of the first smallpox death are known. Because Chardon did not mention smallpox in his journal until July 14, when he recorded its first fatality, I reason there may have been

only one or two initial cases. Chardon probably did not know there was smallpox in Mitutanka Village until the initial death; otherwise, he would have written about it. He wrote about everything else. The first Mandan to become ill may have been the first to die, or the first to die could have been someone he (or she) infected.

12. Chardon described the first smallpox victim as a "young Mandan," which I take to mean a teenage boy, though it is possible the individual was a girl.

13. DeLand, abst., "Fort Tecumseh and Fort Pierre Journal and Letter Books," 9:104 describes how the Mandans abused their bodies while grieving over the death of a loved one. Although there is no record of the young man being shrouded in a raw buffalo hide, it was a common burial custom.

14. Larpenteur, "Journals and Notes," 159. DeVoto, *Across the Wide Missouri*, 287 reports these cases occurred fifteen days after Halsey reached Fort Union. Counting June 24 (the day the *St. Peter's* arrived) as day one, means that the disease finished its incubation on July 8; not counting June 24 makes the completion date July 9. In Jacob Halsey to Pratte, Chouteau & Company, November 2, 1837, reprinted in Chardon, *Journal*, 394-6, Halsey wrote that a second case of smallpox (presuming Halsey meant that his was the first) appeared at Fort Union "Fifteen days after I [he] was taken sick." Since Halsey was probably bedridden with the disease when the steamboat arrived, I assume he meant fifteen days after he landed. Dollar, "High Plains Smallpox Epidemic," 22 states that eighteen days after the *St. Peter's* reached Fort Union, two people at the trading post were prostrate with smallpox and one had died. For his reference, Dollar cites Larpenteur's narrative, *Forty Years a Fur Trader on the Upper Missouri*. My reading of Larpenteur, *Forty Years*, 109; and Larpenteur, "Journals and Notes," 159-61 does not jibe with Dollar's.

15. Dollar, "High Plains Smallpox Epidemic," 22 n. 26 says the book was most likely *The Modern Practice of Physic, Exhibiting the Character, Causes, Symptoms, Prognostics, Morbid Appearances, and Improved Method of Treating the Diseases of All Climates* (8th American Edition, New York, 1825) by Robert Thomas.

16. DeVoto, *Across the Wide Missouri*, 288; and Larpenteur, *Forty Years*, 110.

17. Larpenteur, "Journals and Notes," 160 states that "seven Assiniboine Squaws" and "some half breeds [*sic*]" (probably *engagés*) were living at the trading post at the time. On page 161, the text says that a total of seventeen people were inoculated. In contrast, Larpenteur, *Forty Years*, 109 says that about thirty Indian women were inoculated but makes no mention of their children. Page 111 tells of a small boy at the trading post who had the disease. Logic dictates that the women had children and that the clerks inoculated them, too. DeVoto, *Across the Wide Missouri*, 287-8 report that only seven women were inoculated and do not say if the women had any children who were also inoculated. DeVoto obviously took his numbers from Larpenteur's "Journals and Notes," which were written at the time the events took place. Larpenteur wrote *Forty Years* in 1871 and 1872, using his journal as a reference. Why he inflated the number of Indian women who were inoculated is unknown.

Karen A. Robertson

Fort Union replica, located on the site of the original trading post, about five miles upstream from the Missouri-Yellowstone confluence.

Karen A. Robertson

Bourgeois's house at Fort Union as it looked after a second story was added prior to 1852. The Fort Union site is managed by the National Park Service.

Karen A. Robertson

Indian trade room at Fort Union, showing the open trading wicket added in 1837 to protect traders because of Indian outrage about smallpox deaths.

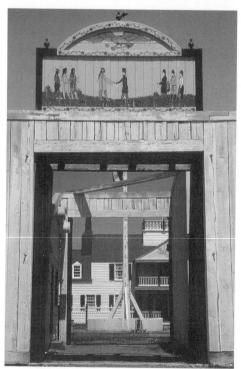

Karen A. Robertson

Main entrance to Fort Union. The painting depicting an Indian and white shaking hands was meant to show friendship to visiting tribes.

Chapter Six

The Village Tribes of the Upper Missouri

For generations before the first European trader came among them, the Arikaras, Mandans, and Hidatsas lived in a string of villages that stretched along the Missouri River Valley from the mouth of the White River to that of the Little Missouri (from just below modern Chamberlain, South Dakota, to the Fort Berthold Indian Reservation in North Dakota). During the Pleistocene, over one million years before the village tribes settled this region, the Missouri River had carved a 200- to 400-foot-deep trench with an alluvial floor that averaged three miles across. Cottonwood groves and willow coppices shared the lush bottomland with ash, burr oak, and box elder.

Above the Missouri floodplain existed an ocean of grass, an expanse so vast the mind struggled to hold it. Reaching from sunrise to sunset, the grass softened the prairie's contours, soothing the eye with green in early June and in late September, with golden brown. Little bluestem, wheat- and needlegrass, and side oats grama cloaked the prairie with a life-sustaining carpet. The land was home to prairie dogs and rattlesnakes, to badgers and wolves, burrowing owls and flycatchers, pronghorns, coyotes, and above all, buffalo and the Indians who depended on them for survival.

During winter when gripped by an arctic chill, the country became a barren wasteland, its swales leveled by drifting snow, its frozen profile stark and unforgiving. Blizzards caromed off the Rocky Mountains, then stampeded over the plains, plunging temperatures and killing all but the most hardy. January cold could freeze the sap in a cottonwood tree, bursting its bark like the snap of a gunshot. Blowing continually, the wind leaned against the land, slanting everything that was rooted down toward the sunrise and demanding of everything else, both man and beast, that it brace an extra bit of muscle just to stand its ground.

Spring on the upper Missouri plain was a season of birth and renewal. Violets and tasseled prairie smoke patterned the countryside in a mosaic of blue, purple, and red. Buffalo cows and pronghorns dropped their young, while wolves—some packs over 200 members strong—stalked the edges of the herds, culling the frail and infirm. Overhead, clouds piled up in cumulus castles that raced across the heavens. Warmed by the sun, ice that had impounded the Missouri since November exploded with the voice of thunder.

For the Mandans, Hidatsas, and Arikaras, the vernal thaw was the time to leave their wind-protected winter camps, which were nestled among the cottonwood groves alongside the river. From early spring until late autumn, the tribes occupied semipermanent towns that were perched on grassy benches located between the open prairie and the Missouri floodplain. These terraced villages afforded the tribes shelter from the scouring wind as well as from their Lakota enemies.

During the early eighteenth century, the Mandans, Hidatsas, and Arikaras had a combined population of around 19,000. Numbering about 7,500, the Arikaras lived in as many as thirty-two villages that were concentrated near the mouth of the Bad River (near modern Pierre, South Dakota) and reached as far south as the mouth of the White. The Mandans totaled about 6,000 people, who occupied between one and two dozen towns along a fifty-mile stretch of the Missouri above the Arikaras. Most of the tribe dwelled near the Missouri's confluence with the Heart River (near today's Bismarck, North Dakota). The Hidatsas, roughly 5,500 strong, resided in a collection of villages near the mouth of the Knife River (just above present-day Stanton, North Dakota).[1]

Unlike their nomadic, hunter-gatherer neighbors, such as the Assiniboines and Crows, the village tribes were primarily agrarian. Each spring after the snowmelt floods had drained from the bottomland, the village women planted their vegetables in the fertile soil. Using hoes made from buffalo or elk shoulderblades, female planters piled dirt atop their seeds instead of placing them in furrows. Mandan, Arikara, and Hidatsa gardens furnished half of the tribes' food. Although the women grew sunflowers, beans, pumpkins, and various other types of squashes, their principal crop was corn, each ear being about the length of a man's thumb. Adapted to the short, arid growing season of the upper Missouri, Indian corn reached maturity in nine or ten weeks.[2]

Indian girls had the chore of frightening hungry blackbirds and crows away from the crops, a duty they performed atop scaffolds that were positioned in the fields. To pass the time, the young women often sang ceremonial songs to the corn and squashes, encouraging their growth. Harvesting began in early August when the squashes were cut into long slices and dried. In late August, the Indians picked a quarter of their corn for roasting ears, celebrating the occasion with the Green Corn Ceremony. The balance was left to mature on the stalk so the dried kernels could be ground into meal. Corn meal was the central ingredient in a popular Indian dish known as four vegetables mixed, which also contained beans, ground sunflower seeds, and squash paste.[3]

The village women supplemented their garden produce with wild foods, such as Indian potatoes, prairie turnips—*pommes blanche* as they were called by the French—chokecherries, wild artichokes, currants, grapes, plums, and the fruit of the prickly pear cactus. Indians especially enjoyed a pudding made from prairie turnip flour that was flavored with buffaloberries. The Missouri River also contributed to the natives' palates, yielding mollusks, terrapins, sturgeon, and catfish. Tribal men hunted pronghorns, deer, elk, plains grizzlies, and buffalo, killing the animals not only for their meat but also for their hides, which the women tanned to make clothing and sleeping robes.[4]

In their summer villages, the Mandans, Hidatsas, and Arikaras lived in dome-shaped lodges, each of which held between ten and thirty members of an extended family. The lodges were supported by an internal skeleton of large wooden posts and beams that were covered with insulating overlays of matted willows and dry grass. A two- or three-foot-thick layer of earth formed the outer shell, which was glazed with clay to make it water-repellent. An earth-covered vestibule permitted passage into the lodge interior, while a hole in the roof allowed smoke to escape from a stone-curbed fire pit in the structure's center. Ranging from thirty to sixty or more feet across and having a useful life of about ten years, the houses were sturdy and could withstand the weight of several dozen Indian adults, who often enjoyed gathering atop the roofs to socialize, bask in the sun, or keep watch for approaching enemies. Family members slept in boxlike beds that ringed their lodge's circular walls. Each bed was screened for privacy with an elk or buffalo hide. A holding pen just off the entry allowed the senior male members of a family to stable their favorite horses inside during cold weather.[5]

Towns ranged in size from a dozen lodges to 150 or more and were laid out at random, often with so little space between adjacent structures that in order to get past, villagers had to walk in single file. In fair weather Mandan men advertised their war triumphs by erecting twenty-foot-tall poles outside their lodges. Scalps from Teton and Yankton Lakotas as well as other enemies adorned the tops of the poles, celebrating victory the same way regimental battle flags herald the laurels of European and American armies.

Most towns contained an open plaza—perhaps fifty paces in diameter—that was used for dances and celebrations, such as the Mandan's four-day *Okipa* ceremony and the buffalo-calling dance. Facing the plaza stood a medicine lodge, which the Mandans used for religious rituals. The Indians built their villages with an eye toward defense, positioning them near steep bluffs that would forestall an enemy assault. Log palisades, constructed from cottonwood trees and driftwood, provided cover for the inland sides that were vulnerable to attack.

To the European eye—and nose—the villages were filthy.

Yet, despite the presence of a horse or two and several dogs, lodge interiors were relatively clean; but outside was a different matter. Families often performed their toilet just beyond their lodge entrances. Nighttime excursions were exercises in caution if one was to avoid stepping in the wrong place. Rain transformed the village pathways into a quagmire of mud mixed with human, dog, and horse dung.[6]

Dogs, at times packs of them, vied with scampering children to see who could create the greatest uproar. Neighs from horses tethered outside their owners' homes added to the pandemonium, as did the shouts of friends and the banter of Indian men and women going about their daily chores. To the European ear it was chaos, but to the Mandans and other village tribes it was the normal bustle of everyday life.

Located just outside the Mandan villages were burial grounds, where the tribe laid its dead to rest. Rather than inter a deceased relative, the Mandans dressed him (or her) in his finest clothes, adorned his face with paint and his hair with bear grease, then wrapped him in a new buffalo robe together with his bow, arrows, knife, shield, tobacco, pipe, and other personal belongings. After binding the body with rawhide, the Mandans enclosed it again, using a raw buffalo hide that had been soaked in water so it would dry into a hard, protective shell. With the deceased now ready to enter the netherworld, the body was placed atop a willow scaffold where its flesh would eventually decay.

Family members came often to the burial ground—called the Village of the Dead—to morn a beloved relative. After the scaffold fell apart, the departed's bones were buried in the ground and his skull was displayed amid a sacred circle of skulls near the scaffold cemetery. Most villages had a couple of these memorials, some up to thirty feet across and containing over 100 skulls. At the center of each circle were two, three-foot mounds of dirt, one displaying the skull from a buffalo cow, the other from a bull. Each mound supported a medicine pole bedecked with feathers and other bric-a-brac that had been blessed with the power to keep the skulls safe.[7]

Tribal warfare often interrupted the tranquillity of the upper Missouri. Although the Lakotas regularly put aside their hostility in order to trade with the Mandans, Hidatsas, and Arikaras, the village tribes considered their eastern neighbor an enemy. They occasionally bickered among themselves and counted coup by stealing one another's horses, but they never allowed their internal squabbles to blur the fact that the Yankton, Santee, Yanktonai, and Teton Lakotas were their common foe.

Although the Lakotas outnumbered the combined population of the Mandans, Hidatsas, and Arikaras, until the late eighteenth century the three tribes were strong enough to hold their own against Lakota raids. Despite the inter-tribal warfare, a balance of power among the Indian nations kept the upper Missouri in a state of equilibrium, but with the coming of the white traders and smallpox, that stability began to erode.

After reaching the western end of the Great Lakes in the early 1600s, French *coureurs de bois* traded matchlock and then flintlock muskets to the Ojibwas, who lived around Lake Superior. Like the Mandans, Hidatsas, and Arikaras, the Ojibwas were also bitter enemies of the Lakotas.

In 1678 and 1679 during his sojourn to the Great Lakes, French explorer Daniel Greysolon Duluth negotiated peace between the Lakotas and Ojibwas, but it was short-lived. At the time, the Lakotas were a populous, woodland people, concentrated in the Mille Lacs country east of the Mississippi River (in central Minnesota), a region just west of the Ojibwas.

The Lakotas and Ojibwas periodically set down their lances and tomahawks in order to trade with their enemies, including each other. Being a spoke in the extended Mandan trading network, the Ojibwas brokered beaver pelts from the western tribes to the French, while bartering French trade goods to the western tribes. But these furs were a fraction of the total number of skins the Ojibwas traded; most came from their own hunters.

Still, this limited commerce gradually allowed the Ojibwas to acquire French guns. Because of the Ojibwas' proximity to the French traders, throughout the late seventeenth century and much of the eighteenth, the Ojibwas were better armed than the Lakotas. The Lakotas resisted as best as they could, substituting aggression and their greater numbers for a lack of firepower. In the late 1600s, the Ojibwas' superior weaponry heated the Mille Lacs region into a raging cauldron.

Unable to best their enemy's muskets, Lakota war parties sought to relieve their frustration by attacking the less numerous Cheyennes, Otoes, and Iowas, who lived along the Minnesota River. Yielding to the more numerous Lakotas, the Cheyennes migrated west to the Sheyenne River (in southeastern North Dakota), while the Otoes and Iowas fled to the country bordering Platte-Missouri confluence (in eastern Nebraska and western Iowa).[8] Once on the Sheyenne River, the Cheyennes slowly evolved from a horticulture economy to one based on buffalo. The acquisition of horses in the early 1740s allowed the tribe's hunters to range farther afield, speeding their transition to equestrian nomads. By allowing the Cheyennes to pursue buffalo and other game over vast distances, horses lessened the feast-or-famine nature of the tribe's nomadic existence.

Around 1750, a string of Ojibwa victories finally drove the Lakotas away from their Mille Lacs homeland. After moving to the western Minnesota prairie, the Teton, Yankton, and Yanktonai Lakotas began acquiring horses and quickly embraced the nomadic ways of the Cheyennes. By now the beaver population within the Ojibwas' territory was showing signs of over-trapping. Knowing that the Ojibwas were increasingly brokering pelts from the Lakotas, Cheyennes, and Missouri River tribes, the French sought to bypass the Ojibwas and open trade directly with their western rivals. Wanting to protect their commerce with the French, the Ojibwas added the Cheyennes to their list of enemies and stepped up their attacks on the Lakotas.

Sometime before 1770,[9] Ojibwa warriors sacked the Cheyenne village on the Sheyenne River. Lacking the Ojibwas' trade guns, the Cheyennes again abandoned their homes and retreated to the Cheyenne River country east of the Black Hills (in South Dakota). The Santee Lakotas also recoiled from the increased Ojibwa onslaught, moving south to the Minnesota River, whereas the Yanktonai Lakotas migrated west to the upper Red River (in southeast North Dakota). Meanwhile, the

Yankton and Teton Lakotas drifted farther onto the plains and closer to the Missouri.

Unable to defeat the Ojibwas, the Lakotas intensified raids against the village tribes, especially the Arikaras and Mandans. These tribes responded in kind and managed to hold the Tetons and Yanktons south of the White River. By 1779, the Tetons had pushed west of the Missouri (into southwestern South Dakota and northwestern Nebraska), while the Yanktons had settled southeast of the Missouri-White River confluence (in southeastern South Dakota).[10]

During the early 1780s, smallpox ravaged the upper Missouri, disrupting the inter-tribal trading network and shattering the village cultures. The once powerful Mandans saw their numbers reduced by between fifty and eighty percent. No longer having enough warriors to defend themselves against raids by the Lakotas, the Mandans abandoned their lodges near the Heart River and moved sixty-some miles up the Missouri, settling beside their Hidatsa allies just below the mouth of the Knife. With the Mandans no longer blocking the Missouri River around its confluence with the Heart, the Santees migrated west and joined their nomadic Teton and Yankton cousins by adopting a horse and buffalo culture.[11]

Severely reduced by smallpox, the Arikaras were also forced to consolidate in order to withstand the Lakota invasion. In 1794, the Arikaras abandoned their villages around the mouth of the Bad River, eventually resettling farther north. From over two dozen towns a generation earlier, the tribe squeezed into two that were about a mile apart at the confluence of the Missouri and Grand rivers.[12]

As competing chiefs vied to retain their authority, Arikara tribal structure often splintered into bickering factions. When tensions between the various family-oriented clans reached an impasse, weaker chiefs left with their kinsmen and established new villages. While trading with the tribe during the winter of 1795 through 1796, Jean Baptiste Truteau watched one Arikara chief take his followers to live beside the Mandans and another move in with the Pawnees.[13]

In less than two years, the smallpox scourge of the early 1780s had destroyed the vitality and wealth of the village tribes. Once commercial rulers of the upper Missouri, the Mandans, Hidatsas, and Arikaras fell into disarray, their leaders dead, their vast trading network in shambles, their spirit numb with grief, and their towns vulnerable to the Lakotas. The survivors—their faces hideously scarred—could now do nothing but dream of their former glory as they huddled together for safety and prayed to their gods for help.

Chapter six notes

[1.] Lehmer, *Selected Writings*, 100-01, 106-07; and Meyer, *Village Indians*, 8-10, 12-14, 21. The population estimates come from Lehmer. Meyer gives the three tribes a total of 25,000 individuals. Citing the work of Alfred W. Bowers, Taylor, "Sociocultural Effects," 65 puts the Arikaras at 24,000 people and the combined Mandans and Hidatsas at 9,000. According to Lehmer, archeologists have discovered at least seventy-five village sites in the upper Missouri Valley that date from 1700 until 1775. The Journal of Jean Baptiste Truteau—a former schoolmaster who turned fur trader—reports that before 1780, the Arikaras occupied thirty-two villages. The typical village contained thirty-five lodges (Lehmer again); each lodge held about ten family members, which gave the average village 350 residents. Applying these ratios to the Mandan population indicates the tribe probably had about seventeen villages, but this is at odds with Meyer, who puts the number between five and nine. In reality, some villages had as few as a dozen lodges, while others had ten times that many. Some lodges housed ten people, whereas others contained thirty or forty. Given the flux of tribal life and the continual combining and breaking apart of various bands, it is impossible to determine with certainty how many villages the three tribes occupied in any given season during the first three-quarters of the eighteenth century.

[2.] Unlike Indian corn of the early 1700s, today's highbred corn has a growing cycle in excess of twenty-one weeks. At thirty-six to fifty inches tall, Indian cornstalks would have looked stunted alongside their modern counterpart, but the forerunner's ability to withstand frost and drought puts designer corn to shame; for more, see Denig, *Indian Tribes*, 44-5; and Meyer, *Village Indians*, 3.

[3.] Meyer, *Village Indians*, 64, 66.

[4.] Lehmer, *Selected Writings*, 97; and Meyer, *Village Indians*, 2.

[5.] Catlin, *Letters*, 1:81-3; Coues, ed., *Alexander Henry*, 1:338-40; and Meyer, *Village Indians*, 60-2.

[6.] Coues, ed., *Alexander Henry*, 1:351; and Dollar, "High Plains Smallpox Epidemic," 26.

[7.] Catlin, *Letters*, 1:89-90.

[8.] Jablow, *Cheyenne*, 4-6.

[9.] See ibid., 8-10 for a discussion of the exact year.

[10.] Bernard DeVoto, *The Course of Empire* (Boston: Houghton Mifflin, 1952), 366; and Josephy, *Indian Heritage*, 116-19.

[11.] DeVoto, *Course of Empire*, 306-7; and Meyer, *Village Indians*, 27.

[12.] Lehmer, *Selected Writings*, 100-01; and A. P. Nasatir, ed., *Before Lewis and Clark: Documents Illustrating the History of the Missouri 1785-1804*, 2 vols. (St. Louis: Historical Documents Foundation, 1952; Lincoln: University of Nebraska Press, Bison Book Edition, 1990), 1:299.

[13.] Meyer, *Village Indians*, 31; and Nasatir, ed., *Before Lewis and Clark*, 1:299. The Arikaras were related to the Pawnees, having broken away from them generations earlier.

Chapter Seven

Mid Summer 1837

On the night of July 16, a booming thunderstorm disrupted sleep at Fort Clark and Mitutanka Village. Lightening zigzagged across the black sky, while sheets of rain pummeled the darkened plain. The storm ended before daylight, leaving behind the sweet smell of wet grass. By mid-morning, the sun and a strengthening southwest wind promised to evaporate evidence of the previous night's rainfall.

Taking advantage of the fair weather, Francis Chardon sent *engagés* to cut hay. The long-stem prairie grasses made a nourishing fodder during the winter when snow prevented the fort's stock from grazing. Nothing seemed able to disrupt the peace of the splendid July day until Chardon penned a final entry in his journal, noting that another member of Mitutanka Village had come down with smallpox.

The next morning, dense smoke from prairie fires hid the distant hills. The acrid smell of burning grass permeated the air, watering eyes and choking lungs. If a Yankton war party wanted cover for a horse raid, it could ask for none better. At dawn the following day, Chardon rode across the plain, searching for buffalo. For the past week, his hunters had brought in no fresh meat, forcing his thirty-man command onto short rations. That evening the *bourgeois* returned to Fort Clark empty-handed. His luck had been as bad as that of his hunters. He had ridden all day without seeing so much as a scrawny calf.

On Thursday, July 20, Baptiste Leclair and William May— both seasoned traders and trappers—arrived at Fort Clark from Fort Pierre, reporting that smallpox had broken out among the Lakotas. The same day, the Arikara war party that had departed Mitutanka Village two weeks earlier came back without a victory. Having no Yankton scalps to show for their effort, the warriors were in an angry mood.

The following afternoon, *engagés* who had been guarding the fort's horses while they grazed on the prairie galloped to the trading post nearly frightened out of their wits. They had stumbled across a Lakota raiding party that was easing its hunger amid one of the Mandan cornfields. The unripened ears were still several weeks shy of harvest and probably provided meager nourishment, but an empty stomach usually demands only to be full. From now on, anyone—white, mixed-blood, Mandan, Hidatsa, or Arikara—who dared ride the prairie alone risked losing his hair.

Earlier in the day, Chardon had sent men to finish cutting hay and haul it to the fort. Given the presence of the Lakotas, he felt greatly relieved when the work detail safely returned with four cart-loads. Meanwhile, the Indians in residence at Mitutanka Village sent word to their tribal hunting camp, begging for food. Game was so scarce, the villagers were in danger of starving. As July ended its third week, the smallpox continued spreading. Every day saw the *Variola* virus begin incubating within a new set of Mandan hosts.

On July 25, a handful of young Mandan warriors returned to Mitutanka Village from the tribe's hunting camp. Each of them carried meat for their elderly fathers and mothers who had remained behind. Ominously, the young men reported that the *rotting face* had spread to their camp. Those who were able to travel were expected to arrive at Mitutanka Village the following day, bringing with them a large supply of dried meat. Despite the presence of smallpox, their buffalo hunt had gone well.

The next day, the Mandan and Arikara hunters and their families who were not too sick to ride left their encampment

George Catlin painting, Smithsonian American Art Museum: Gift of Mrs. Joseph Harrison, Jr.
Mah-to-toh-pa (Four Bears) was a Mandan warrior chief who was a longtime
friend of whites until he and his people were struck down by smallpox.

and returned to their village beside Fort Clark. Although the
Indians had a huge load of meat, their mood was somber. In
addition to the lower ranking members of their party who had
taken ill, the renowned Mandan chief, Four Bears, had also contracted smallpox and seemingly lost his mind. Reacting like a

mad man, he had fled from the hunting camp and vanished on the prairie.[1] Many of his tribesmen feared he would die.

That afternoon, Four Bears willed strength into his aching muscles and reason into his fever-racked brain. Mustering his courage and stamina, he turned his horse toward Mitutanka Village and home. At his arrival, his people gathered around, visibly expressing their joy. But their euphoria was short-lived. During the evening, a party of Mandans rode in from Ruhptare. Mitutanka's smaller, sister village now too had smallpox, and a number of people had already died. The next day, *Variola major* claimed the lives of four Mandans at Mitutanka Village. All afternoon and into the night, the mournful wail of Mandan women drifted from the earthen town toward Fort Clark. The dying had now begun in earnest.

Friday, July 28, dawned to rain. All morning, thick, gray clouds overhung the prairie, adding to the gloom of death. In Mitutanka Village, Four Bears sat in his lodge, his body consumed by fever. The skin on his cheeks and arms had elevated into pus-filled blisters, transforming his noble visage into something horrible and rotten. One by one his wives and children had sickened and died before his eyes. His heart breaking, he realized that he did not have the strength to see to their proper burial. They would have to enter the spirit world without the customary shrouds of raw buffalo hides. Legend says that Four Bears was unable to control his grief, that he wandered alone from his lodge to a nearby hill and prepared to die. To purify his soul, he shunned all food, determined to make his final offering to the Mandan gods a life-ending fast.

In a tragic, but implausible irony, the smallpox had so far primarily attacked the Mandans. Other than a few isolated cases, the Arikaras had yet to become infected, despite living at Mitutanka Village. The Hidatsas were also unaffected, making the Mandans wonder if there was some evil magic at work. The Arikaras thought so, too. Because the traders at Fort Clark were also free of the disease, the tribes reasoned that the whites had employed sorcery to attack the Mandans while keeping everyone else well. Blaming the fur company for the epidemic, the Mandans threatened to wipe out Chardon and the other men at the trading post. Alarmed that the Mandans would carry through on their threats—and perhaps break the spell that was protecting the Arikaras and Hidatsas—Arikara chiefs warned the Mandans that if they killed a single white man, the Arikaras would annihilate their entire tribe.

Francis Chardon took the Mandans' anger seriously, especially when a young Mandan warrior slipped inside the stockade with a musket hidden beneath his robe. Determined to kill the *bourgeois* in revenge for the death of his family, the Indian waited for Chardon to come to the courtyard. Some minutes later, the *bourgeois* opened a door to one of the storerooms, preparing to step outside. As the Mandan raised his gun to his shoulder, a hunter named Mitchel snatched the weapon from his hands and took him into custody. Mitchel turned the young man over to two other Indians—probably Arikaras—who escorted him back to Mitutanka Village. Although Chardon had escaped harm, the episode so unnerved him, he broke out 100 muskets and 1,000 pounds of gunpowder, intending to arm the Arikaras in case the Mandans attacked en masse. As an extra precaution, he urged all post personnel to remain within the fort. Individual Mandans continued making isolated threats, though the tribe as a whole was too wary of the Arikaras to start a war.

Later that afternoon, an Arikara raiding party that had departed on July 7 returned, driving five horses it had captured from the Lakotas. The Arikaras had stolen the animals from a Lakota family they found camping in a single tipi on the Bad River.[2] Before running off the stock, the Arikaras had riddled the Lakotas' tipi with musketballs. Although they boasted that their lead must have killed the occupants, they had no scalps with which to prove their claim. It was unusual for the Arikaras to have found a Lakota family so defenseless. Knowing the risk of attack, Lakotas usually camped in groups for mutual safety. One thing only could have prompted this family to shun the protection of its band—fear of the *rotting face*.

The evening following the Arikaras' return, a group of Mandans put aside their anger and staged a dance outside Fort Clark's palisades. With more of their number succumbing to smallpox by the day, the Mandans had adopted a sad fatalism. Some of the revelers told the whites—those who were bold

enough to venture outside the fort—that since they were going
to die of the *rotting face* anyway, they may as well die dancing.
The flippant response probably masked a more somber reason
for their entertainment. The Mandans no doubt viewed the
dance as a religious rite, an offering to the spirits, beseeching
them to save the tribe from a horrible death.[3] But the dancing
did not help. During the night, more Mandans died.

The next day, two Hidatsas came to Fort Clark from their
tribe's main hunting camp a number of miles away, reporting
that no one there had yet caught the disease. Other Hidatsas
were not so lucky. A small band had moved south a few months
earlier to hunt with some Arikaras, and it had now contracted
the virus. Nearly a dozen of its members were dead—including
two revered Hidatsa chiefs.[4]

July 30 found Four Bears again within Mitutanka Village,
his face a ripened mass of oozing sores. Perhaps the legend is
true, and he had returned from his hillside fast to die among his
people. Then again, maybe he had never undertaken the lonely
vigil. Whatever the truth, Four Bears knew he was dying. At
last he agreed with his tribe: The *rotting face* had come from the
whites.

All his life Four Bears had befriended the white traders.
Never had he raised his hand against them. Instead, he had fed
them when they were starving. He had always served as their
protector. And how had he been repaid? The white man's disease had murdered his family. It had slain his friends. And
unless it was checked, it would surely annihilate his tribe.
Never again would he call a white man friend. From this day
forward, all whites would be his mortal enemy. From now on,
Four Bears considered whites to be nothing but "black-hearted
dogs."

Legend says that Four Bears donned his finest war shirt and
leggings, that he put on his heavy necklace made from the claws
of a giant grizzly. If so, he no doubt crowned his head with his
buffalo-horn headdress and its cascade of feathers. He probably
armed himself with his bow and a quiver of arrows and perhaps
a lance. He may also have stepped into his shield's carrying
strap and pulled it up over his shoulder, then picked up the war
club that had earned him so many honors. Mustering his failing

strength, he left his lodge and marched to the village center. Speaking with a resonant voice that had often rallied the Mandans to war, Four Bears renounced his friendship with the white race. Believing that he would carry his rotting sores to his afterlife, he is said to have lamented that "even the Wolves will shrink with horror at seeing Me."

Calling on his warriors to avenge the Mandans who had died, Four Bears promised to do his part.[5] Tradition claims that after the chief finished his speech, he returned to his lodge. His body weary from the exertion, Four Bears lay beside his deceased wives and children, perhaps hoping to regain his strength so he could avenge his people. But the great Four Bears was never able to carry out his threat. Within a few hours, the *rotting face* claimed his earthly body, releasing his spirit to join those of his dead family and friends.[6]

As July ended, the Mandans were dying faster than the rats at Fort Clark. For the entire month, Chardon had killed only sixty-one.

During the last week of July while Four Bears was living out his final days, upriver at Fort Union Jacob Halsey gradually recovered from his bout of smallpox. His pustules had dried into scabs, which were now peeling. As the scabs fell away, his skin revealed a spiraling pattern of deep-pitted scars. Because of his previous vaccination, Halsey's case had been milder than most. Nevertheless, he would carry his pockmarks to the grave.

Elsewhere within the trading post, *Variola major* had completed its incubation within those who had been inoculated with Halsey's pus.[7] Although the inoculated *engagés* became sick, their conditions were less severe than those of the treated Indian women and their children.

Inside their holding cell, the women and their mixed-blood offspring writhed amid their blankets and robes. Blinding headaches, stabbing pains in the lower back, aching muscles, and temperatures that rocketed past 100 degrees blurred their reality into a hallucinogenic nightmare. Despite the summer heat, their bodies shivered with chills one moment, then the next, burned as if they had been submerged in a lake of fire. Desperate to cool their feverish skin, the Indians unconsciously tore at their tunics and dresses, shredding them with their bare hands. Unable to see to their toilet, the women and children fouled their clothing and blankets, then helplessly tossed and turned in their own filth. A din of misery emanated from the makeshift prison, draping the fort with a doleful pall.

As the disease progressed, rashes spread across the victims' cheeks and forearms, then migrated to their stomachs, breasts, backs, and thighs. Pain blurred day into night as the darkened rashes slowly elevated into hard boils that filled with a watery fluid before changing to pus. One by one the women—including Charles Larpenteur's wife—and children began to die.

Some drowned in their own gore as hacking coughs ruptured their blistered tracheas. Others hemorrhaged to death, the virus having eaten away the lining of their internal organs. Those who hung onto life saw their pustules ripen and split into oozing sores. Soon maggots infested the open wounds, eating the putrefied flesh. Within the fort, clerks, traders, and other post personnel shielded their noses with handkerchiefs or vials of camphor. But nothing blocked the sickening smell. Three hundred yards away from the palisades, the nauseous stench still impregnated the air.[8]

In early August, three dozen Assiniboine warriors approached the fort, led by Chief Co-han. Banging on the main gate, the Indians demanded to be let inside. The traders warned them about the epidemic, but the warriors suspected a trick. Brandishing their muskets and bows, they clamored for whiskey, ordering the whites to open the trade room before they opened it themselves. Hoping to dissuade them, one of the traders went to the makeshift jail and brought out a young, mixed-blood boy whose face was encrusted with scab. Holding the child atop the stockade, the trader told the warriors to leave or they would suffer the same fate. The ploy worked. The Assiniboines departed without their liquor, but they did not escape the *rotting face*. Sometime later, word reached Fort Union that over half the band had died.[9]

The record is unclear on how the Assiniboines first contracted smallpox, but contract it they did. Maybe Co-han's troop encountered a band of contagious Mandans or Arikaras. More likely, if the Assiniboines did not catch the disease from other infected Indians, they may have inhaled the virus by unearthing the bodies of the Fort Union dead.[10]

One story attributes their infection to a prank by Assiniboine warriors. According to the account, a few Indians slipped into Fort Union's horse corrals and tried stampeding the herd. Some men from the post foiled the attempt, but not before the Assiniboines made off with two head. The whites hastily formed a posse and gave chase, quickly surrounding the thieves and recovering the stolen horses. Figuring that humiliation was a sufficient punishment, the whites turned the warriors loose, sending them back to their tribe on foot. But the Assiniboines did not return home empty-handed. The day after the recovery, a mixed-blood member of the posse developed smallpox, which he may have passed to the Assiniboines.[11]

As August wore on, the inoculees within Fort Union who had not died began to recover. Meanwhile, among the nomadic Assiniboines on both sides of the forty-ninth parallel, the *Variola* virus ignited a full-blown epidemic. Indians seeking medical aid from the American traders were sent to deserted Fort William, which several years earlier had been dismantled and rebuilt adjacent to Fort Union.

Fort William had originally been constructed across from the mouth of the Yellowstone in 1833 by the trading firm of William Sublette and Robert Campbell. Unable to compete with the American Fur Company, Sublette & Campbell sold out to it in early 1834. Soon after the transfer, *engagés* removed Fort William's pickets, using them to construct horse corrals at Fort Union. Fort William's buildings were also taken down and re-erected alongside the American Fur Company post. Two years later, fire destroyed a number of Fort William's structures. During the smallpox epidemic of 1837, those rooms that remained were converted into a pesthouse for the Assiniboines.

The makeshift hospital had no doctor. A few old Assiniboine women who had survived the smallpox epidemic of 1801 and 1802 served as nurses, though their care did little to ease the suffering. Compounding the agony of the sick Assiniboines, Charles Larpenteur and Edwin Denig—after Denig had recovered from his own mild bout of smallpox—offered them the white world's medical remedies. To those who were burning with fever, their skin a mass of oozing sores, the clerks gave strong purgatives, adding diarrhea to the Indians' other miseries. When that did nothing to stem the epidemic, Larpenteur and Denig tried bleeding their patients. Still, the smallpox refused to quit. Many of the Indians died before their rashes ever formed pustules. Denig reported that some victims bled from their mouths and ears, a symptom of *Variola hemorrhagica,* the most deadly form of the disease.[12]

The *engagé* John Brazeau was charged with disposing of the dead. Overwhelmed by the numbers, he gave up digging graves and piled the bodies on the prairie or dumped them in the Missouri River. Seeing him every morning, Larpenteur usually asked how many had died during the night. Seemingly amused by his work, Brazeau would typically reply, "Only three, sir; but, according to appearances in the hospital, I think I shall have a full load to-morrow [*sic*] or next day."[13]

Just outside Fort Union, an Assiniboine warrior named Little Dog watched the virus rot the skin of his favorite child, transforming his once-handsome face into a clot of putrid blisters. For several days, the lad battled for his life, ultimately surrendering to death. Distraught with grief, Little Dog lost his will to live. Determined to join his son in the land of the spirits, the warrior proposed to his wife that they and their other children should commit suicide despite none of them being sick. Little Dog argued that if they waited until the pestilence killed them, they would go to the netherworld with rotting faces, an appearance they would wear for eternity. Agreeing, the woman asked her husband to take her life before those of their two remaining children. She had watched her firstborn die and did not have the heart to witness the deaths of her other offspring.

Taking his musket, powderhorn, and bullet pouch, Little Dog went among his horses, shooting them one by one. Next he killed his dogs. While his wife sang her death song, the warrior aimed his gun at her breast and squeezed the trigger. His eyes overflowing with tears, he pulled his knife from his belt and slit the throats of his two young children. His family now dead, Little Dog recharged his musket and placed its muzzle between his teeth. Hopeful that his spirit life would be happier than the one he was leaving, he pressed the trigger and blew out the back of his head.[14]

By Edwin Denig's estimate, the smallpox epidemic of 1837 and 1838 claimed 600 of 1,000 Assiniboine lodges. Of those Assiniboines who survived, half owed their lives to the cowpox vaccine that the Hudson's Bay Company had administered to them a few years earlier.[15] Yet, the immunized Indians were not spared the disease's worst horror. In countless tipis, vaccinated Assiniboine mothers and fathers wept while the *rotting face* consumed their unvaccinated sons and daughters.

By early August, the smallpox at Mitutanka Village no longer confined itself to the Mandans. The Arikaras now too were sick. On Saturday, the fifth, word reached Fort Clark that the virus had also attacked a small Hidatsa hunting camp near Turtle Mountain. Many in the band were already dead.

August 7 saw six more Mitutanka villagers die. With increasing numbers of Mandans and Arikaras coming down with the disease, several Arikara families abandoned the town, deeming they would be safer living in isolation on the prairie. By the following day, two-thirds of the Mitutanka Mandans were ill. Across the Missouri, smallpox was raging among the Mandans at Ruhptare Village, where several Indians had already perished.

At numerous times over the years, Chardon had written about his dislike of the Mandans. But at last, their deaths and anguish softened his heart. In a rare display of well-intentioned—though misguided—charity, the *bourgeois* visited the sick at Mitutanka Village, dispensing large doses of Epsom salts. The magnesium purgative did nothing to relieve the smallpox, but merely added stomach cramps and diarrhea to the malady's other miseries. Two days after Chardon's visit, all the Arikaras still living at Mitutanka Village who were fit enough to travel moved down the Missouri, hoping to distance themselves from the *rotting face*. In addition, Mandans who were not yet ill talked about relocating across the Missouri. Meantime, the daily death toll had climbed from six to eight, to ten, and now fifteen.

From the combined Hidatsa and Arikara hunting band that

had caught the disease late the previous month, news filtered down to Fort Clark that it had lost many members, including several chiefs. After hearing that the Indians blamed him personally for their plight, Chardon dispatched Toussaint Charbonneau to the Knife River with a present of tobacco and "a bag full of good talk." Because Charbonneau had lived among the Hidatsas for a major part of his life, he seemed the perfect ambassador. Later that day, those Mandans at Mitutanka Village who could still ride abandoned their feverish loved ones and forded the Missouri, planning to camp away from the disease. Within the town, the death toll continued escalating, rising so rapidly that Chardon could no longer keep count.

On August 12, word reached Fort Clark that a seventy-man war party of Hidatsas and Arikaras had been defeated by the Saones, a division of the Teton Lakotas.[16] Many of the Hidatsas and Arikaras had been killed. Noting the event in his journal, Chardon reverted to his true Indian-hating form, writing that the Saones had made "quicker work" of the warriors than smallpox would have done.

The next day, an elderly Mandan stood outside the trading post gate, urging his tribe to avenge the smallpox deaths by killing the traders. He had watched his entire family—fourteen people—die, and blamed the whites for bringing the *rotting face* to the upper Missouri. Although the other Mandans undoubtedly sympathized with him, none stepped forward to do his bidding. Eventually, the wrinkled old warrior wandered back to Mitutanka Village, unaware that the pestilence had finally spread to Fort Clark. Several employees within the trading post were now running high fevers.

That night Charbonneau returned from the Knife River, reporting that the Hidatsas were not vengeful toward the whites. To the contrary, they blamed the Arikaras for fomenting trouble. As far as Charbonneau knew, the majority of Hidatsas were still camped farther up the Missouri, where by all accounts, they remained disease-free.[17]

With the smallpox now infecting the Arikaras, they added their threats to those of the Mandans. Nearly every morning a warrior approached Fort Clark's main entrance, brandishing his musket and screaming that the whites had murdered his family with the *rotting face.* Wanting revenge, each of them declared war on the traders, promising to kill any who ventured beyond the palisades. Fearing for his life, Chardon hid within the stockade and prepared the garrison to repel an attack. Any working parties that had to leave the post went heavily armed.

One day a group of Mandan chiefs demanded a parley with Chardon. The *bourgeois* received them in the trade room, where he sat at a small table, his arms resting on its top. Resurrecting a charge they had used before, the Mandans accused Chardon of destroying their tribe with magic. In the midst of the tirade, a dove flew through the open doorway and lit on one of Chardon's outstretched arms. Perhaps it was seeking shelter from a pursuing hawk. Maybe the incident was chance. In any case, the peaceful bird perched on Chardon's arm for nearly a minute as the Indians watched with their mouths agape, too startled to speak. After the dove flew away, the Mandans asked the *bourgeois* why it had come to him. Surely, such a strange occurrence was an omen.

Seeing an opportunity to turn the Indians' superstition to his advantage, Chardon explained that the dove had been sent by his white friends to learn if the Mandans had taken his scalp. As the chiefs listened intently, Chardon told them that he had informed the dove that the Mandans were his brothers, that they would never harm him, and that among them he would always be safe. Believing that the *bourgeois* possessed spiritual power, the Indians filed out of the fort, vowing never again to threaten Chardon's life.[18] Unfortunately for the Mandans, Chardon's power was an illusion. He had no magical potion that would stem the terrible epidemic. The smallpox virus continued to assail the Mandans with unabated ferocity.

Despite the dove and the promise of the chiefs to leave Chardon in peace, on August 15, other Mandans carried a war pipe to the main Hidatsa village on the Knife River, seeking to enlist their allies in an all-out battle against the white traders. Most of the Hidatsas were still at their hunting camps many miles north, but a number of them had recently returned to the Knife.[19]

Turning their backs on the Mandan's pipe, the Hidatsas refused to make war on Fort Clark. Although they were sorry for the suffering of their Mandan friends, the Hidatsas held no animus toward the whites. Perhaps if the smallpox was killing Hidatsas as it was the Mandans, the Hidatsas would have felt differently, but other than a few fatalities among a couple of smaller, outlying bands, the tribe had so far been spared. The Hidatsas saw no reason to anger the spirits by attacking the whites. Their entreaty rejected, the Mandans packed away the war pipe and returned to their homes. By now the Hidatsas had heard enough stories about the *rotting face* to put them on guard. Reasoning that the Mitutanka villagers could be under some sort of evil spell, the Hidatsas' "tribal police" quarantined their Knife River village, refusing to allow any more Mandans or Arikaras to enter.[20]

The same day the Hidatsas rejected the Mandan's call for revenge, the combined Arikara and Mandan war party that had left Mitutanka Village the last week of June returned with seven Lakota scalps. The Lakotas had been camped in two lodges at the mouth of the White River when the Mandans and Arikaras swept in, massacring not only the men, but also the Lakota women and children. Living in such isolation was dangerous, as these two families learned, but they had probably been forced to it in order to escape the smallpox epidemic that was raging around Fort Kiowa and Fort Pierre.

The Mandans and Arikaras may have lifted their enemies' hair, but the dead Lakotas ultimately had their revenge. At least one of them had been sick with smallpox when the war party struck. While the victors headed home with their grisly trophies, the *Variola* virus began to incubate inside several of their bodies. As they neared the Grand River, a number of the warriors fell prey to the high fever, headache, and back pain that marked the onset of the *rotting face*.

At Mitutanka Village the death count continued to accelerate. With so many of the Mandans and Arikaras sick, burial customs were forgotten, and the dead were left to rot. Dogs and rats fed on the corpses as though they were buffalo that had been drowned during the Missouri's spring thaw. The smell of decay draped the Mandan town and neighboring countryside, spreading like a putrefied fog until it permeated every molecule of air. At Fort Clark the stench crept into the storerooms and living quarters, nauseating all except those with stomachs of cast iron.

In mid August, a young Arikara warrior began hanging around outside the trading post, intent on killing Chardon in retaliation for the smallpox. On the morning of August 17, the Indian sat beside the fur press in front of the main gate with his musket cocked, hoping Chardon would present himself as a target.

Thinking he could defuse the young man's anger, a Dutch *engagé* named John Cliver tried talking him into a change of heart, but Cliver's words fell on deaf ears. After a few minutes, Cliver gave up and headed for the stockade. As the Dutchman approached the gate, the warrior raised his musket and fired. The ball shattered Cliver's spine, killing him instantly. As fort personnel rushed to Cliver's side, the Arikara took off at a run. Vowing to avenge the murder, a few of Cliver's friends dashed after the fleeing warrior, overtaking him near a small stream. While the Arikara sang his death song, Antoine Garreau, a French-Arikara interpreter, shot him, tumbling him backwards to the ground. Seeing that the wound was not fatal, Garreau rushed forward with his knife and plunged it in the Arikara's belly, gutting him like a fish.

That afternoon the young warrior's friends cried for revenge. Chardon and the other men of Fort Clark barricaded themselves inside the stockade, wondering if the Arikaras would attack. Although tensions remained high, none of the tribe appeared willing to fire the first shot.

As evening approached, the dead Indian's mother came to the fort, weeping and begging for the traders to put her out of her misery. Vowing to send her to the spirit world with her son, Garreau pulled his hatchet and prepared to split the old woman's skull. As the interpreter raised his arm to strike, his compatriots grabbed him and wrestled him back inside the palisades. Saved from joining her dead son, the old woman headed to her lodge to continue her mourning.

The next day, Chardon and his command cowered within their cottonwood fortress like prisoners under the sentence of death. Attempting to bolster his nerve, the *bourgeois* repeatedly dipped into his whiskey stock as he worried about what the brothers of the murdered Arikara would do when they returned from hunting buffalo. With each glass, Chardon's gloom deepened. Adding to his apprehension, a few members of the garrison vowed to quit the fur company and flee the upper Missouri, lest the Arikaras carry through on their threats. Whether the men would stay or not was anyone's guess.

Desperate to keep the Hidatsas on friendly terms, Chardon asked Toussaint Charbonneau to visit the quarantined Hidatsa village on the Knife River and ask the tribal police to send a messenger, begging the Indians in the main hunting camp to stay where they were. The *bourgeois* hoped that between the ten-pound gift of tobacco he was sending and Charbonneau's speechifying, the Hidatsas would refrain from taking sides with the Arikaras. Afraid to travel during the daylight, Charbonneau departed Fort Clark after nightfall, August 18, accompanied by his Hidatsa wife. No one suspected that the *Variola* virus was incubating within the woman's lungs. In less than two weeks, she would be her most infectious.[21] The Hidatsas' quarantine was about to be rent asunder.

Chapter seven notes

1. Chardon's journal entry for July 26 (Chardon, *Journal*, 123) states that Four Bears "has caught the small pox [*sic*], and got crazy and has disappeared from camp—he arrived here in the afternoon." I interpret "camp" to mean the hunting camp and "here" to mean Mitutanka Village, which sat beside Fort Clark—Chardon's location when he recorded the day's events in his journal. Catlin, *Letters*, 2:258 states that Four Bears left Mitutanka Village after his family had perished, intending to starve to death. According to Catlin, Four Bears fasted six days, then returned to his lodge where he lay beside his dead wife and children, passing away three days later. DeVoto, *Across the Wide Missouri*, 282 recounts Catlin's version, then dismisses it as fiction. Neither Catlin nor DeVoto puts Four Bears at the hunting camp. Although my account of Four Bears's final days relies on Francis Chardon's *Journal* and, to a lesser degree, DeVoto, the facts concerning the death of this great Mandan chief have long since evolved into legend.

2. Although Chardon called the river the Little Missouri (Chardon, *Journal*, 123), he was probably referring to the Bad River. See Chapter 3, endnote 15.

3. Meyer, *Village Indians*, 93.

4. David L. Ferch, "Fighting the Smallpox Epidemic of 1837-38: The Response of the American Fur Company Traders," parts 1 and 2, *The Museum of the Fur Trade Quarterly* 19, no. 4 (winter 1983): 5 says that this band of Hidatsas had joined the Arikaras for a spring buffalo hunt.

5. Dollar, "High Plains Smallpox Epidemic," 30-2 make a strong argument that the speech attributed to Four Bears—the one printed in the front of this book—was fiction, a product, in Dollar's words, "of someone's fertile imagination." Annie Heloise Abel, who edited *Chardon's Journal*, discovered the written speech with the manuscript and inserted it after the entry for July 31, 1837; see Chardon, *Journal*, 124-5, 316 n. 486. By placing the speech at this point in the *Journal*, Abel indirectly credited Chardon as its transcriber. Dr. Abel surely realized that readers would assume Chardon had penned the words, an assumption Clyde Dollar disputes. There are actually three questions that must be considered: Did Four Bears give the speech? If so and given that Four Bears would have been speaking in Mandan, is the written speech a correct translation? And was Chardon or someone else the transcriber? For my part, I agree with Dollar. (I have included it at the front of this book for dramatic effect, not to assert that it is true.) It is doubtful that Chardon or another white man—if Chardon was not the speech's transcriber—was present when Four Bears uttered his denunciation (presuming that he did utter it). Since the chief was calling for armed revenge against Fort Clark, it would have been dangerous for Chardon or any other trader to show his face in Mitutanka Village. As a result, it is nearly impossible for the written speech to be a literal translation of Four Bears's words. More likely, Four Bears, in the grief of watching his family die, vilified the whites for infecting the Mandans with smallpox. *Chardon's Journal* contains numerous entries about Indians seeking to avenge the deaths of their loved ones. No doubt Chardon or someone else heard about Four Bears's condemnation and made up the version that Dr. Abel found with the *Journal*. Until more information comes to light, it is impossible to say if Chardon was the speech's author or if it has a modicum of truth.

6. My version of Four Bears's final days is undoubtedly more legend than fact. Francis Chardon was present at the chief's death—that is Chardon was in residence at Fort Clark when Four Bears died at Mitutanka Village. The artist George

Catlin, who had met Four Bears in 1832, wrote about his death from hearsay; see Catlin, *Letters*, 2:258. Although the noted historian Bernard DeVoto dismisses Catlin's version (DeVoto, *Across the Wide Missouri*, 282), the one he substitutes is probably no closer to the truth than Catlin's. Perhaps all we can know for certain is that Four Bears was a great man and a tower to his people. Like the death of his tribe, his passing was a tragedy.

7. Larpenteur, "Journals and Notes," 161 states that the inoculees became ill on July 20, eight days after their treatment.

8. Ibid., 162; and Larpenteur, *Forty Years*, 110.

9. Larpenteur, *Forty Years*, 110-11.

10. Ferch, "Fighting the Smallpox Epidemic," 20, no. 1 (spring 1984): 7.

11. Larpenteur, "Journals and Notes," 162-3. DeVoto, *Across the Wide Missouri*, 288-9 recount this incident, citing it as the cause for the Assiniboines becoming infected. Arguing against this being the cause for the outbreak among the tribe, smallpox victims are usually not contagious until after the disease completes its incubation.

12. Denig, *Indian Tribes*, 71.

13. Larpenteur, *Forty Years*, 111.

14. Denig, *Indian Tribes*, 71-2.

15. Ibid., 72.

16. DeLand, abst., "Fort Tecumseh and Fort Pierre Journal and Letter Books," 9:122 n. 79 states that Saone was a generic term used to describe the Sans Arc, Two Kettle, Huncpapa, and Blackfoot Lakotas.

17. Chardon, *Journal*, 129 states that the largest band of Hidatsas had yet to move to its summer village on the Knife River, and as of mid August, it was still free of smallpox.

18. Audubon, *Journals*, 2:44. The date this event occurred is open to question. It may have been later than where I place it in my narrative. Chardon made no mention of it in his journal.

19. The location of the various Hidatsa bands is confusing, especially when one attempts to reconcile the Hidatsa entries in *Chardon's Journal* with Ferch, "Fighting the Smallpox Epidemic," 19, no. 4 (winter 1983): 5; and DeVoto, *Across the Wide Missouri*, 284.

20. Chardon, *Journal*, 129; and Ferch, "Fighting the Smallpox Epidemic," 19, no. 4 (winter 1983): 5. Indian tribal police were typically members of a warrior society who were charged with maintaining discipline.

21. For confirmation that Charbonneau's wife was infected with smallpox, see Chardon's journal entry for September 10 (Chardon, *Journal*, 135).

Chapter Eight

Smallpox and the Fur Trade
After the Revolution

In the years immediately following the smallpox epidemic of 1780 and 1781, the American colonies won their independence from Great Britain. The ministers of King George III signed the Treaty of Paris on September 3, 1783, acknowledging that England had lost. Turning their backs on the Iroquois and other tribes that had rallied to the loyalist cause, the British ministers abandoned them to the clemency of their colonial conquerors.

The crown's former subjects quickly consolidated their victory. At Fort Stanwix, New York, a year after the Treaty of Paris, the fledgling nation *persuaded* the Iroquois League to make peace. Although most of the confederation had supported Great Britain during the American Revolution, the Oneidas had fought for the colonies and supplied corn to General Washington's army during its winter bivouac at Valley Forge. But the Oneida allegiance carried no weight with the American negotiators, especially when Indian land was at stake. When the Iroquois chiefs touched pen to paper at Fort Stanwix, their once-powerful federation—including the Oneidas—forfeited its ancestral hunting grounds from New York to eastern Ohio.

In 1787, the American government continued its amalgamation by enacting the Northwest Ordinance. Beyond the ordinance's central purpose of dividing the frontier northwest of the Ohio River into districts and establishing rules under which the districts could attain statehood, the act also sought to protect the rights of Indians living in the partitioned country.

The upheaval of nearly two centuries of Indian and European warfare, together with the westward encroachment of white settlers, had driven a multitude of native refugees to the Northwest Territory. Land that had traditionally belonged to the Potawatomi, Kickapoo, Miami, Wea, Piankashaw, Shawnee, Winnebago, Menominee, Sauk, Fox, Peoria, Kaskaskia, and Illinois was now also occupied by dispossessed Iroquois, Delaware, Ottawa, and Wyandot.

The Northwest Ordinance was meant to protect Indian rights, but its ink was barely dry before American farmers began illegally staking out new homesteads. The Indians of the Ohio country opted to fight rather than relinquish terrain that was theirs by right of birth. At first, the British supported the tribes, eager for them to block American advancement between the Ohio River and Great Lakes, which would ensure that English traders held control of the region's fur trade.[1] By 1790, the northwest frontier reverberated with the tempo of Indian war drums.

On November 3, the following year, Miami and Shawnee warriors shattered the dawn quiet of General Arthur St. Clair's militia encampment on the upper Wabash River. Despite his experience fighting redcoats, St. Clair was no match for the native force that Miami Chief Little Turtle hurled at him that frosty autumn morning. When the killing was finished, 630 American soldiers lay dead, and 283 others bore wounds testifying to the ferocity of the fight. Those who escaped counted themselves fortunate to be alive, having survived the worst defeat an American army would ever suffer at the hands of Indians.[2]

Nearly three years passed before the United States mustered the leadership necessary to bring the Indians of the Northwest Territory to heel. Then on August 20, 1794, General "Mad Anthony" Wayne soundly defeated Little Turtle's replacement, Chief Turkey Foot, at the Battle of Fallen Timbers, just west of Lake Erie. Although the Indian deaths numbered no more than fifty warriors, the Northwest tribes lost heart when nearby British soldiers refused to come to their aid.[3]

The Treaty of Greenville, which the tribes signed in 1795, forced the Indians to cede vast tracts of land (two-thirds of Ohio, a large section of Indiana, several square miles around Fort Detroit, and multiple acres south of Lake Michigan that would one day be Chicago). The Miami, Potawatomi, and other tribes of the Ohio River country were driven toward the Mississippi onto territory owned by the Kaskaskia, Peoria, and other nations of the Illinois Confederation. As waves of newly dispossessed forest Indians fled before the advancing white settlements and their protective armies, ripples of discontent spread westward, as though a pebble had been tossed into the edge of a glassy pond.

Before long, the forest tribes began crossing the Mississippi River, squeezing the hunting ranges of the Great Plains tribes. Reacting to the pressure, the Santee Lakotas drifted onto the Minnesota plains and stepped up their transition to a horse culture. Having been spared the worst of the smallpox devastation that their Ojibwa enemies had suffered in the early 1780s, the Santees—with their Yanktonai brothers—now turned the tables, intimidating any Ojibwa who sought to trade with Canada's North West Company at its new fort near the confluence of the Park and Red rivers (north of Drayton, North Dakota).[4] With muskets, gunpowder, and lead now being funneled through the Santees from British traders along the Minnesota and upper Mississippi rivers, all the Lakotas were well armed.

Among the village tribes, the Arikaras suffered the most from Lakota harassment. Bragging that the Arikaras took "the place of women," Yankton warriors lorded over their weaker neighbor, pillaging their cornfields and gardens, stealing their horses, and beating their wives and daughters. Such trade that existed between the Arikaras and Yanktons was formalized coercion, with the Yanktons imposing the terms of exchange. Seeking to escape their persecution, the Arikaras moved up the Missouri River, settling near its confluence with the Grand. But the move failed to halt the Arikaras' torment. Relishing their role as pirates of the plain, the Yanktons continued their out-rage.[5]

Not content to beleaguer only the Arikaras, Lakota war par-ties attacked Missouri River tribes from the mouth of the Niobrara to that of the Knife. Having access to British-made firearms and Arikara corn, the Lakotas now had no reason to maintain trading relations with the traditional Missouri mid-dlemen—the Mandans. Following the smallpox epidemic of the early 1780s, the Mandans had relocated just below the Missouri-Knife River confluence to be near their Hidatsa allies. For the most part, the Lakotas found it more expedient to steal horses from the village tribes instead of obtaining them through trade. This continual raiding kept the upper Missouri in a state of turmoil.

Farther west, the Blackfoot Confederation, too, had lost many of its sons and daughters to the *rotting face*. For a few years after the smallpox epidemic of the early 1780s ended, the Piegans, Bloods, and Northern Blackfeet forgot about battling the Shoshonis and instead sought to reassemble their lives. Still without firearms, the Shoshonis hunted buffalo herds clos-er to the Missouri River, leaving the South Saskatchewan and its tributaries to their more powerful enemy. The Shoshonis also had been weakened by the epidemic and seemed content to leave the war lance broken—or so the Blackfeet thought.

Sometime around 1785 or 1786, five Piegan families left their main band to search for game along Canada's upper Bow River. When they failed to return as planned, a Piegan scouting party rode to the Bow to pick up their trail. What they found instead were scalped and mutilated Piegan men, women, and children. Nearby, the scouts spotted sticks painted with the images of snakes, the sign of the Shoshonis.[6]

Uniting the other two confederation tribes to their cause, the Piegans launched a war of annihilation against the Shoshoni people. Striking south toward the Missouri River, confederation war parties overwhelmed numerous Shoshoni bands, killing the adult males and capturing the women and children so they could be assimilated into the Blackfeet. Riding west, other Blackfoot warriors attacked the Flatheads and Kutenais, who were occasional allies of the Shoshonis. Lacking the quantity of guns that the Blackfeet had, the two Plateau tribes fled across the Rocky Mountains, surrendering the upper Saskatchewan to the confederation. Likewise, the eastern Shoshonis retreated southwest across the Continental Divide, joining their fellow tribesmen in the Great Basin. By the turn of the nineteenth century, the Blackfeet held sway over the entire western Saskatchewan and western Missouri plains.

East of the Blackfeet, the Plains Crees had also been devastated by the *Variola* epidemic of the early 1780s. For over a century, they had occupied the subarctic homeland of the Chipewyans. Now the Crees were too weak to stop the Chipewyans from reclaiming what was theirs by right of birth. Opting to move south rather than fight the Chipewyans, the Plains Crees invaded the country between the North and South Saskatchewan rivers, driving out the smallpox-diluted Atsinas, who resettled along the upper bend of the Milk River (in southeastern Alberta and north-central Montana).[7] The Plains Crees remained allies with the Assiniboines, who had also suffered from the smallpox. The two tribes now shared a common hunting ground and often wintered together.

As the Plains Crees and Assiniboines attempted pulling their cultures back together in the years following the epidemic, competitive changes in the Canadian fur trade all but wiped out their role as middlemen. After the establishment of the North West Company in 1783, Nor'West and Hudson's Bay Company traders rapidly expanded their western trading houses. The Nor'Westers' supply line stretched from Lachine (next to Montreal on the St. Lawrence River) to within sight of the Rocky Mountains, and the Hudson's Bay Company's reached from York Factory (on Hudson Bay) to the foothills of the Rockies.

With the construction of the Hudson's Bay Company's Edmonton House (now Edmonton, Alberta) in 1795 and Action House (now Rocky Mountain House, Alberta) in 1799, the Blackfeet no longer had to depend on the Plains Crees and Assiniboines to furnish them with European weapons, ammunition, and other manufactured truck. During the same years

that Edmonton and Action houses opened, the North West
Company countered by building Fort Augustus and Rocky
Mountain House in the shadow of the Hudson's Bay establish-
ments.[8]

All these trading posts soon put the Plains Cree and
Assiniboine brokers out of a job. Because the two tribes had
concentrated so heavily on honing their bartering skills during
the most recent decades, they had lost their ability as trappers.
They were still reeling from the impact of smallpox, and now
the fur companies had derailed their livelihood as traders.
Having no alternative, the Plains Crees and Assiniboines upped
their harvest of buffalo and began supplying meat and pemmican to the trading posts and armadas of freight canoes that
plied Canada's inland waterways.

The fur companies' food requirements were staggering, as
demonstrated by the estimated consumption of the trading
houses along the Assiniboine River (located in Saskatchewan
and Manitoba). The combined personnel at these twenty-one
posts annually ate over 660 tons of meat from nearly 3,100 buffalo. Considering that the posts on the Assiniboine River made
up only one portion of the two fur companies' expanding trading
networks, the Crees and Assiniboines had plenty to keep them
busy. A consequence of their stepped-up hunting was that the
Blackfeet now looked on the Plains Crees and Assiniboines as
competitors instead of trading partners. Since the economic
basis of their friendship no longer existed, the Blackfoot
Confederation added its eastern neighbors to its list of enemies.[9]

In the last two decades of the eighteenth century, the fur
trade—like the Indian political landscape—also underwent a
transition. Until that time, French *coureurs de bois* had occasionally visited the village tribes, lived and traded with them
for a season or two, then returned to their home forts with a
load of pelts. But until smallpox disrupted the tribal structure
of the Mandans, Hidatsas, and Arikaras in the early 1780s,
these transient French-Canadian traders were merely minor
participants in a much larger fur trading scheme.

The competitive playing field changed in 1783 with the

organization of the North West Company. Thereafter, Montreal's former Peddlers grappled tooth and nail with their eminent rival at Hudson Bay. Soon both firms were sending roving traders to the upper Missouri. Still reeling from the chaos brought about by *Variola major,* the few Mandan, Hidatsa, and Arikara middlemen who had survived the epidemic watched helplessly as their trading business was swallowed up by the Europeans.

In 1792, Jacques D'Eglise, a French-Canadian trader from Spanish-owned St. Louis, journeyed to the Mandans. Upon returning home, D'Eglise told the Spanish authorities that English fur company traders, operating from forts above the forty-ninth parallel, had invaded the Spanish territory of the upper Missouri.[10] The Spanish governor-general chartered a group of St. Louis merchants to form the Company of Discoverers and Explorers of the Missouri River—or Missouri Company, for short—intending to wrest the upper Missouri fur trade from the British.

Before the new partnership could send an expedition to the Mandans, word reached St. Louis that a Nor'West trader named René Jusseaume had opened a permanent trading fort near the mouth of the Knife River. In the summer of 1796, two years after the establishment of Jusseaume's post, the Missouri Company's John Evans finally reached the Mandans and ousted the North West and Hudson's Bay traders. But Evans's victory was fleeting. The next spring, Jusseaume returned with a fresh supply of merchandise, far more than Evans had on hand.

Not caring which white trader furnished the European products on which they had become dependent, the Mandans and Hidatsas shifted their allegiance back to the Nor'Westers. After Jusseaume threatened his life, Evans fled down the Missouri, abandoning the village tribes to the British. Although René Jusseaume's trading house was small, it and the trading forts that the North West Company had built on the Red River of the North for the Ojibwas ushered in another change in the make-up of the fur trade on the Great Plains: the era of fixed posts.

By 1800, the Indian survivors of the smallpox epidemic of 1780 and 1781 had given birth to another generation that lacked immunity to *Variola major*. Tribes such as the Mandans, Hidatsas, Arikaras, Assiniboines, Plains Crees, and Ojibwas, which had been hardest hit, saw their populations rebound, though none of them came close to the numbers they had known before 1780.

From a societal standpoint, smallpox—by killing so many native storytellers—had partly severed the historical links that coupled the current generation to its past. Traditions, religious beliefs, social mores, hunting and domestic skills, and clan leadership lay in tatters. The *rotting face* had all but shredded tribal structure, leaving the survivors casting about like a rudderless ship. In addition, the disease had spawned an increasing dependence on the fur companies and European technology.

In 1801, another smallpox epidemic swept the Missouri. Although historians have never identified its source with certainty, some think it originated at one of the fur trading enclaves on the west shore of Lake Michigan or Lake Superior.[11] For two years *Variola major* again raged along the central and upper Missouri and into Canada, killing Indians by the thousands. Once more the keens of Native American women draped Indian villages and camps from the Platte River to the North Saskatchewan.

Pockmarked survivors from the epidemic of twenty years before watched helplessly as their sons and daughters sickened, their flesh rotted, and their bodies exuded the putrid odor of decay. As before, the village tribes suffered worse than their nomadic neighbors, whose cultural inclination to disperse held down the number of deaths. Mandan, Hidatsa, Arikara, and Ponca shamans prayed to their spirits for the power to heal, but as had happened two decades earlier, their pleas went unanswered. Once again the tribes along the Missouri saw their ranks cut by half, two-thirds, or more.

Among all the Indians on the Missouri River, none underwent a greater loss than did the Omahas. Dwelling in a cluster of villages about 100 miles above the mouth of the Platte (just north of Decatur, Nebraska), the Omahas had earned a reputation as one of the most fearsome tribes on the central plains.

During the summer of 1794, Jean Baptiste Truteau of the Company of the Discoverers and Explorers of the Missouri River had gone upstream, intending to trade with the Arikaras and winter with the Mandans. As he approached the Missouri's Grand Detour, a band of Teton and Yankton Lakotas blocked his progress. Truteau and his men cached their pirogue and some of their trade goods, then sneaked overland during the cover of night, intending to seek refuge with the Arikaras. Reaching their camp, the traders found it abandoned, the tribe having fled north to escape Lakota raids.

Nearly starving, Truteau and his crew turned south, retrieved their cache, and dropped downriver out of Lakota territory to the mouth of the Niobrara River. Intending to stay upcountry in order to have a jump on the coming trading season, the party built a small cottonwood fort that offered as little in comfort as it did in protection. Then as the winter storms began in earnest, Chief Blackbird—Washing-guh-sahba—arrived with an entourage of Omaha warriors.

Blackbird had risen to prominence by predicting death. Years earlier, a French trader had given him arsenic and taught him how to poison his enemies. When the chief wished to rid himself of a rival, he would summon other members of his tribe to watch while he served his victim arsenic-laced food. During the meal, Blackbird would announce with great fanfare that his guest would die before morning. Since his predictions always came true, his tribe revered him, thinking he possessed magical powers.

During the 1790s, Chief Blackbird capitalized on his ability to foretell death by compelling Omaha warriors to do his bidding. None dared refuse, fearing the chief would use his magic on any who tried. Turning the Omahas into the villains of the middle Missouri, Blackbird coerced tribute and ransom from white traders who ventured upriver from St. Louis. During the winter of 1794 to 1795, he unleashed his warriors on Jean Baptiste Truteau.

Demanding tobacco, lead, gunpowder, and other merchandise on credit—loans he had no intention of repaying—Blackbird harassed Truteau and his men, bidding their acquiescence by threatening to lift their hair. A schoolteacher by training, Truteau was powerless to prevent the chief's thievery. When the spring thaw unlocked the Missouri, the Omahas headed downriver, but not before falsely warning the nearby Poncas that the trader was plotting their destruction. The Poncas painted their faces for war, forcing Truteau to spend more of his dwindling trade goods to soothe their ire.[12]

Six years later, smallpox began its sweep of the Missouri River. Infecting the Omahas, the *Variola* virus killed wantonly, as if it wished to punish the tribe for its sins. While his people died by the score, Blackbird sat in his lodge, seemingly immune to the raging death. Then in 1802, his horrified tribe witnessed the impossible as the *rotting face* claimed the revered and fearsome chief. About 300 Omahas survived the epidemic, too few to ever again menace fur traffic on the Missouri. After carrying Blackbird's body to a bluff of yellow sandstone that overlooked the river, his kinsmen placed him astride his white war horse and raised a mound of dirt and stones over them, marking the grave with a cedar staff and banner. Known as Blackbird Hill, the site served as a beacon for passing keelboats and mackinaws.[13]

In addition to the Omahas, the epidemic of 1801 and 1802 also pummeled the Pawnees, Poncas, Iowas, Kiowas, Arikaras, Mandans, Hidatsas, Assiniboines, and Crows. Carried by Indian hunting and war parties, the disease diffused across the Continental Divide to the Flathead tribe, then west to the Pend d'Oreilles, Kalispels and Spokanes.[14] Hudson's Bay Company factor Peter Fidler, who worked on the South Saskatchewan River, wrote that the Atsinas caught smallpox from a party of visiting Arapahos. The Arapahos lived around the South Platte River (in northeastern Colorado and western Nebraska) and were related to the Atsinas. The tribes regularly visited back and forth. According to Fidler, the Arapahos had been infected by Indians from the lower Missouri River. Among the Atsinas, the disease was especially deadly for the young, who lacked the immunity many of their elders had acquired during the epidemic of the early 1780s.[15]

At every village and camp it touched, *Variola major* rent the fabric of social order, destroying not only Indian families but also tribal direction and continuity. Traditional crafts and cultural links with the past disappeared amid fevers and blistered skin. This second major smallpox epidemic in twenty years completed the destruction of the once-vast native trading system. Indian survivors now had no choice but to turn to the white traders and their manufactured goods. Luxuries of the past became necessities. Smallpox had claimed so many female artisans among the Missouri River tribes that the craft of making pottery vanished. Having no one to teach them to mold clay into pots and harden them with fire, coming generations of Indian women would be compelled to purchase metal kettles from the white traders. Similarly, future ranks of Native American boys would never gain the skills that had permitted their grandfathers' grandfathers to hunt with bows instead of guns.

In the Arkansas River Valley (in eastern Arkansas, above the mouth of the Arkansas River), the Quapaws—who had been ravaged by smallpox in 1698—fell prey to this latest epidemic. So too did their northwestern neighbor, the Osages, who lived near the Marais des Cygnes and upper Osage rivers (in southwestern Missouri). For years the Osages had used the Quapaws as a protective but weak buffer against the aggressive and well armed Choctaws and Chickasaws, who occupied the territory west of the Mississippi River (in western Tennessee and western Mississippi). In the second half of the eighteenth century, the Choctaws and Chickasaws had begun crossing the Mississippi and hunting the game-rich Ouachita and Ozark mountains that straddled the Arkansas River, country the Osages considered their exclusive domain. As in other tribal conflicts in North America, this one also traced its origins to the fur trade.

During the 1700s, the Osages dominated the fur traffic between the lower Missouri and lower Arkansas rivers, supplying Spanish and French traders in St. Louis, New Madrid, Ste. Geneviève, and Arkansas Post (about seven miles southwest of Gillett, Arkansas) with nearly half their annual inventory. Deerskins made up most of the market, supplemented by pelts from black bears, beaver, and bobcats.

Following a scenario that had played throughout the history

of North America, the Osages—because of their domination of the region's fur trade—acquired more muskets than their neighbors. The Osages tolerated the Quapaws in their hunting grounds but brooked no other competition. Although the Osages were powerful enough to battle the Choctaw and Chickasaw interlopers directly, they deemed it more expedient to allow their Quapaw ally to bear the brunt of the fight. While the Quapaws held off Choctaw and Chickasaw war parties, the Osages raided south, routing the poorly armed Caddos, Wichitas, and Kichais, who lived near the Red River (in southern Arkansas and eastern Texas).

For the Osages, the main spoils of these raids were horses, which the three weaker tribes had acquired from the Comanches and Kiowa-Apaches. Over the years, Osage pressure gradually pushed the Caddos, Wichitas, and Kichais south and west from their homeland. During the 1770s through the 1790s, while the Osages grew rich on the fur trade and stolen horses, the Quapaws absorbed repeated attacks from their eastern enemies, blows that weakened the Quapaws and gradually eroded their effectiveness as a buffer. After being hit by smallpox in the spring of 1801, so many Quapaws perished, the tribe lost its ability to hold the line between the Osages and their Choctaw and Chickasaw foes.[16]

As it did to the Quapaws, the smallpox epidemic of 1801 and 1802 also invaded the Osages, killing at least half the tribe, better than 2,000 people by some estimates.[17] After the pestilence died out, the surviving Osages had to face the Choctaws and Chickasaws with almost no help from the Quapaws. Rather than muster their warriors for an all-out battle, the Osages fought a holding action on their eastern border while continuing to raid their weaker, southwestern foes. To these neighbors, the Osages appeared as powerful as ever, but smallpox had dampened much of their eternal fire. Now split into three main bands—the Big and Little Osages on the upper Osage River and the Chenier Osages (among other names) on the lower Verdigris River (northeastern Oklahoma)—the Osages began a long slide toward compromise and subjugation. Within a few decades, this once-powerful tribe would find itself bunched together in the Indian Territory (now Oklahoma) amid its former foes.

Among the Missouri Indians, from whom the Missouri River took its name, the smallpox epidemics of the early 1780s and 1800s so reduced their numbers that their warriors could no longer defend the tribe against the Pawnees and Lakotas. Shortly after the latest epidemic ended, the Missouri Indians threw themselves on the mercy of their Otoe allies, who lived along the lower Platte River. The Otoes welcomed the Missouris into their villages and granted them protection against their common enemies, but the Otoes never accepted the Missouris as equals.[18]

While the Missouris were begging succor from the Otoes, most of the Hidatsas who had survived the epidemic of 1801 and 1802 were dwelling in a large town on the north side of the Knife River, about five miles upstream from its confluence with the Missouri. The nearly 900 lodges the tribe had boasted in the days before its contact with white traders had shrunk to about 130, enough homes for perhaps 2,700 people.[19] The Amatihas (a.k.a. Awatixa), a sub-tribe of the Hidatsas, occupied a village on the right side of the Knife, halfway downstream from the big Hidatsa town and the Missouri. Among the Amatihas' residents were Toussaint Charbonneau and his Shoshoni wife, Sacajawea, who were destined to earn their place in history alongside Meriwether Lewis and William Clark. Another of the Hidatsa relatives, the Amahamis, had a hamlet on the Knife's south bank, a bit above the river's mouth.

Having moved upriver to escape Lakota harassment, the Mandans—numbering between 1,200 and 1,300 people—lived in two villages a few miles downstream from the Knife. The Arikaras occupied three villages, one on a long island a few miles above the mouth of the Grand River, the other two on opposite sides of a small creek that emptied into the Missouri from the west, about four miles above the island village.[20]

Although the Arikaras had hoped their move from the Bad River to the Grand would stop the Lakotas from tormenting them, the intimidation continued. Still viewing the Arikaras as slaves, the Lakotas stole corn from their fields and horses from their pastures. Lakota warriors regularly chased buffalo away from the Missouri, then threatened Arikara hunting parties so they were afraid to venture out after them. Desperate for meat, the Arikaras were compelled to trade the produce of their gardens for Lakota-made jerky, accepting in payment whatever their enemy offered.[21]

Reeling from Lakota hostility, the Arikaras maintained a shaky alliance with the Mandans and Hidatsas, a truce that was often shattered when one side or the other took umbrage at some insult. When not feuding among themselves, the village tribes occasionally raided their common foe in joint war parties, attempting to make the Lakotas pay for their transgressions. But the retaliatory attacks failed to stem the Lakota onslaught.

In slightly more than a generation, smallpox had reduced the Mandans, Hidatsas, and Arikaras from five or six dozen villages to only eight.[22] Before *Variola major,* the three tribes had possessed the strength to safeguard their domain. But after undergoing two major epidemics, they were powerless to do anything except delay the juggernaut of Lakota expansion.

Chapter eight notes

1. Viola, *After Columbus*, 118-19.

2. Utley and Washburn, *Indian Wars*, 113-14; and Waldman, *Atlas of the North American Indian*, 114-15. General St. Clair's losses were nearly three times those of Lieutenant Colonel George Armstrong Custer and the Seventh Cavalry three-quarters of a century later.

3. Utley and Washburn, *Indian Wars*, 114-15; and Viola, *After Columbus*, 123.

4. In 1793, the North West Company's Peter Grant built the first Ojibwa-Red River trading post below the forty-ninth parallel, locating it opposite the mouth of the Pembina River at the site of today's St. Vincent, Minnesota. Within a few years, Grant fled to Canada to escape Lakota hostility. In 1797, Nor'Wester Charles Jean Baptist Chaboillez established Fort Paubna immediately below the mouth of the Pembina River, then deserted it two years later because of the Lakotas. In the fall of 1800, Alexander Henry the Younger became the latest North West Company trader to attempt maintaining a presence among the Ojibwas. The Park River Post—his first fort in the region—lasted from September 1800 until spring 1801, when it was replaced by a new fort at the mouth of the Pembina River. Although he held on longer than his predecessors, in the end Henry too abandoned the effort because of Lakota attacks; for more see Robertson, *Competitive Struggle*, 194-6.

5. Jablow, *Cheyenne*, 52-6.

6. Ewers, *The Blackfeet*, 29.

7. Ray, *Indians in the Fur Trade*, 98.

8. Innis, *Fur Trade in Canada*, 234.

9. Ray, *Indians in the Fur Trade*, 102-04, 130-1. Between 1800 and 1820, the Assiniboines and, to a lesser degree, the Plains Crees gradually drifted south from the Saskatchewan River, drawn by the buffalo herds that became more plentiful as the Indians approached the forty-ninth parallel. With the opening of American trading posts on the upper Missouri River in the 1820s and early 1830s, this south-ward migration accelerated, spurred on by the burgeoning market for buffalo robes; see Ray, *Indians in the Fur Trade*, 182-3.

    The Plains Cree-Assiniboine food monopoly waned in the 1830s when the Métis (a non-derogatory Canadian term for people born from mixed unions between Indians and whites or for individuals whose parents were Métis) population in the Red River Valley (below Lake Winnipeg) began to hunt buffalo on a large scale and sell the surplus meat for less than the prices charged—in trade goods—by the Crees and Assiniboines. Within ten years, the Métis were offering the Hudson's Bay Company more meat and pemmican than it could use.

10. In 1762, realizing that France was going lose the French and Indian War (known in Europe as the Seven Years' War), Louis XV gave New Orleans and the Louisiana Territory west of the Mississippi River to Spain. A year later, the Treaty of Paris, which formally ended the war, forced France to cede Canada (a.k.a. New France) and the Louisiana Territory east of the Mississippi River (other than New Orleans) to Great Britain. In 1783, a second Treaty of Paris handed the land east of the Mississippi to Britain's former colonies, giving rise to the United States of America.

11. Lehmer, *Selected Writings*, 106 postulates that the virus was spread by the Lakotas, who infected other Indians at the annual James River trade fair.

12. DeVoto, *The Course of Empire*, 367-8.

13. Audubon, *Journals*, 1:485-6 n. 2; Bernard DeVoto, ed., *The Journals of Lewis and*

Clark (Boston: Houghton Mifflin, 1953), 18; and Richard Edward Oglesby, *Manuel Lisa and the Opening of the Missouri Fur Trade* (Norman: University of Oklahoma Press, 1963), 111. In contrast with these accounts, Bradbury, *Travels*, 85 n. 47 reports that the Omahas entombed Chief Blackbird and his war horse in a cave at Blackbird Hill, then erected a stone monument on the hill's summit, adding (on page 86 n. 49) that fewer than 600 Omahas—versus the 300 reported by other sources—survived the smallpox out of a pre-epidemic population of between 3,000 and 4,000.

During George Catlin's steamboat voyage up the Missouri in 1832, the artist removed Blackbird's skull from its grave and hid it. Some months later while descending the river in a canoe with two French-Canadian companions, Catlin retrieved the skull and took it to St. Louis; see Catlin, *Letters*, 2:6. Time and weather have long since erased Blackbird's memorial, whose site is about seventy-five miles north of Omaha, Nebraska.

14. Stearn and Stearn, *Effect of Smallpox*, 75-6. North West Company trader François Antoine Larocque estimated that the smallpox epidemics of 1780 through 1781 and 1801 through 1802 reduced the Crow population from 2,000 lodges to 300; see Denig, *Indian Tribes*, 142 n. 6.

15. Martin, "Wildlife Diseases," 57.

16. Willard H. Rollings, *The Osage: An Ethnohistorical Study of Hegemony on the Prairie-Plains* (Columbia: University of Missouri Press, 1992), 136-146.

17. Ibid., 278. After the expedition of Zebulon Pike visited the Osages in 1806, small-pox again hit them, killing 200 more. Later outbreaks occurred in 1827 and 1828.

18. Bradbury, *Travels*, 80.

19. The lodge estimates come from North West Company trader, Alexander Henry the Younger, who visited the tribe in 1806. Henry was actually writing about the lodge reduction in the Hidatsas' main village, but 900 lodges is such a large number, the Indians who provided the information may have been referring to the entire tribe; see Coues, ed., *Alexander Henry*, 1:345, 348. Taylor, "Sociocultural Effects," 65 states that in 1804, Meriwether Lewis put the Hidatsa population at 2,700, the Mandans at 1,250, and the Arikaras at 2,000. Denig, *Indian Tribes*, 43 n. 5 says that Lewis estimated the Arikaras numbered 2,600 people, not 2,000.

20. Denig, *Indian Tribes*, 42 n. 3; and Meyer, *Village Indians*, 37-8, 45-6.

21. Meyer, *Village Indians*, 39-40.

22. Lehmer, *Selected Writings*, 107.

Chapter Nine

Late Summer 1837

By mid August, the upper Missouri smallpox epidemic had become a raging inferno. Like an untethered fire, the deadly affliction would not stop until it had exhausted its reservoir of human fuel.

At Mitutanka and Ruhptare villages, the Indians succumbed to a tragic fatalism. So many were either sick or dead, those who had not caught the disease thought they would. For the Mandans and Arikaras, all hope vanished. Husbands wept as they watched their wives and daughters writhe in feverish agony, their comely visages swollen with pus-filled blisters. Grandmothers and grandfathers screamed out their grief as their warrior sons and grandsons shivered beneath their robes, too frail to stand and too sick to eat—assuming the family still had someone fit enough to hunt. Shamans continued shaking dew-claw rattles and passing sacred eagle feathers over their patients, but few recovered.

Overwhelmed by the suffering caused by the *rotting face,* some fathers vowed to save their loved ones from having to undergo such a terrible ordeal. Since death was inevitable, families saw no reason they should not bring it on sooner. Gripped by despair, parents began to take the lives of their children— including those who were not ill.

At Mitutanka Village a young Mandan warrior looked at his wife, her cheeks crusted in scab. Remembering the beauty of their marriage day, he picked up his musket, primed the pan with gunpowder, closed the frizzen, and pulled back the cock until it locked. Pointing the muzzle between her dark eyes, he told her that she was going to leave him, but not to fear because she would not enter the spirit world alone. He would be her companion. Blinking back his tears, he squeezed the trigger, firing a half ounce lead ball into her brain. After dropping the musket, he seized his knife from its scabbard, then plunged the blade into his stomach and jerked it through his bowels. As his life gushed out between his fingers, he slumped beside his dead wife, happy to be joining her among their ancestors, far from this nightmare world of pain and rotting flesh.[1]

In a nearby lodge, a Mandan father watched the virus claim his only son. Overcome by grief, the father summoned the boy's mother. His eyes brimming with tears, he told her that everything they had loved had been stripped away. Because their son had gone to the spirit world, the sobbing Mandan no longer wished to live. His wife agreed, saying that she too wanted to be with their son. Taking his musket, the Mandan pointed it at his wife and fired. She died instantly. After loading another ball, he placed the barrel in his mouth, no doubt glancing one last time at his dead boy. Reaching his thumb into the trigger guard, the bereaved father resigned himself to the hereafter as he blew out his brains.[2]

In a different lodge, an Arikara warrior burning with fever pulled an arrow from its hide quiver, then shoved the pointed shaft down his throat until he drowned in his own blood. Elsewhere, another Arikara rose from his robes, his head pulsating with pain, his skin erupted in pustules. Gaining his feet, he picked up his tomahawk, then lurched toward his nineteen-year-old wife. Determined that he would not go to the grave alone, he mustered his strength in one final swing, smashing the mallet against her skull. Unconscious, but still alive, the woman sprawled on the earthen floor. Thinking she was dead, the warrior drew his knife and slit his own throat.

Throughout Mitutanka and Ruhptare villages, Indians shot themselves to avoid the *rotting face*. As Mandan and Arikara society disintegrated before their eyes, Indians who were not sick lost their will to live. In one lodge, a Mandan wife, her body gripped with pain, her youthful beauty disfigured by pustules, watched her once-vigorous husband expire in front of her and their two sons. For three days, she stared at her husband's blackening corpse. She was too ill to build a cottonwood burial scaffold or dig him a grave. She had neither the energy to cook nor the stamina to care for her eight-year-old and six-year-old sons. On the fourth day after her husband's death, she summoned her final reserve of strength. Vowing that her children would not suffer as had she and her husband, she killed them. Afterward, she tied a braided rope to a lodge support-beam, slipped a noose around her neck, and hanged herself.

Other Indians jumped to their deaths from high bluffs. Many drowned in the Missouri, some committing suicide, more because they were trying to cool their fevered bodies.

On August 23, Toussaint Charbonneau returned from the Hidatsa Knife River village, reporting that it was still free from smallpox. The quarantine of the tribal police was doing its job. The tribe had accepted the gift of tobacco and had shown no desire to join the Mandans or Arikaras in a blood feud with the traders.

Meantime, the epidemic continued exacting its toll among the Indians at Mitutanka Village. Word soon filtered into Fort Clark that the *rotting face* had broken out among the Arikaras who had moved downriver two weeks earlier. The disease appeared to be everywhere, except among the Hidatsas on the Knife River and at their main northern hunting camp. Still worried about traveling during daylight, Charbonneau returned to the Hidatsas' quarantined town on Thursday night, August 24. Francis Chardon sent along a few loads of ammunition as a present to the Hidatsa chiefs. Although they had declared their friendship for the whites, it never hurt to make sure.

Two days later, Chardon accompanied his interpreter, Antoine Garreau, to a grave that a young Arikara had asked his mother to dig. Ill with smallpox, the boy had crawled into the hole and begun singing his death song. Through Garreau, Chardon begged the young man to return to his lodge, but the lad refused, saying he no longer wished to live because the *rotting face* had killed all his friends. His only desire now was to join them. Nothing Chardon said could dissuade him. He was resolved to die. That evening the Arikara spirits granted the boy's last request.

Elsewhere, another young Arikara warrior was determined to kill himself instead of suffering another day with the *rotting face*. He had survived the smallpox's early stages and was now covered with scabs. Wanting to end his misery, he began scraping them off. Soon his entire body oozed blood. Out of his mind with agony, he threw off his robe and crawled to the fire pit in the center of his lodge. Having no thought other than ending his life as quickly as possible, he rolled in the hot embers. Although he burned his skin, he eventually coated his running sores with a thick crust of ashes. For the next two days while the warrior awaited death, the ashes dried to a hard shell. Exasperated that he was still alive, the young man peeled off his plaster bodysuit and discovered that the smallpox blisters were gone and he was beginning to heal.

Another Indian resorted to a less painful way to save his son from smallpox. Though the child had not yet fallen sick with the disease, his father sought to spare him from its horrors by performing a crude inoculation. Whether he had heard about the procedure or it came to him in a vision is unknown. Using his knife, the father pared two small pieces of skin from the lad's arms and two from his stomach. After obtaining a smallpox scab from a recovering tribesman, the warrior rubbed it in his boy's incisions. As happened to other people who underwent a successful inoculation, the child caught a mild case of the disease and then recovered, his body forevermore immune.[3]

On Sunday, August 27, an Indian hunting party rode past Fort Clark on its way to Mitutanka Village. The hunters had located a large herd of buffalo about a day's ride away and were returning with their horses piled high with fresh meat. The news raised the spirits of everyone at the trading post. With so many Indians fomenting trouble because of the epidemic, Chardon had been wary of sending out his own hunters. It was hoped that the traders would be able to buy some of the excess meat, if not from this hunting party, then perhaps from the next one. A couple of hours later, the men at the fort found something else to worry about besides their hunger. The Indian telegraph brought word that smallpox had broken out in yet another small Hidatsa hunting camp.[4]

Two days after hearing about *Variola* at the Hidatsa hunting camp, Francis Chardon awakened with a fever. He was not alone. Five other men within the fort were running a temperature—including the interpreter, Antoine Garreau—and another one had erupted in smallpox pustules.[5] All that day the *bourgeois* shivered with chills one moment, then the next burned as if in an oven. That evening he drank a hot whiskey punch, wrapped in his blankets, and sweated. By morning, rashes blotched all the men who had been feverish except Chardon. His fever was gone, and he felt well enough to see to his duties. If he had smallpox, as suggested by some historians, his case was extremely mild.

August ended with Chardon thankful that he and his men were still wearing their scalps. Other than a couple of Indians who had come to the trading post armed and intent on murder, most of the Mandans and Arikaras had done nothing but issue threats. Among the Arikaras, the epidemic had yet to hit full stride, but among the Mandans, it was consuming victims with abandon. As the month closed, Chardon noted in his journal that the Mandan death toll was nearing 500, about thirty percent of the tribe. Many of the deaths, particularly among those who had survived past epidemics, were from suicide. Praying that September would bring an end to his constant peril, Chardon recorded that during August, he had dispatched eighty-nine rats. The *bourgeois* certainly had a ways to go if he hoped to match the killing efficiency of the *rotting face*.

As September began, Jacob Halsey felt strong enough to assume his role as Fort Union's acting *bourgeois*. Halsey's case had been light. His cheeks were pockmarked, but not heavily. In contrast, a number of the native women and their mixed-blood children who had been inoculated were dead.[6]

Also included among the deceased was at least one *engagé*, Baptiste Compton. Halsey maintained the quarantine that his clerks had put in effect, and, as an afterthought, sent interpreters among the Assiniboines, urging them to keep away from the trading post. But the warning came too late. The *Variola* pestilence was already loose on the prairie. Spouting the folk science of the day, Halsey blamed the spread of the disease on miasmas. In his words, the air around the stockade "was infected with it for a half mile."[7]

As the Mandans and Arikaras had done, the Assiniboines also accused the whites of starting the epidemic. Screaming for vengeance, the Assiniboines vowed to set fire to Fort Union and kill every trader. Chief Le Vieux Gauche—Old Left Hand—was particularly vocal about seeking revenge, going so far as to burn his American flag. Le Gauche had survived smallpox as a boy, having caught the virus during the great epidemic of the early 1780s. At that time, his band was living north of the forty-ninth parallel.[8] Although the childhood attack protected him from future bouts of *Variola major,* it did not immunize his heart.

Watching his tribe now die from the latest round of the white man's disease, Le Gauche lusted for blood. While the *rotting face* chipped away at the chief's band, eventually reducing it from 300 families to fewer than twenty,[9] he called his people to arms. Although most of his warriors were dead or dying, Le Gauche still commanded enough Assiniboines to pose a threat to Fort Union, especially if the traders allowed them access to the trade room, which was located inside the main gate.

Le Gauche's shouts of an eye for an eye so alarmed Jacob Halsey that he ordered his carpenters to build an inner gate, separating the Indian trade room from the rest of the stockade. As an added precaution, the workmen cut a wicket in the palisade wall so the most hostile Indians could be kept outside the fort when they came to trade.[10] The additions thwarted Chief Le Gauche's calls for reprisal against the traders, but they did not temper his desire for battle. With Fort Union now impregnable, he decided to bide his time and look for an easier target, one that would ensure success.

Although Halsey had worried that the epidemic would severely reduce Fort Union's business, it had the opposite effect. Despite wanting to punish the whites, the Assiniboines continued bringing their buffalo robes to the trading post. As more of the tribe died, those still living resigned themselves to death

Montana Historical Society

Alexander Culbertson, his Blackfoot wife, Natawistacha (Medicine Snake Woman), and their son Joe. Culbertson was the *bourgeois* of Fort McKenzie during the upper Missouri smallpox epidemic of 1837-1838.

and determined to sell all they owned in order to have one last "frolic."[11] Most nights, Charles Larpenteur worked into the wee hours, dispensing watered-down liquor through the newly installed wicket. A few drunken Indians took potshots at the clerk, but he attributed the gunfire to alcohol instead of any purposeful retribution.

While a number of the Assiniboines were drinking themselves into a stupor, Alexander Harvey waited at the mouth of the Judith River with his keelboat of trade goods that were slated for Fort McKenzie. The Blackfoot passenger who had boarded the *St. Peter's* between Fort Clark and Fort Union—and later joined Harvey's keelboat—had come down with smallpox and infected two of Harvey's voyageurs.[12] Not wanting to spread the disease to the Blackfeet who were waiting upriver at Fort McKenzie, Harvey had stopped and sent an express to the *bourgeois,* Alexander Culbertson.

A native of Chambersburg, Pennsylvania, Culbertson had

entered the fur trade in 1830, working as a trader on the Mississippi near its confluence with the Minnesota River (at that time called the St. Peters River). In 1833, he joined the Upper Missouri Outfit of the American Fur Company and journeyed to Fort Union on the firm's steamer, *Assiniboine.* From there a keelboat took him to Fort McKenzie, the UMO's most remote trading post. Culbertson clerked at the fort until 1836, when he received a promotion giving him full command.[13]

When Harvey's express reached Fort McKenzie, there were 500 tipis camped just beyond its palisades.[14] The lodges belonged to between 4,000 and 5,000 members of the Blackfoot Confederation. Most of them were Bloods or Piegans, and they were all eagerly awaiting the keelboat and its store of trade goods and muskets. Alexander Culbertson was well aware that Fort McKenzie remained open only by their good graces. Before going counter to their dictates, a *bourgeois* had better think long and hard about the consequences.

Such as it was, Fort McKenzie stood as the traders' sole line of defense. The fort's cottonwood pickets extended fifteen feet above the ground. Wooden, two-story bastions on the northeast and southwest corners provided cover in case of attack, and each contained a small cannon. Near the rear of the 40,000-square-foot stockade, the *bourgeois,* clerk, and interpreters occupied a long building that was sectioned into three rooms. The clerk's room doubled as a mess hall, and the interpreters' quarters also served as a council room for important Blackfoot chiefs.

All the buildings within the post were constructed from cottonwood logs and roofed with planks and dirt. Fireplaces and chimneys were made from stone and mud. The palisade also enclosed a kitchen; shops for a blacksmith, carpenter, tinsmith, and tailor; warehouses; a fur press room; a meat storage locker; an ice house; and an Indian trade room, which was separated from the post's interior by an inner gate. In addition, the fort contained stables for three dozen horses and a dozen cattle, and pens for several hogs. A separate structure was used for salting and preserving buffalo tongues.

Because the Blackfeet were considered especially dangerous, barter with the visiting bands usually took place through a wicket that had been cut through the trade room wall. Indians passed their furs and robes through this two-foot-square window and received their payment—blankets, tobacco, muskets, lead, gunpowder, fire steels, muslin, fishhooks, brass wire, copper pots, metal knives and tomahawks, metal arrow and spear points, or liquor—from the trader inside the trade room. Hot and dusty in summer, cold and dank at other times of the year, Fort McKenzie had none of the comforts of forts Union and Pierre.[15]

Alexander Culbertson no doubt read Harvey's express with trepidation. The Blackfeet had been camped outside the fort for some time. They knew the keelboat was coming and that it carried a wealth of manufactured goods on which they were dependent. Culbertson realized the prudent decision would be for Harvey to hold the boat at the Judith River until the smallpox was finished. But that could take a month or more, especially if the disease infected other members of the crew. The Blackfeet could not sit idly by at Fort McKenzie, waiting for Harvey's voyageurs to end their quarantine. The buffalo were in rut. In a couple of weeks it would be time for the tribe's fall hunt. If the Blackfeet missed the opportunity, they risked starving to death during the coming winter.

Hoping to persuade the Blackfeet to go hunting and then return to Fort McKenzie for trade, Culbertson sent word to the tribal chiefs that he wished to parley. Speaking through an interpreter, the *bourgeois* explained that the keelboat could not continue upriver because of a deadly sickness aboard. The Indians listened but were not swayed. Figuring that Culbertson wanted to trick them in order to sell the trade goods—particularly the guns and ammunition—to their Crow or Flathead enemies, the Blackfeet demanded that the *bourgeois* call the boat upriver. If he refused, they vowed to destroy Fort McKenzie and kill every white man within the stockade.

As he listened, Culbertson knew the threat was real. Numbering between 16,000 and 20,000 people, the Blackfoot Confederation was composed of three of the most militant tribes in North America.[16] Despite having been ravaged by two epidemics of *Variola major,* the Blackfeet were still the most feared warriors on the upper Missouri. Tribes such as the Arikaras and

Mandans also boasted renowned war chiefs, but no other confederation besides the Teton, Yankton, Yantonai, and Santee Lakotas could field as many men. For decades, the Piegans, Bloods, and Northern Blackfeet had relentlessly expanded their homeland. It now encompassed the western North American prairie between the North Saskatchewan and Missouri rivers. Like a nest of red ants, the Blackfeet attacked anyone, Indian or white, who dared trespass.

For many years, the Hudson's Bay Company had maintained a truce with the Blackfeet. The confederation welcomed the British traders, but it refused them permission to do their own trapping. In 1830, Kenneth McKenzie, then *bourgeois* of Fort Union and head of the American Fur Company's Upper Missouri Outfit, decided to break the British-Blackfoot trading monopoly below the forty-ninth parallel. In a bold gamble, he sent Jacob Berger—an interpreter who had traded with the confederation in years past when he worked for the Hudson's Bay Company—to the Piegans, inviting them to Fort Union for a parley. That December, Berger brought a few dozen warriors to hear what McKenzie had to offer.

McKenzie proposed to undercut the Hudson's Bay Company's prices if the Blackfeet would allow him to open a trading post near the mouth of the Marias River. Being shrewd traders, the Blackfeet agreed, but they forbade the American Fur Company from employing its own trapping brigades in their territory, an edict the firm ignored. In July 1831, James Kipp—fresh from constructing Fort Clark for the Mandans— went up the Missouri to the Marias confluence and built Fort Piegan. That winter business was so good, Kipp exhausted his stock of trade goods. In the spring of 1832, he and his men floated their fur inventory downriver to Fort Union in order to resupply. Angry that Kipp had deserted Fort Piegan, and, most likely, egged on by Hudson's Bay agents, the Blackfeet burned the trading post to the ground.

That summer David Mitchell—who had succeeded Kipp— came up the Missouri with a fresh store of merchandise. Finding Fort Piegan destroyed, Mitchell continued another seven miles upstream and built Fort McKenzie as a temporary replacement. The following year, carpenters constructed a permanent trading post near the interim one. Since then, the Blackfeet had allowed the fort to prosper.[17] Although the confederation kept the peace with the traders, an air of danger overhung the stockade like the implied threats of a school-yard bully. Fort McKenzie's *bourgeois* needed no reminder that he had best watch his step.

Now confronted with the Blackfoot demand that he order the keelboat upriver, Culbertson understood the gravity of his situation. He realized that failure to do the confederation's bidding could cost him and his men their lives. Unwilling to take that risk, Culbertson sent an express to Harvey, directing him to bring the keelboat to Fort McKenzie, the smallpox be damned.

When Harvey and the keelboat arrived at the trading post a few days later, the disease had spread to other members of his crew. For nearly a week the Blackfeet traded, drank watered-down alcohol, and danced, celebrating their coup over the fur company. The Piegans and Bloods relished their victory, unconcerned that two of Harvey's voyageurs were dead.[18]

After their trading and revelry were finished, the Blackfeet struck their tipis and rode north looking for buffalo, eager for their autumn hunt. Still gloating over how they had cowed Pratte & Chouteau's *bourgeois,* none of them suspected that a deadly killer was growing within their lungs.

During the next few weeks, Culbertson and nearly everyone else at Fort McKenzie came down with smallpox. Twenty-seven residents at the trading post died, with the Indian wives of the *engagés* and traders accounting for all but one of them.[19] During the height of the contagion, there were so few healthy workers to care for the sick or see to burials, cadavers were dumped in the Missouri.

Later that fall, Culbertson recovered from his illness. When his scabs fell off, he checked his cheeks in a looking glass, noting the deep pockmarks that radiated outward as if they had been spun off a revolving disk. While the sagebrush flowered in the warm sun of Indian summer and the cottonwood leaves turned as yellow as buttercups, the *bourgeois* scanned the horizon, wondering why no Blackfeet came to the fort to trade. After regaining his strength, Culbertson rode across the upper Missouri plain, searching for his customers. Everywhere he looked, he spotted large herds of buffalo but no Indian hunters. Then near the Three Forks of the Missouri, he sighted a Blackfoot camp with nearly sixty lodges. Studying the tipis from afar, he saw no smoke wafting from their tops. No delegation of warriors dashed forth to ensure he was a friend. No clusters of women knelt alongside buffalo hides, scraping away the fat and sinew in preparation for tanning. The camp appeared as lifeless as a phantom ship on the open sea.

Riding in to investigate, Culbertson listened for the laughter of children but heard only the wind caressing the prairie. Reaching the edge of the encampment, he noticed dead horses and dogs scattered among the lodges, their bodies bloated by the warm autumn air. Most had been shot or had had their throats cut by their owners, who wanted the animals available to them in the netherworld. As Culbertson moved among the tipis, his stomach knotted from the stench. And then he saw them: Blackfoot men, women, and children—putrefied and dead—their arms and legs gnawed to the bone by coyotes and rats. Peering inside the tipis, Culbertson found more people, their bodies swollen with rot, their features disfigured by decay and the horrible curse of *Variola major*. Rushing from one lodge to another, the *bourgeois* searched for survivors, his mind refusing to accept that everyone was dead. Then just when he was ready to admit his worst fears, he discovered two old women— walking skeletons—starving and out of their heads from having witnessed the obliteration of their band. Over a half century old, they had lived through earlier epidemics and were now immune to smallpox but not to its heartache.[20]

A bove the forty-ninth parallel, the *Variola* virus invaded the realm of the Hudson's Bay Company. Carried north by infected parties of Blackfeet and Assiniboines, the *rotting face* quickly spread across the Canadian plains and central lake country. Near the confluence of the St. Mary and Belly rivers (in southern Alberta), so many Blackfeet died, the survivors renamed the location "The Grave Yard."[21] At Fort Pelly on the Assiniboine River (in eastern Saskatchewan), Chief Factor William Todd, head of the firm's Swan River District, had learned of the epidemic on September 20. Three Crees from the Qu'Appelle River region told him that a dreadful sickness had overwhelmed Fort Union. The Americans had bolted the gate and prohibited any Indians from entering.[22]

Although Todd was uncertain if the disease was smallpox, he assumed the worst. The day after hearing about conditions at Fort Union, he called together all the Indians around Fort Pelly and warned them to stay clear of the Missouri River. As a further safeguard, he offered to vaccinate any who were willing. Unlike the American trading companies, the Hudson's Bay Company had stocked many of its larger posts—including Fort Pelly—with cowpox vaccine, instructing its factors to immunize any Indians they could. For the most part, the directive had been ignored, but at least some of the outlying trading houses had vaccine available.

In order to persuade the Fort Pelly Indians that they should be vaccinated, Todd warned them that all who refused would die before the first leaves of spring. Sixty Crees volunteered their arms for the white man's medicine, and Todd's traders made incisions with lancets and applied vaccine, rendering the tribesmen safe from an epidemic that was destroying their brethren below the forty-ninth parallel.

Over the next several weeks, Todd heard conflicting reports about the nature of the disease. One claimed there was nothing amiss at Fort Union, adding that the Americans had locked its gates to shelter a band of visiting Blackfeet from being massacred by the Assiniboines. Then on October 27, Todd received word that eighteen Assiniboines had perished from an illness that had all the symptoms of smallpox. Ten days later, an express reached Fort Pelly from the Beaver Creek post, stating that the malady killing the Assiniboines was something other than smallpox, exactly what, the factor, William McKay, could not say.

Five days before Christmas, Todd finally received an express that confirmed his most dreaded fears. A smallpox epidemic had indeed broken out across central Canada and was hammering tribes over the entire Saskatchewan plain. On December 23, Pierre Le Rocque, one of the express messengers who had brought Chief Factor Todd the news, developed a high fever. Four days after the New Year, 1838, Le Rocque died, another victim of *Variola major*.[23]

Now that the epidemic had been positively diagnosed as smallpox, Todd redoubled his efforts to immunize all the

Indians within his district. During the previous fall while the true nature of the disease was still in doubt, Todd had sent more vaccine to his traders, instructing them to use it at once. Most, such as William McKay at Beaver Creek, had complied, thereby saving many of the Saskatchewan River tribes from the worst of the *rotting face*. Todd had also trained a number of Indians to administer the vaccine, including Chief Chocah of the Qu'Appelle Crees.

Despite the efforts of William Todd, many smaller Hudson's Bay trading houses never received any vaccine and some of the ones that did were staffed with traders unschooled in its proper use. As a result, thousands of Canadian Indians remained unprotected. At Carlton House on the lower North Saskatchewan River, Chief Trader William Small ran into a different problem. His vaccine was inert. Not only did the Indians he had vaccinated catch smallpox but so too did many of the Carlton House personnel. Because of their Native American ancestry, Métis *engagés* were particularly vulnerable.

By late December 1837, smallpox had destroyed over half the Blackfoot Confederation. On the twenty-eighth of the month, Edmonton House Factor, John Rowand, wrote the Hudson's Bay governor, George Simpson, that he had no way of stemming the epidemic and that his command was at the mercy of smallpox and Blackfoot revenge.[24]

In early January 1838, William Todd forwarded a fresh supply of vaccine to Edmonton and Carlton houses, hoping to save those Indians who had not yet contracted the dreaded virus. As winter wore on, Hudson's Bay traders rushed to vaccinate the Plains Indians who were still at risk. By the start of spring, the company had checked the epidemic west of Lake Winnipeg, thereby sparing Canada's eastern woodland tribes. But along the North and South Saskatchewan rivers, the *rotting face* had killed upwards of seventy-five percent of the non-vaccinated native population. At Fort Pelly, Carlton House, Edmonton House, and other Hudson's Bay posts in central Canada, the only Indians coming in to trade were those who had been vaccinated and a handful of pockmarked survivors who now wore the hideous *Variola* brand.

In the midst of the epidemic, while the Hudson's Bay factors were attempting to stem the virus on the Canadian prairie, the *rotting face* invaded the Pawnees. On the plains far south of the forty-ninth parallel, a band of Skidi Pawnees searched for buffalo, finding instead a small party of Ogalalas, one of the seven tribes of the Teton Lakotas and bitter enemies of the Skidis. The two sides immediately circled up, the men painting their faces for battle. After beseeching their spirits for a grand coup or a noble death, the warriors charged one another as they shrieked their war cries and fired their musketballs and arrows.

The Pawnees won the fight, taking many scalps and capturing nearly two dozen Ogalala women and children. As the Pawnees returned to their village, they exulted in their triumph, never suspecting that the victory would be the most costly of their lives. Some of the Ogalala prisoners had been infected with smallpox and now had its virus multiplying within their lungs. Soon the disease showed itself among the Ogalalas and passed to the Pawnees. Before the next moon, Skidi mothers and fathers were mourning the loss of their own sons and daughters.

Reeling with anguish and desperate to stem the epidemic that was destroying their children, Skidi parents called on the tribal shamans, imploring them to save their families. The shamans prayed and searched their hearts, then announced that the gods were punishing the Skidis for having turned their backs on the tribe's ancient religion. Proclaiming that the god Morning Star must be appeased, the medicine men called for a revival of human sacrifice. In years past, the Pawnees had been the only Plains tribe to practice the grisly rite. Now, their shamans told them they must renew the ritual, or they all would be consumed by the *rotting face.* With the approval of the tribal elders, Skidi shamans purified and painted the body of a captive Lakota virgin, then burned her to death atop a ceremonial pyre.[25]

But Morning Star was not appeased. The smallpox continued. *Variola major* eventually spread to the rest of the Pawnee nation, devouring nearly one-fourth of its population—an estimated 2,500 men, women, and children.

Chapter nine notes

[1.] Chardon, *Journal*, 130.

[2.] Audubon, *Journals*, 2:46.

[3.] Chardon, *Journal*, 130-3.

[4.] On August 5, 1837 (ibid., 126), Chardon wrote that the Hidatsas camping near Turtle Mountain had caught smallpox. On Sunday, August 27 (ibid., 132), he penned "News from the Gros Ventres [Hidatsas] of the disease breaking out amongst them." He failed to say if he was writing about the main body of Hidatsas camped far to the north, the Hidatsas' Knife River village—which Charbonneau had gone to visit on August 25—or merely some other hunting camp. I assume he meant another small hunting camp because of his entry for Sunday, September 10 (ibid., 135), which states "Charboneau [*sic*] arrived late last night from the Gros Ventres, all well in that quarter, the disease has not yet broke out among them."

[5.] Chardon's journal entry for August 29, 1837 (ibid., 133), is ambiguous: "there is six of us in the Fort that has the Fever, and one the small pox [*sic*]." I take that to mean seven men were ill, including Chardon. The following day, he wrote, "All those that I thought had the small pox [*sic*] turned out to be true, the fever left them yesterday, and the disease showed itself." DeVoto, *Across the Wide Missouri*, 283 asserts that Chardon had a mild case of smallpox, but given the short time he was sick, he may have had something else.

[6.] Because of the discrepancy between the number of Assiniboine women reported inoculated in Larpenteur, *Forty Years* and the number given in Larpenteur, "Journals and Notes," it is impossible to know how many died from the procedure. DeVoto, *Across the Wide Missouri*, 288 follows "Journals and Notes," stating that of the seven Indian women and ten whites who were inoculated, only three died. Jacob Halsey, who had every reason to downplay the number of deaths, claimed (in Halsey to Pratte, Chouteau & Company, November 2, 1837, reprinted in Chardon, *Journal*, 394-6) that four people at Fort Union died out of twenty-seven who had the disease. Halsey did not say if any of the twenty-seven had been inoculated with his pus. Larpenteur, *Forty Years*, 110 asserts that of those Indian women who were inoculated (by Larpenteur's count in *Forty Years* about thirty) "many died." Ferch, "Fighting the Smallpox Epidemic," 19, no. 4 (winter 1983): 4-6 argue for Larpenteur's count in *Forty Years*. As Ferch points out, Larpenteur had far less reason to inflate the death count than Halsey did in reducing it. Of course Ferch ignores the difference between Larpenteur's two accounts.

Although Larpenteur's *Forty Years* and his "Journals and Notes" never mention the inoculation of the Indian women's children, it is inconceivable that they were not given the same treatment as their mothers. Larpenteur, *Forty Years*, 111 describes a "little boy" who had the disease, but the text does not say who he belonged to. Readers should avoid concluding there were no other children merely because Larpenteur failed to write about them. Most likely, he left them out because he felt they were unimportant.

[7.] Jacob Halsey's quote comes from Halsey to Pratte, Chouteau & Company, November 2, 1937, reprinted in Chardon, *Journal*, 394-6. The belief that miasmas or poisonous vapors caused diseases such as smallpox was old, having gained popularity through the writings of the Greek physician Galen (A.D. 130-200). In addition to discussing the smallpox-infected air, Halsey's letter states that he lost only one man to the disease, Baptiste Compton. DeLand, abst., "Fort Tecumseh and Fort Pierre Journal and Letter Books," 9:110 n. 44 reports that an *engagé* named

Antoine Dauphin also died of smallpox at Fort Union in 1837.

8. Denig, *Indian Tribes*, 73 says that Le Gauche contracted smallpox sometime between 1776 and 1800. Assuming he was a baby or toddler in 1780—his date of birth is unknown—he most likely caught the disease that year or the next. Finally, Le Gauche must have been a common French name for left-handed Indians. Bradbury, *Travels*, 128 reports that John Bradbury met an Arikara chief by that name during the naturalist's keelboat journey up the Missouri with Wilson Price Hunt's Astorians in 1811.

9. J. A. Hamilton to Pierre Chouteau Jr., February 25, 1838, Chouteau Family Papers (St. Louis: Missouri Historical Society, photocopied) cites Chief Le Gauche's losses. English by birth, Hamilton's true name was Archibald Palmer. When he wrote this letter, he worked as Pratte & Chouteau's St. Louis cashier.

10. Erwin N. Thompson, *Fort Union Trading Post: Fur Trade Empire on the Upper Missouri* (Originally published as *Fort Union Trading Post Historic Structures Report*, part 1, National Park Service, 1968; Medora, North Dakota: Theodore Roosevelt Nature and History Association, 1986), 46.

11. Larpenteur, *Forty Years*, 112.

12. Ewers, *The Blackfeet*, 65 states that the Blackfoot who had boarded the *St. Peter's* at the mouth of the Little Missouri River continued up the main Missouri from Fort Union on Harvey's keelboat. As the keelboat neared the Judith River, the Blackfoot became ill with smallpox and infected two others. Giving a different version, DeVoto, *Across the Wide Missouri*, 290 reports that one boatman and an Indian girl became sick.

13. Hafen, ed. *Fur Traders, Trappers, and Mountain Men of the Upper Missouri*, 43, 65.

14. DeVoto, *Across the Wide Missouri*, 290.

15. Audubon, *Journals*, 2:188-95.

16. In 1832, during a trip to the upper Missouri to paint the region's Indians, artist George Catlin estimated the Blackfoot Confederation at 1,650 lodges, each with an average of ten family members. A year later the German nobleman-adventurer, Alexander Phillipp Maximilian, Prince of Wied-Nuwied, journeyed to Fort McKenzie and raised Catlin's population estimate to between 18,000 and 20,000 people; see Ewers, *The Blackfeet*, 60.

17. Robertson, *Competitive Struggle*, 170-1.

18. DeVoto, *Across the Wide Missouri*, 291.

19. Ibid.

20. Ibid. Ewers, *The Blackfeet*, 212 reports that James Doty, assistant to Governor Isaac Stevens, estimated the 1854 Blackfoot population at 7,630, less than half of the 1832 estimates of Catlin and Maximilian.

21. Ewers, *The Blackfeet*, 65-6.

22. Arthur J. Ray, "Smallpox: The Epidemic of 1837-38," *The Beaver* 306, no. 2 (autumn 1975): 9-11.

23. Ibid., 12 reports that Pierre Le Rocque, who was Métis, had been treated with dormant cowpox vaccine.

24. Ibid. Rowand either had no cowpox vaccine or no active vaccine.

25. DeVoto, *Across the Wide Missouri*, 292-4; and Dollar, "High Plains Smallpox Epidemic," 24.

Chapter Ten

Prevention

By the late eighteenth century, most Europeans recognized how vulnerable Native Americans were to infectious diseases such as smallpox. Recognition was one thing, but the collective will and ability to prevent their spread were quite another. The first concerted attempt to protect the New World from smallpox came with the 1776 exploratory voyage of Captain James Cook, who was seeking the fabled Northwest Passage. Before leaving England, the British navigator required every crewman aboard his ships, the *H.M.S. Resolution* and *H.M.S. Discovery,* either to have had smallpox or to have been inoculated.[1] The precaution kept smallpox away from the Eskimos and Aleuts, who Captain Cook encountered while probing the Bering Strait, and the Hawaiians, who later killed him, but it did not serve as a precedent for other Europeans. Safeguards such as Cook's were infrequent, at best.

Seventeen years after the islanders of Hawaii ended the life of Captain Cook, Edward Jenner began experimenting with cowpox as a way to immunize people from the *Variola* virus. At the turn of the nineteenth century, two years following the publication of Jenner's pamphlet about the benefits of cowpox, Dr. Benjamin Waterhouse of the Harvard Medical School performed America's first vaccinations—on his own children—

using vaccine that he had received from England. Impressed by the results, Waterhouse promoted the procedure to the medical community and learned citizenry.

Educated whites saw the benefits of vaccination over inoculation and readily accepted its use. In contrast, the illiterate poor usually rejected both treatments, viewing periodic outbreaks of smallpox as the will of God. Sitting at the bottom of the social pecking order, most Indians and black slaves came no closer to being vaccinated than did a tree stump.

An early disciple of Dr. Waterhouse, President Thomas Jefferson directed that eighteen members of his household undergo the newfangled procedure. At Jefferson's behest, Dr. Edward Gantt—the Congressional chaplain—vaccinated a party of visiting Indian chiefs, who toured Washington City in April 1802. Dr. Gantt may have used vaccine that Jefferson had cultured. Jefferson grew his own stock of vaccine at his Monticello home, and readily offered it to southeastern physicians.[2]

After hearing the alarming news of the Missouri River smallpox epidemic of 1801 and 1802, Jefferson ordered Meriwether Lewis and William Clark to take a measure of cowpox vaccine (called kinepox vaccine by Jefferson; the word kine is an archaic plural for cow) with their Corps of Discovery and vaccinate any Indians they encountered during their exploration of the Louisiana and Oregon territories. At the time, most vaccine culture came from the Vaccine Institution of London or from Dr. Waterhouse, who had also gone into the vaccine distribution business. The culture was transported on cotton thread that had been repeatedly submerged in eight-day-old cowpox virus.[3]

Despite President Jefferson's good intentions, the humanitarian mission of Lewis and Clark failed. Before the explorers reached their first Missouri tribe, their vaccine culture was dead. Faulty storage is the most likely cause of its loss. The problem was so common, many physicians of the day vaccinated directly from the blistered arm of a cowpox-infected donor to that of the intended recipient.[4] Yet, if the captains' stock had retained its potency, Lewis and Clark may not have been able to persuade the Indians to undergo the procedure.

Although the Missouri tribes allowed the two explorers to

treat their visible physical disorders, they may have been less willing to allow them to scratch the skin of a perfectly healthy arm and rub it with the white man's medicine. The degree of trust required for Indians to submit to such a treatment varied from tribe to tribe.

President Jefferson and Dr. Waterhouse were not the only Americans to become excited about the benefits of vaccination. A Baltimore physician named James Smith also recognized the value of Jenner's research and administered his first vaccination on May 1, 1801. In 1809, Smith received an agency charter to vaccinate the citizens of Maryland. When an attempt to bring Pennsylvania under his agency umbrella failed, he decided to go national.

Because of Smith's lobbying, Congress directed President James Madison on February 27, 1813, to appoint a vaccination czar. The czar was to oversee the nation's vaccine supply and supervise a platoon of agents who would immunize the populace. Madison picked James Smith, making him the country's primary source for cowpox vaccine and authorizing him to hire twenty vaccination practitioners. Unfortunately for Smith, Congress failed to appropriate funding for his position, instead allowing him to charge for his services. As an afterthought, the politicians granted him a franking privilege so he could mail his vaccine free of postage.

Frustrated that Congress refused to pay him—because a cadre of lawmakers thought doing so would be unconstitutional—Smith established his own foundation, the National Vaccine Institution. Although the politicians nixed his petition for a federal charter, Smith secured enough private financing to begin operation, albeit on a limited scale.

The National Vaccine Institution limped along until 1821, dispensing cowpox vaccine but coming nowhere near the grand designs envisioned by its founder. Then in November that year, disaster struck when Smith mailed some vaccine to Dr. John Ward, his agent in Tarborough, North Carolina. Somehow, Ward inadvertently substituted smallpox scabs for Smith's vaccine and started a mini-epidemic, which resulted in several deaths.

In an argument that quickly reached the House of Representatives, Ward blamed Smith for sending infected medicine, while Smith accused Ward of maintaining a sloppy laboratory. When the press started covering the quarrel, the public began to question the safety of vaccination. Needing a scapegoat, Congress stripped Smith of his commission. Private donations to the National Vaccine Institution dried up immediately, and the vaccine repository failed within a year.[5]

In 1818, before James Smith and his National Vaccine Institution ran into trouble, the federal government again attempted to vaccinate the Indians of the upper plains, this time directing the Army's Yellowstone Expedition to carry out the work. Commanded by Colonel Henry Atkinson, the two-year undertaking was intended to project the power of the United States by building a military stockade at the confluence of the Yellowstone and Missouri rivers (near where Fort Union was eventually located).

From the moment the force started up the Missouri, logistical ineptitude caused repeated delays. Then the keelboat carrying the cowpox vaccine sank, soaking the culture and rendering it useless. Army doctors tested the inert vaccine on some Pawnees near the Loup River, but the treatment would not take. Meanwhile, the main body of the expedition grew concerned about the approaching winter and sputtered to a halt at Council Bluffs, never to reach the mouth of the Yellowstone. After Congress refused to allot additional funds to the fiasco, the expedition hobbled back to the settlements, leaving a garrisoned cantonment at Council Bluffs as its only tangible success.[6] By failing to successfully vaccinate the tribes of the upper Missouri, the leaders of the Yellowstone Expedition were unable to protect the Lakotas along the White River (in South Dakota) from a minor *Variola* outbreak that beset them in 1819.[7]

By the mid 1820s, many years had passed since the Omaha Indians were the pirates of the Missouri River. Their bravado having been pulverized by the smallpox epidemic of the early 1800s, the surviving Omahas clung peacefully to their toehold on the central Missouri, no longer a threat to the keelboats and mackinaws that plied the river north of Council Bluffs. Having become dependent on the traders' wares, the Omahas at last made a formal truce with the United States. After signing a treaty in 1825, tribal elders granted permission for government agents to immunize those who had been born after the death of their revered Chief Blackbird. By doing so, the Omahas saved their young people from a bout of smallpox that swept the central plains in the early 1830s.[8]

In 1831 and 1832, this latest round of smallpox attacked the nomadic Arapaho, who roamed the prairie bordering the South Platte River (northeastern Colorado and western Nebraska). At the time, their Atsina relatives were visiting, as they had done every few years since separating from the Arapahos generations before. Although the Arapahos welcomed their cousins, their periodic visits must have strained Arapaho resources, for the Arapahos referred to their guests as beggars and spongers. The Atsina trait of quelling their hunger at the campfires of their friends had earned them a reputation of having "big bellies." French trappers, who first learned about the tribe through its neighbors, had mistranslated this insulting term for the Atsinas into the name Gros Ventres.[9]

As the smallpox spread among the scattered Arapaho bands and their Atsina visitors, it exacted a terrible toll, killing better than a quarter of both tribes. Terrified that the *rotting face* would soon destroy them all, those Atsinas who could ride fled northwest to their home territory alongside the upper curve of the Milk River (in northern Montana and southern Alberta). That the epidemic did not envelop the upper plains was fortunate. Still, it touched the Cheyennes, Pawnees, and a few bands of Arikaras.[10]

The artist and prairie traveler George Catlin blamed white fur traders for accidentally infecting the Pawnees with smallpox in 1832, although it is just as likely that they caught it from the Arapahos or Atsinas. By Catlin's count, the disease destroyed nearly one-half of the Pawnee tribe, which seems a gross exaggeration in light of the number of Pawnees who died during the epidemic of 1837 and 1838.

Years earlier, a trader had shown some Pawnee chiefs a stoppered bottle, claiming it contained smallpox. The tribal elders remembered what the pestilence had done during the epidemic of 1801 through 1802 and were frightened. When the trader demanded that the Pawnees grant his wishes—probably give him more buffalo robes than his supply of trade goods would warrant—or he would open the bottle, the tribe complied. After the Pawnees caught the *Variola* virus in 1832, they probably assumed that some trader had unleashed it from a bottle.[11]

By the early 1830s, vaccination was seen as a necessary preventive for Indian delegations visiting America's eastern cities. In the autumn of 1831, Indian agent John F. A. Sanford and two interpreters escorted four Indians to St. Louis, the first leg of their journey to Washington, D.C. In the river town, agent Sanford introduced his four charges to Indian Superintendent William Clark, then took them to the most important white man they would meet on their entire trip, a Doctor Tiffin. The doctor persuaded the Indians to be vaccinated against smallpox, lest they catch the disease in some eastern city. His bill to the government for the procedure was thirty-five dollars.[12] Considering the epidemic that would sweep the upper Missouri within six years, Dr. Tiffin's treatment was a godsend.

The same year Sanford and his Indian delegation headed east on their grand tour, the Upper Missouri Outfit of the American Fur Company sent cowpox vaccine to Fort Tecumseh, but there is no record of it being widely administered to the neighboring Lakotas.[13]

In the spring of 1832, the Twenty-second Congress debated the feasibility of vaccinating all the nation's Indians, guessed to be upwards of 290,000 people. On May 5, the House and Senate approved $12,000 for the operation, directing its execution to the Secretary of War. To contemporary eyes the sum seems paltry, but at the time the funds would have gone a long way toward preventing the epidemic that was to hit the upper Missouri just five years later. In the midst of that tragedy, the Commissioner of Indian Affairs, T. Hartley Crawford, put the cost of vaccinating the western tribes at six cents per person. In 1832, the appropriated funds should have been sufficient to vaccinate 200,000 Indians, about sixty-nine percent of the country's estimated native population.[14]

Although Congress appropriated the money, its good intentions fell prey to bureaucratic indifference and, perhaps, wanton prejudice. The Army did send a physician to the Osages soon after the moneys were authorized. Although heat and humidity damaged much of his vaccine, the doctor managed to treat about one-third of the tribe.[15]

Among other tribes, government officials adopted a less humane policy. On May 9, 1832, Secretary of War, Lewis Cass, wrote John Dougherty, the senior Indian agent for the upper Missouri, that he should not vaccinate any tribes above the Arikaras.[16] A kind interpretation of Cass's directive would assume the Secretary wanted to husband his resources. On the other hand, cynics could argue that he more likely wanted to see the Blackfeet annihilated, especially since they regularly harassed American trapping brigades. For friendly tribes such as the Mandans, Hidatsas, and Assiniboines who lived between the Arikaras and Blackfeet, Cass's order was just bad luck.

Despite the Secretary's injunction, a small amount of vaccine reached the upper Missouri. During the summer of 1832, Army Major Jonathan L. Bean and a detail of troops escorted a physician and some cowpox vaccine as far as Fort Union. Although the doctor tried persuading the various Indian bands that he encountered to be vaccinated, most declined, fearing it was a trick to make them ill. The Lakotas, in particular, rejected the procedure, telling the physician that they felt fine. They saw no reason to take the white man's medicine until they became sick.[17]

On September 30, the same year, a Doctor Martin journeyed from the Indian agency at Fort Kiowa to Fort Pierre in order to try again vaccinating the Yankton Lakotas. Earlier that summer, the American Fur Company had shipped vaccine to the new post, along with directions for its use. On October 2, the doctor returned to Fort Kiowa, having spent only one full day on his mission. It is doubtful that he could have immunized any more than a fraction of the Indians living around the Missouri-Bad River confluence—even if they had been willing.[18]

In the mid 1830s, the Reverend Samuel Parker, a Congregational missionary, toured the Columbia Territory and reported that in the six years prior to his visit smallpox had destroyed nearly ninety percent of the Indians living between The Dalles (a famous series of rapids on the Columbia River) and the Oregon coast. According to reports, the Indians perished so rapidly, the banks of the Columbia were littered with the dead. Entire villages were wiped out as the epidemic enveloped the Pacific shoreline, eventually touching the tribes of northern California.[19] Perhaps at the behest of the Reverend Parker, a few bands of Christian Indians dwelling near Kettle Falls (in northwestern Washington) were vaccinated around the time of his tour. For these lucky "believers," the treatment enabled them to survive the smallpox epidemic of the late 1830s, which spilled over the Continental Divide from the upper Missouri, destroying vast numbers of Spokane and other non-Christian Indians.[20]

Another early effort to vaccinate the Native Americans enjoyed a modest success. In 1836, government emissaries signed a peace treaty with the Ottawas and Ojibwas living near the Red River of the North (the river divides Minnesota from North Dakota). Among the treaty's many covenants, one called for the United States to furnish a physician and $300 per year to vaccinate those Indians who remained on their reservation.[21] In light of the horror that was to consume their upper Missouri neighbors a year later, the Ottawas and Ojibwas probably considered themselves fortunate to have swapped their freedom for protection from the *rotting face.*

Chapter Ten notes

1. Ramenofsky, *Vectors of Death*, 138.
2. Shurkin, *Invisible Fire*, 190, 192. Disagreeing with Shurkin, Hopkins, *Princes and Peasants*, 265 states that the visiting Indians were vaccinated in late 1801.
3. Shurkin, *Invisible Fire*, 193; and Stearn and Stearn, *Effect of Smallpox*, 57-8.
4. Stearn and Stearn, *Effect of Smallpox*, 58.
5. Shurkin, *Invisible Fire*, 194-7.
6. Chittenden, *The American Fur Trade of the Far West*, 2:560-79; and Stearn and Stearn, *Effect of Smallpox*, 61-2. The Army cantonment at Council Bluffs eventually became Fort Atkinson.
7. Stearn and Stearn, *Effect of Smallpox*, 78-9 state that the epidemic occurred during the winter of 1818 and 1819. Dollar, "High Plains Smallpox Epidemic," 24 puts it between 1819 and 1820.
8. Stearn and Stearn, *Effect of Smallpox*, 75.
9. Josephy, *Indian Heritage*, 116. The Atsinas were usually called the Gros Ventres of the Prairie to differentiate them from the Hidatsas, who were also called the Gros Ventres; for more see Chapter 3, endnote 15.
10. Taylor, "Sociocultural Effects," 66, 78, fig. 1.
11. Catlin, *Letters*, 2:24, 25 n. (n.n.).
12. Ewers, *Indian Life*, 81, 83.
13. Chardon, *Journal*, 319 n. 507; and Stearn and Stearn, *Effect of Smallpox*, 64.
14. Ferch, "Fighting the Smallpox Epidemic," 19, no. 4 (winter 1983): 4.
15. Rollings, *Osage*, 278-9.
16. Chardon, *Journal*, 319 n. 507.
17. Stearn and Stearn, *Effect of Smallpox*, 63-4; and Taylor, "Sociocultural Effects," 59. It is interesting to note that shortly after the US Government halfheartedly attempted to vaccinate America's Indians, the British Government passed the Act of 1835, requiring the vaccination of all newborns in England and Wales; see Cartwright, *Disease and History*, 128.
18. DeLand, abst., "Fort Tecumseh and Fort Pierre Journal and Letter Books," 9:161. While it is possible that Dr. Martin was the same physician that Major Bean took to Fort Union during the summer, the Journal contains no record of an earlier visit. Although the Journal puts the Lakota Agency at Fort Lookout instead of Fort Kiowa, the two posts were one and the same.
19. Catlin, *Letters*, 2:255 n. (n.n.).
20. Stearn and Stearn, *Effect of Smallpox*, 64.
21. Ibid., 65.

Chapter Eleven

Autumn 1837

On September 1 outside Mitutanka Village, Arikaras swarmed over the ripening Mandan cornfields, helping themselves to the harvest. Reduced by the *rotting face,* the Mandans were too weak to make them stop. The Arikaras had also watched their own kinsmen perish from the deadly virus, but their numbers of dead came nowhere near those of the Mandans. So many Mandans were now sick, it would be a miracle if any pulled through. More important to the tribe's well-being than buffalo, their corn was their staff of life. Without it, they were doomed. Any Mandan lucid enough to know of the theft must have regretted ever allowing the Arikaras to share his lodge. Mandan hospitality had been repaid with Arikara deceit.

At Fort Clark the cooks were so low on firewood that Chardon opted to risk an attack by sending out a wood-cutting detail. The party completed its task without incident, returning to the post with several cords. Deeming the danger from Indian retaliation to be subsiding now that so many Mandans were either dead or dying, the *bourgeois* dispatched other men to retrieve the prairie grass that had previously been cut but left in the fields. Again, the Indians allowed the *engagés* to work in peace.

On September 4, three white trappers arrived at Fort Clark, reporting that the plains were overrun with buffalo. In normal times, Indian hunters would have been hot after the herds, but that was before the smallpox. Because entire families were stricken, there were few native men able to hunt and few women available to butcher meat or tan hides. With most of their corn lost to the Arikaras, the Mandan survivors faced starvation.

By now Chardon had begun to fear for the welfare of his son, Andrew Jackson. Seven men at Fort Clark were still bedridden with smallpox, including the interpreter, Antoine Garreau. If the boy remained at the trading post, he was sure to become infected. Hoping that Fort Pierre was now free of the disease, Chardon ordered his workmen to build a bull boat, intending to send the lad away from the contagion. On September 7, Chardon bid his son good-bye as the child headed downriver, escorted by two *engagés*.

Two nights later, Toussaint Charbonneau returned to Fort Clark from the main Hidatsa village on the Knife River. To Chardon's relief, the old trader reported that the Hidatsas' quarantine was still holding. Although smallpox had broken out in a couple of the tribe's smaller hunting camps, it had not yet attacked the core of the Hidatsa nation. Ominously, Charbonneau announced that his wife had come down with the disease soon after they reached the village. She had died September 6. Thankful that the tribe was—for the most part— still safe, Chardon gathered a store of trade goods, and again sent Charbonneau to the Knife River.

If Chardon suspected the danger that Charbonneau's deceased wife posed for the Hidatsas, he never confided it to his journal. Instead, the *bourgeois* expressed his hope that the tribe would barter enough robes to salvage the trading season. As on his previous trip, Charbonneau traveled at night in order to avoid any Mandan or Arikara warriors who were set on avenging their dead relatives.

On September 12, an Arikara chief named Bloody Hand stopped by Fort Clark, having come from his camp near the Hidatsa Knife River village.[1] His news undoubtedly sent a chill down every spine inside the trading post. The Hidatsa quarantine had failed. Smallpox had erupted on the Knife. Most likely, the wife of Chardon's emissary, Toussaint Charbonneau, had been the carrier. It remained to be seen if the Hidatsas would seek revenge. The next day, the weather turned as cold and gloomy as the traders' mood. No longer were the fort personnel concerned about attaining their quota of buffalo robes. Now their central concern was whether they would keep their hair.

On September 15, a two-man express arrived at Fort Clark from Fort Union, reporting that the smallpox epidemic had spread to the Assiniboines and Blackfeet. The messengers said that a number of Indians in both tribes had already died, and that fatalities were mounting by the hour. Two days later, an early frost destroyed most of the corn and pumpkins remaining in the Mandans' gardens. The untimely weather portended a belt-tightening winter for Indians and traders alike. Chardon had planned to buy a few dozen bushels of Mandan corn in order to bolster Fort Clark's food supply, but the hard freeze dashed that possibility. Now if he bought ten bushels, he would count himself lucky.

As the month wore on, Chardon did the work of his *engagés,* since most of his command was still bedridden with smallpox. He found the labor physically demanding, prompting him to note in his journal that he had not toiled so hard in years. But hay had to be cut and hauled, and firewood had to be chopped and stacked, for winter loomed on the horizon, and the blizzards had their own timetable and would not wait for the *rotting face.* On September 19, a young Mandan from Ruhptare Village came to Fort Clark, saying that all but fourteen members of the town had perished. On hearing the news, Chardon raised his estimate of Mandan dead to 800—one-half of the tribe—noting sarcastically in his journal, "What a bande [*sic*] of RASCALS has been used up."

Now the surviving Mandans began to fear that their fickle Arikara allies might join the Saone Lakotas for an all-out attack on Mitutanka Village. The Saones had not yet been touched by the epidemic. For the past week, Arikara and Saone ambassadors had smoked the calumet, negotiating a truce between their tribes. Weakened by smallpox, the Mandans would have no chance against such a duo. Accordingly, all the

Mandans who were able forded the Missouri River on September 21, leaving behind forty-one members of their tribe who were too sick to cross.[2] No one at Fort Clark had any idea about what the fleeing Mandans planned to do. The epidemic had set Indian against white and tribe against tribe, turning the entire upper Missouri into a powder keg.

The next day while Chardon fretted about the strong upriver wind that prevented him from rafting firewood down the Missouri, at Fort Pierre his mixed-blood son, Andrew Jackson, died from smallpox. At least the child's older brother, Bolivar, was attending school in Philadelphia. Perhaps if Chardon had also sent Andrew Jackson to live with his aunts and grandmother, both boys would still be alive.

On September 27, Charbonneau returned to Fort Clark from the Hidatsa Knife River village, having traded for eighty-five buffalo robes and four beaver pelts. Chardon appreciated the robes and furs, but the news Charbonneau related did far more to buoy the *bourgeois's* spirits. Although ten Hidatsas had recently died from smallpox, the disease was nowhere near as rampant among them as it was among the Mandans. In contrast, the Knife River Arikaras were faring worse than their Hidatsa hosts, with two or three Arikaras joining the spirit world every day. To Chardon's relief, none of the Knife River Indians had threatened to attack the trading post—so far. After a couple of days at Fort Clark, Charbonneau headed back to the Hidatsas, taking along stores for the winter trade.

As September drew to an end, David Mitchell and thirty other Pratte & Chouteau employees stopped for the night at Fort Clark. Mitchell was traveling overland to take command of Fort Union from Jacob Halsey. The newly appointed *bourgeois* could not have been heartened by the number of deaths at Mitutanka Village. Chardon had recently raised his estimate of Mandan dead to seven-eighths of the tribe—nearly 1,400 men, women, and children.

Among the Arikaras who had been living with the Mandans, Chardon put the losses at fifty percent, with more of them becoming sick by the day. Of the Hidatsas and the Arikaras who were residing with them along the Knife River, he guessed that at least half would die before the epidemic was finished. Only the elderly of the three tribes who had survived the outbreaks of the early 1780s or early 1800s were safe. For the month, Chardon had exterminated seventy-four rats, a mere pittance compared with the number of Indians killed by the *rotting face*.

On October 1, David Mitchell and his party departed Fort Clark, continuing their journey to Fort Union. Two nights later, a heavy autumn rain turned to snow in the early morning hours. Although the upper Missouri could yet expect a spell of Indian summer, winter had flexed its muscles, letting everyone know it would soon be at hand. Feeling a sense of urgency, Chardon redoubled his effort to lay in a store of firewood. With so many of Fort Clark's employees recovering from smallpox, the labor fell to two *engagés*. They would be hard-pressed to complete the task before the river froze solid.

On October 4, the Arikaras living on the Knife River started south, intending to take possession of Mitutanka Village now that so many Mandans had died and the rest had fled across the Missouri. The opportunity to acquire the Mandans' wealth without a fight far outweighed any perceived danger from living in a place that had witnessed so much death and misery. Having no concept of germ theory, the Arikaras were unaware that the *Variola* virus lurked within the bodies and former possessions of the deceased Mandans. For the Arikaras, Mitutanka Village was too valuable a plum to be left unplucked.

Those Knife River Arikaras who were too ill to travel remained behind in their lodges. Most would eventually succumb to starvation if not to the epidemic. The Hidatsas also deserted their sick, reasoning that their fate was in the hands of the spirits. With winter approaching, the tribe needed to leave its summer village and move to a sheltered camp farther up the Missouri. The prairie would soon be in an icy grip, and if the Hidatsas wished to live through it, they had to lay in a store of dried buffalo meat before the herds drifted south. Though seemingly callous, the decision to abandon its dying kinsmen gave the tribe a chance at survival. Yet as the Hidatsas rode away from the Knife River, few of them realized how slim that chance was. They were leaving their sick relatives, but they were not escaping the *rotting face*.

Some days afterward, a number of the migrating Hidatsas

developed high fevers and aching muscles, compelling their families to camp below the mouth of Lucky Mound Creek. Again the *Variola* terror raged among its new victims, killing them by the score. Eventually, the beleaguered survivors pressed on to their winter quarters, but not before naming their Lucky Mound campsite "Where People Died of Smallpox."[3]

Meanwhile, reports continually reached Fort Clark about large herds of buffalo and pronghorns grazing on the nearby prairie. With so few Indians able to hunt, game was more abundant than it had been in years. Any warrior fit enough to sit a horse headed onto the plain, preparing to give chase. Their women went too, that is the ones who had the strength to walk. Feeling the press of winter, the village tribes were desperate to build up their stock of dried meat. In addition, the women needed to begin dressing buffalo robes to trade at Fort Clark. Otherwise, their families would have to do without the knives, kettles, lead, gunpowder, and other manufactured truck on which they had become dependent.

Throughout the first week of October, Francis Chardon parleyed with the Mandans—most of whom now kept to the left side of the Missouri—and Arikaras, urging them to put away their grudges against the fur company and to tan many buffalo robes for the coming trading season. On October 7, a few Arikara families forded the Missouri and joined the Mandans, preparing to go with them to their winter camp. A week later, the Mandans and their Arikara guests headed upriver. Although Chardon tried learning where they had gone, he was unsuccessful. If the Mandans still had any worries about having to fight a joint Arikara-Saone war party, they could breathe easier. The Saones had recently come down with smallpox, which they blamed on the Arikara ambassadors. The Arikaras had fled the Saone encampment under the cover of night, fearing for their lives.

On October 16, a majority of the Arikaras went downstream from Fort Clark and established their winter camp in a sheltered nook known as the Point of Woods. The location offered more protection from the winter winds than did Mitutanka Village. By now the smallpox epidemic among the Mandans and Arikaras had begun to subside, its reserve of potential victims nearly exhausted. Outbreaks continued to occur, but in nowhere near the numbers of a month ago. Similarly, the Indians ceased their call to arms, having lost their desire to kill Chardon and his men.

With so few warriors able to hunt and so few women left to cook, dress hides, and make clothes, the tribes needed to look to their future. Instead of viewing Fort Clark and the fur company as the root of their ills, the Mandans and Arikaras now saw them as the means to their survival. *Variola major* had rent the social order of the upper Missouri. The old ways were dead and would never again be reborn.

On the fourth Sunday of October, Jacob Halsey and three voyageurs came down the Missouri in a pirogue and stopped for the night at Fort Clark. Halsey had been relieved as *bourgeois* of Fort Union by David Mitchell and was heading to Fort Pierre, where he would renew his duties as senior clerk. Wanting to see his friends at Fort Pierre and perhaps the grave of his son, Andrew Jackson, Francis Chardon decided to accompany Halsey downriver. The following morning, they left at ten o'clock and arrived at Fort Pierre the last day of the month.

At Fort Pierre the conversation undoubtedly focused on the smallpox and how it was affecting the company's trade. Halsey worried about his role in the epidemic, especially since he had introduced the disease to Fort Union. Since David Mitchell was certain to critique Halsey's activities as Fort Union's interim *bourgeois,* Halsey most likely felt compelled to write his own report first.

On November 2, Halsey hurriedly penned a letter to Pratte & Chouteau headquarters in St. Louis, giving his side of the disaster.[4] In it, he mentioned that he had caught a mild case of smallpox while aboard the *St. Peter's.* Although he wrote that twenty-seven people at Fort Union eventually caught the disease, he failed to state that they had been inoculated with his own pus. He put the fort's smallpox deaths at four, adding that only one was a company employee—Baptiste Compton. Halsey noted that the other three fatalities were Indian women, and he disclosed nothing about their mixed-blood children.[5]

No doubt preparing Pierre Chouteau Jr. and the fur company's other senior partners for a year of dismal returns,

Halsey observed that although the prairies were thick with buffalo, there were few Indian hunters. Ignoring the death of Chardon's son, Andrew Jackson, Halsey stated that Fort Pierre was free of smallpox, although the disease had infected the neighboring Lakotas. Halsey ended his report by begging the partners to rush cowpox vaccine to the upper Missouri trading posts. In an effort to push responsibility for the disaster on David Mitchell, Halsey concluded with "had Mr. Mitchell brought some [when he came to Fort Union to take command,] thousands of lives might have been saved."

On November 12, Francis Chardon left Fort Pierre, returning to Fort Clark; he arrived twelve days later, having waded through knee-deep snow drifts. By now most of Fort Clark's employees had recovered from the epidemic and were back at work.[6] The interpreter, Antoine Garreau, was well enough to search for two horses that either had wandered off while grazing or had been stolen. Although the quest took him three days, on November 28, he returned to the trading post with the missing mounts.

By month's end, Fort Clark had slipped into the comfortable routine that marked late autumn. Hunters kept the cooks' larder supplied with fresh buffalo humps, tongues, and ribs; *engagés* chopped firewood, molded bar lead into rifle balls, and did a host of other manual chores; and traders headed to outlying Indian camps, taking supplies that they would advance on credit against the robe production of Indian women.

Among the Mandans and Arikaras, the *rotting face* had nearly exhausted its stock of victims. Isolated cases continued to occur, but the conflagration that had consumed nearly all the Mandans and close to half of the Arikaras had burned itself out. No word about the Hidatsas had reached the fort since the tribe left the Knife River, so Chardon had no way of knowing that among them the epidemic was far from over. As the *bourgeois* closed out his journal for November, he tallied up the rats he had killed for the month, adding to them the number he had dispatched in October. They totaled 268.[7]

On December 1, a trader returned to Fort Clark from the Point of Woods, reporting that the Arikaras had recently killed three Lakotas who were caught attempting to steal their ponies. In celebration, the Arikaras had staged a scalp dance. Chardon welcomed the news. Although the Arikaras had stopped railing against him and his men in retaliation for the smallpox, their lust for revenge had not waned. Like a mountain stream that occasionally disappears beneath a rockfall, the Arikaras' desire for vengeance flowed just below the surface, ready to burst forth at the first opportunity. By giving the Arikaras a way to vent their pent-up anger, the Lakotas had redirected the Arikaras' rage away from Fort Clark.

On December 4, the Missouri River froze. The December solstice and March equinox bracketed winter in the settlements, but on the upper Missouri, they were arbitrary dates that had been sanctified by an almanac. Winter on the upper Missouri began when the river turned to ice and ended with its spring thaw.

With the freezing of the Missouri, life at Fort Clark lapsed into a mind-numbing lethargy. The men continued their chores, though they did them more by rote than with zeal. Unlike eight months earlier when buffalo were nowhere to be found, they now grazed within an hour's ride of the trading post. Chardon's hunters easily kept the fort kitchen supplied with fresh meat.

On December 16, a chimney fire in the *engagés'* quarters produced a break from the winter tedium, though it was quickly extinguished and caused only limited damage. Chardon stayed busy treating with Indians who stopped by to visit, sending expresses to company headquarters in St. Louis, and seeing to it that his men did what they were told. His few diversions came from killing rats and trapping the foxes and wolves that prowled the fort dump, searching for scraps of food. For the month he exterminated eighty-five rats, bringing his total for the year to 1,021.

On the final day of 1837, Toussaint Charbonneau returned to the fort after trading with a ten-lodge band of Hidatsa. His news was grim. Far from being over, the smallpox epidemic continued its rampage. Although the Hidatsas had dispersed into small units, hoping to preserve some of their members, the old trader feared that few would be left alive come spring.

Chapter eleven notes

1. Chardon's entry (Chardon, *Journal*, 135-6) about the location of Chief Bloody Hand's infected camp is ambiguous. Chardon stated that the chief "arrived from his camp, at the Gros Ventres [Hidatsas]." I infer that the camp was located near the Hidatsas' Knife River village.

2. Denig, *Indian Tribes*, 59 n. 27.

3. Meyer, *Village Indians*, 99.

4. Jacob Halsey to Pratte, Chouteau & Company, November 2, 1837, reprinted in Chardon, *Journal*, 394-6.

5. In contrast, Larpenteur, *Forty Years*, 109-10 state that about thirty Indian women and a few fort employees were inoculated (neither Larpenteur nor Halsey mentioned fatalities among the women's mixed-blood children), adding that "the operation proved fatal to most of our patients." This, of course, differs with Larpenteur, "Journals and Notes," 161, which reports that only seventeen people were inoculated.

6. Chardon's entry for November 25 (Chardon, *Journal*, 141)—"Men all employed sawing wood"—implies that the post personnel were no longer convalescing.

7. Although Chardon wrote that he had killed 268 rats in November 1837 (ibid., 142), the number probably represents the total for October and November. Because of Chardon's visit to Fort Pierre, there is a break in his journal between October 23 and November 24. Since no dead-rat count is given for October, I assume the number Chardon recorded for November includes that month as well as October.

Chapter Twelve

Technology and Change

The horse was the most important technological improvement in Native American transportation until the invention of the automobile. Before the Europeans arrived, the Indian tribes of the North American heartland bartered with one another through a sophisticated, Mandan-dominated trading system. Spanish conquistadors introduced horses to Mexico and the Pueblo Indians of the Southwest. First stolen for food by the Apaches and Navahos, horses eventually became items of exchange as they were dispersed from south to north by Indian traders.

Tribes on the Great Plains adopted the horse into their cultures for the same reason they incorporated the Europeans' metal products—efficiency. Just as metal knives, arrowpoints, guns, scrapers, awls, and kettles were labor-saving devices, so too were horses. Horses sped travel and allowed Indians to transport more equipment than they could using dogs. The impact on native society of going from a pedestrian culture to a horse culture was immense, similar in many ways to that experienced by the early twentieth-century world when it switched from horses to cars. Yet, by increasing Indian mobility, horses also aided the diffusion of *Variola major*.

The fur trade produced changes in Indian life equal to those brought about by horses. By the end of the smallpox epidemic of the early 1780s, the trading prowess of the upper Missouri's village tribes was in shreds. Over the next twenty years, French-Canadian *coureurs de bois* stepped into the void, displacing the few Mandan, Hidatsa, and Arikara middlemen who had survived. Beginning with the North West Company trading houses of Peter Grant on the Red River of the North in 1793 and René Jusseaume's trading post among the Mandans a year later, fixed posts also supplanted the Indian trading system. At the same time, these trading forts brought increasing numbers of white men among the Indians, greasing the skids for the further spread of smallpox.

July 27, 1817, ushered in another technological leap in transportation—this one indirectly affecting the Indians. On that day the steamboat *Pike* moored at St. Louis, marking the first time a steamer had come to the burgeoning fur capital. Two years later, the ninety-eight-ton *Independence* became the first steamboat to venture up the Missouri, embarking on a trip that took it to the hamlet of Franklin. Within months of that voyage, the *Western Engineer* steamed to the Yellowstone Expedition's cantonment near Council Bluffs.[1]

By the end of 1829, the American Fur Company had sewn the Missouri River with trading posts from the mouth of the Kansas to that of the Yellowstone. Each spring, French-Canadian voyageurs laboriously hauled the annual trading supplies to the firm's distant forts, using keelboats. Although the sturdy craft were equipped with a mast and sail, more often than not their crews manhandled them against the Missouri's current, using oars, setting poles, and the *cordelle*—a long rope that ran from mid mast to a gang of boatmen who trudged through the shallows, dragging the vessel upstream. Labor intensive, keelboats normally covered twelve or fifteen miles per day, taking them between seventeen and twenty-one weeks to complete the 1,800-mile journey from St. Louis to Fort Union.

In 1830, Kenneth McKenzie, *bourgeois* of Fort Union and managing partner of the American Fur Company's Upper Missouri Outfit, persuaded his fellow partners to purchase a steamboat. On April 16 the following year, the side-wheeler *Yellow Stone* departed St. Louis on its maiden voyage up the

Missouri, reaching its highest point, Fort Tecumseh, two months later. On March 26, 1832, the steamboat again headed upriver, this time making it to Fort Union. The voyage took eighty-four days, a savings of several weeks over the typical keelboat trip.[2] Five years later, the *St. Peter's*—during its fateful journey that infected the upper Missouri with smallpox—cut the time to sixty-nine days. Over the next decade, the time would be further reduced, eventually dropping to forty days.[3] Because steam transportation was faster and needed fewer boatmen than that powered by muscle, shipping costs per mile plummeted.

Among the native tribes along the Missouri River, steamboats made a profound impression. Calling them "fire boats that walk on water," the Indians deemed them "powerful medicine." Since the American Fur Company possessed this new technology and the rival Hudson's Bay Company did not, tribes living near the forty-ninth parallel that had previously traded exclusively with the British firm began bringing their pelts and robes to the American Fur Company's trading posts on the Missouri.

In addition to speeding the rate at which diseases such as smallpox could spread, steamboats also aided the next evolution in the fur trade. By the time the American Fur Company began using steamers to supply its upcountry trading posts, the dominance of beaver was drawing to a close. Among style-conscious gentlemen in European and American cities, silk hats were replacing those made from beaver. Further eroding the market for beaver pelts, hatters who used fur increasingly relied on nutria, a South American rodent, whose underhair had felting properties similar to those of its northern cousin.

The slide in the price of beaver spelled the end of the large, company-supported trapping brigades, whose colorful mountain men had given birth to the raucous summer trade fairs, known as rendezvous. Although a number of mountain men would cling to their trapping life into the 1840s, their heyday ended in June 1834 when the American Fur Company's Western Department and Upper Missouri Outfit became Pratte & Chouteau.

Fortunately for Pratte & Chouteau, as the demand for

beaver declined, a market arose for buffalo robes.[4] Used to make coats and lap covers, buffalo robes that Indians bartered for a few trade goods brought an eighteen percent return (eventually expanding to 135 percent) in St. Louis. Compared with the profits per hide that had been earned in the glory years of the beaver trade, the gain was small, but with modern business practices, such as economies of scale and volume production, the potential existed for a fur company to reap a great deal of money. Pratte & Chouteau paid $1.35 in trade goods for each robe the Indians bartered, either to the partnership's roving traders or at one of its fixed trading houses.

The expenses of running the trading posts, paying an army of traders and other employees, shipping the robes to eastern markets, and transporting supplies and merchandise to the outlying forts increased the firm's cost per robe to $2.55. In the late 1820s, buffalo robes fetched about $3.00 each, a price that peaked at $6.00 in the 1840s. Because of such low receipts—in dollars per hide—a fur company needed a massive supply of robes if the trade was to make economic sense.

Unlike small, high-margin furs such as beaver and otter, low-margin buffalo robes were too bulky to be efficiently moved in quantity by horses or canoes. Cargo shipped across Canada's rivers and lakes required backbreaking portages. In contrast, transport on the Missouri River was comparatively easy. The use of steamboats and mackinaws enabled Pratte & Chouteau to sell a buffalo robe for a fraction of what the Hudson's Bay Company could. As a result of this cost advantage, Pratte & Chouteau—despite competition from a few other American trading companies—dominated the robe market.

For the tribes of the Great Plains, the buffalo robe trade heralded yet another change in their lives. Indian women were the linchpin of the robe business, as important to its good order as were the whites who ran its distribution system. Indian husbands and fathers killed the buffalo, but to their women fell the arduous task of skinning, fleshing, and curing the hides. Working alone, an Indian woman could dress ten skins per year, but two or more women functioning as a team could each tan between fifteen and eighteen.

Although Indian women used many of the robes for their

own families, any surplus was bartered to the fur companies. By providing the women metal knives and scrapers in lieu of implements fashioned from flint and bone, the fur trade made the chore of finishing a hide easier, but it did nothing to ease their workload. Instead, it made the women's lives more difficult. Because the buffalo robe trade needed a volume production in order to turn a profit, it bound Indian women to a repetitious cycle of hard labor.

The native masters of this buffalo capitalism were Indian men. Owning the output of their spouses and daughters,[5] Native American men sought to boost production. Many recognized the economic benefit of having more than one wife. Rather than condemning polygamy as did most Europeans, the Plains tribes had always accepted it as a way to absorb their excess female members. Hunting accidents and warfare took a heavy toll on Indian males, leaving most tribes with more women than men. But wanting additional wives and having the wherewithal to buy them were different matters. Fortunately for Indian men, the bride-price of a new wife could be paid in horses.

By the early 1830s when the demand for buffalo robes began to explode, a number plains warriors had accumulated large horse herds, far more than were required for hunting, warfare, or moving camps. Blackfoot Chief Sachkomapoh purportedly owned between 4,000 and 5,000 head.[6] Many Horses, a Blackfoot warrior who died while fighting the Crows, had over 500 in his remuda.

With the fur trade spurring the demand for robes, and horses providing the means to purchase more wives, Indian men saw that they could increase their wealth through multiple marriages. Blood Chief Seen-From-Afar had ten wives and 100 horses. Charles Larpenteur reported seeing a number of Blackfeet men, each with five or six wives and two dozen or more children spread between several lodges. The annual trade from such families often approached $2,000 in merchandise.[7]

Widows, especially attractive, hardworking widows, did not stay single long. Likewise, unwed teenage sisters were considered prime candidates to marry their older sister's husband. If the girls' parents liked their son-in-law, they typically encouraged such marriages in order to avoid the problems associated with having multiple sons-in-law. An Indian wife usually accepted her sisters into her household far more easily than a non-relative, an important consideration for a man seeking a second or third wife.[8] Just like other husbands worldwide, Indian husbands also prized matrimonial harmony.

As the value of female labor rose, many warriors stopped selling women captives, preferring instead to adopt them into their households as subordinate wives—in reality, slaves— whose main job was to dress buffalo robes. In addition to buffalo hides, Indian women tanned skins from deer, wolves, muskrats, otters, ermine, and beaver, which were also bartered to the white traders.

Salted buffalo tongues found a market with the fur companies, as well. Pratte & Chouteau sold them by the thousands to consumers in Boston, New York, Baltimore, and other eastern cities. The manufacture of pemmican was also a tipi industry. Most trading posts stored numerous bags of this staple of the prairie, holding it for times when game was scarce. Above the forty-ninth parallel, Hudson's Bay Company voyageurs, who paddled the firm's large freight canoes across Canada's waterways, lived on pemmican during their journeys, having no time to hunt.

In addition to speeding transportation and enabling Indian men to acquire multiple wives, horses also altered Native American hunting practices, particularly on the Great Plains. The twin beliefs that Indians wasted no part of any animal they hunted and that the white buffalo skinners alone destroyed the continent's vast bison herds are Hollywood myths.

As soon as the Indians acquired horses, they ceased depending on *piskuns* (buffalo jumps) for their kills and began hunting from horseback. No longer having to harvest buffalo at random, mounted Indians could ignore the bulls and go after the cows. A cow's meat was more tender than a bull's, and its hide was easier to tan. Although hunting from horseback negated the need for Indians to slaughter an entire band of buffalo at a *piskun,* by making cows their primary target, Native Americans eventually upset the sexual balance of the herds. But until the fur trade sent the demand for buffalo robes into the strato-sphere, the typical mounted Indian hunter killed fewer buffalo than in the days before he had horses.[9]

After obtaining muskets, most Plains Indians continued hunting buffalo with bows and arrows. A skilled archer could shoot fifteen or twenty well-placed arrows in the time needed for him to reload a flintlock musket—an operation made dou-bly-difficult on a galloping horse. As an added benefit of the bow over the gun, Indian hunters could positively identify their kills because of their individually-marked arrows.

In 1806, generations before white buffalo skinners added a methodical efficiency to the bison massacre, North West Company trader Alexander Henry the Younger observed the wasteful hunting practices of the Mandans.[10] Appearing to hunt more for sport than sustenance, mounted Mandans slew far more buffalo than their families needed for food. Nomadic tribes such as the Crow and Arapaho were no better at conservation than were the sedentary Mandans. As the nomads acquired more horses, they drove the buffalo away from the prime graz-ing pastures, further stressing the herds.

When the buffalo were scarce, native women used everything from a hunt, but when the animals were plentiful, the women collected only the hides—if needed for tanning—and choicest cuts of meat, abandoning the rest to the coyotes and wolves. Eighteenth- and nineteenth-century Plains Indians had no con-cept of waste as it is understood by modern society. They believed that a guardian spirit—the Manitou to some tribes—controlled the herds, sending or withholding them as it saw fit. Perhaps because of such beliefs as well as commercial gain, Indian hunters of the 1830s through 1850s slaughtered tens of thousands of buffalo, taking nothing but their skins and tongues.

In May 1832, a couple of hundred mounted Lakota warriors attacked a large buffalo herd across the Missouri River from Fort Pierre. Near sunset the Lakotas rode to the trading post with 1,400 tongues, which they swapped for a few gallons of whiskey. They had removed nothing else from their kill, neither hides nor meat. Except for the tongues, the Lakotas had left the

1,400 carcasses to rot.[11]

Indian bands used "soldiers" to ensure that everyone hunted in concert. Soldiers were typically members of a tribal warrior society and functioned as a police force. Their duty was to prevent one or two hotheads from scattering a herd in advance of the main body of hunters. But soldiers had no responsibility to see that none of the meat was wasted.

The rise of the buffalo robe trade in the nineteenth century dramatically increased the number of animals that Indians killed. From an annual shipment of 25,000 robes in the late 1820s, the volume of dressed hides the American Fur Company and its successors sent east steadily increased, reaching 45,000 in 1839, 67,000 the next year, 90,000 per year in the second half of the 1840s, and 100,000 per year during the 1850s and early 1860s.[12]

Writing in his journal in 1832, artist George Catlin made an impassioned plea for an end to the carnage brought on by the robe trade. He correctly foresaw the demise of America's bison herds years before the white buffalo skinners descended on the plains.[13]

Another example of the unwillingness of Indians to conserve their natural resources occurred in the beaver trade. Indian hunters had begun using steel traps and castoreum bait (a strong-smelling secretion from a beaver's perineal glands) by the 1790s. Before that, the most common way Indians obtained beaver was by walking onto frozen ponds in the winter and breaking into the animals' lodges from the top. As the North West and Hudson's Bay companies gradually introduced the new trapping technology across their territories, the best Indian hunters switched to baited steel traps. The efficiency of these traps led many tribes to deplete the beaver within their territories.[14]

In the 1820s, the Hudson's Bay Company governor, George Simpson, tried putting the Canadian beaver harvest on a sustained-yield basis, but he ran into native resistance when he attempted to restrict hunting in over-trapped regions. Not only did the tribes believe that the spirits determined if game was plentiful, but they also feared that if they did not hunt a particular locale, their neighbors would.[15]

The marriage of steamboats and the buffalo robe trade in the mid 1830s brought a commercial boom to many Indians on the upper Missouri. But the prosperity did not flow equally to all tribes. Past smallpox epidemics had severely reduced the population of the Mandans, Hidatsas, and Arikaras and at the same time toppled their trading monopoly. With the Mandan-dominated trading system in shambles, fur companies such as Pratte & Chouteau and its predecessors had stepped into the vacuum, substituting fixed trading posts and a riverine distribution system for the native brokers.

With the influx of the white traders, nomadic tribes such as the Lakotas, Crows, and Assiniboines no longer needed the village tribes to act as middlemen. When the demand for buffalo robes increased, the nomadic tribes upped the robe output of their women, swapping it directly to the fur companies at their far-flung trading posts. Having lost their livelihood as brokers, the village tribes were compelled to produce buffalo robes in order to acquire the white-manufactured merchandise on which they had become dependent. This put them in direct competition with the nomads. Because the village tribes and their nomadic neighbors had lost their link as trading partners, their ancient hatreds intensified.

The smallpox epidemics of the early 1780s and 1800s had brought the Mandans, Hidatsas, and Arikaras to their knees. The epidemic of 1837 and 1838 all but destroyed their identity as three separate tribes.

Chapter twelve notes

[1.] Chittenden, *The American Fur Trade of the Far West*, 1:106, 337; and Hunter, *Steamboats*, 47.

[2.] My count of eighty-four days follows Chittenden, *The American Fur Trade of the Far West*, 1:339, which assumes the *Yellow Stone* reached Fort Union around June 17.

[3.] Ibid., 2:956.

[4.] Unlike the demand for beaver, which had been international, the market for buffalo robes ended at the western edge of the Atlantic Ocean. Europeans found it more economical to fashion their coats and lap covers from locally-raised sheep.

[5.] A general statement such as this is certain to generate a basketful of exceptions. Here are two. Alexander Henry the Younger noted that Hidatsa women swapped their garden produce for leather goods, deerskin dresses, and similar products offered for trade by the Crows and other Indian visitors. According to Roe, *Indian and the Horse*, 326-7, in 1863, F. V. Hayden wrote about Arikara women selling corn and squashes at Fort Berthold (in central North Dakota) in exchange for hoes and beads. Obviously, some Indian men allowed their wives to trade a portion of their labor for items the women wanted—for example, iron kettles and metal scrapers to ease their labor and vermilion, mirrors, and metal bells to please their vanity. The reasons for the men being so "generous" no doubt ranged from love to a desire to promote domestic tranquillity, motivation for males of every race, including those in the modern world.

[6.] An Indian informant gave these figures to Alexander Phillipp Maximilian, Prince of Wied-Nuwied, during his 1833 visit to Fort McKenzie. Roe, *Indian and the Horse*, 283 cautions readers from taking this or any other Indian estimate of large numbers literally. According to Roe, Sachkomapoh's herd probably counted in the low hundreds—150 were sacrificed at his burial—still enough to have made the chief a wealthy man.

[7.] Larpenteur, *Forty Years*, 331; and Roe, *Indian and the Horse*, 289, 292.

[8.] McClintock, *Old North Trail*, 190.

[9.] Roe, *Indian and the Horse*, 356. In James A. Hanson, "The Myth of the Wasted Meat," *The Museum of the Fur Trade Quarterly* 34, no.3 (fall 1998): 3, the author reports visiting the Olsen-Chubbock *piskun* site in eastern Colorado where Indians had butchered fewer than one-quarter of their prey, leaving the remainder of the buffalo for scavengers. McNeill, *Plagues and Peoples*, 29; and Crosby, *Columbian Exchange*, 19-20 discuss how Paleolithic Native American hunters may have exterminated North America's vast herds of woolly mammoths, giant sloths, mastodons, and other now-extinct large mammals.

[10.] Coues, ed., *Alexander Henry*, 1:336-7.

[11.] Catlin, *Letters*, 1:256.

[12.] John E. Sunder, *The Fur Trade on the Upper Missouri, 1840-1864* (Norman: University of Oklahoma Press, 1965), 17.

[13.] Catlin, *Letters*, 1:262-4. Although the horse allowed native hunters to alter the sexual mix of the bison herds, Roe, *Indian and the Horse*, 192 contends that the Indians never would have annihilated them the way the white buffalo skinners did.

[14.] Innis, *Fur Trade in Canada*, 263-4. Robin F. Wells, "Castoreum and Steel Traps in Eastern North America," *American Anthropologist* n.s., no. 74 (1972): 479-83 argue that the English developed the use of steel traps and castoreum bait sometime before 1728, sixty-five years earlier than anthropologists originally thought.

15. Ray, *Indians in the Fur Trade*, 201-03. For a detailed description of Indian beaver-hunting techniques before the introduction of steel traps, see Carl Russell, *Firearms, Traps, & Tools of the Mountain Men* (New York: Alfred A. Knopf, 1967; Albuquerque: University of New Mexico Press, 1977), 97-102.

Chapter Thirteen

1838

As the new year began, Assiniboine losses to smallpox surpassed one-third of the tribe. Still the disease refused to quit. Each day saw another Indian family journey to the makeshift hospital at old Fort William. The post's dilapidated buildings stood in sharp contrast with the whitewashed stockade of nearby Fort Union.

Despite its appearance, Fort William symbolized the promise of healing. Grandparents who had survived past epidemics came with their sons, daughters, grandsons, and granddaughters. The elders had heard that the traders possessed medicines, magic cures that could restore the infirm. It must be true, the storytellers said; otherwise, how else could so many of the whites at Fort Union have caught the disease and yet survived? The old ones clutched the tales to their hearts, refusing to let them go. They had to believe, for not doing so would have been to abandon hope. But such beliefs were as useless as trying to grasp the wind. There was no magic antidote for smallpox. The traders had nothing to offer but purges and bleeding. The epidemic seemed destined to continue until the Assiniboines were no more.

The old women who nursed the sick in the rotting cabins of Fort William could do little for their patients besides dispense water and a bite of food, and then wait for their charges to recover or die. So many died, tribal burial customs were forgotten, making them just another victim of the *rotting face*. With the Missouri River frozen and the prairie blanketed with snow, the hospital's stopgap mortician, John Brazeau, collected the dead each morning and dumped their bodies on the barren plain.[1]

Inside Fort Union, clerk Edwin Denig had recovered from his mild bout of smallpox and was now back at his duties. Denig's fellow clerk, Charles Larpenteur, continued dispensing alcohol to those Assiniboines who wanted a final fling before their bodies were defiled by the *Variola* virus. In their drunken exuberance, Indian customers occasionally discharged their muskets at the newly installed trade window, but so far Larpenteur had kept out of the line of fire. His job was risky, but the large number of buffalo robes that the liquor trade brought in made it acceptable. The fort's take of robes matched that of an average winter season,[2] a fact that pleased the new *bourgeois,* David Mitchell.

The previous November, Mitchell's predecessor, Jacob Halsey, had warned Pratte & Chouteau's managing partners that the smallpox deaths would cause severe losses,[3] but so far Halsey had been wrong. Mitchell, too, had thought the company would suffer a production shortfall, and wrote that what few robes Fort Union took in would be "a mere drop in the ocean." When he relieved Halsey, Mitchell had sent an express to St. Louis, telling of the epidemic and suggesting that expected shortages ought to enhance the value of Pratte & Chouteau's existing robe inventory, once word of the disaster reached the fur market.[4]

Yet, a reckoning was coming, if not this winter then certainly the next. Many of the Assiniboines' most productive robe manufacturers were dead. The robes that were now being bartered with such abandon came from household stocks, robes that were intended for personal use instead of trade. The future would demonstrate the extent to which smallpox had harmed the fur trade and Pratte & Chouteau's profits.

Karl Bodmer painting, Library of Congress.
Piegan Blackfoot encampment near Fort McKenzie.

Far up the Missouri at Fort McKenzie, *bourgeois* Alexander Culbertson and his employees were enduring a winter of frozen loneliness. Few Blackfeet came to the post to trade. In isolated camps from the Three Forks of the Missouri to Canada's North Saskatchewan River, *Variola major* was exacting a heavy toll. Other than the Mandans, no other Indian nation suffered such losses as did the three tribes of the Blackfoot Confederation.

As January 1838 began, the number of Blackfoot dead climbed to the thousands. Culbertson eventually estimated the Blackfoot fatalities at 6,000, while the noted Indian historian Henry R. Schoolcraft put them at 8,000. The exact count will never be known, although it may have approached two-thirds of the combined tribes.[5] The Blackfeet had once rivaled the Lakotas with the ranks of warriors they could field, but smallpox had the Blackfeet reeling. Never again would they have the strength to block migration into their homeland. The *rotting face* had done in a few months what a regiment of dragoons could not have accomplished in a decade.

East of the Blackfeet in the border country between them and the Assiniboines lived the Atsinas. Allies of the Blackfeet and considered by most whites of the day to be members of the Blackfoot Confederation, the Atsinas had caught smallpox in 1832 while visiting their Arapaho kin on the South Platte River. Although the epidemic destroyed a quarter of the Atsinas, it left the survivors immune to further attacks. As a result, in early 1838 most of the tribe was safe from the pestilence that was now killing its neighbors. Yet, the *Variola* virus did not leave the Atsinas untouched. Atsina children who had been born in the years after the early 1830s were not protected. Among them, many died.[6]

South of the Atsinas—in the region of the Yellowstone, Tongue, Bighorn, Power, and Wind rivers—dwelled the mighty Crows, or as they called themselves, the *Apsaruke*.[7] In late 1837, smallpox had infected the Pratte & Chouteau personnel at Fort Van Buren.

Intended for the Crow trade and named after Vice President Martin Van Buren, Fort Van Buren had been built in the autumn of 1835 and sat on the north side of the Yellowstone River, across from the mouth of Rosebud Creek (about ten miles east of Forsyth, Montana). When the epidemic struck the trading post, the Crows were away from the Yellowstone, hunting. After rumors about the contagion reached the scattered bands, their elders who had lived through previous scourges recounted the disease's terrible effects, cautioning their people to stay clear of Fort Van Buren. For the most part, the Crows listened and that winter remained deep in their country, avoiding their infected neighbors and the trading post. As 1838 began, Crow mothers and fathers had no cause to weep for their young.[8]

On January 6, 1838, an old Mandan warrior came to Fort Clark, searching for his young wife who had run off with an Arikara. When the traders told him they had not seen her, the jilted husband departed, although it is doubtful that he had the courage to carry his pursuit to the Arikara winter camp, which was located downstream. That night, a daughter of Chief Starapat (Little Hawk with Bloody Claws, the Arikara's highest ranking warrior) died within the trading post, another casualty of the *rotting face*. Nearly three months earlier, smallpox had claimed her younger sister. Unlike other members of his tribe,

Chief Starapat accepted the deaths of his children without seeking retribution against the whites. He remained friends with Chardon and served as a liaison between the *bourgeois* and the various Arikara bands.

The night after the old Mandan came looking for his estranged wife, she showed up at Fort Clark, accompanied by her Arikara lover. They had just arrived from his tribe's winter quarters. The Arikara told the traders there was a large buffalo herd near his band's lower camp. Yet, despite the abundance of buffalo, the Arikaras had few robes.[9] Smallpox had so ravaged the tribal ranks, Arikara hunters could barely kill enough animals to keep their families fed. Those women who were able to work were needed for butchering and drying meat. They had no time to dress hides for Pratte & Chouteau.

The presence of so many buffalo ensured that Fort Clark's hunters rarely returned to the trading post empty-handed. Chardon and his men may have had to worry about meeting their robe quota, but at least they could do so on full stomachs. The company hunters kept the cooks well supplied with fresh meat, enough to make the dinner tables groan beneath pans of roasted hump and boiled tongues.

On January 17, a mixed-blood *engagé* developed a high fever and aching head, making him Fort Clark's latest victim of smallpox. To Chardon and the other men at the trading house, the epidemic seemed as though it would never end.

Ten days later, a trapper and trader named William May came to the fort from the Hidatsas. Although there were buffalo aplenty across the tribe's territory, few Hidatsa men were able to hunt. As it had done to their neighbors, *Variola major* was also thinning the ranks of the Hidatsas. In each of the tribe's winter camps, the disease continued to rage. Chardon must have realized that if the epidemic did not stop soon, the Hidatsas could easily go the way of the Mandans. The Mandans were now a tribe in name only.

By the end of the month, the post traders had taken in only 400 robes, a fraction of their normal haul. Paralleling the inventory of robes, Chardon's monthly tally of dead rats also declined. During January, the *bourgeois* had killed but twenty-four.

Following in lockstep with January's weather, the first week of February remained bitterly cold. The mixed-blood *engagé* who had come down with smallpox on January 17 began to improve, showing every sign of being fit enough to return to work within a day or so. Large herds of buffalo continued to graze on the neighboring prairie, using their massive heads to clear snow off the winter grass. During blizzards, their thick coats became cloaked in white, making them resemble four-legged ghosts. With buffalo in such abundance, it was no surprise to Francis Chardon when on February 9 over 200 wolves crossed the frozen Missouri to cull the bison herds of their sick and young. As he noted in his journal, "the running season [had] commenced."[10]

Despite the ravages of smallpox and the cold, raw weather, the Arikara robe trade began to show signs of life. Trader William May, interpreter Antoine Garreau, and Arikara Chief White Horse arrived at Fort Clark on February 11, leading three ponies bearing robes and tongues from the lower Arikara camp. Toussaint Charbonneau also rode in that day, bringing two pack-loads of buffalo tongues from the Hidatsas. He reported that the tribe's robe production had nearly ground to a halt because so many Hidatsa women were either sick or dead. Five days later, Charbonneau stocked his horses with more goods and headed back to the Hidatsas, hoping to keep the trading season from turning into a complete bust.

Among the Arikaras who had survived or so far escaped the *rotting face,* the lure of counting coup on their enemies was like a magnet. A stolen horse or a scalp cut from an Assiniboine or Yankton Lakota could make a grieving warrior forget, for a moment, the devastating losses he had so recently witnessed. Wanting such a release, an Arikara war party nearly seven dozen men strong rode west up the Missouri in late winter, planning to raid the Assiniboines.

February ended at Fort Clark with Chardon's dead rat count reaching sixteen. It was his lowest monthly total since arriving at the trading post in 1836. March began with a snow shower and the continuation of a heated row between the trapper John Newman and his Arikara wife. The pair had been at each other's throats for the past five days, disrupting the usual winter torpor. Far from being a youthful boy who was easily swayed by the opposite sex, Newman was at least in his early fifties and had served with Lewis and Clark in the westward exploration of the Corps of Discovery. On March 2, the feuding couple called it quits. Newman's wife—his third since the previous autumn—rode to her people's winter camp, seeking sympathy and solace among her own kind. John Newman followed close on her heels, determined to purchase another bride, one he prayed would be more amicable. The following day, the personnel at Fort Clark were surprised to see Newman and his wife return to the post, their marital discord settled—permanently, everyone hoped.

By now, the *rotting face* had exhausted its store of vulnerable Mandans and Arikaras. Like a blazing fire that has consumed its fuel, the epidemic dwindled to a flicker and then went out. Smoldering in the ruins were the human ashes of its devastation. From a pre-smallpox population of about 1,600 people, the Mandans had been reduced thirteenfold. *Variola major* and its attendant complications—suicide, starvation, accidental drownings, and pneumonia—had destroyed over ninety percent of the tribe. In less than three generations, the Mandans had gone from a robust people, whose trading prowess gave them sway over the upper Missouri, to a few dozen supplicants who would forever live by another's leave.

For reasons that cannot be explained, the same virus that had all but annihilated the Mandans killed only half of the Arikaras.[11] "Only half"—the words bring to mind one of every two warriors; fifty percent of all female robe producers; four sons and daughters out of a family's eight children; every other Arikara mother and father. But the death ratios were not so statistically neat. Because many of the tribe's elders had survived the smallpox epidemics of 1780 and 1781 or 1801 and 1802 and were immune to the virus's latest rampage, the *rotting face* claimed a disproportionate number of the young. For the most part, *Variola major* had feasted on the most productive members of the tribe—mothers and fathers in their late teens, twenties, and early thirties—and on their children, the seed corn of the Arikaras' future. Although the Arikaras—unlike the Mandans—were still a functioning tribe, their society lay in pieces.

During the first two weeks of March, when Francis Chardon

would normally have expected to garner buffalo robes by the hundreds, Fort Clark's trade was barely a trickle. Of the few robes that found their way to the trading post, most had come from the Arikaras. The Mandans had produced next to nothing, whereas the Hidatsas were too busy fighting the ravages of smallpox to worry about trading. Although the epidemic had died out among the Arikaras and Mandans, among the Hidatsas it was now hitting full stride.

Midmorning, March 18, the Missouri River awakened from its winter freeze. With a thundering clap, its ice shattered, heaved, and began flowing downstream. Spring had arrived on the upper Missouri. Two days later, a small band of Arikaras came up from their winter camp and moved into the deserted lodges at Mitutanka Village. The following day, the remainder of the Arikaras abandoned their winter quarters, preparing to take possession of the Mandan town. On reaching Mitutanka Village, the Arikaras spread among the lodges, appropriating this one and that until they had gained control of the entire town. The few Mandans who continued to live with them now became guests in their own homes.[12]

While the Arikaras were taking possession of Mitutanka Village, upriver at Fort Union, Charles Larpenteur secured a leave of absence, intending to visit his parents. They lived near Baltimore, Maryland, and he had not seen them in ten years. On March 22, he left the trading post in a canoe, accompanied by two voyageurs and an adventurer named Robert Christy. Christy was returning to St. Louis after having wintered at Fort Union as a guest of Pratte & Chouteau.

With the spring runoff strengthening the Missouri's current, their canoe made good time. Although the river ice at Fort Union had broken up earlier in the month, the water was barely above freezing.[13] Because the Missouri did not thaw all at once, ice posed a continual danger. Hitting a thick chunk of floating ice could capsize a canoe in a heartbeat. In addition, the combination of ice floes, a constricted channel, and a rapid drop in temperature often caused ice dams, which were hazardous to boats of any size. Being sucked beneath one usually meant certain death.

As the minutes drifted by, Larpenteur focused on the river, unconcerned about Indians. Smallpox had reduced the Assiniboines by as much as half,[14] lessening a traveler's chance of encountering a war party. Still, it paid to be cautious. Although the voyageurs attempted keeping the canoe in mid channel, occasionally sandbars and sawyers compelled them to edge closer to shore than was prudent.

A few hours into their first day, the paddlers drove the canoe to within twenty yards of a willow- and brush-tangled bank. Suddenly, several dozen Indians rose from the foliage, their bowstrings nocked with arrows. Unbeknownst to Larpenteur, they belonged to the eighty-man Arikara raiding party that had headed upriver in late winter, intending to count coup among the Assiniboines. For an instant, Larpenteur thought the warriors would turn him and his companions into pincushions. Then he noticed one of the Indians running along the bank, urging his tribesmen not to shoot. Grudgingly, the Arikaras lowered their bows, allowing the canoe to pass. Each paddler bent to his strokes, happy to escape with his hair.[15] Most of the warriors had lost members of their families to smallpox. Blaming the white traders for causing the disease, the Arikaras had exerted a full measure of self-control to keep from taking their revenge on so convenient a target.

Two days later, Larpenteur and his fellow travelers were hailed from the riverbank by a party of Canoe Band Assiniboines, who requested that the whites ferry them across the Missouri. Fearing the Indians would rob them, Larpenteur ordered his voyageurs to paddle faster. When the boat did not stop, the Indians opened fire. Along with the rest of their tribe, the Canoe Assiniboines had also been beset by the *rotting face* and no doubt figured that four scalps would ease their sorrow.

Although the warriors' musketballs and arrows missed their mark, the gunshots alerted the band's main camp farther downriver. Indians from the encampment raced to the water's edge just as the canoe passed out of range. Hoping to catch the whites at the next bend, the warriors dashed cross-country and set up on the bank. When the canoe came into view, they unleashed a hailstorm of arrows and lead. Fortunately for Larpenteur and his companions, the Missouri had widened out, allowing them to maneuver close to the far shore. Three musketballs embedded in the near-side gunwale, but either by Providence or luck, no one was hit. Some miles later, the paddlers relaxed, allowing their boat to drift while they caught their breath, smoked, and wondered what other dangers would befall them before their trip was finished.

Late the following morning, the canoe came on another band of Indians, this one gathered on a small rise overlooking the Missouri's right flank. Expecting to be attacked once again, yet compelled by the channel to continue, Larpenteur piled a few carrots of tobacco on the bow and directed the voyageurs to head toward the screaming horde. As the boat neared the Indians, Larpenteur saw an aged white man in their midst, beckoning him to land. Wearing a red flannel shirt and trousers, the man looked as old as Methuselah. When the canoe put in to shore, he scrambled down the bank and introduced himself as Toussaint Charbonneau. The Indians were his Hidatsa friends. Larpenteur gave the tobacco to the Indian elders who Charbonneau designated. Had the ancient trader not been among them, the Hidatsas may have murdered Larpenteur and his fellows in order to avenge the smallpox epidemic that was still crippling their tribe.

Now seventy miles above Fort Clark, the canoeists pressed on, determined to reach the trading post before evening the following day. The next afternoon, the current slowed to a standstill, blocked by sheets of curdling ice. Slowly snaking their way among the floes, the paddlers worked through the bottleneck and continued toward the fort. When they were about two miles above the mouth of the Knife River, the ice dam broke and came hurtling downstream ahead of the freed-up water. Certain that their luck had finally run out, the boatmen rode the flood surge and prayed they would not capsize. About a mile above Fort Clark, they finally maneuvered to shore, happy to have escaped with their lives for the fourth time in as many days.

Deciding to delay their trip until the ice disappeared for good, Larpenteur, Christy, and the two voyageurs hiked to the trading post and prepared to wait. Francis Chardon hosted his visitors in fine style, no doubt happy to do so because of a two-gallon keg of whiskey that Christy had brought along to ward off the cold. To Chardon's delight, Christy showed no hesitation about sharing. The *bourgeois* relished the liquid offering, finding it the perfect antidote for his most unusual medical condition. Every few minutes, Chardon refreshed his cup, claiming that he had "a great many worms in his throat" that needed to be cleared.[16]

The next day, March 26, the Arikaras departed Mitutanka Village, intending to hunt buffalo and make dried meat. Remaining behind were forty old women who were too frail to butcher or tan hides. Most likely, their sons and grandsons had fallen victim to smallpox, and there was no one to care for them. The tribe's surviving hunters were hard put to provide enough food for their own families and considered the women an unnecessary burden. Without someone to feed them, the old grandmothers would die.[17]

The following morning, the Missouri flushed away the last of its ice, permitting Larpenteur, Christy, and the voyageurs to continue their journey. Chardon escorted them to their canoe, pleading with them to stay a bit longer. Larpenteur felt Chardon's motive had less to do with hospitality than a desire by the *bourgeois* to rid himself of his remaining worms. Because the whiskey keg was nearly empty, Christy gave it to him. Clutching the unexpected gift as though it might escape, Chardon bid his visitors a hasty good-bye, turned on his heel, and carried the liquor back to his quarters "in double-quick time."[18]

The canoe proceeded downriver, passing Fort Pierre and Fort Kiowa. Twenty miles below Vermilion Post, the tactic of keeping in mid channel saved the travelers from yet another disaster. In this stretch, the Missouri had spread over the bottomland, allowing the men to stay well clear of both banks. Seeing the craft and thinking it was in musket range, a band of Omaha warriors opened fire from shore. Instead of revenge for smallpox, their motive was more likely robbery. The shots fell short, but they gave Larpenteur and his companions a healthy rush of adrenaline.

Some days later as the canoe neared the mouth of the Platte

River below Council Bluffs, Larpenteur spotted the Pratte, Chouteau & Company steamboat, *Antelope,* coming upstream with provisions for the firm's trading posts. On board was Kenneth McKenzie, the retired former head of the Upper Missouri Outfit. He was going to Fort Union for a visit. Also included among the passengers was Doctor Joseph R. DePrefontaine and his escort, Indian agent Joshua Pilcher.

During the late summer of 1837, Pilcher and a delegation of Fox, Sauk, and Yankton Lakota representatives had toured the nation's capital. That fall Pilcher led his delegates back to Missouri, then sent them to their home tribes. Deciding it was too late in the season to return to his Indian agency at Fort Kiowa, Pilcher took rooms in St. Louis, opting to remain there for the winter.

Throughout the fall and into January 1838, word filtered down the Missouri, hinting at the calamity being wreaked by *Variola major.* As January faded into February, rumors about the epidemic permeated the city. Pierre Chouteau Jr., who was traveling in the east, had already taken steps to slow the epidemic around Fort Pierre. Using his own funds, he had ordered vaccine shipped to his traders at the mouth of the Bad River so they could immunize the Lakotas. His benevolence was but a cup of water tossed on a raging inferno; yet, for those Indians who submitted to the treatment, Chouteau's gift was a godsend.[19]

Alarmed by news that the disaster was worse than he had feared, Pilcher penned a letter to William Clark, Superintendent of Indian Affairs, on February 5, begging him to send a doctor and cowpox vaccine to the tribes of the upper Missouri.[20] After reading Pilcher's letter, Clark forwarded it to C. A. Harris, Commissioner of Indian Affairs, in Washington, D.C. Along with Pilcher's correspondence, Clark added his own summary of events, stating that he had been powerless to stem the epidemic.[21]

On February 24, longtime fur trader Etienne Provost brought the latest upcountry express to Pratte & Chouteau's headquarters, reporting that the tragedy exceeded everyone's worst nightmare.[22] On February 27, Pilcher again wrote Clark, telling him that smallpox had turned the upper Missouri into "one great grave yard [*sic*]." Once more Pilcher urged the government to send cowpox vaccine to the tribes. In addition, he also asked Clark to provide $2,000 worth of gifts to induce the Indians to submit to vaccination.[23] By now, word of the epidemic was attracting the attention of the eastern clergy, who began pestering Joel R. Poinsette, the Secretary of War, demanding to know what the government was doing to relieve the Indians' suffering.[24]

While Clark waited for the government to match rhetoric with action, he appointed Pilcher temporary head of the Mandan subagency. The appointment filled the vacancy left by William Fulkerson, who had recently quit during a spat over his salary and because Pratte & Chouteau's traders refused to treat him in the manner he deemed his position was entitled.[25] In late March 1838, the War Department finally authorized Superintendent Clark to send cowpox vaccine to the upper Missouri. Clark outfitted Pilcher and Indian agent John Dougherty each with $500 worth of the medicine, dividing a like sum between two other agents. All were instructed to use the vaccine as they saw fit. At the same time, Clark ordered Pilcher to escort Doctor DePrefontaine up the Missouri so the physician could vaccinate all the Indians he encountered. Pilcher and the doctor booked passage on Pratte & Chouteau's annual supply boat, the *Antelope,* which was scheduled to depart St. Louis in a few weeks.[26]

In early April, the *Antelope* steamed north from St. Louis, turned into the mouth of the Missouri River, and headed upstream. Pilcher and Doctor DePrefontaine hoped it was not too late for the vaccinations to do some good.

The *Antelope* encountered the canoe of Charles Larpenteur and Robert Christy just below Fort Bellevue and Council Bluffs. The two men came aboard the steamer, where they were resupplied with much-needed provisions. While on the boat, Larpenteur talked with his former boss, Kenneth McKenzie,[27] and undoubtedly with Joshua Pilcher and Doctor DePrefontaine. Nothing Larpenteur could have told them about the epidemic would have been encouraging. Assuming that Francis Chardon had related the full extent of the smallpox disaster among the Mandans, Hidatsas, and Arikaras during

Larpenteur's stopover at Fort Clark, Larpenteur probably passed that information to Pilcher, as well. Larpenteur certainly could describe the disease among the Assiniboines.[28]

After a short visit aboard the *Antelope,* Larpenteur and Christy continued down the Missouri. A couple of days after leaving the steamboat, their canoe reached the small settlement of Camden, Missouri, where Larpenteur and Christy secured passage on a packet steamer for the remainder of their journey to St. Louis.[29]

Meanwhile, the *Antelope* proceeded to Council Bluffs, where crewmen slid out its gangplank at Fort Bellevue. Realizing that the epidemic was nearly finished on the upper Missouri, Pilcher probably reasoned that he and the doctor should try to prevent it from spreading south. There was nothing they could do for the Indians who were already sick or dead. While deckhands unloaded supplies and annuities, Pilcher urged the nearby Otoe and Omaha chiefs to allow their people to take the white man's medicine. The Indian leaders heeded Pilcher's plea, and a number of their tribesmen were vaccinated.[30]

From Fort Bellevue, Pilcher and Doctor DePrefontaine continued upriver on the *Antelope,* performing their humanitarian errand everywhere the steamboat stopped. During the next few weeks, the doctor scratched Indian arms and applied cowpox vaccine from Council Bluffs to Fort Kiowa. Having witnessed the death and misery brought about by the disease, the tribes along the central Missouri willingly extended their arms, eager for any white-made magic that would save them from the *rotting face.*

After exhausting Pilcher's store of government vaccine, Doctor DePrefontaine dipped into his own stock as he immunized Indians as far north as Fort Pierre. By his own count, the doctor vaccinated about 3,000 members of the Otoe, Omaha, Ponca, Yankton, and Santee tribes. At Fort Pierre, Pilcher enlisted an interpreter for Doctor DePrefontaine, sending them to the Teton Lakotas, who ranged along the South Fork of the Platte River. On the journey the doctor became ill and aborted his mission, leaving most of the Tetons unprotected.[31]

Earlier, on March 28, the day after Charles Larpenteur and Robert Christy had left Fort Clark in their canoe, Francis Chardon visited the Arikara grandmothers who had been abandoned by their tribe at Mitutanka Village. Having no one to hunt for them, the women were starving. Although Chardon peppered his journal with his distaste for Indians—except those he took to bed—for once, he displayed an alien streak of charity. He gave the old women enough food for a single meal. After presenting them with a "feast"—by his description—he returned to Fort Clark, unconcerned that without further aid, the women would die. Since he was unwilling to become their permanent protector and because they were too feeble to fend for themselves, his kindness merely prolonged the inevitable.

Despite the hand-to-mouth existence that the *rotting face* had forced on the village tribes, the robe trade limped along. On March 29, Toussaint Charbonneau returned to Fort Clark from the Hidatsas, dropped off a few buffalo robes, and awaited orders to go back upriver with more trade goods. By now the smallpox epidemic among the Hidatsas had wound down to a couple of isolated cases. Although the *Variola* virus had been slow in attacking the Hidatsas, once it started, it had killed with the same wanton efficiency that it had used on the Arikaras. The Hidatsa death rate stood at fifty percent of the tribe.[32]

Thanks to Charbonneau's contribution, the month ended with Fort Clark collecting 125 packs of buffalo robes and three and a half packs of beaver. In contrast with February when Chardon had killed only sixteen rats, his tally for March rebounded to 101.

On the first day of April, Charbonneau and two *engagés* headed upriver to the Hidatsas for more robes. At the same time, another trader rode to the Mandan winter camp, hoping to persuade the tribe's survivors to renew their trade. Three days later, five Mandan families came to Fort Clark and were treated to a banquet—probably lye-soaked corn and a few pieces of dried buffalo. The next day, they bartered sixty robes. Twenty-four hours later, the balance of the Mandans turned over another forty robes to the trading post. Faced with a shortage of manpower and shattered cultures, the surviving

Mandans, Hidatsas, and Arikaras had no choice but to embrace the robe trade and look to Pratte & Chouteau as their savior.

While Chardon busied himself bartering with the Mandans, Toussaint Charbonneau enjoyed better luck among the Hidatsas. During the first week and a half of April, he garnered 600 buffalo robes. On April 11, he loaded a bull boat with his bounty and started down the Missouri for Fort Clark. That evening a thunderstorm whipped the river to a froth. Waves battered Charbonneau's boat, splitting its rawhide-stitched seams and sinking its valuable cargo. Chief Starapat, who was either traveling with Charbonneau or happened by, brought word of the disaster to Chardon. The *bourgeois* sent two *engagés* to help the old trader salvage what he could from the wreck. The men saved most of the load, although 400 robes had to be re-dressed by native women, an effort that cost Charbonneau and Chardon an eighty-robe fee. April ended without further excitement. While not up to pre-epidemic levels, the fort's robe trade exhibited signs of recovery. Likewise, Chardon's rat-killing effort was also blessed with an upswing. Aided by a single day in which he had dispatched sixteen, his monthly total topped out at 217.

Rats were not the only species exhibiting an upturn. Unlike the spring before when the buffalo had shunned the prairie around Mitutanka Village, this year the herds grazed everywhere. During the first week of May, the men at Fort Clark sighted so many bison, they nearly wore out their horses, giving chase. With game in such abundance, the trading post cooks turned every meal into a feast, setting mouths to watering with savory brisket and slow-roasted hump ribs.

On May 8, the Arikaras returned to Mitutanka Village from their dried meat camp and swapped Chardon several beaver pelts and 106 buffalo robes. The following day, a small band of Hidatsas stopped by the fort and traded a couple of dozen more robes. During the ensuing week, robes continued trickling into the post, fifty-two one day, seventy-five the next. Always eager to count coup, Arikara war parties again headed east, each hoping to steal a few horses and lift the hair from some unsuspecting Lakotas. Most came home with little to brag about.

The night of May 17, several unknown Indians struck a coup

against Mitutanka Village that would be sung around their campfires for a generation. Two or perhaps more enemy warriors sneaked into the lodge of the Arikara chief, Long Horn, and shot him dead. Before departing, the assailants also fired at another chief, wounding him twice. With the assistance of Chardon and other men from Fort Clark, the Arikaras scoured the landscape for the killers, but they had been swallowed by the gloom. The moonless evening had provided the perfect cover for such a daring raid. Although the attackers could have been Assiniboines, they were more likely Yankton Lakotas.

The next day, a feud that had been simmering for some time between Chardon and his Arikara wife exploded. He had taken her to his bed a month after the death of his Lakota wife, Tchon-su-mons-ka.[33] Tiring of matrimony—or perhaps of her *bourgeois* husband—the young woman stormed out of Fort Clark, divorcing Chardon Indian-style by returning to her people at Mitutanka Village. Their marriage had lasted a year.

On May 20, an Arikara war party rode triumphantly into Mitutanka Village, having been gone five weeks. This time the warriors did not return empty-handed. Exulting in their prowess, they paraded through the town, waving their battle trophy for all to see. It was the scalp from a Lakota woman, who they had killed on the Bad River.[34] That afternoon, the warriors' wives extolled the victory with a spirited dance. Scalping a Lakota woman was less of a coup than scalping a Lakota warrior, but of late the Arikaras had had nothing to celebrate. They would take what the fates offered, including the gift of a woman's hair.

Over the ensuing week, snow and wind buffeted the upper Missouri, providing a reminder of winter. One particularly brutal storm caught Chardon and his hunters on the plain as they were returning to Fort Clark with their horses laden with freshly butchered buffalo. Refusing to discard the meat in order to lighten their horses' loads, the men struggled through the swirling snow, endeavoring to reach the trading post before they froze. Though nip and tuck, their epic ended successfully in the early evening. They made it home alive, happy to thaw out before a roaring fire.

The following day or the day after, while Chardon and his

hunters warmed themselves and recounted their near disaster amid the recent blizzard, a young Arikara warrior came to Mitutanka Village to visit his friends.[35] He had wintered with a band of Hidatsas somewhere farther up the Missouri. On Sunday, May 27, the young man developed a blinding headache and burning fever. By now everyone had seen enough symptoms to know he had smallpox. Most likely he had contracted the virus from the Hidatsas, and it had incubated during his journey. The next day the visitor died, another victim of the *rotting face*.[36] To the men at Fort Clark, it seemed as if the pestilence would go on forever.

Despite the presence of buffalo, the fur trade continued slow. On May 30, Indian hunters slaughtered over three hundred animals for meat and sport, yet it is doubtful that there were enough healthy women to dress more than a fraction of the hides. Fort Clark had accumulated 2,700 robes for the season, a mere pittance of what should have been traded. The shortfall was but another example of the effects of *Variola major*. As Chardon inspected his ledgers, he hoped the Hidatsas would increase the robe count to something reasonable. It was unfortunate he could not include the post's dead rats in the total. For May, he had killed another 146.

In early June, the main body of Hidatsas returned to their summer village near the Knife River. Eager for the tribe to barter its buffalo robes, Chardon sent Charbonneau—who was again at Fort Clark—to bribe the chiefs with tobacco so they would urge their people to trade. A bit after the old trader had left on his mission, Hidatsa warriors came to the trading post and begged admission, saying they had a letter for the *bourgeois*. The Hidatsas had been members of a war party that had gone to the mouth of the Yellowstone in late winter, intending to raid the Assiniboines.

David Mitchell, the *bourgeois* of Fort Union, had asked the Hidatsas to deliver the letter to Chardon. In it, Mitchell wrote that two war parties—one Hidatsa and the other Arikara or possibly a combination of the two tribes—had stopped by Fort Union after failing to count coup among the Assiniboines. Mitchell treated with the Indians and persuaded them to be vaccinated against smallpox. Having witnessed the terrible effects of the disease among their people, the warriors probably needed minimal persuasion. How and when Mitchell obtained his vaccine remains a mystery. As Chardon read Mitchell's letter, he must have wondered why none of the vaccine had been sent to Fort Clark.[37]

The next day, the sky released a barrage of rain and hail, interspersed with jagged veins of lightning and the throaty rumble of thunder. Using the storm for cover, a Lakota warrior crept into Mitutanka Village, but before he could earn his coup, a Hidatsa sprang on him and wrestled him to the ground. The Hidatsa was about to kill him, when an Arikara joined the fray and stayed the Hidatsa's hand. Within moments, other Arikaras swarmed from their lodges and surrounded the three men. Knowing that he was as good as dead, the Lakota claimed he had come to warn the Arikaras that a large Lakota war party planned to attack the Hidatsas' Knife River village early the following morning. The Lakota informant wanted the Arikaras to remain in Mitutanka Village and not go to the Hidatsas' aid. Believing the warrior's story, the Arikaras gave the man two ponies and sent him on his way.[38]

Only time would tell if the Lakota had spoken the truth. Still, it never hurt to be on guard. The Arikaras decided to heed their enemy's advice and stay inside Mitutanka Village if the assault took place. Just to be safe, they intended keeping their bows and muskets close at hand. Francis Chardon heard about the encounter, so it is likely that the Lakota's story was also conveyed to the Hidatsas.

On June 8, gunfire pierced the pre-dawn quiet as a large Lakota war party swarmed into the Hidatsa village. Hearing the popping sound of distant muskets, the Arikaras at Mitutanka Village grabbed their weapons in case the Lakotas widened the assault. Instead of rushing to the Hidatsas' aid, the Arikaras stood pat, content to let their ally shoulder the battle. The Lakotas had counted on surprise and may have thought a majority of the Hidatsas were still at their hunting camps, but the only ones surprised were the Lakotas. The Hidatsas easily repelled the outnumbered invaders, slaughtering a dozen and a half or more. The Lakotas wounded six Hidatsas and killed a Mandan, the villagers' only fatality.

Carrying their wounded and some of their dead, the Lakotas soon broke off the attack and ran, leaving fourteen of their fallen warriors to be mutilated by the victorious Hidatsas. After hacking the Lakota bodies into pieces, the Hidatsas burned them in a large pyre. The smoke and flames lit up the sky, adding to the humiliation of the fleeing Lakotas. The Hidatsas had won a great coup, one that would be told and retold for years. The defeated Lakotas would have no victory dance, merely an increased lust for revenge. Although they had lost this skirmish, in the long run the numbers were on their side. *Variola major* had seen to that.

Before the smallpox epidemic, the Lakotas had been more populous than all the village tribes combined. Afterward, the ratio was more lopsided. Although the *rotting face* had decimated the Lakotas, its toll came no where near what it had extracted from the Hidatsas and their neighbors. The Hidatsas had carried this fight, but the victory was fleeting. They no longer had enough warriors to hold the Lakotas at bay. In time, the Hidatsas would have to yield.

Later that day, Pratte & Chouteau's steamboat, the *Antelope*, came in view of Fort Clark. As the steamer maneuvered to make land, Chardon ordered his gunners to fire ten salutes from the post's four-pounder cannons. Gunners on the *Antelope* answered in kind. After the boat's gangway had been run out, deckhands off-loaded Indian annuities and stores. If cowpox vaccine was included among the supplies, Francis Chardon never wrote about it in his journal. Joshua Pilcher and Doctor Joseph DePrefontaine had left the steamer at Fort Pierre in order to vaccinate the Lakotas, but former company partner Kenneth McKenzie was still aboard.

At eight o'clock the next morning, the *Antelope* continued its journey to Fort Union. Toussaint Charbonneau went along, intending to go ashore when the steamer reached the mouth of the Knife River.

On June 15, four weeks to the day after splitting with his Arikara wife,[39] Chardon grew tired of the bachelor life. Feeling that a younger woman would cause him less trouble than an older one, he cast his eye on a fifteen-year-old Arikara "virgin." The girl's father sold her to him for $150 in trade goods. That afternoon a violent rainstorm complete with thunder and lightening provided the newlyweds with a spectacular shivaree.

Two days following Chardon's wedding, the *Antelope* returned to Fort Clark, having completed its voyage to Fort Union. The steamer laid over for the night and continued downriver just after dawn. Later in the day, seven mackinaws arrived at Fort Clark, filled to the gunwales with buffalo robes. Despite the smallpox epidemic, forts Union, Van Buren, and McKenzie had eked out a middling trade. Chardon had garnered 2,870 robes, which his *engagés* stowed aboard another mackinaw. The robe harvest was below average, but not as bad as had been feared. The next morning, voyageurs poled the flat-bottomed flotilla into the Missouri's current and began their long float to St. Louis.

A few hours before dawn on June 21, a large Yankton Lakota war party opened fire on Mitutanka Village. No doubt wanting to redeem their tribe's humiliating loss to the Hidatsas two weeks before, the Yanktons probably figured that the Arikaras and sprinkling of Mandans living among them would be an easy mark. For four hours the two sides exchanged musketballs, with the Yanktons sporadically taking potshots at Fort Clark. No one was hit. Finally running low on ammunition, the attackers retreated, their quest for a great coup again foiled.

Any elation the village tribes felt by twice forcing their enemy to withdraw was tempered by reality. The Lakotas had no fear of bringing the fight to their opponents' home ground. The village tribes could launch an occasional raid against a small Yankton or Santee camp, but it was clear that the Lakotas now had them on the defensive. The recent smallpox epidemic had permanently altered the tribal power structure of the upper Missouri.

Three days after the bloodless engagement, a half dozen young Arikara warriors rode out of Mitutanka Village, searching for buffalo. They had journeyed but a short distance across the plain when a Lakota war party jumped them, killing one and chasing the others back to the river. Hearing shots, the teenagers' kinsmen boiled out of the town and drove off the Lakotas. The prairie was no longer safe. From now on, anyone not traveling in a large group risked losing his hair. Because

Fort Clark was allied with the village tribes, the danger also applied to Francis Chardon and his men.

The next day, a party of Hidatsas rode to the trading post from the Knife River and bartered 120 buffalo robes and a few beaver pelts. The *rotting face* had killed so many Hidatsa women, those that remained were redoubling their tanning efforts, knowing that their families' welfare depended on an increased robe production. Although direct commerce with *coureurs de bois* had started over 100 years earlier, the Hidatsas' economic prowess had not begun to erode until the introduction of smallpox.

In 1780 and 1781 and again in 1801 and 1802, the deadly virus had pared the tribe's population, making future generations increasingly dependent on the fur trade. Each year, the Hidatsas—together with the Mandans, Arikaras, and a host of other tribes—had steadily broadened their reliance on the white world's manufactured goods. Now in the wake of this most recent epidemic, the Hidatsas lost all semblance of self-sufficiency. Not only had the disease undermined their security and tribal unity, but it also made the survivors virtual slaves of the fur companies. In this regard, the Hidatsas were not alone. To varying degrees, the latest bout of *Variola major* bound the Arikaras, Assiniboines, Blackfeet, and other tribes of the upper Missouri to Pratte, Chouteau & Company and its rivals. Yet far worse, the pestilence had all but erased the Mandans as a separate people.

The same day the Hidatsas bartered ten dozen robes at Fort Clark, Chardon's Arikara wife—the one who had run off on May 18—returned to the trading post, no doubt missing her life of comparative ease. As the wife of a *bourgeois,* she had to endure her husband's temper and an occasional beating, but the physical comforts he provided far exceeded anything she would have among her own tribe. If she was surprised by Chardon's new teenage bride, there is no record. After a "few reproaches on both sides," Chardon took his older wife back. Since he made no reference in his journal to his fifteen-year-old bedmate leaving the fort, one must assume that he and the two women lived as a threesome.

On June 26, Lakota raiders descended on a herd of Arikara

horses, using a rainstorm for cover. While the Lakotas tried to stampede the herd, Arikara guards alerted their tribesmen. Most Arikara warriors owned multiple horses and kept one or two tethered in or beside their lodges. Within minutes, a swarm of Arikaras galloped out of Mitutanka Village toward the Lakotas. While the foes fired at one another from horseback, the Lakotas drove a number of Arikara mounts across the prairie. The running battle lasted for some time and produced non-fatal casualties for the Arikaras and Lakotas alike. But in the end, the Lakotas won the day, escaping with several Arikara horses.

Unable to defeat the Lakotas, the Arikaras had turned their frustrations on the few Mandan families who continued residing at Mitutanka Village. The *Variola* epidemic had trimmed the Mandans from 1,600 people to eleven dozen or so.[40] Because there were so few surviving Mandan men, the Arikaras used their women at will, refusing to pay for the privilege. Tiring of their allies' sordid behavior and too weak to stop it, most of the Mandans left Mitutanka Village, moving to the Knife River to live among the Hidatsas.[41]

June ended with Chardon tallying another sixty-eight dead rats. Yet the carnage was not limited to Fort Clark's rodent population. The Lakotas now smelled an opportunity to step up their raids on their smallpox-weakened enemies. Foreshadowing the expanding struggle for dominance of the upper Missouri, word reached the fort on July 1 that the Yanktons had killed the old trapper, John Newman. That same day, Lakota and Arikara warriors traded shots outside Mitutanka Village, the Arikaras garnering three scalps, the Lakotas one. Delighted with their victory and seeking to humiliate the Lakotas further, the Arikaras burned the bodies of the Lakota dead.

Soon after sunrise the next morning, a pulsating tom-tom of drums joined in unison with the voices of Arikara women. Throughout the day, the throbbing tempo droned over Mitutanka Village as Arikara warriors danced around their three-scalp coup. At Fort Clark, the din cast a cloud over the stockade, making Chardon and his men feel as though they were again under siege. Despite the three-to-one casualty advantage of the Arikaras, the eastern prairie now belonged to the Lakotas. No one pondered if they would attack, merely when. The following day, Arikaras from Ruhptare Village crossed the river, adding their bows and muskets to those of their Mitutanka brothers. As each hour passed without a fight, the Arikaras increasingly feared that the Yanktons were summoning their Santee and Teton brothers for a final, all-out assault.

On July 6, a heavily armed group of Arikaras rode to the Knife River and invited the Hidatsas to join them at Mitutanka Village for the summer. Unless the two tribes fought side by side, the Arikaras argued, the Lakotas would attack their villages separately, destroying them piecemeal. Safety in numbers, including with the fickle Arikaras as an ally, certainly had merit, but the idea of living among them may have given the Hidatsas pause. No doubt the Mandan smallpox survivors had reported how they had recently fared at the hands of the Arikaras. On July 9, the Hidatsas and their Mandan guests relocated closer to the Arikaras, but the Hidatsas declined the invitation to move into Mitutanka Village. Instead, the Hidatsas and Mandans decamped to Ruhptare Village, thinking that was close enough for the tribes to support one another if the Lakotas struck in concert.[42]

The Hidatsas shift to Ruhptare may have had as much to do with Assiniboine aggression as with concern about the Lakotas. Earlier in the month, Assiniboines had murdered a lone Hidatsa while he was hunting. Then the day after the Arikaras had asked for their help, the Hidatsas lost three more warriors to Assiniboine scalping knives. Like the Lakota hostility, the Assiniboine onslaughts were also rooted in the *rotting face*.

By the spring of 1838, Assiniboine Chief Le Vieux Gauche had lost nearly ninety percent of his followers to *Variola major* and with them much of his power. Too weak to avenge their deaths by sacking Fort Union, he instead planned to regain his position as a tribal leader by commanding a raid on the smallpox-ravaged Hidatsas. In early July, the chief recruited warriors from outlying Assiniboine bands and moved down the Missouri. As the Assiniboines awaited the order to pounce on their enemy's Knife River village, they scouted the countryside, killing four Hidatsas and wounding four others. But before Chief Le Gauche could coordinate a general assault, the Hidatsas abandoned their lodges and relocated to Ruhptare Village. Undeterred, the chief positioned his warriors around Ruhptare and prayed to the spirits for a great coup.

On July 12, Le Gauche signaled his warriors to open fire and charge the town. Hearing the gunshots, Arikara warriors from Mitutanka Village swam their ponies across the Missouri and joined the fray, tilting a victory to their Hidatsa allies. That night, the Hidatsas, Arikaras, and a couple of dozen Mandans danced and sang over sixty-four enemy scalps, while eight Assiniboine female captives wept at their tribe's loss. Chief Le Gauche fled with remnants of his war party, but his defeat was more than he could stand. The *rotting face* had destroyed most of his band, and now the Arikaras and Hidatsas had crushed his warriors. His world in pieces, Chief Le Gauche lost hope. Shortly after the battle, he swallowed a vial of poison, ending his own life.[43]

Two days after the fight with the Assiniboines, Chardon and two of his hunters rode across the prairie with fourteen Arikaras, searching for buffalo. About a mile away from Fort Clark, the party was fired on by Lakota warriors, who had been laying an ambush. In a hail of Lakota lead, the *bourgeois* and his Indian and white companions galloped back to the safety of the trading post, thankful they all made it with their hair.

With the smallpox now only a bitter memory, the Arikaras and Hidatsas sought to renew the world they had known before the epidemic. For the depleted Mandans such a goal was impossible. Adult Mandans had to satisfy themselves with dreams about their tribe's past glory, while they and their children assimilated into the Hidatsas. Among Arikara and Hidatsa warriors, the desire to invade their enemies was eclipsed by the necessity of feeding their families. Still, the lure of stealing horses died hard.

On the first day of August, a small group of Arikara warriors rode east from Mitutanka Village, searching for Lakota ponies and scalps. Compared with the war parties the village tribes had fielded before the *rotting face,* this one cast a mere shadow.

Filled with bravado, the young men probably had no idea that for every coup they counted, the Lakotas would answer tenfold.

Meanwhile, at Fort Clark the *bourgeois's* journal recorded that 137 more rats had perished during the month of July. With summer half over, the post's *engagés* kept busy making charcoal and laying in an ample store of hay. On August 3, Chardon's on-again, off-again marriage to his older Arikara wife once more sailed into troubled waters. While Chardon was away from the fort hunting, the woman loaded her belongings on her pony and skedaddled back to her tribe. Finding her gone when he returned home, Chardon noted her desertion in his journal.[44] Perhaps to ease his frustration, the *bourgeois* took a canoe to Fort Pierre for another vacation, departing Fort Clark on August 18 and reaching his destination six days later.

On September 1, Indian Superintendent William Clark died in St. Louis of natural causes, leaving his office vacant. Because the superintendent controlled the trading licenses for the upper Missouri, Clark's replacement was of paramount interest to Pratte & Chouteau and its competition. Every fur company wanted someone who would be sympathetic to its cause. For Pratte & Chouteau, Joshua Pilcher seemed the perfect choice. He knew the upper Missouri Indians as well as anyone, and he was a former employee of the American Fur Company, having managed its trade at Council Bluffs. In the eyes of the Pratte & Chouteau partners, the Senate could do a lot worse than pick Joshua Pilcher for the plum position.

While Pierre Chouteau Jr. and his trading rivals lobbied for their candidates, Francis Chardon returned to Fort Clark from Fort Pierre, arriving in mid October. Accompanying him was another new wife, a teenage Lakota, who he had wooed away from his friend, Jacob Halsey.[45] During Chardon's absence from Fort Clark, the Arikaras had left Mitutanka Village, shifting to their winter camp.

With the upcountry blizzards pressing ever closer, Chardon ordered work details to cut firewood, and kept his hunters busy harvesting buffalo. On October 22, he sent Toussaint Charbonneau up the Missouri, looking for the Arikara and Hidatsa encampments. As a successful trading post command-er, Chardon knew the importance of maintaining friendly relations with his customers. Three days later, the Arikara Chief Two Bulls rode to Fort Clark from his tribe's winter quarters. Chardon could not have been happier with the chief's news, for Two Bulls told him that the prairie around the Arikara camp was overrun with buffalo. He assured the *bourgeois* that the Arikara women would dress many robes during the coming months. At long last, it appeared the trading doldrums were nearing an end.

That night, Charbonneau returned from his reconnaissance, having located the Hidatsas and Arikaras. During the next couple of days, Chardon supervised the fort's *engagés* as they assembled two cart-loads of trade goods for the Indian camps. Meanwhile, Charbonneau focused his attention on matters other than commerce. He was now at least eighty years old, long beyond the age when most men think about matrimony. But Toussaint Charbonneau was not like most men. He had known the upper Missouri when it belonged to the English. He had seen the Pacific Ocean with Lewis and Clark. And he had been married to a Shoshoni teenager who would eventually become one of the most famous women in American history. Although he had packed several lifetimes of adventure into his eight decades, Charbonneau wanted more. In him, the juices still flowed.

After the battle at Ruhptare Village the previous July, Francis Chardon had purchased a fourteen-year-old Assiniboine girl who had been taken captive by the Arikaras. In the months that followed, she had lived at Fort Clark[46] and caught Charbonneau's eye. To everyone's surprise, the aged trader announced that he and the girl were going to marry. No doubt his fellow traders snickered behind his back as they speculated about his wedding night. On Saturday evening, October 27, the deed was done. Two Arikara friends of Charbonneau joined the fort's French-Canadian *engagés* and traders, giving the old man a raucous shivaree. After the kettle-banging, gun-firing, and loud hee-haws had died down, Charbonneau thanked his well-wishers, hosting them to a fine meal that was topped off with whiskey. The celebration complete, Charbonneau bid his guests good night and escorted his young bride to bed, intent on "doing his best."

On October 29, Chardon and six of his men took two carts of trade goods to the Arikaras and Hidatsas. Late that afternoon, they reached the Arikara camp, which set four miles below that of the Hidatsas. The tribes were probably wintering near each other for mutual security against the Assiniboines and Lakotas. Chardon was relieved to see that Chief Two Bulls had told the truth. The prairie around the encampments was thick with buffalo. Over the next two days, the *bourgeois* smoked and talked with the Arikara and Hidatsa tribal leaders, giving them presents and accepting their declarations of friendship. The Hidatsas apologized for having threatened to kill the *bourgeois* because of the *rotting face*. They continued blaming the whites for starting the epidemic, but claimed they no longer thirsted for revenge. In the months since the pestilence had ended, they had spilled the blood of their Indian enemies. Now their hearts were satisfied. Henceforth, the white traders would be their friends.

On the last day of October, Chardon left the Hidatsas and returned to the Arikaras, planning to make an early start back to Fort Clark the following morning. That afternoon, the small war party that had left Mitutanka Village on August 1 arrived at the Arikara camp with fourteen horses that its members had stolen from the Lakotas. It was a good coup, one the returning warriors recounted during an evening feast that featured the roasted ribs from fat buffalo cows. Chardon joined the festivities, not only relishing the delicious food but also a spirited dance that the Bull Band warrior society performed. After bidding his good-byes the next day, the *bourgeois* headed downriver with his men, confident that the coming trading season would be a success.

Chardon reached Fort Clark the following afternoon, November 1. Seven days later, the Missouri River froze, signaling the start of winter. Life at Fort Clark now slowed as the men wished away the weeks until spring. Buffalo hunting provided the main diversion for the days, while the nights were passed trapping wolves and foxes or enjoying the warm embrace of an Indian wife. Traders regularly visited the Arikara and Hidatsa camps, delivering presents and supplies, and ensuring the tribes remained friendly. Because of the abundant buffalo herds, robe production proceeded at a brisk pace despite the reduced number of Indian hunters and female tanners. Having more meat than they could eat, the tribes bartered the excess to the whites. When the traders returned to Fort Clark, their pack horses usually carried not only buffalo robes but also freshly butchered humps and hundreds of tongues.

November slipped into December with no more notice than an entry in Chardon's journal. For the month, Chardon and his men had killed forty-seven wolves and thirty-six foxes. In addition, the *bourgeois* had personally exterminated forty-two rats. As 1838 crept toward a close, the days passed with a mind-numbing sameness, a monotony that was interrupted only by Christmas. December 25 began with a few salutes from the fort's four-pounder cannon. Then in keeping with the spirit of giving, Chardon presented each of his men a glass of whiskey and a special ration of coffee, sugar, and flour. Although spartan, the gift was appreciated.

For all of 1838, Chardon had killed 1,129 rats. His total since coming to Fort Clark exceeded 3,400. As he had hoped, the trading season appeared well on the road to recovery. The New Year began with the press room bristling with 1,000 buffalo robes and 300 fox and wolf skins. There were no beaver pelts because all the native trappers were dead.[47] The Lakotas had killed a few, but most had died from smallpox.

Just before dawn, January 9, 1839, a cluster of Indians outside the Fort Clark stockade awakened Chardon from a deep sleep. Hearing their shouts, he donned his clothes and wandered into the courtyard to see what had them so excited. The night sky glowed orange, lit by flames from the Mandan's former town. Under the cover of darkness, a Lakota war party had slipped into Mitutanka Village and set it ablaze. Fire leapt from its empty lodges, fed by their bone-dry timbers and grass-insulated walls and ceilings. Sparks danced above the conflagration, each living its momentary existence in a burst of light. Roaring in a combustible frenzy, the inferno consumed the village the way the *rotting face* had consumed the Mandan nation. By daylight, all that remained were smoldering ashes and burned-out shells. Like the Mandans, Mitutanka Village was no more.

Chapter fthirteen notes

1. DeVoto, *Across the Wide Missouri*, 289; and Larpenteur, *Forty Years*, 111.

2. Larpenteur, *Forty Years*, 111.

3. Jacob Halsey to Pratte, Chouteau & Company, November 2, 1937, reprinted in Chardon, *Journal*, 394-6.

4. D. D. Mitchell to P. D. Papin, December 1, 1838, Chouteau Family Papers (St. Louis: Missouri Historical Society, photocopied).

5. DeVoto, *Across the Wide Missouri*, 291.

6. Ibid. and Taylor, "Sociocultural Effects," 66.

7. According to Robert H. Lowie, *The Crow Indians* (New York: Reinhart, 1935; Lincoln: University of Nebraska Press, 1963; Bison Book Edition, 1983), 3, *Apsaruke* is more often spelled and pronounced *Absaroka,* which early French traders misinterpreted as *gens de corbeaux,* meaning Crow.

8. DeVoto, *Across the Wide Missouri*, 290, 418 n. 6; and J. A. Hamilton to Pierre Chouteau Jr., February 25, 1838, Chouteau Family Papers (St. Louis: Missouri Historical Society, photocopied). DeVoto cites Fort Cass, but Fort Van Buren had replaced Fort Cass in 1835; see Robertson, *Competitive Struggle*, 89, 236. Denig, *Indian Tribes*, 170 n. 29 also reports that, for the most part, the Crows avoided the smallpox epidemic of 1837 and 1838.

9. Chardon, *Journal*, 146.

10. Ibid., 149.

11. Trimble, "Spread of Smallpox," 45 puts the Arikara fatality rate at fifty percent as does Stearn and Stearn, *Effect of Smallpox*, 94. For an in-depth analysis, see this chapter, endnote 40.

12. Chardon, *Journal*, 153; and Denig, *Indian Tribes*, 59 n. 27.

13. Larpenteur, *Forty Years*, 113 reports that the ice broke up in front of Fort Union in early March. Chardon, *Journal*, 153 states that downstream at Fort Clark, the river did not thaw until March 18.

14. Larpenteur, *Forty Years*, 111; and Stearn and Stearn, *Effect of Smallpox*, 94 use this estimate, whereas Ray, *Indians in the Fur Trade*, 187-8 put the Assiniboine fatalities at 6,000, some two-thirds of the tribe. In reality, no one knows for certain how many Assiniboines died in the epidemic.

15. Larpenteur, *Forty Years*, 114-15.

16. Ibid., 115-20.

17. Chardon, *Journal*, 154, 318-19 n. 504. DeVoto, *Across the Wide Missouri*, 286 states that the women were left at the Arikaras' winter camp before the tribe moved into Mitutanka Village. DeVoto's conclusion is at odds with Chardon's journal entry for March 26, which reads "All the Rees, except a few Old Women have left the Village." Since the Arikaras had deserted their winter camp nearly a week earlier, I take Chardon's reference to "village" as meaning Mitutanka Village.

18. Larpenteur, *Forty Years*, 120.

19. Sunder, *Joshua Pilcher*, 138. Joseph Picotte to P. D. Papin, April 21, 1838 (in French), Chouteau Family Papers, trans. anonymous (St. Louis: Missouri Historical Society, photocopied) reports that Picotte vaccinated a number of Lakotas at his trading outlet on the Cheyenne River, but he did not have enough medicine to immunize all the Indians who sought protection.

20. Joshua Pilcher to William Clark, February 5, 1838, reprinted in "Spread of Smallpox," by Trimble, 68-71.

21. William Clark to C. A. Harris, February 6, 1838, reprinted in "Spread of Smallpox," by Trimble, 71-3.

22. J. A. Hamilton to Pierre Chouteau Jr., February 25, 1838, Chouteau Family Papers (St. Louis: Missouri Historical Society, photocopied).

23. Joshua Pilcher to William Clark, February 27, 1838, reprinted in "Spread of Smallpox," by Trimble, 73-7.

24. For an example, see John Stows to Joel R. Poinsette, March 29, 1838, reprinted in "Spread of Smallpox," by Trimble, 77-8.

25. Sunder, *Joshua Pilcher*, 137-8.

26. Ibid.

27. Larpenteur, *Forty Years*, 122.

28. Although Larpenteur's *Forty Years* makes no mention of a conversation with Pilcher, it is inconceivable that Pilcher would not have pumped the clerk and Robert Christy for everything they knew. After all, the two men were eyewitnesses to the epidemic that Pilcher had been charged to contain.

29. Larpenteur, *Forty Years*, 121-2.

30. Sunder, *Joshua Pilcher*, 138.

31. Meyer, *Village Indians*, 96, 282 n. 38; and Sunder, *Joshua Pilcher*, 138-9.

32. Trimble, "Spread of Smallpox," 45. In contrast with Trimble's estimate of fatalities, Stearn and Stearn, *Effect of Smallpox*, 94 sets the Hidatsa death rate at thirty-three percent.

33. Chardon, *Journal*, 160, 319 n. 506. It is interesting to note that Chardon made no mention in his journal if his Arikara wife caught smallpox during the epidemic. It seems inconceivable that she could have avoided it, given the number of people within the fort who became sick.

34. Chardon, *Journal*, 160 states that the woman was scalped on the Little Missouri River. As pointed out in Chapter 3, endnote 15, South Dakota's Bad River was often called the Little Missouri.

35. I infer the man was an Arikara, although Chardon, *Journal*, 161 does not specifically say so.

36. Ibid. reports that "an Indian died at the Village of the Small Pox [sic]." I assume the Indian was the young warrior, since the *Journal* mentions no other cases.

37. Jacob Halsey to Pratte, Chouteau & Company, November 2, 1837, reprinted in Chardon, *Journal*, 394-6 states that had David Mitchell arrived at Fort Union with cowpox vaccine, "thousands of lives might have been saved." Since Mitchell had no vaccine when he reached the post in mid October 1837, some must have been sent between then and the following spring when he vaccinated the two war parties. Halsey's letter begged Pratte & Chouteau to rush vaccine to the upper Missouri. Responding to Halsey's message or, perhaps, to other reports about the smallpox epidemic, Pierre Chouteau Jr. (according to Sunder, *Joshua Pilcher*, 138) sent a supply to Fort Pierre, where Halsey was serving as senior clerk. Joseph Picotte to P. D. Papin, April 21, 1838 (in French), Chouteau Family Papers, trans. anonymous (St. Louis: Missouri Historical Society, photocopied) reports that Picotte vaccinated Indians (probably Lakotas) on the Cheyenne River in the late winter or early spring of 1838. Therefore, Halsey or the Fort Pierre *bourgeois* probably forwarded some of Chouteau's vaccine to Mitchell via a winter express. That in itself would have been unusual, since most winter expresses went downriver instead of up. Accepting this scenario begs the question, why no vaccine was forwarded to Fort Clark, or if it was, why Chardon never mentioned it in his journal?

    According to Chardon, *Journal*, 319 n. 507, the American Fur Company had sent vaccine to Fort Pierre in 1832, but it is doubtful any of that culture would have still been active by the winter of 1838. Larpenteur, "Journals and Notes," 160 reports that seven Assiniboine women and several mixed-bloods at Fort Union were vaccinated either before or right after Jacob Halsey and the *St. Peter's* arrived in 1837, but the vaccine was inert.

38. Readers rolling their eyes in disbelief at this encounter are encouraged to read Chardon's journal entry for June 7, 1838 (Chardon, *Journal*, 162).

39. In his journal (ibid., 160, 164) Chardon erroneously wrote that his Arikara wife had left him two months earlier, but they had separated on May 18, which was only one month prior.

40. J. A. Hamilton to Pierre Chouteau Jr., February 25, 1838, Chouteau Family Papers (St. Louis: Missouri Historical Society, photocopied), puts the adult male Mandan survivors at thirty-one, making no mention of the women or children. Although other sources use different numbers, Meyer, *Village Indians*, 95-6 list the Mandan survivors at twenty-three men, forty women, and between sixty and seventy children, which indicates the Mandan tribal death rate exceeded ninety percent. In addition to estimating the Mandan population at 1,600 before the epidemic began in 1837, Meyer places the pre-epidemic Hidatsa population at 2,000 and that of the Arikaras between 2,750 and 3,000. On page 97, Meyer claims that the Hidatsas and Arikaras lost half their populations during the pestilence. In contrast, Stearn and Stearn, *Effect of Smallpox*, 94 puts the pre-epidemic Arikara population at 3,000 and the Hidatsas' at 1,500, adding that the Arikaras were reduced by half and the Hidatsas by one-third. Lehmer, *Selected Writings*, 107 places the pre-epidemic combined populations of the Mandans, Hidatsas, and Arikaras at 7,000, reporting that the number dropped to 2,000 by mid 1838. Subtracting the Mandans from Lehmer's count gives the combined Hidatsas and Arikaras a pre-epidemic population of 5,400 (7,000 minus 1,600) and a post-epidemic population of around 1,870 (2,000 minus 130), which translates into a death rate of sixty-five percent for the combined Hidatsas and Arikaras. Finally, Taylor, "Sociocultural Effects," 62 cites Joshua Pilcher, who claimed that suicide contributed to the high number of Mandan fatalities.

41. Chardon, *Journal*, 165; and Denig, *Indian Tribes*, 59 n. 27.

42. Denig, *Indian Tribes*, 59 n. 27.

43. Chardon, *Journal*, 167-8 state that Chief Le Gauche attacked "the Camp on the other side" of the Missouri from Fort Clark. The Arikaras, "all eager to help their friends the Gros Ventres [Hidatsas]," crossed the river and joined in the battle. Denig, *Indian Tribes*, 77-9; and Taylor, "Sociocultural Effects," 64 report that Chief Le Gauche fought the Mandans. Although it is true that some surviving Mandans were living with the Hidatsas at the time, there were far more Hidatsa warriors in the battle than Mandan.

44. Although Chardon made no mention in his journal if he was still enjoying the arms of his teenage wife, it can be surmised that he was not, since he soon acquired another.

45. Chardon, *Journal*, 175. The whereabouts of Chardon's fifteen-year-old Arikara wife, who he purchased for $150 on June 15, 1838, is a mystery.

46. I base this conclusion on Chardon's journal entry for October 27 (ibid., 173). Writing about the girl, Chardon penned that she was "bought by me of the Rees."

47. Ibid., 180.

Chapter Fourteen

AFTERMATH

The smallpox virus that came up the Missouri River on the *St. Peter's* ignited a western North American pandemic that killed Indians from the Canadian subarctic to New Mexico. On America's southern plains and in the southwest, the *rotting face* eventually infected the Osages, Choctaws, Comanches, Apaches, and Pueblos. Among the Kiowas, December 1839 through February 1840 is remembered as *Tä dalkop Sia*—the smallpox winter.[1]

Although *Variola major* dealt its death and misery over a broad section of the North American West, its most virulent assault fell on the upper Missouri. By mid 1838, the Mandans—for all practical purposes—had ceased to exist as a separate tribe. Needing protection from their enemies, surviving remnants of this once-wealthy nation sought refuge with their allies. The social structure of the Hidatsas and Arikaras remained intact, though barely. Reeling from their world turned upside down, the Hidatsas and Arikaras struggled to reassemble their lives. So many of their male hunters and female gardeners had been killed by the virus, starvation would dog the village tribes for years to come.

Farther west, the situation was much the same. The nomadic Assiniboines had seen their numbers reduced by at least half. The Plains Crees had also suffered, but thanks to the vaccinations provided by the Hudson's Bay Company, their losses were less than those of their western and southern neighbors. The Crows were more fortunate than the Plains Crees. They had escaped the epidemic. After hearing about smallpox among the traders at Fort Van Buren, the Crows had stayed in the Absaroka foothills during the contagion, thereby keeping themselves safe.

Among the Atsinas, the illness had confined itself to the tribe's young children. Most older members had caught smallpox in the early 1830s while visiting their Arapaho cousins during a mini-epidemic that ravaged the South Platte River. Although the earlier virus had winnowed the Atsinas' ranks, it protected the survivors from the more virulent attack of 1837 and 1838.

Unlike the Atsinas, the Piegans, Bloods, and Northern Blackfeet had had no defense. *Variola major* had cut through their confederation as though it were a scythe mowing the late summer hay. Of all the tribes on the upper plains, only the Mandans suffered a higher percentage of fatalities than did the Blackfeet. Estimates of their dead are but guesses, ranging from well over half to two-thirds of the entire confederation.[2] In the wake of the epidemic, the Blackfeet lost their swagger. Never again would they have the warriors to prevent white incursions. No longer would their enemies tremble before their bows. What brigades of mountain men had failed to do during twenty years of strife, smallpox had accomplished in one. The Blackfeet were subdued.

No one knows how many Indians perished in the smallpox epidemic of the late 1830s. Among the tribes of the upper Missouri, the fatality consensus ranges from 17,000 to 20,000.[3] Add to this the untold host that perished on the central Canadian plains, the southern American plains, and the southwest, and the number staggers the mind.

Because history demands a reckoning, ethnologists, anthropologists, and historians conjure up estimates in the "umpteen thousands" or "tens of thousands." But such statistics are antiseptic. They produce no understanding of smallpox's terrible ordeal. On the contrary, numerical rhetoric acts as a fine-mesh filter, cleansing the past of its cankers, its odors, and its screams. Statistical tabulations of death insulate history's spectators from their emotions, and allow modern man to claim empathy without shedding a tear. No matter how many zeros the numbers contain, they will never recount the heartbreak of a Mandan husband hugging the emaciated body of his small-pox-ravaged wife.

In mid February 1839, the Arikaras and Hidatsas were living side by side when an Arikara warrior killed—by accident or otherwise—a Hidatsa woman. In retaliation, some young Hidatsa warriors captured two teenage Arikara girls and put them to death. The Hidatsas immediately broke camp and moved up the Missouri, feeling it would be wise to put distance between themselves and their capricious ally. After learning about the girls' murder, Arikara warriors painted their faces for battle, vowing to avenge their tribe's honor. Realizing that war between their people would spell disaster, Arikara and Hidatsa elders called for calm, arguing that the Assiniboines and Lakotas were the true enemy. Somewhat mollified but still lusting for revenge, an Arikara raiding party set out against the Hidatsas, intending to take their horses instead of their scalps.[4]

The trouble between the two erstwhile friends festered for the rest of the winter and into spring. Fortunately for both tribes, horse raids satisfied their warriors' need for vengeance, precluding the outbreak of a full-fledged war. That May, the Arikaras rebuilt Mitutanka Village and again used it as their summer home. Although a few Mandans put aside their differences with the Arikaras and also moved into the town, most of them continued living with the Hidatsas, who reoccupied their old village near the confluence of the Knife and Missouri rivers. In time, several Hidatsa families established a village on the lower Little Knife River (now beneath North Dakota's Garrison Reservoir), and others joined their Crow relatives and gradually assimilated into their tribe.[5]

Smallpox had destroyed so many Indians on the upper Missouri plains, tribal hegemony was forever changed. As had happened during earlier epidemics, the Lakotas fared better than the village tribes. Now allied with the Northern Cheyennes and Arapahos, who had also come through the recent epidemic with relatively few deaths, the Lakotas accelerated their western migration, filling the void created by the *rotting face*. Far from being heartless villains, the Lakotas were merely reacting to pressure from a westward-expanding white society.

Waves of white emigrants were staking out farms in Minnesota and Iowa, driving away the buffalo on which the Lakotas depended for food and shelter. Unable to halt the white onslaught, the Lakotas pushed west against the weakened Arikaras and Hidatsas, taking advantage of the power vacuum that had been created by smallpox. With so many of their warriors dead, the village tribes lay prostrate before Lakota aggression, capable of offering only token resistance. For generations the Mandans, Hidatsas, and Arikaras had acted as a buffer between the Lakotas and Assiniboines, but now that the villagers were no longer able to hold back the Lakota hordes, Teton and Yankton raiding parties increasingly invaded the Assiniboine domain.

Despite the large death toll exacted by the smallpox epidemic of 1837 and 1838, the buffalo robe trade on the upper Missouri recovered quickly. *Variola major* had destroyed so many of the tribes' skilled male hunters and female artisans, it made the survivors all the more dependent on the fur companies and their manufactured trade goods. Needing the output of America's factories in order to live, the upper Missouri Indians increased their robe production at the sacrifice of their traditional handiwork.

Like the once-noble Mandan nation, the *St. Peter's* also failed to outlast the smallpox epidemic of the late 1830s. The steamboat was dismantled for parts in 1838.[6]

That same year, Bernard Pratte Jr. withdrew from active service in Pratte & Chouteau, devoting his energy to his newly elected position in the Missouri State Assembly. The next year, Pierre Chouteau Jr. reorganized Pratte & Chouteau into Pierre Chouteau Jr. & Company. Four years later, Bernard Pratte Jr.

and John Cabanné Jr. formed a partnership and began competing with the Chouteau enterprise. Their venture was far from a
success. Renewing his interest in politics, Pratte won election
as the mayor of St. Louis in the mid 1840s and ended his business association with Cabanné.[7] Bernard Pratte Jr. died in
1887.

On February 28, 1839, the United States Senate appointed
Joshua Pilcher Superintendent of Indian Affairs, filling the
vacancy left by the death of William Clark. Pilcher resigned his
Lakota-Cheyenne-Ponca Agency position, unaware the government would allow it to stand empty for another three years.
Pilcher held the job of superintendent until September 1841,
when he was replaced by David Mitchell. Pilcher died twenty-
one months later.[8]

After returning to Fort Pierre from Fort Union in the fall of
1837, Jacob Halsey worked as a clerk until late summer 1842.
That September while visiting William Laidlaw—a former
bourgeois of Fort Pierre—at his home near Liberty, Missouri,
Halsey went riding while drunk. Galloping down a hill, he fell
from his horse and smashed his head against a tree, dying
instantly.[9]

Toussaint Charbonneau remained on the upper Missouri at
least through the summer of 1839. In August of that year,
Joshua Pilcher wrote that the old trader was "tottering under
the infirmities" of his advanced age.[10] Soon thereafter,
Charbonneau disappeared from the rolls of history.

Francis Chardon remained *bourgeois* of Fort Clark through
1842, and in 1843, he took command of Fort McKenzie.
Alexander Harvey was still employed at the post as clerk and
senior trader, while Jacob Berger continued working there as
an interpreter. The following January, Blackfoot Bloods murdered a black slave belonging to Chardon. Wanting compensa-
tion for the loss of his "property," Chardon hatched a plot with
Harvey and Berger whereby they would massacre and rob the
Bloods when they next came to the fort to trade. A few weeks
later, a party of Bloods gathered outside the palisades, shouting
for *engagés* to open the main gate.

Seeing his chance for revenge, Chardon directed Harvey to
load the post cannon with grapeshot and aim it at the trading

room door. When the gate was opened, the Indians hurried inside, bunching together before the trade room entrance. They usually paid no mind when the *engagés* shut and locked the front gate, a standard policy for controlling the number of Indians allowed within the stockade. But this time, something about Harvey's demeanor signaled a warning. Sensing danger, the chiefs yelled for their warriors to flee.

As the Bloods broke toward the stockade wall, Harvey ignited the powder in the cannon's touchhole. Like a giant shotgun blast, the grape tore into the Indian ranks, killing three and severely wounding two others. Seeing a chief who was about to climb over the pickets, Chardon fired his pistol, shattering the man's thighbone. Within minutes the fight was over. Those Indians who had not escaped or been killed outright, lay in the dirt, writhing in pain. Showing no mercy, Harvey knelt beside each one and slit his throat before lifting his hair. Acting as though he were a fiend in a vampire novel, he then licked the blood from his knife. Chardon, Harvey, and Berger looted the dead of their robes and other property, delighted at how well their plan had worked. As a final insult to the fallen warriors, Harvey ordered the Indian wives of the trading post's employees to dance around the Blackfoot scalps.[11]

Word of the massacre quickly spread from the surviving Bloods to the rest of the Blackfoot Confederation. Almost overnight, trade at Fort McKenzie dried up. The Blackfeet embraced Pierre Chouteau Jr. & Company's competition, swapping their robes at the Union Fur Company's Fort Cotton (located five miles above modern Fort Benton, Montana). In addition, any Chouteau man who ventured alone on the prairie risked having his hair decorate a Blackfoot lodgepole. Under pressure from Alexander Culbertson—now head of the Upper Missouri Outfit—to rekindle the trade, Chardon torched Fort McKenzie and built Fort Chardon as its replacement near the mouth of the Judith River (in central Montana).

The Blackfeet shunned Fort Chardon as they had done Fort McKenzie. Then in 1845, the Union Fur Company sold out to Pierre Chouteau Jr. & Company. Determined to restore the Blackfoot trade, Culbertson closed Fort Chardon and sent Francis Chardon downriver. A short time later, Culbertson established a new Blackfoot trading post—Fort Lewis—near the recently abandoned Fort Cotton. That year, smallpox again struck the Blackfeet, although most of the cases occurred above the forty-ninth parallel. With Pierre Chouteau Jr. & Company now holding a trading monopoly on the western upper Missouri plain, the Blackfeet living south of the so-called "medicine line" faced trading with their Chouteau enemy or taking their robes to the Hudson's Bay Company's forts in Canada and risk their children catching the *rotting face*. Not surprisingly, they opted to do business at Fort Lewis.

In the meantime, a shortage of firewood around the mouth of the Knife River compelled a majority of Hidatsas—and their handful of Mandan guests—to move forty-two miles up the Missouri to Fishhook Bend, a place the Indians called *L'Ours qui Danse* (Dancing Bear). For years the Hidatsas had held their bear dance at this north shore site. Here they found land for their cornfields and gardens. The thick cottonwood groves provided ample fuel, and the country could be defended from Assiniboine and Lakota war parties. The Hidatsas and Mandans named their new home Like-A-Fishhook Village. That autumn Pierre Chouteau Jr. & Company sent James Kipp and Francis Chardon to Fishhook Bend where they built Fort James. Some months later, the trading post was renamed Fort Berthold. Chardon died at Fort Berthold in 1848. He was probably in his early to mid fifties.[12]

During the 1840s, the Arikaras and a few families of Mandans continued living in the rebuilt Mitutanka Village and trading at Fort Clark. In 1846, measles struck the town, further reducing the Indians' numbers.[13] Each year, Lakota influence and hostility grew more powerful. Although Lakota war parties occasionally raided the Hidatsas at Like-A-Fishhook Village, they focused most of their aggression on the Mitutanka residents.

In 1846, Alexander Harvey formed a partnership with Charles Primeau and other former Pierre Chouteau Jr. & Company traders. Known as Harvey, Primeau & Company, the new firm sought to challenge the Chouteau empire on the upper Missouri. In the late 1840s, the opposition firm established Fort Primeau, placing it midway between Fort Clark and Mitutanka

Village. Although the competition offered the Arikaras better prices for their robes, most of the tribe stayed loyal to the Chouteau post.

In 1848, the Shoshonis caught smallpox from emigrants on the Oregon Trail. The Shoshonis then passed the virus to the Crows, where it was most deadly among the children. Three years later, California-bound emigrants again gave smallpox to the Shoshonis, who infected a band of Crows on the upper Powder River (in central Wyoming). The number of Shoshoni deaths are unknown, but in the second epidemic, the Crows lost 400 tribesmen.[14]

In 1851, the steamer *St. Ange* of Pierre Chouteau Jr. & Company brought another epidemic to the upper Missouri, this one cholera. At Like-A-Fishhook Village, the Hidatsas died by the score, but in fewer numbers than had perished from small-pox in the late 1830s. Rudolf Kurz, a clerk at Fort Berthold, put the cholera death rate at seven percent—one out of fourteen. Cholera losses at Mitutanka Village were said to have been higher.[15]

That September, while cholera buffeted the Arikaras and Hidatsas (and the few families of Mandans who had not yet assimilated into their hosts), government agents called the western tribes to Fort Laramie (on eastern Wyoming's Laramie River just above its confluence with the North Platte). The peace parley included over 10,000 Indians and was the largest one ever held. Lakota, Shoshoni, Arapaho, Crow, Cheyenne, Assiniboine, and Atsina chiefs accepted presents and touched pen to paper, promising to live in peace with one another and to allow white emigrants passage over their land on the white man's road, known as the Oregon Trail.[16] Yet the ink on the treaty was barely dry before Lakota war parties were again raiding the residents of Mitutanka and Like-A-Fishhook vil-lages. Indian agents such as Thomas Moore preached peace, but there were never enough soldiers to prevent the Lakota attacks. Seeing their outnumbered young men dying in battle, the Hidatsas and Arikaras seethed at a government policy that refused to arm them and allow their warriors to fight in their own defense.

Amid the inter-tribal warfare, Chouteau's steamboats

continued bringing government annuities to the village tribes, but the presents were always too few and lacked guns. In 1853, grasshoppers descended on the cornfields and gardens of Like-A-Fishhook Village, eating the crops.[17] Powerless to stop the devastation, the Hidatsas looked on with dismay, knowing their harvest would be meager and that during the coming winter, their children would cry from hunger. Meanwhile, Fort Pierre was showing its age. Wanting to unload the post instead of waste money on its repair, Pierre Chouteau Jr. & Company sold the fort to the Army in April 1855, for $45,000.

In 1856, a violent hailstorm pummeled the unripened corn, squashes, and other crops at Like-A-Fishhook Village, destroying another year's bounty. Adding to the misery, smallpox again invaded the upper Missouri, further reducing the Hidatsas and Arikaras. Less terrible than the epidemic of the late 1830s, this latest outbreak attacked the children and young adults of the tribes, those under the age of nineteen. Anyone older had survived the previous scourge and was immune. In 1857, as the smallpox spread to the Blackfeet on the Canadian plains,[18] a shortage of firewood and grazing pastures at Fort Pierre prompted the Army to abandon its two-year-old purchase. Soldiers dismantled many of the post's structures and shipped the timbers 150 miles down the Missouri to the new Fort Randall.

Fort Primeau—which sat between Fort Clark and Mitutanka Village—passed through several iterations of Pierre Chouteau Jr. & Company's competitors before the last one folded in 1860. Soon afterward, a large section of Fort Clark burned, prompting the Chouteau traders to annex abandoned Fort Primeau. Over the next two years, the Arikaras at Mitutanka Village grew increasingly weary of the Lakota onslaught. Finally deserting their lodges, they fled up the Missouri, eventually joining the Hidatsas at Like-A-Fishhook Village. With the Arikaras gone from Mitutanka Village, Pierre Chouteau Jr. & Company closed Fort Primeau and what remained of Fort Clark, consolidating their trade at Fort Berthold.[19]

In 1738, when the French trader Pierre Gaultier de Varennes, the Sieur de La Vérendrye, first visited the Great

Plains, the Mandans, Hidatsas, and Arikaras had numbered 25,000 people and lived in dozens of villages between the Knife and Bad rivers. Together, the three tribes dominated the upper Missouri, controlling everything from egress to commerce. But within five generations, smallpox had reduced their collective population tenfold, and among the Mandans, the virus had nearly eliminated them entirely. Their numbers repeatedly reduced by disease and war, the survivors of these formerly powerful tribes were forced for the sake of security to huddle together in a single town, Like-A-Fishhook Village. Their past glory forever destroyed, the village tribes now lived by the tight-fisted largesse of an indifferent government and its fur company agent.

With the start of the American Civil War, the demand for buffalo robes collapsed. In addition, escalating Lakota hostility disrupted the upper Missouri's native robe manufacturers, further harming the trade. Pierre Chouteau Jr. & Company now made more profit distributing Indian annuities than it did from buffalo. In 1864, the Army positioned supplies at Fort Union—guarded by soldiers of the Thirtieth Wisconsin Infantry—anticipating that Congress would authorize a permanent post near the Yellowstone-Missouri confluence. In the spring of 1865, the Chouteau firm sold Fort Union to the Northwest Fur Company (not to be confused with the old North West Company of Canada). That August, the soldiers left the aging Fort Union trading post, giving the stored materials to its new owner. In June 1866, the Army began constructing Fort Buford across from the mouth of the Yellowstone River, on the original site of old Fort William (whose re-located buildings had been used as a hospital during the smallpox epidemic of the late 1830s). The following summer—1867—the Northwest Fur Company sold Fort Union to the Army, which dismantled it and used the material to enlarge Fort Buford.[20]

As the 1860s came to a close, smallpox again invaded the Blackfeet. Among its victims was the aged Blood Chief Seen-From-Afar, brother-in-law of Alexander Culbertson. Earlier, in 1855, in concert with other confederation chiefs, Seen-From-Afar had added his mark to a government document titled the Treaty with the Blackfoot Nation. Known by the Blackfeet as

Lame Bull's Treaty, the agreement forbade the Piegans, Bloods, and Northern Blackfeet from making war on their Indian neighbors. Further, it granted white Americans nearly unlimited trespass across Blackfoot land below the forty-ninth parallel. When Seen-From-Afar and the other chiefs made their marks on the treaty paper, they signed away the Blackfeet's birthright, forfeiting the sovereignty of what had once been one of the strongest Indian powers in North America.[21]

During the fourteen years following the signing of Lame Bull's Treaty, confederation war parties ignored the covenant that prevented them from raiding the horse herds of the Crees, Flatheads, Crows, and other tribes. Officials from Indian Affairs protested the forays, but the tribal chiefs said their young warriors refused to heed the treaty, claiming they needed to prove their manhood. On August 17, 1869, as the Blackfeet underwent the latest visit of *Variola major,* a small party of Piegans killed a former Fort Union *bourgeois,* Malcolm Clark, at his Montana ranch. When the Piegan leader, Mountain Chief, refused to surrender the murderers, General Philip Sheridan, commander of the Military Division of the Missouri River, ordered a winter campaign to bring them to justice.

On January 23, 1870, as the temperature dipped twenty degrees below zero along the Marias River, blue-coated soldiers mistakenly attacked the friendly Piegan camp of Chief Heavy Runner. Many of the camp's inhabitants were suffering from smallpox. By the time the troopers finished their slaughter, 173 Indians lay dead, many of them women and children. Although the assault lacked all justification, it did bring a lasting peace to the Montana Territory.[22] Beset by the *Variola* virus, the Blackfeet realized they were too weak to seek revenge. The soldiers were too many and too well armed. If the Blackfeet retaliated, the Army would finally accomplish what repeated bouts of the *rotting face* had failed to do, wipe their confederation from the face of the earth.

By the early 1870s, the ancestral tribes of the middle and upper Missouri—the Omahas, Poncas, Pawnees, Arikaras, Mandans, Hidatsas, Assiniboines, and Blackfeet—had been subdued. Weakened by smallpox and harassed by their enemies, these previous rulers of the Great Plains no longer held sway in their own land. White farmers and Montana gold miners now filled the margins of the vacuum they had left behind. Usurping its center were the Lakotas and their Northern Cheyenne and Arapaho allies. Yet soon, they too would yield to the white invasion.

Chapter fourteen notes

1. Hopkins, *Princes and Peasants*, 271-2; and Stearn and Stearn, *Effect of Smallpox*, 86-7. Differing with Hopkins and the Stearns, DeVoto, *Across the Wide Missouri*, 294 argues that the epidemic that hit the Choctaws—and by inference the Kiowas, Osages, Comanches, Apaches, and Pueblos—came from a different source than the one that infected the upper Missouri.

2. DeVoto, *Across the Wide Missouri*, 291; and Ewers, *The Blackfeet*, 66.

3. DeVoto, *Across the Wide Missouri*, 295; Ferch, "Fighting the Smallpox Epidemic," 20, no. 1 (spring 1984): 7; Stearn and Stearn, *Effect of Smallpox*, 94; and Sunder, *Joshua Pilcher*, 139.

4. Chardon, *Journal*, 188.

5. Ibid., 193; and Meyer, *Village Indians*, 97, 99-100.

6. Casler, *Steamboats*, 35.

7. Sunder, *The Fur Trade on the Upper Missouri*, 5, 7-8. Bernard Pratte Jr. served as the mayor of St. Louis from 1844 to 1846.

8. Sunder, *Joshua Pilcher*, 143, 166.

9. Chardon, *Journal*, 211 n. 50.

10. Ibid., 282 n. 280.

11. Robertson, *Competitive Struggle*, 173-4. There are nearly as many versions of this massacre as there are historians; this is but one of them.

12. Chardon, *Journal*, xviii, xxix n. 29; and Meyer, *Village Indians*, 100. Honore Picotte to Pierre Chouteau Jr. & Company, December 7, 1845, reprinted in "Fort Tecumseh and Fort Pierre Journal and Letter Books," abst. DeLand, 9:212 calls Fishhook Bend *L'ours gen clans* (Bears that dance). Chardon's date of birth is unknown.

13. Meyer, *Village Indians*, 104. The death count is unknown.

14. Denig, *Indian Tribes*, 185-6 and 186 n. 35.

15. Meyer, *Village Indians*, 104.

16. David Lavender, *Fort Laramie and the Changing Frontier*, Handbook 118 (Washington: Division of Publications, National Park Service, 1983), 69-73.

17. Meyer, *Village Indians*, 105-06.

18. McClintock, *Old North Trail*, 444.

19. Robertson, *Competitive Struggle*, 71-2, 210-11.

20. Ibid., 236.

21. Ewers, *The Blackfeet*, 224.

22. Ibid., 246-53.

Chapter Fifteen

BLAME

Before the modern historian can assign blame for the deaths of so many Native Americans, it is important for him or her to appreciate the state of scientific knowledge during the eighteenth and early nineteenth centuries. Physicians of the day had no understanding of bacteria, let alone viruses such as *Variola major*. No one had seen a microorganism until 1683, when Dutch naturalist Antonie van Leeuwenhoek looked at one under the newly invented microscope. At the time, the concept of blood circulation was a newfangled theory that had been suggested by the Spanish theologian and physician, Michael Servetus (or Miguel Serveto), in the previous century. Servetus had published his heretical hypothesis in the *Christianismi Restitutio*, for which the religious zealot John Calvin burned him at the stake in 1553.[1]

Building on Servetus's work, English physician and anatomist, William Harvey, furthered the concept pulmonary circulation in 1628 with his publication of *De motu cordis et sanguinis* (The Motion of the Heart and Blood). Fortunately for him, the church had recently tempered its treatment of scientists who challenged accepted dogma. Seventeenth-century English physician Thomas Sydenham blamed disease on "peccant matter" that had corrupted the blood. Although his cures relied on bleeding and laxative purges, he was ahead of other doctors of the day in that he did not cover feverish victims under piles of heavy blankets.[2]

Contemporary medicines, if they can be called that, leaned toward mercury, opium, and rattlesnake root. Calomel was a preferred purgative, and ipecac was used to induce vomiting. Some drugs, such as water soaked with South American cinchona bark (a.k.a. Jesuit's bark)—which contained quinine, a treatment for malaria—actually did some good. Those made from human or animal dung and urine usually made the patient's condition worse. One of the more novel panaceas for smallpox involved drinking vast quantities of water that for two days had been left in contact with tar.[3] While being no more of a cure than other absurd elixirs, tar water probably caused those who drank it far less discomfort than did an excrement cocktail. Given the large doses in which some of these so-called remedies were administered, it is a wonder any of the sick survived.

Following Leeuwenhoek's work with the microscope, nearly a century passed before a few physicians first suspected that a particular organism was responsible for a specific disease. The Hidatsas had already established Like-A-Fishhook Village before Ferdinand Cohn published his study of bacteria in 1853. And Louis Pasteur did not succeed in immunizing animals against bacteria-borne disease until 1880.

The knowledge of viruses came after that of bacteria. The existence of non-bacterial infectious agents gained acceptance only after Russian bacteriologist Dmitri Ivanovski proved that the cause of tobacco mosaic disease—a virus—could penetrate a series of porcelain filters that blocked bacteria. As a result of Ivanovski's 1892 experiments and those of Dutch bacteriologist Martinus Beijerinck six years later, scientists knew that infectious agents existed that were smaller than bacteria, but they had no idea of their makeup. That had to await the invention of the electron microscope in the late 1930s, 100 years after *Variola major* had all but annihilated the Mandans.

S hortly after the epidemic of 1837 and 1838 ended, stories
began to circulate that an Indian had stolen a smallpox-
infected blanket from a dying deckhand when the *St. Peter's*
first stopped at Fort Clark. According to some of the tales, the
Indian caught the disease from the blanket and introduced it to
his tribesmen at Mitutanka Village. On September 20, 1837,
Mandan subagent William Fulkerson wrote the Superintendent
of Indian Affairs, William Clark, that an Arikara had taken a
blanket from a *St. Peter's* crewman who was recovering from
smallpox. Fulkerson seemingly wanted Clark to think he had
penned the letter while on the upper Missouri, but Clark suspected that he had composed it in St. Charles, Missouri, after
returning from his agency. According to some historians, Clark
dismissed the blanket incident as fiction.[4]

In 1843, Francis Chardon related a similar story to John
James Audubon, during the naturalist's tour of the upper
Missouri. According to Audubon, Chardon claimed that when he
boarded the *St. Peter's*—which Chardon mistakenly called the
Assiniboine—there were "many victims" of smallpox aboard.
Chardon added that after the steamboat arrived at Fort Clark,
an Indian chief stole a blanket from a contagious crewman, who
was deathly ill. Knowing the danger to the neighboring tribes,
Chardon offered to replace the blanket, but the chief refused.
The chief caught smallpox from the blanket and infected the
Mandans before dying.

Although the story is plausible—one can catch smallpox by
inhaling spores from a scab-contaminated blanket—Chardon
made no mention in his journal of there being multiple cases of
smallpox when he boarded the *St. Peter's* on April 18, 1837. If
there had been, it seems likely he would have written about
them, but his journal entries from mid to late April lack any references to illness on the steamer or to the stolen-blanket incident. The account Chardon related to Audubon has the ring of
a tale intended to shield its teller from culpability. Once the
Indians at Mitutanka Village became sick, they held Chardon
and Pratte, Chouteau & Company responsible. In truth,
Chardon probably had no idea how the smallpox spread to the
Mandans and other tribes. But a story about a chief stealing an
infected blanket clearly shifts the blame for the ensuing

epidemic to the Indians.[5]

In another version of the blanket episode, the notorious liar and mountain man, James Beckwourth, claimed to have traded a smallpox-laced blanket to a band of Blackfeet, who then came down with the disease and gave it to the rest of their confederation. The story is fantasy.[6] In yet another rendering, Thomas J. Farnham, an Oregon-bound overland emigrant, substituted a Blackfoot warrior for Chardon's Indian blanket thief, alleging that the epidemic reached the Blackfeet because of the dishonesty of one of their own members.[7]

History is silent about how the rumors began. While it is possible that an Indian slipped aboard the steamboat at Fort Clark and carried off a contaminated blanket, the more likely cause of smallpox at Mitutanka Village was the three Arikara women and their children, who contracted the illness while en route from Council Bluffs. Stories of stolen blankets were probably meant to ease white guilt. If the Indians could be implicated in spreading the virus, then Pratte & Chouteau and the United States government would not have to shoulder the blame.

As owner of the steamboat *St. Peter's,* Pratte, Chouteau & Company was responsible for introducing smallpox to the upper Missouri. But a business concern is a legal fabrication that can do nothing on its own. The employees and shareholders of an enterprise act on its behalf. To accuse a corporation or partnership is to accuse the workers and owners.

Inanimate bodies cannot be held to account; that is reserved for living people. Historians seeking to assign fault to Pratte & Chouteau must step behind the firm's corporate veneer and examine the actions of its members. In that regard, no blame attaches to the St. Louis partners of Pratte & Chouteau. There is no evidence that they knew the black deckhand aboard the *St. Peter's* was infected with smallpox. Had they known, they probably would have never allowed him on the boat. They certainly had no desire to see their native customers die. Apart from any humanitarian considerations, it was bad for business. Captain Pratte's decision to keep the sick man on board—after his condition was confirmed—and continue the voyage was made without consulting company headquarters. Once word of the epidemic reached St. Louis, Pierre Chouteau Jr. purchased cowpox vaccine with his own money and sent it to Fort Pierre. Could he and his partners have done more? Certainly. But whether they should have anticipated the full extent of the epidemic entails the worst sort of second-guessing.

In 1837, when Bernard Pratte Jr., master of the *St. Peter's,* made the decision to continue up the Missouri River despite the presence of smallpox, the white world was well acquainted with the devastating effect the disease had on Native Americans. Although the history of the western hemisphere has a few examples of whites deliberately releasing the *Variola* virus among Indians, there is no proof Captain Pratte plotted such a horrible deed. On the contrary, as a partner in Pratte & Chouteau, he had every reason to see the tribes of the upper Missouri remain disease-free. Indians were the producers of his firm's primary commodity—buffalo robes—and the consumers of its trade goods. Indians were the lifeblood of Pratte & Chouteau's existence. It is inconceivable that Bernard Pratte Jr. or any other rational businessman would intentionally kill his own customers and, thereby, destroy his livelihood.

Still, Captain Pratte knew his riverboat carried smallpox, and it must be assumed that he realized what the contagion could do if set loose on the plains. The concept of quarantining the *St. Peter's* was not new. Ships with smallpox and other communicable diseases had been ordered quarantined since 1647, though the best doctors of the day lacked a scientific understanding of why quarantining worked. By the eighteenth century, Boston, Portsmouth, and other Atlantic coastal towns regularly enacted maritime quarantine laws. Other colonial statutes required smallpox patients to be confined to their homes or to specially-built pesthouses. In 1747, New Hampshire established an isolation hospital for its smallpox-infected citizens. Rhode Island did so in 1751, followed by South Carolina in 1754.[8] Despite such medical traditions, Captain Pratte went on with his journey, and for that he is culpable.

Pratte faced two choices—to continue the voyage or not to continue—both potentially detrimental to his fur company. On the one hand, by allowing the *St. Peter's* to proceed, he ignited an epidemic that ultimately ate into Pratte & Chouteau's profits and threatened its future. Yet, if he had stopped the steamer until the virus exhausted itself, he also would have put his partnership at risk. Although the buffalo robes at the firm's upcountry posts were shipped downriver aboard mackinaws, the forts needed the trade goods and other supplies that the *St. Peter's* was carrying. The annual window to ascend the Missouri was short. Any delay, such as laying over and sending word to St. Louis for the company to dispatch another boat— assuming one was available—increased the odds that the river would drop, stranding the steamer with its cargo undelivered.

If Pratte had paused until his passengers and crew recovered from the smallpox, he would have needed to burn almost everything on board to ensure that none of the *Variola* spores survived to be distributed in a contaminated blanket or bolt of cloth.

In the modern world cloaked with revisionist hindsight, such a course of action begs to have been taken. But the 1837-era upper Missouri refuses to conform to such a mold. Had Pratte merely tarried along the river until the sick regained their health and were no longer contagious, Indian bands such as the Lakotas would most likely have ridden to the boat and demanded their annuities. Later, Indian agent Joshua Pilcher sent interpreters among the Yanktons and Santees, cautioning them to keep clear of Fort Kiowa and the other posts because of smallpox. Despite the warning, most Lakotas were not frightened away from the trading houses until they saw the *rotting face* among their own kinsmen.

In spite of vigilance by the *St. Peter's* crew, some Indians would have sneaked aboard the steamer—they did on every other upcountry steamboat—exposing themselves to the deadly virus. On the middle or upper Missouri, a layover would have failed to keep the Indians free from smallpox, and Captain Pratte probably knew it. The foolproof way to have prevented the epidemic would have been for Pratte to turn the *St. Peter's* around and descend to Fort Leavenworth, where the Army could ensure the boat's quarantine.

Unfortunately for the Indians of the upper Missouri, Pratte made the worst decision amid two bad choices. Had he dropped downstream, Pratte & Chouteau would have suffered trading losses, but they probably would have been far less than those it suffered as a result of the epidemic. Captain Pratte was not guilty of premeditated genocide, but he was guilty of contributing to the deaths of thousands of innocent people. The law calls his offense criminal negligence. Yet in light of all the deaths, the almost complete annihilation of the Mandans, and the terrible suffering the region endured, the label criminal negligence is benign, hardly befitting an action that had such horrendous consequences.

Beyond Captain Pratte were a number of others who played roles in the smallpox tragedy. At first blush, William Fulkerson, Mandan subagent, appears wholly innocent. Had Pratte heeded the agent's advice and put the infected black deckhand ashore on the lower Missouri, the epidemic may have been avoided. But Fulkerson lacked the authority to order Pratte to do his bidding, and there is no evidence that senior Indian agent, Joshua Pilcher, supported Fulkerson's recommendation. In 1837, early diagnosis of smallpox was hit-or-miss, at best. Perhaps Pilcher sided with Captain Pratte and thought the deckhand's illness was only a bout of river ague.

When the *St. Peter's* reached Council Bluffs, the nature of the disease was no longer in doubt. Leaving the deckhand quarantined at Fort Bellevue may have spared the Lakotas, Mandans, Arikaras, and other tribes of the upper plains from the epidemic, but only if the quarantine held. If any Indians around the trading post had caught smallpox from him, it is probable they would have passed it to others, allowing the virus to move upriver in any case. Nevertheless, entrusting the sick crewman to the trading post would have been a prudent decision (not as good as returning to Fort Leavenworth, of course, but certainly better than continuing upriver).

In contrast, if Pratte had dropped the man and someone to care for him at an uninhabited point above Council Bluffs, a roving Indian band would likely have stumbled across them and become infected. The window of opportunity to contain the disease slammed shut once the *St. Peter's* steamed away from Fort Bellevue.

Twenty-twenty hindsight dictates that Pratte, Pilcher, and Fulkerson should be faulted for allowing the three Arikara women to come aboard the steamboat at Council Bluffs. No doubt Pratte and the two agents figured that quarantining the deckhand in a portion of the cargo hold would keep the disease from spreading. Tragically for the Indians of the upper Missouri, they were wrong. Assuming the man was sequestered, his quarantine leaked like a gun-shot water bucket. Again, blame falls most heavily at the feet of the *St. Peter's* captain.

At Fort Kiowa, Joshua Pilcher distributed annuities to the Yankton and Santee Lakotas who had been awaiting the steamer. Although his decision to do so may have been fatal—assuming the Lakotas caught the virus from contaminated annuities and not from a contagious passenger or crewman—in his defense, he probably had no other choice. The Indians were expecting the government presents. Warnings that they could be infected would have been fruitless. The Lakotas knew nothing about contagion. Had Pilcher attempted to withhold the annuities, the Indians would have reasoned that he was trying to cheat them and, no doubt, have taken the stores by force. Pilcher should be credited for sending interpreters to the outlying Lakota bands, pleading with them to keep away from the trading posts. Although many refused to heed his advice, some undoubtedly did and were spared.

In contrast with Pilcher, Fulkerson did nothing to warn the Indians of his agency about the risk of smallpox. Other than handing out a few trinkets and making a couple of speeches urging his native charges to keep the peace, he exited the upper Missouri as fast as the *St. Peter's* could whisk him downstream. His crime, if it can be called one, was that of benign neglect.

Francis Chardon, the *bourgeois* of Fort Clark, was one of the most Indian-hating traders ever to venture up the Missouri. His journal overflows with vitriol. On April 8, 1835, he described the Mandans as "the meanest, dirtiest, worthless, cowardly set of Dogs—on the Missouri." And on June 6, the same year, he wrote of a Mandan war party, "May they never return to their Village, is the Wish of Your Humble Servant."[9] Yet despite Chardon's animus, his only crime during the epidemic was a lack of humanity. He was callous, without a doubt, but coarse indifference is hardly a felony.

Some may argue that Chardon bears guilt because he

dispatched Toussaint Charbonneau and his infected wife to the Hidatsas' quarantined village. While there, the woman sickened and died and was, presumably, the source of the Hidatsas catching the virus. If Chardon is at fault, then Charbonneau deserves more blame. Certainly, Charbonneau ought to have known better than the *bourgeois* if his wife had been exposed to smallpox. The old trader could have left her at Fort Clark and gone to the Hidatsas alone. That he took her along reeks of bad judgment, but it in no way indicates that he wished the Hidatsas ill. On the contrary, as the tribe's principal trader, Charbonneau had every reason to see the Hidatsas remain free of the disease.

At first glance, indictment hangs heavier on Charles Larpenteur—clerk at Fort Union—than it does on Chardon or Charbonneau. Together with other members of Pratte, Chouteau & Company, Larpenteur understood the dangers of smallpox. Because the acting *bourgeois,* Jacob Halsey, had the disease, everyone else at the trading post who had neither had *Variola major* nor been recently vaccinated was in jeopardy. Having no active cowpox vaccine available, Larpenteur scraped pus from Halsey's sores in order to inoculate the Indian women who were living at the trading post and those *engagés* who were not immune. On the surface, the decision to inoculate was not criminal. The procedure had been employed for centuries. But for Native Americans, inoculation posed a far greater risk than it did among other populations. Having no hereditary resistance to smallpox, inoculated Indians were more likely to develop a full-blown case than were Old World races. Larpenteur may have suspected this, since he noted in his personal narrative, "This was done with the view to have it all over and everything cleaned up before any Indians should come in, on their fall trade, which commenced early in September."[10]

Given the cold-blooded tenor of Larpenteur's statement, modern readers are apt to claim that the clerk ought to have anticipated the fatalities. Perhaps he did, since he wrote that his Indian wife—one of the women who was inoculated—had "death put in to her harm [arm]."[11] Yet, if he had not inoculated the Indian women and they had remained within the fort, they could have caught the virus from Halsey or someone else. After all, within two weeks of Halsey's arrival, the disease passed naturally to his young son and clerk Edwin Denig.

At least by inoculating, Larpenteur took some action to prevent the smallpox from spreading, a defense that cannot be applied to Francis Chardon at Fort Clark. One could argue that Larpenteur should have sent the women away when Halsey first arrived. That he failed to do so is unfortunate. After Halsey's son and Denig caught the disease, Larpenteur did consider sending the women back to the Assiniboines, but never pressed his plan. By then he was less concerned with the women taking sick than with their families blaming the fur company if they became ill within the confines of Fort Union.[12]

Where blame does attach to Larpenteur and others at Fort Union is in the imprisonment of the Indian women after they were inoculated. Larpenteur locked the women in a small room to prevent them from escaping to the prairie and infecting the neighboring tribes. His description of the stench of rotting flesh, insanity, and maggot-infested sores tells of suffering beyond belief. The few women who survived the ordeal bore such deep scars that their mothers would have had difficulty recognizing them.[13]

Efforts to reproach Jacob Halsey must take into account his physical condition. When the *St. Peter's* reached Fort Union, Halsey was sick with smallpox. He had previously been vaccinated against the disease, but the immunization had lost its potency. Although Halsey's vaccination caused his case to be far milder than those of the Indians, it was still a jolt to his constitution. He was probably bedridden when he arrived at the trading post and may have been out of his mind with fever. The decision to inoculate the Indian wives at the fort was made by Charles Larpenteur and one or two other clerks. If they secured Halsey's permission to perform the procedure, it is doubtful the *bourgeois* was in full command of his reason.[14]

After Halsey recovered, he ordered carpenters to install a wicket in the stockade and an inner gate to separate the Indian trade room from the post courtyard. Other than allowing the abandoned buildings of Fort William to be converted into a makeshift hospital, Halsey devoted most of his energy to ensuring the security of Fort Union. The regret he later expressed for the dying Assiniboines appears rooted in his concern for the robe trade instead of in any compassion for the victims.

The senior partners of Pratte & Chouteau levied more blame for the epidemic on Jacob Halsey than he deserved. In barely four months after he had assumed command of Fort Union, he was replaced by David Mitchell. Demoted from acting *bourgeois,* Halsey was summarily recalled to Fort Pierre, where he served as a clerk until his untimely death. His November 1837 report to company headquarters in St. Louis downplayed the number of fatalities at Fort Union, while blaming smallpox for the expected falloff in the robe trade. The letter was defensive and was meant to restore Halsey to the good graces of his superiors. It came to naught, since Mitchell wrote his own report, painting "a woeful picture of Halsey's conduct during the summer."[15]

No fault for the Blackfeet catching smallpox imputes to Alexander Culbertson or Alexander Harvey. While taking a keelboat of supplies from Fort Union to Fort McKenzie, Harvey recognized that one of his voyageurs and an Indian passenger had come down with the disease. Prudently, he halted near the mouth of the Judith River and sent word to Culbertson that he intended waiting until the pestilence had passed.

Camped near Fort McKenzie were several thousand Blackfeet, eagerly anticipating the trade goods that Harvey had on board. Culbertson warned the Indians that Harvey had stopped because of smallpox, but the Blackfeet refused to heed the danger and threatened to destroy the trading post unless the keelboat arrived. Only when faced with the probable annihilation of his command did Culbertson order Harvey upriver and doom the Blackfeet to the *rotting face.*

It is easy for the modern world to second-guess Culbertson, suggesting that had he been more persuasive, the Blackfeet may have taken his warning to heart. But such reasoning is hindsight. The Blackfeet had no cause to trust Culbertson or any other American trader. For nearly three decades, various fur company trapping brigades had trespassed on Blackfoot land, stolen beaver from tribal streams, and killed confederation warriors. The Blackfeet had first allowed an American trading post within their country only six years before—Fort

Piegan at the mouth of the Marias River—and they burned it after one season. Its replacement, Fort McKenzie, was the most hazardous assignment on the Missouri River.

When Culbertson told the Blackfeet that Harvey's voyageurs were infected with smallpox, they probably figured the *bourgeois* was attempting to trick them so he could sell the keelboat's trade goods to their enemies, the Flatheads and Crows. It is doubtful that the grandest oratory could have persuaded them otherwise.

The case for blaming the United States government for the epidemic is similar to the case against Pratte, Chouteau & Company. Just as a corporation or partnership is a collection of employees and shareholders, a government is an amalgamation of bureaucrats and politicians. Government policy is set and carried out by individuals, and it is the individual who must be held accountable. At his office in St. Louis, Superintendent William Clark probably first learned about the smallpox from Joshua Pilcher in late summer 1837, during the Indian agent's sojourn to Washington, D.C., with his delegation of Foxes, Sauks, and Yankton Lakotas.[16] By then, the disease was raging among the Santee Lakotas and Mandans and was claiming its first victims among the Arikaras. Every day more Indians became infected.

Clark notified the Secretary of War, Joel Poinsett, who eventually authorized him to send vaccine to the upcountry tribes. But as the letters of Clark and Poinsett crisscrossed the nation, summer turned into fall. On his return to St. Louis from the eastern United States, Joshua Pilcher found that the epidemic was worse than his wildest fears. Meanwhile, autumn slipped into winter. In February 1838, Pilcher sent two missives to Clark, begging him to rush vaccine and doctors to the upper Missouri. Finally armed with Poinsett's authorization, Clark gave Pilcher permission to take Doctor Joseph DePrefontaine and some vaccine upriver. Pilcher and the doctor were compelled to wait for Pratte & Chouteau's steamboat, the *Antelope,* which began its voyage in early April 1838. By then the death toll had climbed to the thousands.

To modern readers accustomed to computers and digital switches that relay information in nanoseconds, such delays may appear unconscionable. Yet in the 1830s, they were commonplace. Francis Chardon typically waited four months or more to receive answers to his letters. Two-way correspondence between Fort McKenzie and St. Louis took longer. Some critics may argue that Clark should have rushed vaccine to the Missouri tribes as soon as he heard about the disease. Perhaps so if it was available and if he could have persuaded a physician or some other person who knew how to vaccinate to ascend the Missouri on horseback (by late summer the upper river was too low for steamboats). Even then, winter would have caught such a samaritan before he was much above the Missouri's Grand Detour.

A far greater indictment falls on governmental officialdom for failing to vaccinate America's Indians before the smallpox epidemic started. Although the War Department did attempt to immunize a few tribes, its efforts were halfhearted at best. Indian-agency policy reserved the government's vaccine for tribes that were considered friendly. Such an understanding may have been behind the 1832 decision of Secretary of War, Lewis Cass, who directed that no Indians above the Arikaras were to be immunized. The order intentionally left the belligerent Blackfeet unprotected, and by doing so, it condemned the peaceful Mandans to annihilation.

Some historians have questioned whether the Indians would have submitted to vaccination had the government mobilized the resources to carry out the procedure. In early 1838, Joshua Pilcher voiced that concern when he urged William Clark to authorize $2,000 worth of presents so agents could bribe the Lakotas into accepting the treatment.[17] In Pilcher's eyes, the greatest risk of immunizing the Indians came from their superstitions. If a vaccinated Indian died or fell ill—from whatever cause—his tribe would point to the white man's medicine as the culprit.

While Pilcher's worry had merit (a number of Lakotas had balked at being vaccinated in 1832), it may have been overblown. The United States government vaccinated the Omahas in the late 1820s and the Ojibwas and Ottawas in 1836 without any major difficulties. In addition, many Canadian Assiniboines and Crees readily submitted to vaccination by the

Hudson's Bay Company in 1837 and 1838. It was not Indian opposition that prevented the widespread vaccination of Native Americans, merely a lack of political and bureaucratic will. Although unilaterally condemning Congress and the War Department for failing to safeguard all of America's Indians invites charges of revisionist hindsight, not doing so ignores the fact that thousands of native deaths could have been prevented.

Of all the people who had a hand in the smallpox epidemic of the late 1830s, Captain Bernard Pratte Jr. deserves the most blame. His decision to continue up the Missouri despite the presence of *Variola major* aboard the *St. Peter's* was heinous. Had he turned the steamer around any place below Fort Kiowa and dropped downriver to quarantine the boat at Fort Leavenworth, the ensuing tragedy could have been averted.

While the mores of modern society make it tempting to second-guess other participants in this calamity, in reality, most were guilty of only ignorance and apathy. Certainly, if the politicians and bureaucrats had done more to vaccinate the Indian population before the epidemic began, many lives could have been saved. But after the *St. Peter's* carried the deadly contagion to Fort Clark and Fort Union, the limitations of transportation and communications ensured that any government response would be too late.

The smallpox epidemic of 1837 and 1838 reshaped the tribal hegemony of the upper Missouri. This latest visitation of the disease all but exterminated the once-powerful Mandans and left their Hidatsa and Arikara neighbors so weak, they had to cleave to each other for mutual security. The Lakotas stepped into the void left by the *Variola* virus, abandoning their traditional hunting grounds to the swelling tide of white migration. Weakened by smallpox, the Assiniboines recoiled from the Lakotas, gradually forfeiting the western North Dakota and eastern Montana plains to their more numerous enemy. And in the eastern shadow of the Rocky Mountains, the Blackfoot Confederation helplessly wrung its hands as its vast domain shriveled like a water-starved melon.

As had happened in past epidemics, the fur trade had opened

the way for *Variola major's* latest rampage. When the scourge finally ended, Indian survivors found their societies in shreds. Having no other choice, they increased their buffalo robe production and became joined at the hip with the fur companies. The alliance lasted until the mid 1860s, when the demand for buffalo robes ebbed and with it, the fur trade. Following the Civil War, white hunters methodically destroyed what remained of America's bison herds. Faced with starvation and harassed by the Army, the Indian tribes of the upper Missouri surrendered their land to white ranchers and homesteaders, and forfeited their freedom on government reservations. As America prepared to enter the twentieth century, her native people lived in defeat.

Much of popular history credits European arms for subduing the Indians. But in truth, they were conquered by a far more efficient killer than the white man's guns. The Indians of the western hemisphere were vanquished by smallpox—a disease many of them called the *rotting face*.

The End

Chapter fifteen notes

1. Ashburn, *Ranks of Death*, 45 n. (n.n.).

2. Duffy, *Epidemics in Colonial America*, 5; and Shurkin, *Invisible Fire*, 72-3.

3. Duffy, *Epidemics in Colonial America*, 82.

4. William Fulkerson to William Clark, September 20, 1837, reprinted in "Spread of Smallpox," by Trimble, 67; and Dollar, "High Plains Smallpox Epidemic," 33.

5. Audubon, *Journals*, 2:42-3. While admitting that the blanket theft could have occurred, Dollar, "High Plains Smallpox Epidemic," 32-8 cast doubt on whether it ever happened.

6. DeVoto, *Across the Wide Missouri*, 295-6.

7. Dollar, "High Plains Smallpox Epidemic," 33.

8. Duffy, *Epidemics in Colonial America*, 101-02.

9. Chardon, *Journal*, 28, 34.

10. Larpenteur, *Forty Years*, 109-10.

11. Larpenteur, "Journals and Notes," 161.

12. Ibid., 160-1.

13. Larpenteur, *Forty Years*, 110.

14. Jacob Halsey to Pratte, Chouteau & Company, November 2, 1837, reprinted in Chardon, *Journal*, 394-6 reports that although Halsey did not "have the disease in its most malignant form[,] . . . it was far from being light."

15. J. A. Hamilton to Pierre Chouteau Jr., February 25, 1838, Chouteau Family Papers (St. Louis: Missouri Historical Society, photocopied).

16. Dollar, "High Plains Smallpox Epidemic," 32 n. 91 speculates that Clark would not have heard about the epidemic until early autumn 1837, when he received a letter from William Fulkerson, but it seems likely that Pilcher would have notified Clark while passing through Missouri on his way to the nation's capital.

17. Joshua Pilcher to William Clark, February 27, 1838, reprinted in "Spread of Smallpox," by Trimble, 73-7.

BIBLIOGRAPHY

Abel, Annie Heloise, ed. Tabeau's *Narrative of Loisel's Expedition to the Upper Missouri*. Norman: University of Oklahoma Press, 1939.

Ambrose, Stephen E. *Undaunted Courage: Meriwether Lewis, Thomas Jefferson, and the Opening of the American West*. New York: Simon & Schuster, 1996.

Ashburn, M. *The Ranks of Death: A Medical History of the Conquest of America*. Edited by Frank D. Ashburn. New York: Coward-McCann, 1947.

Audubon, John James. *Audubon and His Journals*. Edited by Maria R. Audubon. Notes by Elliott Coues. 2 vols. Charles Scribner's Sons, 1897. New York: Dover Publications, 1960.

Axtell, James. *The European and the Indian: Essays in the Ethnohistory of Colonial North America*. New York: Oxford University Press, 1981.

———. *The Invasion Within: The Contest of Cultures in Colonial North America*. New York: Oxford University Press, 1985.

Boucher, François. *20,000 Years of Fashion: The History of Costume and Personal Adornment*. New York: Harry N. Abrams, 1967.

Bradbury, John. *Travels in the Interior of America in the Years 1809, 1810, and 1811*. London, 1819. Vol. 5 of *Early Western Travels, 1748-1846*. Edited by Reuben Gold Thwaites. Cleveland: Arthur H. Clark, 1904. Lincoln: University of Nebraska Press, Bison Book Edition, 1986.

Brazeau, J. E. to P. D. Papin, April 21, 1838 (in French). Chouteau Family Papers, trans. anonymous. St. Louis: Missouri Historical Society. Photocopied.

Campbell, Colin to P. D. Papin, March 14, 1838. Chouteau Family Papers. St. Louis: Missouri Historical Society. Photocopied.

Cartwright, Frederick F., in collaboration with Michael D. Biddiss. *Disease and History*. New York: Thomas Y. Crowell, 1972.

Casler, Michael M. *Steamboats of the Fort Union Fur Trade: An Illustrated Listing of Steamboats on the Upper Missouri River, 1831-1867*. Williston, North Dakota: Fort Union Association, 1999.

Catlin, George. *Letters and Notes on the Manners, Customs, and*

Conditions of the North American Indians: Written during Eight Years' Travel (1832-1839) amongst the Wildest Tribes of Indians in North America. 2 vols. Philadelphia: published as Field Notes, 1841. London: 1841, 1844. New York: Dover Publications, 1973.

Chardon, F. A. Chardon's Journal at Fort Clark, 1834-1839. Edited by Annie Heloise Abel. Pierre: Lawrence K. Fox, Superintendent, Department of History, State of South Dakota, 1932. Lincoln: University of Nebraska Press, Bison Book Edition, 1997.

———. to P. D. Papin and J. Picotte, December 12, 1837. Chouteau Family Papers. St. Louis: Missouri Historical Society. Photocopied.

———. to Pierre Chouteau Jr., June 14, 1838. Chouteau Family Papers. St. Louis: Missouri Historical Society. Photocopied.

Chittenden, Hiram Martin. The American Fur Trade of the Far West. 3 vols. New York: Francis Harper, 1902. Reprint (3 vols. in 2), New York: Press of the Pioneers, 1935. 2 vols. Lincoln: University of Nebraska Press, Bison Book Edition, 1986.

———. History of Early Steamboat Navigation on the Missouri River: Life and Adventures of Joseph La Barge. 2 vols. New York: Francis Harper, 1903.

Cockburn, Aidan, M.D. The Evolution and Eradication of Infectious Diseases. Baltimore: Johns Hopkins Press, 1963.

Coues, Elliott, ed. The Manuscript Journals of Alexander Henry, Fur Trader of the Northwest Company, and of David Thompson, Official Geographer and Explorer of the same Company. 2 vols. Minneapolis: Ross & Haines, 1897. Reprinted, 1965.

Crooks, Ramsey to Pierre Chouteau Jr., March 4, 1838. Chouteau Family Papers. St. Louis: Missouri Historical Society. Photocopied.

Crosby, Alfred W. Ecological Imperialism: The Biological Expansion of Europe, 900-1900. Cambridge, Great Britain: Cambridge University Press, 1986.

———. Jr. The Columbian Exchange: Biological and Cultural Consequences of 1492. Westport, Connecticut: Greenwood Press, 1972.

Crutchfield, James, A. Mountain Men of the American West. Boise: Tamarack Books, 1997.

DeLand, Charles Edmund, abst. "Fort Tecumseh and Fort Pierre Journal and Letter Books," ed. Doane Robinson. In South Dakota Historical Collections. Vol. 9. Pierre: South Dakota State Department of History, 1918.

Denig, Edwin Thompson. Five Indian Tribes of the Upper Missouri:

Sioux, Arikaras, Assiniboines, Crees, Crows. Edited by John C. Ewers. Norman: University of Oklahoma Press, 1961.

DeVoto, Bernard. *Across the Wide Missouri.* Boston: Houghton Mifflin, 1947.

———. *The Course of Empire.* Boston: Houghton Mifflin, 1952.

———, ed. *The Journals of Lewis and Clark.* Boston: Houghton Mifflin, 1953.

Dobyns, Henry F. *Native American Historical Demography: A Critical Bibliography.* Bloomington: Indiana University Press, 1976.

———. *Their Number Become Thinned: Native American Population Dynamics in Eastern North America.* Knoxville: University of Tennessee Press, 1983.

Dollar, Clyde D. "The High Plains Smallpox Epidemic of 1837-38." Reprint, *The Western Historical Quarterly* 8, no. 1 (January 1977): 15-38.

Duffy, John. *Epidemics in Colonial America.* Baton Rouge: Louisiana State University Press, 1953.

———. "Smallpox and the Indians in the American Colonies." *Bulletin of the History of Medicine* 25 (1951): 324-41.

Dyer, Robert L. "A Brief History of Steamboating on the Missouri River with an Emphasis on the Boonslick Region." *Boone's Lick Heritage* 5, no. 2 (June 1997). Published on line: http://members.tripod.com.

Eckberg, Scott B. "Artist, Clerk, Chronicler: Rudolf F. Kurz and His Fort Union Sojourn." *North Dakota History: Journal of the Northern Plains* 61, no. 3 (summer 1994): 41-52.

Ewers, John C. *The Blackfeet: Raiders on the Northwestern Plains.* Norman: University of Oklahoma Press, 1958.

———. *Indian Life on the Upper Missouri.* Norman: University of Oklahoma Press, 1968.

Ferch, David L. "Fighting the Smallpox Epidemic of 1837-38: The Response of the American Fur Company Traders." Parts 1 and 2. *The Museum of the Fur Trade Quarterly* 19, no. 4 (winter 1983): 2-7; 20, no. 1 (spring 1984): 4-9.

Frazer, Robert W. *Forts of the West.* Norman: University of Oklahoma Press, 1965.

Giblin, James Cross. *When Plague Strikes: The Black Death, Smallpox, Aids.* New York: HarperCollins, 1995.

Goetzmann, William H. and Glyndwr Williams. *The Atlas of North American Exploration: From the Norse Voyages to the Race to the Pole.* Derby, England: Swanston Publishing, 1992. Norman: University of Oklahoma Press, 1998.

Hafen, LeRoy R., ed. *French Fur Traders and Voyageurs in the American West*. Compiled from *Mountain Men and the Fur Trade of the Far West*. Edited by LeRoy R. Hafen. 10 vols. Glendale, California: Arthur H. Clark, 1965-72. Lincoln: University of Nebraska Press, Bison Book Edition, 1997.

————, ed. *Fur Traders, Trappers, and Mountain Men of the Upper Missouri*. Compiled from *Mountain Men and the Fur Trade of the Far West*. Edited by LeRoy R. Hafen. 10 vols. Glendale, California: Arthur H. Clark, 1965-72. Lincoln: University of Nebraska Press, Bison Book Edition, 1995.

————, ed. *Fur Trappers and Traders of the Far Southwest*. Compiled from *Mountain Men and the Fur Trade of the Far West*. Edited by LeRoy R. Hafen. 10 vols. Glendale, California: Arthur H. Clark, 1965-72. Logan: Utah State University Press, 1997.

————, ed. *Mountain Men and Fur Traders of the Far West*. Compiled from *Mountain Men and the Fur Trade of the Far West*. Edited by LeRoy R. Hafen. 10 vols. Glendale, California: Arthur H. Clark, 1965-72. Lincoln: University of Nebraska Press, Bison Book Edition, 1982.

————, ed. *Trappers of the Far West*. Compiled from *Mountain Men and the Fur Trade of the Far West*. Edited by LeRoy R. Hafen. 10 vols. Glendale, California: Arthur H. Clark, 1965-72. Lincoln: University of Nebraska Press, Bison Book Edition, 1983.

Hamilton, J. A. to Pierre Chouteau Jr., February 25, 1838. Chouteau Family Papers. St. Louis: Missouri Historical Society. Photocopied.

Hanson, James A. "The Myth of the Wasted Meat." *The Museum of the Fur Trade Quarterly* 34, no. 3 (fall 1998): 3-7.

Heidenreich, Virginia L., ed. *The Fur Trade in North Dakota*. Bismarck: State Historical Society of North Dakota, 1990.

Henige, David. *Numbers from Nowhere: The American Indian Contact Population Debate*. Norman: University of Oklahoma Press, 1998.

Hopkins, Donald R. *Princes and Peasants: Smallpox in History*. Chicago: University of Chicago Press, 1983.

Hunt, William J. "Fort Floyd: An Enigmatic Nineteenth-Century Trading Post." *North Dakota History: Journal of the Northern Plains* 61, no. 3 (summer 1994): 7-20.

Hunter, Louis C. *Steamboats on the Western Rivers: An Economic and Technological History*. New York: Dover Publications, 1949.

Innis, Harold A. *The Fur Trade in Canada: An Introduction to Canadian Economic History*. New Haven: Yale University Press,

1930. Revised, 1956. Yale Western Americana Special Contents Edition, 1962.

Jablow, Joseph. *The Cheyenne in Plains Indian Trade Relations, 1795-1840*. Published as "Monograph 19" of the American Ethnological Society, 1950. New York: J. J. Augustin, 1951. Lincoln: University of Nebraska Press, Bison Book Edition, 1994.

Josephy, Alvin M., Jr. *The Indian Heritage of America*. Boston: Houghton Mifflin, 1968. Revised, 1991.

———, ed. *America in 1492: The World of the Indian Peoples Before the Arrival of Columbus*. New York: Alfred A. Knopf, 1992.

Larpenteur, Charles. *Forty Years a Fur Trader on the Upper Missouri: The Personal Narrative of Charles Larpenteur, 1833-1872*. Edited by Elliott Coues. 2 vols. New York, 1898. Re-edited by Milo M. Quaife (2 vols. in 1). Chicago: R. R. Donnelley & Sons, Lakeside Classic, 1933. Lincoln: University of Nebraska Press, Bison Book Edition, 1989.

———. "White Man Bear (Mato Washejoe), Upper Missouri Trader: Journals and Notes of Charles Larpenteur between 1834 and 1872." Transcribed by Edwin T. Thompson. National Park Service Library, Denver. Photocopied.

Lass, William E. *A History of Steamboating on the Upper Missouri River*. Lincoln: University of Nebraska Press, 1962.

Lavender, David. *Fort Laramie and the Changing Frontier*, Handbook 118. Washington: Division of Publications, National Park Service, 1983.

Leduc, Adrienne. "Dear Sieur de La Salle." *The Beaver* 79, no. 2 (April-May 1999): 8-12.

Lehmer, Donald J. *Selected Writings of Donald J. Lehmer*. Lincoln: J & L Reprint, *Reprints in Anthropology* 8, 1977.

Lowie, Robert H. *The Crow Indians*. New York: Reinhart, 1935. Lincoln: University of Nebraska Press, 1963; Bison Book Edition, 1983.

Martin, Calvin. "Wildlife Diseases as a Factor in the Depopulation of the North American Indian." *The Western Historical Quarterly* 7, no. 1 (January 1976): 47-62.

McCaa, Robert. "Spanish and Nahuatl Views on Smallpox and Demographic Catastrophe in the Conquest of Mexico." *Journal of Interdisciplinary History* 25, no. 3 (winter 1995), 397-431. Published on line: http://www.hist.umn.edu/~rmccaa/vircatas/, 1-21.

McClintock, Walter. *The Old North Trail: or Life, Legends and Religion of the Blackfeet Indians*. London: Macmillian, 1910.

Lincoln: University of Nebraska Press, Bison Book Edition, 1968. Reprint, 1992.

McNeill, William H. *Plagues and Peoples*. New York: Doubleday division of Bantam Doubleday Dell, 1976. New York: History Book Club, Monticello Editions, 1993.

Meyer, Roy W. *The Village Indians of the Upper Missouri: The Mandans, Hidatsas, and Arikaras*. Lincoln: University of Nebraska Press, 1977.

Mitchell, D. D. to P. D. Papin, December 1, 1837. Chouteau Family Papers. St. Louis: Missouri Historical Society. Photocopied.

Morgan, Dale L. *Jedediah Smith and the Opening of the West*. Indianapolis: Bobbs-Merrill, 1953. Lincoln: University of Nebraska Press, Bison Book Edition, 1964.

Nasatir, A. P., ed. *Before Lewis and Clark: Documents Illustrating the History of the Missouri 1785-1804*. 2 vols. St. Louis: Historical Documents Foundation, 1952. Lincoln: University of Nebraska Press, Bison Book Edition, 1990.

Newman, Peter C. *Caesars of the Wilderness: Company of Adventurers*. Vol. 2. New York: Viking Penguin, 1987. New York: Penguin Books, 1988.

————. *Empire of the Bay: An illustrated history of the Hudson's Bay Company*. Toronto: Viking Studio/Madison Press Books, 1989.

Oglesby, Richard Edward. *Manuel Lisa and the Opening of the Missouri Fur Trade*. Norman: University of Oklahoma Press, 1963.

Picotte, Joseph to P. D. Papin, April 21, 1838 (in French). Chouteau Family Papers, trans. anonymous. St. Louis: Missouri Historical Society. Photocopied.

Ramenofsky, Ann Felice. *The Archaeology of Population Collapse: Native American Response to the Introduction of Infectious Disease*. Ann Arbor: University Microfilms International, 1982.

————. *Vectors of Death: The Archaeology of European Contact*. Albuquerque: University of New Mexico Press, 1987.

Ray, Arthur J. *Indians in the Fur Trade: their role as trappers, hunters, and middlemen in the lands southwest of Hudson Bay, 1660-1870*. Toronto: University of Toronto Press, 1974.

————. "Smallpox: The Epidemic of 1837-38." *The Beaver* 306, no. 2 (autumn 1975): 8-13.

Robertson, R. G. *Competitive Struggle: America's Western Fur Trading Posts, 1764-1865*. Boise: Tamarack Books, 1999.

Robinson, Doane. "The LeSueur Tradition." In *South Dakota Historical Collections*. Vol. 9. Pierre: South Dakota State

Department of History, 1918.

Roe, Frank Gilbert. *The Indian and the Horse*. Norman: University of Oklahoma Press, 1955.

Rogers, J. Daniel. *Objects of Change: The Archaeology and History of Arikara Contact with Europeans*. Washington: Smithsonian Institution Press, 1990.

Rollings, Willard H. *The Osage: An Ethnohistorical Study of Hegemony on the Prairie-Plains*. Columbia: University of Missouri Press, 1992.

Ross, John F. "Picturing Pocahontas." *Smithsonian* 29, no. 10 (January 1999): 34-6.

Rozwenc, Edwin C. *The Making of American Society*. Vol. 1 to 1877. Boston: Allyn and Bacon, 1972.

Russell, Carl. *Firearms, Traps, & Tools of the Mountain Men*. New York: Alfred A. Knopf, 1967. Albuquerque: University of New Mexico Press, 1977.

Ryan, Frank, M.D. *Virus X: Tracking the New Killer Plagues Out of the Present and into the Future*. New York: Little, Brown, 1997.

Schuler, Harold H. *Fort Pierre Chouteau*. Vermillion: University of South Dakota Press, 1990.

Shurkin, Joel N. *The Invisible Fire: The Story of Mankind's Victory Over the Ancient Scourge of Smallpox*. New York: G. Putnam's Sons, 1979.

The Spirit World. Alexandria, Virginia: Time-Life Books, 1992.

Stearn, E. Wagner and Allen E. Stearn. *The Effect of Smallpox on the Destiny of the Amerindian*. Boston: Bruce Humphries, 1945.

Sunder, John E. *Bill Sublette: Mountain Man*. Norman: University of Oklahoma Press, 1959.

———. *The Fur Trade on the Upper Missouri, 1840-1864*. Norman: University of Oklahoma Press, 1965.

———. *Joshua Pilcher: Fur Trader and Indian Agent*. Norman: University of Oklahoma Press, 1968.

Taylor, John F. "Sociocultural Effects of Epidemics on the Northern Plains: 1734-1850." Reprint, *The Western Canadian Journal of Anthropology* 7, no. 4 (1977): 55-81.

Thompson, Erwin N. *Fort Union Trading Post: Fur Trade Empire on the Upper Missouri*. Originally published as *Fort Union Trading Post Historic Structures Report*. Part 1. National Park Service, 1968. Medora, North Dakota: Theodore Roosevelt Nature and History Association, 1986.

Trimble, Michael K. "An Ethnohistorical Interpretation of the Spread of Smallpox in the Northern Plains Utilizing Concepts of Disease

Ecology." Columbia: University of Missouri Department of Anthropology Study, 1979. *Reprints In Anthropology* 33. Lincoln: J & L Reprint, 1986.

Urdang, Lawrence, ed. *The World Almanac Dictionary of Dates*. New York: Longman, 1982.

Utley, Robert M. and Wilcomb E. Washburn. *Indian Wars*. New York: American Heritage, 1977. Boston: Houghton Mifflin, 1987.

Ver Steeg, Clarence L. *The Formative Years: 1607-1763*. New York: Hill and Wang, 1964.

Viola, Herman J. *After Columbus: The Smithsonian Chronicle of the North American Indians*. Washington: Smithsonian Books, 1990; distributed by Orion Books.

Waldman, Carl. *Atlas of the North American Indian*. New York: Facts On File, 1985.

Ward, Geoffrey C. *The West: An Illustrated History*. New York: Little, Brown, 1996.

Wells, Robin F. "Castoreum and Steel Traps in Eastern North America." *American Anthropologist* n.s., no. 74 (1972): 479-83.

Williams, Glyndwr. "The Hudson's Bay Company and the Fur Trade: 1670-1870." *The Beaver* 314, no. 2 (autumn 1983). Reprinted (1991): 3-81.

Wintemberg, W. J. "Was Hochelaga Destroyed or Abandoned?" *American Anthropologist* 29 (1927): 251-4.

Wishart, David J. *The Fur Trade of the American West, 1807-1840: A Geographical Synthesis*. Lincoln: University of Nebraska Press, 1979; Bison Book Edition, 1992.

Wolkomir, Richard. "In Vermont, A Valiant Stand for Freedom." *Smithsonian* 29, no. 4 (July 1998): 54-64.

Wood, W. Raymond. "An Introduction to the History of the Fur Trade on the Northern Plains." *North Dakota History: Journal of the Northern Plains* 61, no. 3 (summer 1994): 2-6.

INDEX

THE AUTHOR

R. G. Robertson served as a U.S. Marine Corps officer in the Vietnam War, and then earned an MBA from the University of Michigan. During a nineteen-year career in the investment business, he was a partner at Hambrecht & Quist in San Francisco and a self-employed options market maker on the Pacific Stock Exchange.

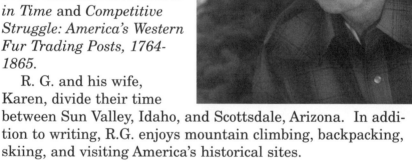

In 1992, he retired and began writing. His other books include *Idaho Echoes in Time* and *Competitive Struggle: America's Western Fur Trading Posts, 1764-1865*.

R. G. and his wife, Karen, divide their time between Sun Valley, Idaho, and Scottsdale, Arizona. In addition to writing, R.G. enjoys mountain climbing, backpacking, skiing, and visiting America's historical sites.

THE PHOTOGRAPHER

Karen A. Robertson was born and raised in Oregon, where she earned BS degrees in history and political science from Portland State University. Following her career in the investment business in Oregon and California, Karen and her husband, R. G., moved to Sun Valley, Idaho. They now divide their time between Sun Valley and Scottsdale, Arizona.

Karen developed her interest in photography when she and her family modeled for their friend, Ray Atkeson, Photographer Laureate of Oregon. Her photographs have accompanied R. G.'s newspaper and magazine articles, as well as his other books.

OTHER BOOKS FROM CAXTON PRESS

Massacre Along the Medicine Road

ISBN 0-87004-387-0 (paper) $22.95
ISBN 0-87004-389-7 (cloth) $32.95
6x9, 500 pages, maps, photos, bibliography, index

The Oregon Trail
Yesterday and Today

ISBN 0-87004-319-6 (paper) $12.95
6x9, 200 pages, illustrated, maps, index

On Sidesaddles to Heaven
The Women of the Rocky Mountain Mission

ISBN 0-87004-384-6 (paper) $19.95
6x9, 268 pages, illustrations, index

Dreamers: On the Trail of the Nez Perce

ISBN 0-87004-393-5 (cloth) $24.95
6x9, 450 pages, photographs, maps, index

Yellow Wolf: His Own Story

ISBN 0-87004-315-3 (paper) $16.95
6x9, 328 pages, illustrations, maps, index

Outlaws of the Pacific Northwest

ISBN 0-87004-396-x (paper) $18.95
6x9, photographs, map, 216 pages, index

For a free Caxton catalog write to:

CAXTON PRESS
312 Main Street
Caldwell, ID 83605-3299

or

Visit our Internet Website:

www.caxtonpress.com

Caxton Press is a division of The CAXTON PRINTERS, Ltd.